AF674869

SOUTH ASIA
IN
NEW ERA

South Asia in New Era

Edited by

Dr. R. B. Singh

Raj Publications

New Delhi - 110002 (INDIA)

South Asia in New Era

First Published in 2011

ISBN 978-81-86208-76-2

Published by : ***Poonam Goel***

Raj Publications

108, 4855/24, Ansari Road,

Daryaganj, New Delhi - 110002

Tel. : 011- 23250939, 9811010939

E-mail- rajpublications@yahoo.co.in

Laser Typesetting : Sky Computers, Delhi-110 009

Printed at : G S Offset, Delhi

Printed in India

CONTENTS

PREFACE

The subject of South Asia in New Era has dynamic tinge attached to it, it implies that problem of a South Asia nation can not be left to a few set of rigid rules and policies being implemented by a few million of uniformed men. In today's scenario, economic, politics, security and somewhat related all the issues which have to be taken immediate Note of to ensure comprehensive and wholesome security of a nation. Here, change is the key word. With every possible development which affects our security as a whole, we have to remodel our security policies and ensure that it has compatible resource to implement the change in letter and spirit.

South Asia in New Era is a edited Book and could not have been written without the generous assistance of so many seniors, friends, well-wishers and colleagues. It is simply not possible to list them all.

I am very thankful to Prof. A.K.Sen Gupta, Dean & Head of the Department of Defence Studies and Dr. S.N. Rai for providing me the moral support to undertake this book.

I am thankful to Dr. O.P. Shukla for valuable guidance given to me for the completion of this book.

I am thankful to Dr. S.K. Mishra, Dr. L.K. MIshra, Dr.

Abhaya Kumar Singh, Dr. Vijay Khare, who always provided me the necessary moral and material support as and when required.

I would like to express from the core of my heart my sincere thank to my professors and Army Officers to Brig. Rajeev Pant, Brig. S.K. Singh, Brig. O.P. singh, Brig. P.N. Verma for their valuable suggestions and provided the material support for the book.

Finally I am thankful to my wife Smt. Veena Singh for her moral support and also I am thankful to my Publisher for publishing the book in a short time.

Dr. R.B. Singh
Lucknow University
Lucknow

Chapter 1

PROSPECTS FOR PEACE & SECURITY IN SOUTH ASIA

Dr. R.B. Singh

Conflict to the Region

This Subject is central to the goals of the United States, and to the interests of the International Community in the region. I know that a principal concern of this subject today is the continuing crisis between India and Pakistan, and I will review current administration thinking on this issue.

But it is also important to keep in mind that there are other, quite serious conflicts in South Asia. I think that these also need to be included in any discussion of stability and the prospects for peace in the region. I know that the situation in Afghanistan is very serious, there continuous faced irregular war for as national & International Terrorism from long time. About Myanmar, faced the fiulurs of democracy and military dictatorship. Bangladesh also disturbed by local infiltration. About Sri Lanka, where there are some indication that an almost twenty-year conflict may be on the way to resolution and about Nepal, where a rural insurgency has grown over the past five years to threaten the future of a country struggling to establish prosperity and democracy.

India-Pakistan

Throughout South Asia, the search for prosperity and democracy is too often overshadowed by the specter of war. The most prominent case in the region, of course, is the continuing crisis between India and Pakistan. Twice so far this year, the possibility of war between India and Pakistan became very real. Hundreds of thousands of Indian and Pakistani troops were mobilized along their border and the Line of Control in Kashmir. These crises were generated by extremely provocative terrorist attacks, first against the Indian Parliament in New Delhi in December, 2001 and then against families of Indian soldiers in Jammu, in May, 2002. The forces of extremism once again sought to exploit the deep and long-standing differences between India and Pakistan over Kashmir.

They did not succeed, and tensions have been reduced since then thanks to decisions made in Islamabad and New Delhi, with the encouragement of the international community. But we and the rest of the international community remain deeply concerned. The military mobilization continues. The rhetoric, though muted, could bubble up again. Another major terrorist attack or a significant surge in violence could still spark a military confrontation, with long-lasting and devastating consequences for the entire region. The enemies of moderation in the region are aware of this fact and have already tried to exploit it through high-profile terrorist attacks. They could very well try again.

We need to recognize that an important factor in the current crisis is the willingness of extremists and terrorists to go to any length to reach their goals. Our efforts to prevent conflict between India and Pakistan are made even more urgent by the global war on terrorism. President of Pakistan recognizing the danger that extremism poses to his country, has denounced the senseless ideology of violence. Pakistani authorities have moved against extremist groups. The extremists, showing how threatened they feel by President of Pakistan actions, have struck back. The government has not been intimidated; instead it has continued its campaign against terrorists and their supporters. We are standing by Pakistan as it faces this brutal challenge.

Both sides have reaffirmed their desire for a peaceful political solution to their differences. President Jardari has pledged that his government will provide no support for infiltration across the line of control and that he will not permit Pakistan to be used as a base for terrorist attacks in any other country. Pakistan needs to sustain that pledge in order to begin a process of resolution of the immediate crisis and of its more fundamental differences with India. We also look to India to take further de-escalatory actions, as Pakistan carries through with its commitments. As tensions begin to subside, New Delhi should agree to resume talks with Islamabad on all issues, including Kashmir. During his recent meetings with Indian leaders in New Delhi, Ex. Secretary Powell saw that there was a solid commitment to dialogue. He said that India understands that their dialogue had to include all the issues between the two nations but especially it had to include Kashmir.

Terrorism

Much is made of threats from terrorism and Pakistan inspired proxy war in J&K. If Pakistan hasn't been able to achieve her desire of wresting Kashmir from India in the last 20 years, it is unlikely she would be able to achieve much in the next 20 years also. What with her own failing health. Terrorists can hardly bring down a strong and thriving democracy like India. At the most, terrorist outrages are no more than wasp stings, painful but hardly dangerous.

Kashmir

The problems of kashmir cannot be resolved through violence, but only through a healthy political process and dialogue between the parties. We look forward to India holding free and fair state elections beginning later in the month. We also encourage a continuation and expansion of the nascent efforts to engage Kashmir separatist leaders. Kashmir's Pakistanis and Indians must do their part to ensure that the upcoming elections can be held in safety and without interference from those who would like to spoil them. Recent attacks on officials and political party activists in Kashmir cannot be allowed to derail the election.

State elections can be an important step in a political process, but they alone cannot resolve the problems between India and Pakistan, nor can they erase the scars of so many years of strife. Only a productive and sustained bilateral dialogue on all issues, including Kashmir, will prevent future crisis and finally bring peace to the region. We are committed to staying engaged, in the months and years ahead, helping both parties resolve their differences so that everyone in the region can live with dignity, prosperity and security.

Pakistan

Pakistan is being considered first for no other reason except that India has a morbid fixation with that country. A country about to collapse under its own weight, saddled with an army "best trained for staging coups" rather than defending the country hardly poses a major military challenge to India. At present, its ability to mount even a

Kargil type operation is doubtful. Pakistan army has nine corps comprising 19 infantry divisions, two armoured divisions, two artillery divisions, a number of independent brigades and supporting units. More than half of this force is deployed on the country's western border and in frontier tribal areas. Another 25 per cent is involved in Internal Security duties. There is hardly any military surplus available for offensive designs against India.

Pakistan has an up and running nuclear establishment capable of fielding nuclear warheads. As per various estimates, Pakistan could have built about 50 HEU based nuclear warheads with HEU reserves for another 50 warheads or so. Given the present instability in Pakistan, specter of nuclear weapons falling into wrong hands ought to be taken into account. The danger though real is vastly exaggerated. Notwithstanding nuclear blackmail, even the jihadis couldn't be unaware of consequences should they be foolhardy enough to use the weapon. This calls for contingency planning and adroit management but can hardly be the cause for a palsied security response.

China

China's military foci are Taiwan, Japan, and Russia in that order. India ranks fourth alongwith Vietnam. China has a 2.5 million strong army. 40 per cent of this faces Taiwan and Japan, 20 per cent faces Russia, 25 per cent are reserves and barely 15 per cent force is available opposite India. As per intelligence estimates China maintains 16 to 18 mountain divisions in Tibet facing India in Arunachal Pradesh and Aksai Chin. Facing this, India has deployed about eight divisions. China would also have to contend with Tibetan nationalists. Though China has connected Lhasa by train to mainland China, her ability to quickly move reserve forces to Tibet is vastly over estimated. Besides, West is unlikely to stay neutral in any future Sino-Indian conflict.

Today, almost 45 per cent of all new world's oil demand is attributable to the rising needs of China. Over 70 per cent of China's oil imports come from West Asia and Africa and all of this must pass through the Indian Ocean. India can easily strangulate this supply. Indian Navy recently held co-operative exercises with the United States, Japan, Australia, and Singapore in this area, and this should checkmate China's purported string-of-pearls strategy against India.

China deploys approximately 130 nuclear warheads for delivery by land-based missiles, sea-based missiles, and bombers. Additional warheads are thought to be in storage for a total stockpile of approximately 200 warheads. As per one estimate, China could have deployed 20 MRBMs and 60 short range surface-to-surface missiles against India. Even so, China wouldn't be foolhardy enough to risk a world war over an almost relegated from memory border dispute with India.

Sri Lanka

As I said earlier, there are other serious conflicts in South Asia, in which thousands have died, and thousands more can die if they are not resolved. I will touch briefly on the situations in Sri Lanka and Nepal. I hope that our discussion after the opening remarks will include some attention to these situations. Recent developments in Sri Lanka have been encouraging and give us cause for cautious optimism. After almost two decades of war, costing well over 60,000 lives, a serious peace process is now under way. A cease fire has been in place since late last year. Norway, which has been acting as a facilitator, recently announced that the Sri Lankan government and the Liberation Tigers of Tamil Eelam have agreed to begin the first round of formal talks on September 16,2002 in Thailand. The government's announcement that it was lifting its ban on the Tamil Tigers as part of the peace process is another welcome development.

The United States has supported Norway's effort and we are continuing to watch developments very closely. We hope that the talks will eventually bring to an end this bitter conflict. The Norwegian government has played a key role in bringing the two sides together in what appears to be a major step forward. We wish them, and the Sri Lankan parties, continued success in their efforts towards peace. A negotiated political settlement to this conflict would be the best demonstration that negotiation not violence provides the most effective means for dealing with contentious issues that divide and separate peoples throughout the world.

We believe that such a settlement is possible if both parties continue to demonstrate the constructive and serious approach that has brought the process to this point. The people of Sri Lanka deserve nothing less. Everyone should understand, however, that the path to peace will not be smooth and that this is just the first step on that journey. The United States strongly supports the Sri Lankan peace process, as the President affirmed in July when he met with the Sri Lankan Prime Minister in Washington. Deputy Secretary of State Armitage recently concluded a successful visit to Sri Lanka, which included meetings with the government, the opposition, and Tamil leaders. Mr. Armitage emphasized the U.S. commitment to peace in Sri Lanka and our desire to help that country realize its great potential. We will continue to urge a negotiated settlement, which has as its goal a nation that is whole, at peace, and respects the rights of all of its citizens.

Nepal

I wish we could have as much optimism over an early end to conflict in Nepal. That country continues to confront a violent Maoist insurgency, now in its sixth year, which has left over 4000 dead. The Maoists have employed ruthless tactics in the field and conducted terrorist government's right and duty to protect its citizens, within the framework of its constitution.

Unfortunately, the leaders of Nepal's ruling political party are locked in a power struggle that inhibits the government's effectiveness in dealing with the insurgents and undertaking development initiatives to start restoring its authority in the countryside. The United States is finalizing plans for assistance as part of an international response to end this brutal conflict and help bring peace to Nepal. Our programms are intended to facilitate the government's effort both to restore security and to focus on development and poverty reduction.

To truly end this conflict, the government and people of Nepal must build a better future for their country. Nepalis must hold their officials accountable for good governance and ending corruption. All must work to find the common ground on which to begin rebuilding what the Maoists have destroyed. We can assist in that reconstruction by continuing aid to Nepal's economic development. Peace can provide the space in which Nepal can diversify its economy, attract foreign investment and seek sustainable and environmentally sound ways to tap the potential of its natural resources. While much remains to be done, many in the international community stand ready to assist.

Continued U.S. Engagement:

These then are three of the four major conflicts in South Asia. All need to be resolved to truly have peace in the region. It is our intention that the United States does what I can to move toward resolution of each one. As Ex-Secretary Powell said in his visit to the region in July, what the United States is trying to do is to play the role of a friend, a good friend to all the nations of South Asia. He observed that our relations with all of the nations of the region are perhaps better than at any time in the last quarter century. And noted that if we are seen as a good partner then we can be in a position to perhaps assist nations in resolving their differences. Not as a meddler nor as a mediator, but somebody whose good offices can help bring people to the table to deal with their differences. We hope that we will be able to play this role in the region.

IRREGULAR CONFLICT AS AN TERRORISM

A. Extremist Islamist Terror & Subversion

1) Terror in very slow-motion
2) The Islamist Extremist End game
3) The Assembly lines of Jehad
4) The myth of the locus of Terror
5) Pakistan : A forth line State
6) The web of Terror : Erosion & Encirclement

Pakistan—The Core Issue

a. **Militarized Islamist - Fundamentalist State**
b. **Footprints of Terror**
c. **The State as Suicide Bomber**
d. **Face of 'Moderate' Dictatorship**
e. **An ideological Conflict in Kashmir**
f. **Pakistan in Occupied Kashmir (PoK) & the Northern Area**—The Northern Areas in Pakistan Occupied Kashmir (PoK) have been split into five districts. Gilgit, Baltistan, Dimir, Ghizer and Ghanche. A population of 1.5 million inhabits a vast

area of 72,495 square kilometers. Sprasely populated as the area is the ethnic groups are varied—Baltees, Vashkuns, Mughals, Kashmiris, Pathans, Ladakhis and Turks, speaking a multiplicity of languages including Balti, Shina Brushaki, Khawer, Wakhi, Turki, Tibeti, Pushto and Urdu.

(i) Structure of Governance (ii) Departments (iii) Judiciary (iv) Setrian Violence (v) Development

g. **Failures of Democracy**

h. **Vice of Jehad**

2. Impact on India

a. Face the major terrorist attack by Pakistan based groups as a Parliament attack & Mumbai blast recently.

b. **The Kashmiri Pandit : An Ethnic cleansing the world forgot-** Since late 1989, the Indian State of Jammu and Kashmir (J&K) has been in the grip of a vicious movement of Islamist extremist terrorism. As many as 36, 289 [till December 30, 2003, Source] lives have been lost in this conflict over nearly 14 years of a sub-conventional war that has inflicted enormous suffering on the people of the State, and transformed this confrontation between South Asia's traditional rivals into a potential nuclear flashpoint.

c. Major terrorist attack in North East Indian states by terrorist groups supported by ISI.

d. **Bangladesh - A Lengthening Shadow of Terror -** Bangladesh soil is increasingly being used for terrorist and for subversive activities by religious extremists, pan-Islamist terrorist groups, and insurgents operating in India's Northeast, substantially through the active collusion of Pakistan's Inter Service Intelligence (ISI) and

(MAP NO. 3) STATE SPONCER TERRORISM & PAKISTAN MAP

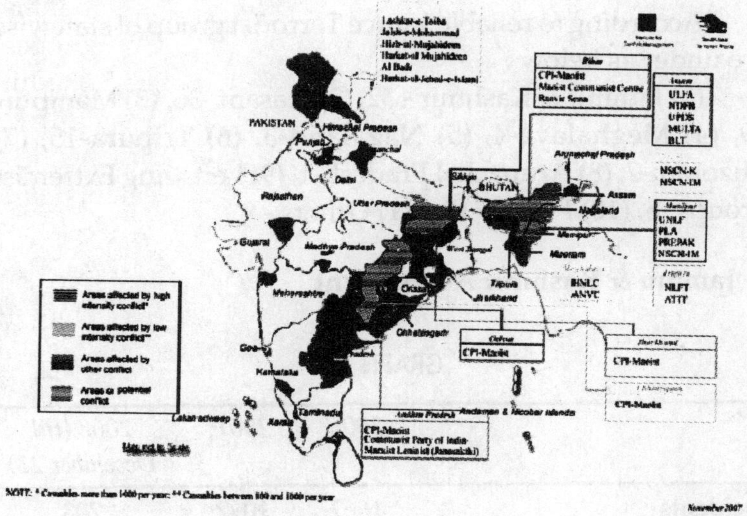

Bangladesh's Directorate General of Field Intelligence (DGFI).

e. (Graph No. 4) Civilian Fatalities—

D- Major conflicts and terrorist groups operating in India

(MAP NO.4) INDIA CONFLICT MAP

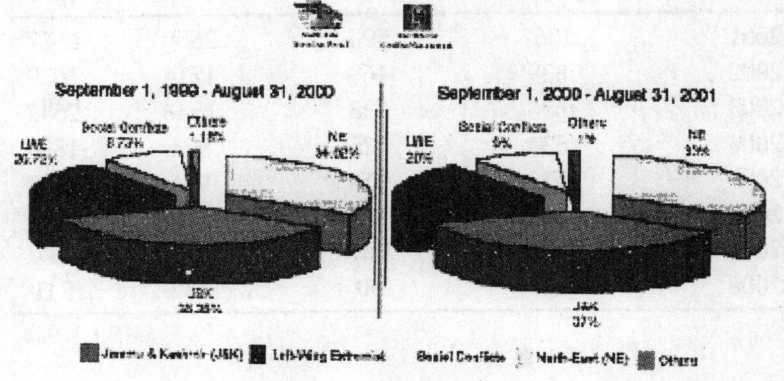

E- India - Terrorist, Insurgent and Extremist Groups

According to reliable source Terrorist group of statewise are under as below :

(1) Jammu & Kashmir - 32, (2) Aasam -36, (3) Manipur-39, (4) Meghalaya-4, (5) Nagaland-3, (6) Tripura-15, (7) Mizoram-2, (8) Arunachal Pradesh-1, (9) Left wing Extremist groups -6, (10) Punjab-12, (11) Others - 9

F- Jammu & Kashmir Assessment

GRAPH - 5

	2006	*2007*	*2008 (till December 23)*
Incidents	1667	1092	703
Civilians Killed	387	164	89
Police personnel killed	49	18	10
VDCs/SPOs* Killed	31	12	10
SF personnel killed	102	92	65

- VDC - Village Defence Committee SPO - Special Police Officer
- *Source :* Jammu and Kashmir Police

GRAPH - 6 COMPARATIVE FATALITIES IN J&K 2001-2008

Year	*Civilians*	*SF Personnel*	*Terrorist*	*Total*
2001	1067	590	2850	4507
2002	839	469	1714	3022
2003	658	338	1546	2542
2004	534	325	951	1810
2005	520	216	996	1732
2006	349	168	599	1116
2007	164	121	492	777
2008	69	90	382	541

G - Reason of Rise of Terrorism

1) A Silent Conflict
2) Media
3) Specific Forms
4) Weak administration
5) Finance and weapons
6) Establishment of Political Power.
7) Crime
8) The only alternative
9) Suitable ethos of society and state
10) Foreign Support
11) Repression
12) Religion

H - Terrorist Profile

1. They are young.
2. They belong to a fatherless family.
3. The women terrorist are fanatical.
4. They are from the minorities.
5. They have a belief that they are martyrs and special laws apply for them.
6. They are mystical (they believe they shall gain eternal-life e.g. IRA or they believe they shall go to heaven e.g. Islamic terrorists)
7. They are mentally imbalanced—aggressive, bored, confused.
8.- Psychological factors like ego, anger, feeling being lost, narcissism, tendency towards groupism and warrior dreams play a role in the development of the terrorist.

I - The Tactics of Terrorism

This is due to the constantly changing state of terrorism,

Traditional, terrorism consists of six terrorist tactics : bombing, hijacking, arson, assault, kidnapping and taking hostages. Terrorist tactics work on these guidelines :

1. Watch target
2. Procure weapons
3. Establish safe houses
4. Central command outside country
5. Central command outside country
6. Small units (to prevent infiltration, to prevent splits in large groups)
7. Anonymity of big city.
8. Finance is from the following source — 'well wishes' abroad governments, robbery, kidnapping for ransom, drugs and legitimate businesses.
9. Terrorist leaders keep the theorist lean, hungry, unexposed to temptations and riches.
10. Terrorists select the victims e.g. tsars, politician.
11. Terrorists employ intelligence officers—penetrate the government targets for maps.
12. Terrorists often try to liberate their fellow comrades from prisons.

J-Type of Terrorism

1) Chemical Weapon Terrorism
2) Biological Weapon Terrorism
3) Nuclear Terrorism
4) Cyber Terrorism

K - Classification of Terrorism

(a) Ideological :

1) Left wing
2) Right wing
3) Others

(b) Religious nationalistic

1) Nationalistic separatist
2) Exotic
3) State sponsored
4) Ethnic

L - Impact of State Sponsored Terrorism on India

1. ISI sponsored terrorists' activities :

   a. Espionage
   b. Subversion and sabotage
   c. Terrorism
   d. Money Action
   e. Internal/External encirclement of India

2. ISI Strategy :

   (i) Proxy War
   (ii) Balkanize India
   (iii) Narco Terrorism
   (iv) Suicide Squads - Fidayeens.

3. ISI Objective :

   a. Create heavy burden on India and deployment of more troops to safeguard every inch of border.
   b. To press on other places causing thinning out of SF's out of Kashmir and Jammu so that more infiltration can take place.
   c. Creating tension in Kashmir and other parts of India to annex Kashmir.
   d. Manipulating the internal political situation in Pakistan to advantage of Army.
   e. Make Afghanistan & confederation of Pakistan to give Pakistan Army Generals a concept of so called 'Strategic depth in Defence.'

M - Source of Funding

(Graph No. 7) Source of Terrorist Funding in J & K

	Source	Fund Contribution
a.	Direct from Pakistan	20%
b.	From Narcotic	20%
c.	Through Counterfeit Currency	10%
d.	Through External Charities & Donations	15%
e.	Through Internal Charities & Donations	10%
f.	Protection Money	10%
g.	From Islamic & other Countries	15%

(Graph No. 8) Payments Made to Terrorist Operating in J&K

[In Indian Rupees]

S. No.	Type of payment	Foreigners	Locals (including Pakistanis)
1.	Given at the time of recruitment	Up to 50,000	Up to 25,000
2.	Monthly Payment	10,000 to 12,000	8,000 to 10,000
3.	End of Tenure Payment	2,00,000 to 2,50,000	
4.	For a spectacular act of terrorism	1 lakh - 2 lakhs	
5.	Payment given to a supreme leader	Up to 50,000 per month	

(Graph No. 9) Miscellaneous Estimated Costs in Terrorist Activities

[In Indian Rupees]

S.No.	Nature of Cost	Amount
1.	Cost of training of a terrorist	25,000

2.	Clothing and equipment	25,000 to 30,000
3.	Relief for family of deceased militants in Pakistan	Ex. gratia 2,00,000
4.	Relief for family of deceased Kashmiri in J & K	Ex. gratia 20,000- plus monthly subsistence allowance Rs. 3,000-5,0000 some extra money on festivals like Id.
5.	Payment to each guide	10,000-20,000
6.	Motivating to join militancy	5,000 - 10,000

(Graph No. 10) Terrorists Hierarchy and Monthly Payment

S.No.	*Appointment*	*Monthly Payment*
1.	Divisional/District Commander, Finance Secretary/ Launch Commander	Rs. 50,000/-
2.	Area/Tehsil Commander	Rs. 20,000/-
3.	Section/Group Commander	Rs. 10,000/-
4.	Rank & File (aa) PT/FT	Rs. 6,0000/-
	(ab) Trained LT	Rs. 5,000/-
	(ac) LT without weapon	Rs. 2,000/-
	(ad) During Training	Rs. 1,500/-

N - Government Response to Terrorism

1) Counter terrorism response has been disjointed without a coherent national policy. 2) More often than not situation has been left to drift and get out of hand due to lack of political will. 3) Faced with critical situation, the SF's have to launch operations against terrorist, but in most of the cases simultaneously political initiative has failed to take off.

O- Adequacy of Police and PMF as Anti Terrorist Force

a) Role ambiguity/multiplicity of forces
b) Outdated weapons/equipments
c) Lack of coordinated training
e) Lack of Continuity
f) Poor Intelligence

P - Involvement of Army in Countering Terrorism

1) Though primary role of Army is to defend country from foreign aggression and in its secondary role it can be called to assist authorities if so requisitioned. It should be exception rather than rule but army find itself embroiled in combating terrorism in North East., i.e. Assam, Tripura, Mizoram and Manipur not to mention J&K. 2) The continued requirement of presence of Army in anti terrorist role in J&K necessitated rising of Rashtriya Rifles. 3) Army has rendered valuable assistance in Punjab terrorism period by hitting the shelter places of Punjab Terrorists.

Q - Inadequacy of Existing Response/Strategy

(a) Policy of appeasement of terrorists
(b) Terrorism/Insurgency generally dealt as Law and Order problem
(c) Absence of political will
(d) Resorting to knee jerk operations
(e) Lack of long term perspective
(g) Absence of coordinated efforts because of following:
  (i) No apex body
  ii) Lack of Unity of command
  (iii) Intelligence/gathering is week link
  iv) Psychological Operations

v) Role of Media
vi) Judicial System—absence teeth in various Law/Acts

R - International Response and Strategy

(i) UN Conventions of Terrorism
(ii) SAARC Convention on the Suppression of Terrorism
(iii) International Strategy
  a. Whether conduct limited war against sponsored terrorism - Israeli example.
  b. Force the sponsor to bear the unbearable expenditure
  c. Use the special ground forces i.e. Mossad, Delta Force, GSG, SAS.
  d. Collective efforts by nation-states as under are required
    i. Collective extradiction treaty.
    ii. Joint action against terrorist bases by specially trained International forces.
    iii. Economic sanctions.

S - Indian National Strategy

(a) **Preparation** - Formulation of policies for fighting terrorism and delegations of responsibility.
(b) **Prevention** - Development of political climate making difficult for terrorist to take shelter. It also involves :
  (i) Intelligence gathering.
  (ii) Denying access/opportunity to terrorist.
(c) **Priorities** - Balancing of opposite objectives.
(d) **Operation** - The attitude of Govt. should be decisive. Even one single terrorist should not be set free.
(e) **Adjudication** - The Judiciary and the Law should

be stern for the terrorist and related actions. Terrorist should not escape from dragnet of judicial system unpunished.

(f) **Education** - The Govt. official and public should be educated to demystify the intimidating image of terrorist. Public be educated regarding such threats. Authority must place facts open regarding terrorist incidents.

Thus India can pursue the following :

(a) To use carrot and stick policy
(b) Leading world countries be forced to put sanctions against terrorism sponsoring country in Indian context i.e., Pakistan.
(c) Negotiate multilateral accords against terrorism.

T - Evolving Counter Measures

Following measures are required for defeating State Sponsored Terrorism:

(a) Strong Administrative Measures.
(b) All state organs to function at optimum level.
(c) State functionary should be made accountable.
(d) Morality and neutrality to be reemphasized in the states especially.
(e) Screening/weeping out anti national elements in the administration.
(f) Separation of terrorist from general public and no excesses to be committed on innocent masses.
(g) Normalizing Civil/Police-Security Forces relationship.
(h) Posting of most competent officers in terrorist hidden area and reward them suitably.
(i) Quick redressal of public grievances.
(j) Traditional sources of information and influence are tapped.

(k) Psychological and Sociological inputs be taken care.
(l) Extraordinary administrative and legislative measures required
(m) Eradication of corruption.
(n) Role of opinion make i.e., media and local influential citizens be recognized and exploited.
(o) Sophisticated weapon and eqpt for forces and training be given due importance.
(p) Intelligence coordination among various intelligence agencies be properly done.
(q) Requirement of integrated counter terrorist strategy and proper coordination.
(r) Raid on training camps across the border should be through off.
(s) Restoration of demoralized situation be done.
(t) Involvement of Security Forces for well being of public and relief.

U - Suggested Remedial Measures

Following are some suggested remedial measures :

(a) Gear up law and order machinery.
(b) Launch public awareness programme.
(c) India should use internal condition in Pak for its own advantage.
(d) To counter disinformation campaign of Pak build strong counter propaganda machinery and media be grossed up.
(e) Proper moral and physical support be given to SF's.
(f) Enactment of suitable Ordinance/Laws.
(g) Deal terrorist and sympathizers family
(h) Human right organizations to be properly briefed and looked after.
(i) Improve coordinating machinery.
(j) Effective intelligence system based on spies,

electronic and photo reconnaissance.

(k) Diplomatic offensive.

(l) Proper checks on the routes of infiltration and use of electronic gadgets.

References

1. Henery Kissinger, the White House years, (London, Weidenfild & Nicoloson & Machael Joseph, 1979), p. 85.
2. Mautaza Rizvi, editor with Dawn, Karachi, Pakistan, "Indian Express, Chandigarh, September, 11, 2007, p. 8.
3. From Wikipedia, "Pakistan Army" At accessed on Nov. 15, 2007.
4. Hari Sood, "China's military prowess in Tibet," October 23, 2007. At accessed on November 18, 2007.
5. NRDC Nuclear Notebook Chinese Nuclear Forces, Bulletin of the Atomic Scientists May/June 2006. At http://the bulletin.matapres.com/ content/I w035m8u644p864u/ fulltext.pdf accessed on November 15, 2007.
6. www.satp.org
7. The DISAM Journal, fall 2002/winter 2003.
8. Ibid.
9. Ibid.
10. www.satp.org.
11. Ibid.
12. Indian Journal of Strategic Studies, Vol. XXVIII - 2007, p. 99.
13. Indian Journal of Strategic Studies, Vol. XXVIII - 2007, p. 102.

Chapter 2

PEACE AND SECURITY CHALLENGES IN SOUTH ASIA

Dr. S.K. Mishra[1]

From all points of view, South Asia play a significant part in world affairs and their importance in all spheres of human activity continues to increase. South Asia is the epitome of third world and occupies juxtaposed problems, assets and culture with distinguished variance in economics, scientific and technological levels and factors accompanying development. In concepts, ideology and philosophy and hypothesis of international relations the South Asia sub-continent interacts with dimensions uncommon in the developed North. The security dynamics is the region not just in military terms but also political, economic and environmental security.

South Asia is the home of 1.2 billion people and accounts for over one-fifth of the world's population. With a GNP per capital of $ 309, which is only one-third the average for the

1. Reader, Department of Defence Studies, Government P.G. College, Hisar (Haryana).

developing world and less than one-fiftieth of the industrial world, South Asia is indeed 'the most deprived region' of the world. South Asia not only lags behind other regions not only in income levels but also in human development levels. Nearly one-half of the world's illiterate population lives in South Asia. This is partly because of the relatively higher levels of military expenditure due to the arms race between Pakistan and India and ongoing ethnic conflict in Sri Lanka, Fundamentalist in Bangladesh and Maoists in Nepal.

South Asia is a unique region from global perspective. Its problems and conflicts have their own dynamics and most, if not all, of these created within the region, by its history, its geo-politics, its geo-strategy, its economy and ecology. Marginalized to some extent from the main stream of global development South Asia continues to be less active in-so-far as its relation with other powers and regions are concerned. However, India's policy of economic liberation making it an integral part of international global development has brought India into international limelight in the 1990s. The United States sees India as a potential market for its products and services. As a result, though it is unhappy over India's nuclear pursuits, it is willing to accommodate India because of its own long term economic interests.

South Asia comprises of India, Pakistan, Nepal, Bhutan, Bangladesh, Sri Lanka and the Maldives. As a term 'South Asia' has been in use only for past five decades or so. It is the 'Indian sub-continent' that has been longer use. The political divisions of the Indian sub-continent brought about at the time of British withdrawal in 1947 gave rise to the use of the term South Asia for the Indian sub-continent. Area studies programmes in the West which divided the world into regions—South Asia, South-East Asia, West Asia, East Asia, etc., popularised the use of the term South Asia. The emergence of Bangladesh in 1971, from what was hitherto

East Pakistan, reinforced this use.

Geographically, South Asia is a natural strategic unit surrounded by the great chain of mountains—The Himalayas, Karakorum, Hindukush in the North and by the Indian Ocean in the South, East and West. Historically from the earliest times, the people of this region have been intimately by race, culture, religion and sometimes by political allegiance. Political boundaries have not been constant in South Asia. Empires have grown and fallen. There have been different foci of political authority, through Delhi has the longest history of being the imperial capital. The territorial boundaries of the seven countries of the region are thus colonial creations. The most conspicuous feature on the face of South Asia is India, a veritable power house in the region. In size, population, natural resources, level of economic development, standard of education, scientific and technological progress, gross national product (GNP) and evolution of democratic political institution, India is a relative giant.

The South Asian firmament is in a unique situation when a growing India is surrounded by smaller neighbours in various stages of development, facing challenges that require to be responsive to their needs without sounding like Big Brother. There are two intertwining strands to India's neighbourhood policy—security and development. Former foreign secretary Shyam Saran said, "Politically, our neighbourhood policy is based on the recognition that what can best secure India's interests in the region would be building a web of 'dense interdependencies' with our neighbours. We must give our neighbours a stake in our own economic prosperity."

This is the new bottom line for India's neighbourhood policy to help neighbouring States long on to India's economic prosperity. It used to be India's position earlier that the neighbours should reciprocate by being sensitive to India's security concerns. Since that found no resonance with the neighbouring states, India's new neighbourhood mantra is "Liberal and Proactive."

Question arises that how will this be organised? Well, MEA has taken the first step to bring the scope of India's foreign policy to the border. This means better development, better connectivity and hence better trade with neighbours. Saran said, "India must start looking at national boundaries not as impenetrable walls which protect us from the out side world, but as 'connectors', bringing India closer to its neighbours. This needs a mindset change, "The flip side is Indian agencies will need to be on the ball in guarding India's security interests on the borders. Borders should be seen as points of contract not as walls between people of two nations. Border trade, integrated checkpoints, easier travel, trade and investment norms, more tourism—these are routes to a more harmonious South Asia.

India's regional security environment continued to remain unstable throughout 2006. Marked by the collusive nuclear weapons-cum-missile development programme of China, North Korea and Pakistan, the strident march of Islamist fundamentalism, the diabolical nexus between narcotics trafficking and terrorism, the proliferation of small arms, the uncertainty inherent in the risk of despotic regimes and a host of other vitiating factors, regional instability remain a cause for serious concern. Indian's immediate security concerns also remained basically the same though tempered by positive developments with its two largest neighbours. Inter instability, authoritarian and/or military rule, extremist political or religious movements, weak state structures, and insurgences and internal of ethnic conflicts continued to characterize many of the countries of the region. Despite the operations against the Al Qaeda and Taliban elements on the Pak-Afghan border, the principal threats to peace and stability in the region remains the combination of fundamentalism and terrorism nurtured in madarssas and training camps in the area, and the danger of proliferation of weapons of mass destruction (WMD) and of them by fundamentalists and terrorists.

With Bhutan, India already has a very successful economic and political relationship. But Bhutan is moving to a constitutional monarchy in 2008 and has already sought to rework its friendship treaty with India; India has agreed. Bhutan continues to display exemplary good neighborliness in preventing the return of insurgent groups that had set up military camps and bases of operations within its territory.

With regard to Nepal, India will need to adjust to the political realignment in the Himalayan State. The best way to do this is to assist in Nepal's economic development- but MEA is careful to say that India needs to keep its neighbours 'comfort level' in mind. Nepal's fledgling democracy, shaky at the best of times, has been further undermined by a palace coupled by King himself on February 1, 2005. A spontaneous people revolution in April 2006 restored Parliament and led to a rapprochement with the Maoist leaders and an agreement on a new Constitution. Simmering discontent and low-key opposition to China's repressive regime continue in Tibet. The military regime in power in Myanmar still shows no signs of acknowledging the people's nascent movement for democracy. But Myanmar too co-operated in undertaking co-ordinated operations against Indian insurgent groups in the north-east that take refuge or operate from campus in Myanmar.

It is with countries like Bangladesh and Sri Lanka that Indian diplomacy faces some real challenges. Partly because Pakistan is becoming rather hot for international terrorist groups to use as a base and partly because the government of Bangladesh has helplessly stood by and ignored a growing Islamist influence, if not supported and abetted it actively. Bangladesh is quickly sinking deeper into the morass of fundamentalist Islamist terrorism. It has also been willy-nilly providing safe havens to Indian terrorist groups despite India's exhortations to desist from such un-neighbourly acts. There has been an almost unending influx of migrants from Bangladesh into India's North-eastern states over several decades. This has upset the demographic balance and led to tensions in the region. Clashes between India's Border Security Force (BSF) and the Bangladesh Rifles (BDR) have been fairly frequent. In case the situation inside Bangladesh spins out of control and refugees once again pour into India, military intervention may again need to be considered. Bangladesh has remained indifferent to the rising influence of political parties and organisations of fundamentalist and radical Islamist orientation in Bangladesh society and government. It has been insensitive and unresponsive to India's concern regarding the presence and activities of Indian insurgent groups from the North-East and the Pakistani Inter Service Intelligence (ISI) on the Bangladesh soil, large-scale illegal immigration and the criminalization of the border.

Sri Lanka's continued involvement in the vicious Tamil insurgency and its inability to find a lasting solution to the conflict in the north-east is slowing down its economic recovery. The uneasy truce between government forces and the LTTE appears to have broken down irretrievably and incidents of violence are growing by the day. Bangladesh is gradually but perceptibly emerging as the new hub of Islamist fundamentalist terrorism. Its struggle for economic upliftment to bare subsistence levels is being hampered by deeply divisive politics to bare subsistence levels is being hampered by deeply divisive politics and poor governance.

India will have to find a way to open a channel of communication with the LTTE without hurting key sections in India, or even lifting the ban on the organisation. It's a huge challenge but, it's clear that without some Indian help Sri Lanka could be headed down a slippery slope, particularly if the Rajapakse government is intent on imposing a military solution.

The most urgent international issue in Afghanistan prior to September 11, 2001 was Pakistan's continued, visibly overt military support to the Taliban militia and the unprecedented covert support that it was providing to prop up and perpetuate a fundamentalist and fanatical Islamist regime. If the Taliban experiment had been allowed to succeed, the virulence of Islamist fundamentalism would have soon reverberated all over the Southern Asian region, including the Central Asian Republics (CARs). Though the cruel and repressive Taliban militia was disbanded and the popularly elected Kanai regime installed in power, the US and its coalition forces are still only partly in control of the security situation in Afghanistan.

The new regime's writ runs only in Kabul and the surrounding areas. Pakistan is once again suspected to be providing material support to the Taliban and this has emboldened its cadres to launch large-scale frontal attacks on North Atlantic Treaty Organisation's (NATO's) forces, though with heavy casualties. The campaign for a strong and stable Afghanistan under a truly representative government has to be fought on all fronts- political, diplomatic, moral and, if necessary, military—by the international community.

The Pakistan army has been deeply hurt by the almost 2,000 casualties that it has suffered in fighting a high-intensity insurgency in the NWFP in its quest to join the global war against terrorism, in September 2006. The Pakistan government quite unexpectedly signed a 'peace accord' with the tribal leaders in Waziristan and agreed to suspend hostilities against them. This has enabled the largely Pushtun 'new Taliban' to upgrade the number and intensity of its encounters with NATO forces by launching forays from Waziristan and retreating to Pakistani territory when pursued. The US and NATO countries are naturally upset at this turn of events as Pakistan has evidently gone back on its promise to provide all possible help in the war against terrorism. It is apparent that the year 2007 will be a year of reckoning for Pakistan to deliver or face the consequences.

There are many bilateral problems between the countries of South Asia; some of them result from the competition for power, security and prestige. Conventional arms build-up and nuclear rivalry between India and Pakistan can be cited as an example. Then there are open bilateral conflicts in South Asia over territory and water resources. Importantly, given the Indo-centric nature of the region, these conflicts are between India and its South Asian neighbours. South Asian region presents a grand theatre where conflict takes place even at the sub-tactical levels. Terrorism, however, has an inherent definitional problem as often these act—and the actors, the motives and the processes—blur and distinctions between insurgency, struggle for self determination and other manifestations of low intensity conflicts.

On the basis of their duration and intensity, territorial conflicts in South Asia can be divided into two categories—protracted and peripheral conflicts. Protracted conflicts include India's disputes with Pakistan, especially over Kashmir and Siachen. Peripheral conflicts are those between India and its smaller neighbours such as Sri Lanka. Again, one can make a further categorisation in terms of the nature of the contested territory: most of the conflicts are related to border demarcations and only Kashmir has the distinct character of being an irredentist dispute. The India-Pakistan territorial conflict is a multipronged affair in the sense that both countries have competed for more than one part of territory at a time. If Kashmir, according to the Pakistanis, is a 'core issue' between India and Pakistan, Siachen, Kutch and Sir Creek have been crucial issues from the standpoint of their national security. The dispute between India and Sri Lanka over Kachchativu was less contested, at least from the Indian side. This made the task of its resolution easy.

As we know, open bilateral conflicts in the region centre on territory and water sharing. While all the three methods of conflict management, arbitration, mediation and bilateral negations have been tried with some success, since the 1960s, India has rejected arbitration and mediation, and preferred to resolve conflicts with its neighbours through bilateral negotiations. This Indian mode of peacekeeping has practically become the regional approach. The Indo-Sri Lanka territorial dispute and the Indo-Bangladesh dispute over the Ganges water were successfully resolved through bilateral negotiations. However, bilateral negotiations with Pakistan to resolve territorial disputes have so far not yielded results. But one cannot give up peacemaking ventures out of frustration. There are no quick fix solutions to intractable problems and the process of peacemaking should continue until the goals are reached. The experience the world over is that success comes only in the process and as a result of bitter failures. South Asian countries accept this reality; breakdowns in peace processes do not normally undermine their interest in conflict management.

Indeed, the adoption of concept of peace and security in South Asia is not a transient cause but a long-term task which is to be accomplished stage by stage, by moving from simple things to more complex problems. The important thing is that the state of the region join in the common quest for mutually acceptable agreements.

The conflict situations prevailing around India's borders have led to regional instability and an uncertain security environment in the Southern Asian region—that is neither conducive to unhindered economic development nor contributes to human security. Private investors naturally hesitate to risk launching large-scale projects in an unstable region that has also been described as a nuclear flashpoint. India can sit back and watch helplessly from the side-lines as instability creeps up to its borders or it can choose to shape the environment through selective intervention. The latter course will call for some hard policy options and a strong political will as well as political consensus to execute them successfully. India remains fully committed to maintaining peace with its neighbours and stability in the region through a combination of defence preparedness, unilateral restraint, confidence building bilateral interaction.

References

1. Cohen, Stephen P. (ed.) 1987 The Security of South Asia: American and Asian perspectives, Vistaar, New Delhi.
2. A.R. Deo (1991) South Asian Neighbours—World Focus, Vol. 12, No. 11-12.
3. Time of India, 16 Dec. 2006, New Delhi (Edition).
4. George Kin: Peace and Security for Asia. Allied Publisher (1986), New Delhi.
5. Ganguli, Sumit (1986), The origins of war in South Asia: Indo-Pakistani conflict since 1947, Boulder Westview Press.
6. Sahadivan P. (2001), Conflict and Peacemaking in South Asia, Delhi Lancers.
7. Raghvan V.R. (2002), Siachen: Conflict without End, New Delhi, Penguin Books.

8. Gurmeet Kanwal, India's unstable neighbourhood in Sahara Times, Jan 6, 2007.
9. Mishra and Ghosh, Terrorism and Low Intensity Conflict in South Asian Region (2003), Manak Publication, Delhi.
10. Anuradha M. Chenoy, Militarism and Women in South Asia (2002), New Delhi, Kali for Women.

Chapter 3

SOUTH ASIA'S STRATEGIC INCOMPATIBILITIES

Dr. R. B. Singh[1]

Introductory Observations

South Asia at various times has been termed by the United States and Western Countries as a "conflict prone region", as a "nuclear flash point", "Kashmir as a nuclear flash point" and as a "politically unstable region". The rest of the world dittoes this viewpoint as a matter of habit used as they are to accept the formulations of the major powers.

Regrettably India gets lumped together with Pakistan's strategic delinquencies and American permissiveness of the same, as one of the major culprits impeding peace in South Asia. Not only is it a travesty of truth and strategic realities, it also betrays the vested strategic interests of the United States and China primarily, which desire to draw a veil on

1. Editor, Guest Lecturer, Department of Defence Studies, University of Lucknow, Lucknow.

the strategic incompatibilities in South Asia, in which both USA and China have extensively contributed.

Equally regrettable is when prominent members of India's strategic community for reasons not apparent, also assume American positions/ stances on South Asian strategic issues to the effect that India as the larger state should make concessions to Pakistan, or that India should not become paranoid about United States military alliance and arms supplies to Pakistan or that it is in India's interests to keep General Musharraf in power and offer him concessions as the Americans desire.

Such formulations and advocacy of such formulations betray a lack of grasp of the strategic incompatibilities that prevail in South Asia primarily between Pakistan and India. It also betrays a lack of penetrative insight or closing one's eyes to the strategic incompatibilities generated in South Asia by the two prominent external intrusive powers namely United States and China.

This paper attempts to highlight these facets in a bid to promote a truer picture of the strategic realities in South Asia whose conflictual overtones are not of India's making.

Pakistan's Strategic Incompatibilities With India

Pakistan's strategic incompatibilities with India are of Pakistan's own creation. It has been led by the United States and China to believe in an obsessive strategic illusion that Pakistan is India's strategic equal in South Asia. It is this illusion which still persists in the Pakistan Army and its Generals, that even after their defeats in four wars (1947, 1965, 1971,1999) they refuse to admit that they are not India's strategic equal, nuclear weapons not withstanding.

Further, Pakistan's following political incompatibilities with India fuel Pakistan's strategic incompatibilities with India:

- Pakistan was conceived and born in religious hatred as a nation. This hatred was primarily directed against the Hindus.
- Pakistan did not emerge as a homeland for Indian Muslims as millions of Indian Muslims elected to stay back in India rather than opt for Pakistan.
- The partition of India was bloody leading to the total expulsion of the Hindu and Sikh population from the areas which now constitute the Pakistan state.
- Islamic Jehad is the battle cry for Pakistan's over a decade old proxy war against India in Jammu and Kashmir and India's North East.

Pakistan's implacable hatred of India has led it to become a failed state. The Kashmir issue was only a convenient excuse for Pakistan to continue its conflicts with India. As General Musharraf himself once said that even if Kashmir is solved, there will be many more Kashmirs which India will have to face.

The United States and China, India's liberal establishment, India's peaceniks and India's starry-eyed media conveniently ignore that peace with Pakistan is well-nigh impossible. They refuse to see the realities of Pakistan, but focus on the promotion of their own personal interests.

To bring "strategic realism" in the picture, this author would like to enlist the conclusions on Pakistan by the respected Pakistani journalist Khaled Ahamad, who besides being earlier in the Pakistan Foreign Service has also been a founder member of Track II Neemrana Dialogue. His most significant observations on Pakistan in his writings have been:

- "Pakistan is falling, because it is a warrior state and is not supposed to last. It is wedded to the ideal of war in which its ideological rulers accept the possibility of annihilation (shahadat) as a consequence of righteous war."

- "Pakistan's ideology invests the state with the passion of war. There is no normal functioning of the strategic mind in Pakistan."
- "The Army in Pakistan owed its status (paramountcy) to confrontation with India. It developed a vested interest in this confrontation and "guaranteed" the anti-Indian nature of Pakistani politics"
- "Pakistani nationalism has been described by certain writers as being akin to nationalism in the Balkans. Its textbook version is based on an anti-West and anti-Hindu interpretation of Indian history."
- "Pakistan has walked into a blind alley because of its compulsion to adopt a hawkish foreign policy totally out of sync with its growing weaknesses.
- "It (Pakistan) has now in the sad position to predict that talks with India over Kashmir would be non-productive and in consequence of this failure of talks, the risk of nuclear war in South Asia becomes real."
- " This is the response of a state breaking from within but desperately relying on its "nuclear status" to scare the world into delivering Kashmir to it."

Pakistan will continue to be strategically incompatible with India if it persists to exist in the mould outlined above. Changes if any can only be brought about by the United States and China and by a massive political mobilization of the Pakistani masses themselves.

Concluding on Pakistan, Khaled Ahamad's sobering thoughts again need to be quoted and these are:

- "Pakistan is sad nation today because it is compelled to experience reality being created by other powerful states in their own interests."

- "It is a depressed nation unwilling to accept reality because it was not trained to look at it inductively."

It is the United States and China which for their own interests that are shielding and blanking out Pakistan's face-to-face with strategic realities. This is strategically incompatible with India's national security interests.

United States-India strategic partnership strategically incompatible with a United States-Pakistan Military Alliance in South Asia:

> In the last few weeks, when India has cautioned the United States not to supply advanced combat aircraft and other weapons systems to Pakistan, the United States and its apologists in India have taken the plea to what amounts to saying that a US-Pakistan military alliance (which includes advanced weapons sales) is strategically compatible with the building up of a US-India strategic partnership. This is not so as the basic parameters of a strategic partnership stand undermined.

The basic parameters of the United States-India strategic partnership were defined/visualized/envisaged by the two nations as under:

- Strategic convergence of interests
- Shared democratic values of democracy and human rights
- War against terror of the 9/11 variety
- Prevention of WMD proliferation

Strategic convergence of interests denotes mutually shared strategic perceptions, first, regionally and then globally. United States fails in the very first litmus test of a strategic partnership and that is regional strategic convergence of interests in South Asia.

India strongly believes that any over-militarisation of

Pakistan generates the conflict potential of Pakistan, increases its propensity for military adventurism and impedes peace in South Asia. The United States ignoring India's strategic sensitivities designates Pakistan as a Major Non-NATO Ally to facilitate the supply of advanced weaponry. All this on grounds of strategic expediency. As for the United States ignoring the return of democracy to Pakistan, the involvement of Pakistan in 9/11 and Global Islamic Jehad and WMD proliferation sanctioned by the Pakistani General, the less said the better of United States double standards.

As this author wrote in the last paper, how can India have a strategic partnership with USA, when it (United States) is not ready to share "regional convergences of interest in South Asia" itself. How can then India share convergences with USA globally. The connotations of all United States policy / attitudes / formulations / statements after 9/11 are:

- Pakistan is United States' choice of a strategic ally in South Asia, notwithstanding all its strategic delinquencies which endangered US security.
- India's strategic sensitivities are inconsequential in United States' strategies of expediency in South Asia.
- India has no choice but to lump it and make India's national security interests subservient to US strategic priorities in South Asia.

Therefore, if the above be the underlying premises, a US-India strategic partnership is strategically incompatible with a United States-Pakistan Military Alliance in South Asia i.e. within the region itself.

China-Pakistan Strategic Nexus Strategically Incompatible with Dynamic Build up of China-India Political Relationship:

China and India have given a dynamic impetus to the build up of a vibrant economic relationship between the two countries. Two way trade is set to touch the $10 billion mark.

China and India have, however, to think whether an economic relationship is enough. The rapidly changing strategic environment in West Asia, South Asia and East Asia all dictate that China and India also work towards a more dynamic political relationship which could greatly contribute to political stability in Asia's strategic regions.

However, a politically dynamic China-India relationship can only emerge if China reviews its South Asia's strategic policies as under:

- China must view South Asia now as a "region of opportunity" and not as a region where "regional spoiler states" like Pakistan have to be built as counter-weights to India.
- China must re-assess the strategic utility of Pakistan in China's grand strategy.
- China has to consider whether it accepts Pakistan's promiscuous relationships with both USA and China.
- China has also to consider whether in its strategic calculus, a Sino-Pak strategic nexus is compatible with Pakistan's status as a "Major Non-NATO Ally" when NATO is creeping Eastwards into China's preferred sphere of influence.
- China has to accord strategic pre-eminence to India in South Asia and say so.

Till the above review takes place in China's grand strategy, a dynamic China-India political relationship is strategically incompatible for India.

Concluding Observations

Some of the readers in their feedback have maintained that India can demand its regional pre-eminence only by first building up its strategic strength and ridding its governance of corrupt and criminal politicians. This point is well taken and it would be recalled that this author has repeatedly in his papers has called for building India's strategic assets like ICBMs, SLBMs, nuclear submarines and its Air Force combats squadrons. The other aspects of need for building India's political will, will to use power, declaratory strategic policies and good governance stand reflected in this author's SAAG Paper No. 1118 dated 16-09-2004 entitled "India's National Security and Defence: Prescriptions." It was an abridged reproduction of the concluding chapter of this author's book: "India's Defence Policies and Strategic Thought: A Comparative Analysis."

Building up national power is an evolutionary and on-going process. It needs to be recalled that the United States, China and others took strategic notice of India only after 1998 nuclear weapons test. It was the first defining moment in India's post-Independence strategic history.

A second defining strategic moment is now called for and that is the ICBM and SLBM arsenal build-up. Once India achieves this, all the strategic incompatibilities analysed in this paper will evaporate and United States and China would be prompted to grudgingly grant India's strategic pre-eminence in the region. It is time to shrug-off external pressures impeding the development of India's strategic assets stated above.

India must begin learning to air its strategic declarations forcefully, even while it evolves its strategic strengths. The United States did not have to be cautioned that it should not provide advanced weaponry to Pakistan. India should have made a firm strategic declaration that a "US -India Strategic Partnership" is incompatible with a "US-Pakistan Military Alliance" in South Asia and hence a strategic partnership with USA is not acceptable to India. Similarly, China too needs to be strategically declared to that a China-Pakistan strategic nexus needs a review, if China wishes to work with emerging major Asian powers.

India has all the cards even while awaiting evolution of its strategic assets. It needs to play them adroitly. One of the many being that India will not make military purchases from foreign countries which sell or provide arms to Pakistan.

Chapter 4

SOUTH ASIA EXTREMIST ISLAMIST TERROR & SUBVERSION

*Dr. K.N. Shukla**

Terror in Very Slow Motion

Despite the shock and outrage the September 11, 2001, attacks inspired, a point that must clearly be noticed is that, other than their timing and the specific contours and character of the co-ordinated terrorist operations, these attacks were not as entirely unanticipated as they may have been projected to be in the post-Black Tuesday phase. While, in many ways, they did constitute a watershed in history, they lay along an interrupted continuum that extended several years into the past. In a sense, indeed, this was terrorism in very slow motion, and its inevitability had long been remarked by the strategic and intelligence communities. John Deutch, a former Director of the Central Intelligence

* Senior Lecturer, Jawahar Lal Nehru P G College, Maharaj Gunj, Gorakhpur, Uttar Pradesh.

Agency (CIA) had— in a joint paper with Ashton Carter and Phillip Zelikov—warned in November 1998 that:

An act of catastrophic terrorism would take place, which would be a watershed event in American history. It could involve loss of life and property unprecedented in peacetime and undermine America's fundamental sense of security. Like Pearl Harbour, this event would divide our past and future into a before and after. The United States might respond through draconian measures, scaling back civil liberties, allowing wider surveillance of citizens, detention of suspects, and use of deadly force. More violence would follow. Belatedly, Americans would judge their leaders' negligent for not addressing terrorism more urgently...[1]

The literature on catastrophic terrorism and on Weapons of Mass Destruction (WMD) terrorism targeting USA has burgeoned in recent years, but the language and idiom of the particular citation above has an uncanny precision when it is compared with the discourse and events in the wake of Black Tuesday.

Even the method used by the terrorists in the US attacks was not entirely unprecedented. Ely Karmon notes that a coordinated hijacking of four planes has, indeed, already taken place. In September 1970, the Popular Front for the Liberation of Palestine diverted a Pan-Am airliner to Cairo while three others—TWA, Swissair and BOAC planes—were diverted to Dawson airport in Jordan. All were blown up on the ground.

Based on intelligence, the hijacking of a plane in order to crash it in a populated area has been feared in Israel since the mid-1970's. This is why, in 1972, a Libyan plane that penetrated Israeli airspace was downed by Israeli warplanes when it failed to react to Israeli warnings. A similar incident occurred on May 24, 2001, when a small Lebanese civilian plane was shot down north of Tel-Aviv by Apache attack helicopters, because it was feared to be part of a Hizballah suicide operation. In December 1994 an Air-France Airbus was hijacked by Algerian GIA terrorists, landed in Marseille for refueling and was stormed by French counter-terrorist teams when it became clear that they were planning a suicide mission over Paris.[2]

Furthermore, the US has, rightly or otherwise, long regarded itself as the primary target of what it narrowly defines as "international terrorism." Those who have, moreover, studied the pattern and expanding networks of terrorist organisations across the world are clear that, while September 11 represented a major event, a critical development in the unfolding extremist Islamist agenda, it did not constitute a radical discontinuity.

In the discourse on catastrophic terrorism targeting the US, the arguments have focused overwhelmingly on technologies—nuclear, chemical and biological weapons, cyber-terrorism, etc. The gravest evidence of the mounting danger, however, comes from the spread of the ideologies and networks of terrorism.

The manner in which we look upon and interpret these recent events is of crucial strategic significance and has critical impact on the strategies of response against terrorism in what the US has dubbed the "Global War on Terror". In significant measure, the strategies of response that are currently being manifested appear to be flawed, and this is at least in part a consequence of a conceptual failure to correctly define and interpret the catastrophic terrorism witnessed on September 11, 2001.

The Myth of the Locus of Terror

It is perplexing to note that the idea of a "geographical shift of the locus of terror from the Middle East to South Asia"[3] had been increasingly and vigorously propounded, identifying Afghanistan, Pakistan and Kashmir as the new loci and primary sources of extremist Islamist militancy. This idea has survived, if not been reinforced, in US strategic perceptions by the events of Black Tuesday. There are, however, some difficulties with this notion. The first and more obvious is the fact that there is no evidence of any sudden or abrupt 'shift', or a radical discontinuity in the situation—Afghanistan's spiral into chaos had been an inexorable fact for over a decade, as had Pakistan's complicity and steady decline. Even a cursory glance at fatalities in Kashmir would confirm, moreover, that terrorism has been at comparable - albeit escalating—levels in this theatre for over a decade.[4]

More significantly, however, it is dangerous to focus inordinately on the transient geographical location or concentrations of terrorist incidents, activities and movements, to the exclusion of their ideological and material sources, their state sponsors, or their intended targets and proclaimed goals. The error here is the belief that the threat of Islamist terrorism is contained within the regions of its most visible manifestation. Extremist Islam must, however, be recognised for its essential character as an ideology, and terrorism as a method that it accepts and justifies. A method will be adopted wherever it is perceived to have acceptable probabilities of success. An ideology extends wherever it has believers. These are the actual limits or foci of extremist Islamist terrorism. The identification of the locus of terrorism with the transient geographical location where it finds the largest number of victims, is a grave error of judgement.

A closer analysis would indicate that it is more accurate to speak of the spread or expansion of the sphere of terrorism, rather than any dramatic 'shift'. Indeed, as terrorists and their state sponsors secure even limited successes in one region, their methods are adopted in others, threatening an ever-widening spectrum of nations and cultures. It is, now, increasingly clear that no nation in the world is entirely free of the threat from extremist Islamist terrorism. This includes not only the affluent—or 'decadent' as the Islamist would have it—West, but also Muslim majority 'Islamic' nations that do not conform to the extremist Islamist's notion of his Faith and its practices. The extremist Islamist vision is not limited to its current sphere of militancy, or to the economic and political jockeying for control of Central Asia that some 'Great Game' theorists believe, but to God's 'universal empire'. "The world is divided into opposing forces," Altaf Gauhar insists, "there is no common ground between secularism and Islam."[5] Allah Buksh Brohi is even more explicit:

Many Western Scholars have pointed their accusing fingers at some of the ... verses in the Qur'an to be able to contend that world of Islam is in a state of perpetual struggle against the non-Muslims. As to them it is sufficient answer to make, if one were to point out, that the defiance of God's authority by one who is His slave exposes that slave to the risk of being held guilty of treason and such a one, in the perspective of Islamic law, is indeed to be treated as a sort of that cancerous growth on that organism of humanity, which has been created "Kanafsin Wahidatin" that is, like one, single, indivisible self. It thus becomes necessary to remove the cancerous malformation even if it be by surgical means (if it would not respond to other treatment), in order to save the rest of Humanity... The idea of Ummah of Mohammad, the Prophet of Islam, is incapable of being realised within the framework of territorial states much less made an enduring basis of viewing the world as having been polarised between the world of Islam and the world of war. Islam, in my understanding, does not subscribe to the concept of the territorial state... [6]

The 'surgical' removal of the 'cancerous malformation' that is the non-Islamic world is what the Islamist terrorists believe they are engaged in.

Unfortunately, the 'loci of terrorism' thesis lends itself to local, capricious and fitful responses, often dictated by transient political pressures or short-term (and potentially counter-productive) considerations. Thus, the US and its primary allies, conceding that all terrorism is reprehensible and demands a global response, have not really commended measures that can be situated in a multilateral and pre-emptive framework. The US State Department's annual report, Patterns of Global Terrorism (PGT) and its subsequent addendum are flawed in their inherent logic. For instance, the PGT 2000 explicitly elaborates on the long and enduring support that the Musharraf regime has extended to the Taliban and terrorist groups active in Jammu and Kashmir (J&K). At the same time, it also alludes to the 'fact' that the Government of Pakistan "generally has cooperated with US requests to enhance security for US facilities and personnel."[7] Pakistan's role in fuelling and sustaining terrorism in J&K and persisting mischief in Afghanistan are clearly recognised in the report: "Pakistan's military government, headed by Gen. Pervez Musharraf, continued previous Pakistani Government support of the Kashmir insurgency, and Kashmiri militant groups continued to operate in Pakistan, raising funds and recruiting new cadre... The United States remains concerned about reports of continued Pakistani support for the Taliban's military operations in Afghanistan. Credible reporting indicates that Pakistan is providing the Taliban with material, fuel, funding, technical assistance, and military advisers. Pakistan has not prevented large numbers of Pakistani nationals from moving into Afghanistan to fight for the Taliban. Islamabad also failed to take effective steps to curb the activities of certain madrassas, or religious schools, that serve as recruiting grounds for terrorism."[8] And yet, Pakistan is the principal ally and frontline state in the US Global War on Terror.

Such contradictory observations are not surprising since US counter-terrorism perspective has for long been steeped in a myopic view - it proposes to attack/counter only if its own citizens are victims. The US has been consistently reluctant—and in substantial measure remains so—to accept the fact that any effective strategy to counter terrorism must be premised on global efforts supplementing national and bilateral strategies, however resilient and effective the latter may be. US counter-terrorism perspectives have critically failed to recognise that the combination of chaos and paralysis that terrorism produces, affects not only particular 'victim' societies, but the composite global order.[9]

The US Secretary of State, Colin Powell, indicated at a hearing of a special Senate Appropriations Sub-committee, that the US "seeks to create an environment that is intolerant of terrorism and isolate those who threaten the US, its friends and allies." But, he also added that "I think you lose credibility when you do it (target the nation of origin) that way."[10] Even as the US acknowledges convincing reports of Pakistan's complicity in supporting terrorist activity in J&K and to the Taliban, it rules out any action against Pakistan. By stating that targeting the nation of origin produces a 'loss of credibility', it effectively places Pakistan beyond the purview of its proposed new policy. The relative lack of consistency in the US policy is revealing. Powell, at a Press briefing, observed that State sponsors of terrorism are increasingly isolated. The PGT report, on the other hand, clearly points to the contrary.

The Islamist Extremist Endgame

The impact of the catastrophic terrorist attack of September 11, 2001, in USA, is still reverberating across the world, and subsequent events have left a trail of unanswered questions in the public mind, and among the strategic community. The most important of these relate to what it was, precisely, that the terrorists sought to achieve in terms of definable strategic gains. True, some 4,000 people were killed in a simultaneous multi-strike operation, and two among the great symbolic edifices of the United States of America - the World Trade Centre representing its economic might, and the Pentagon its military prowess—were successfully targeted. But, what precisely had this act of apparently wanton destruction achieve? How did it undermine or detract from the overwhelming military and economic power of the US? How did it further the Islamist extremist cause?

To many Western strategists, the suicide attacks, and the subsequent and apparently related cases of bio-terrorism in the US, are acts of unadulterated evil, of a rage that finds its justification and end in the suffering it inflicts. They are acts, equally, that inescapably condemn not just their perpetrators, but their entire network of support, their ideological bases, and the causes they represent, to an inevitable and possibly hideous end at the hands of a wounded and righteous global community. Considering the firepower, the technologies and the resources available to America, on the one hand, and the poverty, the isolation and the primitive conditions in which Osama bin Laden's cohorts and the Taliban subsisted, the attacks on the US appear suicidal, not only for the 19 hijackers who went down with the planes in New York, Washington and Pennsylvania, but for the Pan-Islamist extremist movement itself.

In some measure, this point of view is reinforced by the

apparent and increasing isolation of the Islamist extremists within the Muslim world, as even collaborators and state sponsors, such as Pakistan, turn their back against the intemperate excesses of what is evidently the most rabidly fanatical element among them. The over-arching malignancy of the Black Tuesday attacks and the accumulating evidence of bio-terrorism in USA (and in an increasing number of other countries as well) [11] have driven a wedge between those who have, for decades, used limited doses of terrorism to further their political or strategic objectives, and the fundamentalist or millenarian terrorists who seek goals that go far beyond the tangible world and all existing structures of contemporary human, social and political organisation, to a vision that seeks to establish the 'Empire of Allah' through acts of extreme violence. Within this millenarian vision, a final, apocalyptic confrontation between the 'armies of the faithful' and of the 'unbelievers' is not only a conceivable eventuality, it may even be a desired end envisaged by their interpretation of the Holy Book, an objective to be actively pursued. This malignant worldview has created deep apprehensions in much of the Muslim world, as it has among non-Muslims, though it may have inspired a small minority of fanatics to an emulative frenzy.

This has crucial repercussions on the character and scale of violence that would be acceptable to the fundamentalist terrorist. No 'strategic terrorist' would resort to violence beyond a certain scale, because in doing so, he would destabilise the situation to a point where he cannot make any rational calculations of the outcome, and hence of strategic gains and losses. Pakistan and its leader, Gen. Pervez Musharraf, fit well into this paradigm—they have, for decades, used measured doses of terror to further their objectives in J&K and in other parts of India. In the wake of the September attacks, however, they have found it entirely convenient to join (albeit under pressure) the US coalition against terrorism. In doing this, they apparently turned directly against their own proteges and long-time partners and friends—bin Laden's Al Qaeda and the Taliban—because no useful strategic purpose could be served by a continuing overt association with these groupings. Indeed, in the emerging situation, such an association could, in fact, place Pakistan's own survival at risk.

The fundamentalist or millenarian terrorist, on the other hand, conceives of no limit to his potential violence. In his perverse vision, the existing world order is corrupt beyond redemption, and must be destroyed—calculations of relative strategic advantage and loss are in the hands of a 'higher power' to whose 'will' he 'submits'. The lives of men and women—both of those who are loyal to the fundamentalist cause, and those of the 'enemy'—have no intrinsic worth, but are mere instrumentalities to the will of God (of which the fundamentalist alone is apparently aware). In other words, he operates within a context in which physical, material and political consequences do not have the same significance or weight that they would have in the planning and projections of conventional parties in conflict.

This is, of course, a reductionist portrait, and strategic and fundamentalist motives combine in various proportions in different actors in the theatre of terror. To the extent, however, that the one or the other set of motives dominates, it is necessary to understand the dramatic shift in patterns of behaviour and strategies this would provoke, and the radically different tactics and policies that are necessary to deal with these patterns.

It is within this context that the American gameplan evolved. Briefly, the US formulated a staged policy which envisaged a long-term struggle, and which sought to bring into being the broadest conceivable coalition of nations into the campaign against global terrorism. The first stage focused on Afghanistan, on the one hand, and on a painstaking investigative process to document and dismantle the international support structures of terrorism, on the other. Within Afghanistan, the military infrastructure of the Taliban was to be destroyed, an interim government installed at Kabul with control of the towns and cities of the country, consigning the Taliban and Al Qaeda forces to a fugitive existence, from where they can be 'smoked out' and 'brought to justice', or where 'justice can be brought to them'. Thereafter, the world community could dedicate itself to systematically, if gradually, destroying the global network of terror that is presently in existence.

There is both clarity and simplicity in this scheme, and given America's overwhelming technological, military and economic might, and the apparent and emerging counter-terrorist consensus across the world, these would appear to be realistic and entirely achievable projections. War, however, is a notoriously unpredictable business and a war against terrorism even more so.

And to return to original theme of this section, moreover, if there was such an easy inevitability to events, what, precisely was it that led the fundamentalist terrorists to escalate the scale of violence to a level that would provoke such overwhelming retaliation—and their own certain defeat? Was this a disastrous miscalculation? Or the design of a small group of hate-impelled fanatics who were beyond caring about consequences?

It is more than evident that months, if not years of planning went into the Black Tuesday attacks, and that this planning reflects a high—if perverted—level of intellectual and strategic capabilities. It is difficult to understand how such planners could have failed to foresee the outcome of a direct and dramatic attack on the heart of America. Indeed, subsequent events and statements emanating from the Al Qaeda and the Taliban are sufficient proof that these repercussions were not only foreseen, but were to be welcomed as links in the chain of events that was intentionally initiated through the September 11 terrorist strikes. Roland Jacquard, President of the International Observatory on Terrorism at Paris, notes that bin Laden intended the '9/11' attacks to be so "audacious, impudent and massively inhumane" as to ensure a "massive, inordinate" US retaliation that would further inflame Muslim opinion against the US and against the Arab regimes allied with Washington. "His design," Jacquard asserts, "is to create sufficient instability to bring about Islamic revolution."[12] This, it appears, is the general interpretation of the Islamist extremist gameplan, and there is, certainly, an element of truth in it. It is too much of a gamble, however, to be the entire truth.

The fundamentalist terrorists' own projections and motives go well beyond how they hope to benefit from the current violence directed against them, and must comprehend clear ideas regarding where their own violence would be directed in future. Whether or not they succeed in their plans will depend substantially on the world's ability to out-guess them, and to create appropriate and effective defences that can contain the impact of such future violence.

To the Islamist fundamentalist terrorist, the present World Order is not only irrevocably unjust, it is utterly debased, a challenge and insult to God's will on earth. It cannot be reformed through any progressive accretions of good, through conciliation and compromise. The power of what he regards as evil is too great in the present arrangement for any limited measure to succeed. The system cannot, in other words, be 'improved'; it must be swept aside, destroyed, whatever the costs.

Crucially, moreover, he does not share the popular assessment of the strength and stability of this system, or of the power of those who dominate it. He is, consequently, not awed into impotent acceptance by the spectacle of America's might, its smart missiles and planes, its nuclear arsenal, its unending destructive power. It is a power that is undermined, in his eyes, by its corruption, by its deviation from 'God's Way', its 'infidelity'.

The apparent stability of the world order, in this view, is a stagnant pool; the act of terror, a rock, or even a pebble, thrown into it. What matters is not the immediate or direct impact, but the ripples it will create. And, with a thousand little pebbles, the wasted, crumbling, degenerate walls and structures of this system will collapse, and a deluge will wash away the 'evil of the world'.

Today's fundamentalist terrorist, consequently, does not seek to mobilise masses before a great rebellion. He is a catalyst. He destabilises the situation, provides a model for action, and consequences follow - and are clearly envisaged by him—even if and after he dies. His personal survival is not essential or integral to the success of his cause. You cannot, in fact, 'decapitate' the new and global insurrection of terror. Where one head falls, others will spring to fill the breach.

The great empires of history did not collapse at the height of their powers through cataclysmic upheavals from within or without. They declined gradually through a process of erosion at the peripheries and of corruption and corrosion at the Centre. The leadership of Islamist millenarian groupings has a fairly sophisticated, though possibly intuitive, understanding of this dynamic. Accurately or otherwise, they point to Russia; one of the two 'Great Powers' of the world that, in a matter of years—its armies, its missiles, its tanks and planes, its great nuclear arsenals, all intact—

collapsed to the status of a Third World country, barely capable of managing its own internal contradictions, its economy surviving on the fitful injection of capital and aid from the affluent West. If this can be the fate of one 'Evil Empire', so can it be engineered for another.

Both the September 11 strikes and the US attacks on Afghanistan can, consequently, be examined as part of a meticulously planned chain of events. The strikes in US were intended to attract retaliatory violence; they were expected to result in a consolidation of the extremist Islamist forces, to undermine US prestige and that country's sense of invulnerability, and to catalyse a chain of events that would destabilise the emerging unipolar world order in unpredictable ways, in order to create a space of political uncertainty in which the Islamists could make a focused bid for power.

What we have seen as yet is thus only the first phase of an elaborate endgame of the Islamists' imaginings, and its fundamentals were articulated by its ideologues decades ago —as far back as in the 1920s—in what was then undivided India, and in Egypt. Its principles have only gradually translated themselves into political violence, militancy, terrorism, and an incipient pan-Islamic movement in widening areas across the world.

The timeframes of this gameplan are in the decades, if not the centuries, and the Western orientation that has, in the past, sought closure in a confrontation of a few weeks, months or even the projected two years that the Americans believe their Afghan campaign will last, can lead to grave miscalculations, and will have to be abandoned for a slower, unwavering and consistent war against terrorism on all fronts. In the absence of such a coherent and sustained response, the economies and the political and social structures of Western nations will suffer gradual erosion; and each phase of such progressive erosion will lead to a consolidation of the extremist position.

This is the process of induced collapse that terrorist actions seek to create through a new 'war of a thousand cuts'. For this, they will not require spectacular exhibitions of the kind that brought down the Twin Towers in New York. A continuous succession of incidents of low-grade violence - an anthrax scare that affects a few score of people, a little suitcase or car bomb in a shopping mall, an innocuous IED that blows up a restaurant, a bus or a train—with each incident claiming no more than a few lives, can undermine popular confidence, create a paralysis of terror in public and institutional responses, and, more importantly, destroy the competitive advantages of the US economy. This is crucial. The terrorist intent is eventually to take the war onto American soil, and to hurt American interests overseas, wherever this is possible. Osama bin Laden clearly articulated these objectives in his statement on the Al Jazeera television network, saying "The US will never know security or safety unless we know security and safety in our land and in Palestine."[14]

If these campaigns can be sustained, however fitfully, over an extended period of time, there will eventually be a flight of capital from US soil and US corporations, as transaction costs increase unbearably, undermining the economy. Events in the wake of '9/11' have also demonstrated that the US is substantially vulnerable to communal and ethnic polarisation. Continued terrorist violence will also be calculated to aggravate such trends, to induce the 'ghettoisation' of American society, and an eventual reverse migration of specialised human resources—particularly those of Asian origin—creating new problems for the viability of American enterprise. Needless to say, such processes can be expected, over time, to undermine the

American power across the world, notwithstanding the overwhelming military arsenal at the disposal of the US Forces.[15]

Terror is at the heart of this vision, conceived of, by the ideologues of extremist Islam, not merely as a transient tactic, but as the essential objective of their 'war to advance God's purpose on earth.' And it is crucial that we understand the concept behind this strategy, and its projected intent and impact. Brigadier S K Malik, unsurprisingly a Pakistani, writes in his Quranic Concept of War:

Terror struck into the hearts of the enemies is not only a means, it is the end in itself. Once a condition of terror into the opponent's heart is obtained, hardly anything is left to be achieved. It is the point where the means and the end meet and merge. Terror is not a means of imposing decision upon the enemy (sic); it is the decision we wish to impose upon him.[16]

Islamist extremist terrorists had been active in many countries—particularly in Asia—long before September 11, 2001, and their activities continue. In addition, there are sleeper and sympathetic cells in an estimated 70 countries world-wide. Strong Islamist extremist networks exist in Canada, Australia, France, UK, and Germany, and there is also a very significant, though largely passive presence in several other European nations. Europe has been at risk for a long time. Islamist extremist networks have been consolidating themselves throughout the continent for decades now, and have been encouraged substantially by regimes that have maintained an ambivalent official attitude towards terrorists whose activities target countries other than their host countries in Europe. These European nations have, for all these years, acted on an assumption that they would never be targeted by the Islamist extremists, and have tolerated or even sought to manipulate these forces in terms of their perceived 'strategic interests'. In the process, they have permitted the build up of these forces on their own soil. It is known that a number of terrorist cells have survived Black Tuesday on US soil as well. It can be expected that these will be activated in the uncertain future.

At the same time, as the memory and the horror of the September 11 incidents recedes and the images of the victims of the war in Afghanistan are reiterated with greater frequency, the moral consensus in favour of US actions will be diluted. In the first days after the terrorist strikes in USA, hardly a voice could be heard offering even a qualified justification of the outrage. After less than a few weeks of US bombings in Afghanistan, these voices began to emerge, albeit on the periphery of the world community. Thus over 60 clerics in Iraq issued a Fatwa against all Muslim nations that offered any assistance to the US 'blasphemers' in their campaigns against the 'innocent Afghans'. There were widespread street protests against the US action in a number of countries, though most prominently in Pakistan and Indonesia. Even in the relatively includes the Harkat-ul-Jehad-e-Islami, which was established by Shawkat Osman, alias Sheikh Farid in 1992 with bin Laden's backing, and which has an estimated strength of about 15,000. The Harkat maintains several camps in the hilly areas of Chittagong, where the cadres are given arms training. Several hundred recruits have also been trained in Afghanistan. The cadres, recruited mainly from among students of various madrassas, style themselves as the 'Bangladeshi Taliban.' Reports suggest that foreign-aided religious fanatics are actively conspiring to establish 'Islamic hukumat' by waging war and killing progressive intellectuals, as well as various minority groups and 'heretical' sects, such as the Ahmadiyas.

In addition to the JEI, the prominent fundamentalist Islamist political parties in Bangladesh include the Muslim

League, Tabligh Jamaat, Jamaat-e-Tulba and Jamaat-ul-Muderessin. One significant pro-Iranian group, the Islamic Shasantantra Andolan (Movement for Islamic Constitution) is also active. The subversive activities of the ISI and foreign extremist Islamist agencies in Bangladesh increased radically after Sheikh Hasina's broadly secular Awami League came to power in June 1996, and this has contributed to an upsurge in militant and fundamentalist political activity. Superimposed over a history of military coups, a politics dominated by the rhetoric of Islam, and increasing international linkages, including networks with insurgent groups operating in India's Northeast, extremist Islamist militancy constitutes the most serious existing internal security threat in Bangladesh.

The recent Bangladesh elections have brought a new right wing regime, backed by Islamist fundamentalist forces, into a clear majority. Apart from the BNP itself, which has exploited an Islamist platform for political ends since its inception, the new Parliament has 16 members from the militant Islamist Jamaat-e-Islami, which has been linked to several acts of extremist violence over the past years, and that runs several training camps for pan-Islamist militants in the country. The Jamaat is overtly pro-Pakistan, and reportedly secures substantial support from the ISI, including funding, arms flows and technical and training assistance. Eclectic and moderate Muslim community in India, at least some voices spoke out in favour of bin Laden and the Taliban, and overtly against the US. Over time, these voices will strengthen, not only among moderate Muslims, but within the Western democracies and the US itself, questioning the morality of the US campaign, sowing confusion in the minds of policy makers in the US and among its allies. As the American position on a number of issues has already demonstrated, moreover, old patterns and calculations of geo-political advantage are already re-emerging, and conventional considerations of strategic 'interests of state' may reassert their priority over a principled and concerted war against all manifestations of terrorism.

As these trends consolidate, terrorist actions will seek to secure a greater convergence, first among extremist Islamist groups, and then among larger Muslim communities, projecting the ideal of a new Khilafat or caliphate. There have already been significant moves in the direction of such convergence, with the more virulent fundamentalist Islamist elements virtually across the world throwing in their lot under bin Laden's banner. Osama bin Laden had, moreover, increasingly reiterated his Pan-Islamist agenda, linking himself to a variety of emotive 'Muslim causes'—including, for instance, Palestine and Kashmir—in different countries, and had also sought to project himself as 'Shiekh-ul-Islam', a title last held by the Caliphs.

The Islamist endgame envisages, consequently, an eventual and decisive confrontation between a corroded and declining Western power, and an increasingly united Islamist force.

There are, of course, a number of possibly grave miscalculations in this grand design. In the first instance, a variety of conflicting forces that undermine the extremist cause have also been brought into increasing operation by recent events. Secondly, even with a substantial degradation of western powers, the gap between the technological and destructive capabilities of these and any eventually consolidated 'Islamic World', is virtually unbridgeable in the foreseeable future. A direct confrontation would be unimaginably bloody, but the defeat of the comparatively primitive forces of fundamentalist Islamist extremism would, consequently, be inevitable. This gap may, however, be wiped out at a stroke if the Islamist terrorists are able to weaponize certain bio-technological strains that may not be entirely outside their competence in coming years.

Most significantly, however, the projected Islamist endgame underestimates the resilience of countries such as the US, in particular, and of democratic societies in general. While Islamist fundamentalism has created a banner under which many 'Muslim' grievances and frustrations are articulated today, the promise of the ideologies of liberal democracy offer a strong and attractive incentive to millions who are equally distressed by authoritarian and oppressive regimes—including fundamentalist regimes—in different parts of the 'Muslim World.'

What we are seeing, consequently, is a global struggle that seeks, on the one hand, the preservation and evolution of the present world order, and, on the other, its unqualified destruction. Eventually, neither vision can be expected to emerge unscathed or unamended, and the unipolar New World Order will have to accommodate alternative perspectives to create a more balanced and humane system.

This is an immensely complex war, and understanding its various dimensions—military, political, social, economic, and most importantly, ideological—is the first step towards securing an acceptable outcome. The fight against terrorism is as complex as the support structures of terrorism, and will have to be extended into the areas of ideology, social structures, finance, coalitions and affiliations, development and various aspects of the international economic and political order. There is, in this, no 'either-or' conflict between military and non-military means. Military means will remain necessary to contain the immediate threat and impact of terrorism. In the absence of such a response, successive waves of terror will simply demolish the structures of governance and order in target societies, undermining and eventually eliminating even the possibility of non-military solutions.

Excessive emphasis on military means, to the exclusion of all others, however, will always leave a residual potential for revival. The world will have to adopt a composite, balanced and graded response to all facets of terrorism, its support structures, and its underlying motives and incentives.

Pakistan: A Frontline State?

Pakistan has been declared, by the US, as a 'frontline state' in the Global War on Terror and, by virtue of its geographical location, it is certainly located on the 'frontline' of what the US currently conceives of as the primary locus of terrorism. The unanswered question, however, is which side of the battlelines does it stand on? The '9/11' terrorist attacks and the subsequent and critically fluid response strategies have not resulted in any perceptible change in Pakistan's policies with regard to India, and there is no evidence that the Pakistani jehad in J&K has been reversed, or even diluted. Pakistan's raison d etre remains inexorably tied to the ideologies of hatred and religious exclusion that led to its creation as a separate nation over half a century ago, and there is little indication that Pakistan has, despite apparent US pressure, chosen to alter the ideologies that defined the perverted course of its history.

Unfortunately, Western perspectives have yet to come to terms in full measure with what they have known for decades, and what they have found to be politically or strategically expedient to deny. In the foreseeable future, it is more than likely that Pakistan would continue its present agenda of bleeding India. Indeed, Pakistan may even reduce the relative levels of terrorist violence in J&K, even as it initiates lethal terrorist attacks at metropolitan centres such as New Delhi, Mumbai, Kolkata, Chennai, etc. A shift in the pattern of violence from Kashmir to other centres would offer

Pakistan greater 'deniability', and enable it to argue that Indian Muslims have been pushed to a point of no return by the government's 'atrocities'. However, such a shift in strategies should not be perceived as a radical departure or even as a 'nuanced' reorientation of the jehadi agenda. It lies entirely within the paradigm that has been sustained since the Zia-ul-Haq regime, and has progressively translated itself into the Islamist fundamentalist agenda in the region. As Fazl-ur-Rahman, Chief of the Harkat-ul-Mujahideen (HuM), expressed it, "Delhi, Calcutta, Mumbai and Washington are the real targets of Militants. Muslims should co-operate with militants for dominance of Islam in the world."

Apprehensions that the current military operation in Afghanistan and turmoil in Pakistan will result in increased cross-border infiltration of terrorists are not misplaced. Recent reports indicate that Pakistan's Inter Services Intelligence (ISI), has shut down or transferred terrorists from nearly a dozen terrorist training camps in Pakistan occupied Kashmir (PoK) and planned to push these terrorists into India through the Line of Control and international borders in J&K, Punjab and Rajasthan. Moreover, the defeat of the Taliban in Afghanistan has released a large number of terrorists from that theatre. At least part of this dispersal may seek shelter and relocate their terrorist operations on Indian Territory.

It is within this context that the US strategies of response have to be assessed. The conventional 'pick and drop' Cold War stratagem has been revitalised in the new 'great game' that is being played out in familiar geographical terrain, and this represents a crucial failure of critical understanding. Pakistan and its ISI, with their deep and continuous involvement in Afghanistan and with the Taliban, have, it was argued, the most 'reliable' intelligence that could help locate America's most wanted man, Osama bin Laden and his network of terrorist camps. Pakistan was, consequently, cast in the unlikely role of a 'frontline state' in the war against terrorism. The fact is, it has long been the frontline state sponsor of terrorism in this region. Any objective assessment of the internal conditions and long-term policies of the Pakistani State would demonstrate a fundamental and irreducible opposition between what that country's ruling elite perceives as its strategic interests, and those of the emerging alliance against terrorism. This implies that the US reliance on Pakistan could be one of the worst strategic blunders for a multiplicity of reasons. Even as US Forces were deeply engaged in Afghanistan, there was continuing evidence of continued Pakistani military presence there in support of the Taliban, as well as the ongoing mobilisation of Islamist fundamentalist forces from J&K, PoK and within Pakistan. There was at least some evidence to suggest that these forces were actively, if 'unofficially', being encouraged to join forces with the Taliban.

Pakistan's ambivalence is evident in the 'neutralisation'[20] of three senior Islamist Army commanders reportedly sympathetic to the Taliban who were superseded or sidelined with great publicity. The most significant of these changes was the removal of Lt. Gen. Mehmood Ahmad, Director General of the ISI, who had extensive linkages with the Taliban regime. Gen. Ahmad, who was in the US during the '9/11' terrorist attacks, also led a delegation of Pakistani mullahs (clerics) to Afghanistan apparently to negotiate Osama bin Laden's surrender. Reports from Islamabad indicated that instead of asking for bin Laden to be handed over unconditionally, Gen. Ahmed praised the efforts of Taliban Chief, Mullah Mohammed Omar, in his fight against the 'Great Satan',[21] and advised him on ways to counter Washington's planned offensive. Media reports also indicate that the US administration had complained to Pakistan that Gen. Ahmad was not providing the US with real-time intelligence inputs that were crucial to track bin Laden, despite a firm commitment in this regard during his recent visit to Washington.[22] After his dismissal, Ahmad is said to have crossed over into Afghanistan to continue to advise the Taliban regime on the course of the war, and there are at least some suggestions that his dismissal was, in fact, intended to facilitate such a role. Indeed, Ahmad's linkages with the Taliban represent a continuation of the Pakistan covert and overt terrorist agenda in the region. As Shireen Mazari noted, "So obsessed is the [Pakistani] military with ensuring the military success of the Taliban that it is dragging Pakistan into a confrontation the country does not need and cannot afford."[23]

Amidst the increasingly volatile anti-US protests in various parts of Pakistan during the initial phase of the Afghan campaign, the religious leadership had appealed to the Muslims of the world to be prepared for waging a jehad against the US and its allies. The attacks on Afghanistan, they asserted, cannot be considered to be an intervention in an individual Islamic country but are a direct and open aggression on the Islamic world. Reports from various parts of the North West Frontier Province (NWFP) of Pakistan indicated that that hundreds of youth had left for Afghanistan to join the Taliban militia in the 'holy war' against the US and its allies,[24] and thousands of others were in readiness to do so. The Jamaat-Ulema-e-Islam (JUI) had claimed that hundreds of thousands of people had 'volunteered' to fight against US ground forces in Afghanistan. Pakistani media reports indicated that cadres of the JUI, the Jamaat-e-Islami (JeI) and the Pakistan-Afghanistan[25] Defence Council (PADC), occupied footpaths and street corners where they exhorted the local populace for jehad and to mobilise donations for their Afghan campaign.[26] Announcements in this regard were also made over loudspeakers from mosques

and camps set up on highways. The Fazlur Rahman faction of the JUI is reported to have received more than Rs 3 million in cash from the tribal areas alone.[27] The JUI (Fazlur), a staunch supporter of the Taliban regime, reportedly established approximately 1,000 camps in tribal areas and in 24 districts of the NWFP, where cadres recruited 'volunteers' for jehad and collected donations. Haji Jalil Jan, Provincial Deputy General Secretary of the JUI (Fazlur), indicating that his party had prepared lists of jehadis at district level and in tribal areas, added that the Taliban regime had, however, advised the party leadership not to send more jehadis to Afghanistan unless the US landed its ground forces in the country. [28]

In Malakand division, the Tehreek-Nifaz-e-Shariat-e-Muhammadi (TNSM), led by Sufi Muhammad, had announced that in case an attack was launched on Afghanistan from Pakistan, jehad would be launched against the Pakistan government. Sufi Muhammad said that TNSM activists would join the Taliban militia in a 'holy war' against the 'infidels'. "Preparations for jehad have started already and the registration of youth has commenced throughout the Malakand division."[29]

The concentration of madrassas (religious seminaries), run by the pro-Taliban Jamaat-Ulema-e-Islam (JUI), factions of Maulana Fazlur Rahman and Maulana Sami-ul-Haq, in the NWFP also mobilised strong opposition to the air strikes on Afghanistan. The academic sessions in the religious schools had ended at the time of the initiation of the US campaign, and students, mostly Afghans, were ready to leave for Afghanistan. Elders and religious leaders from Orakzai, Kurram, Khyber, North Waziristan and South Waziristan agencies also supported the July. At a meeting at Darul-ul Uloom Zargari in Hangu, they had vowed to work under the leadership of Maulana Fazlur Rahman to prepare people for jehad in Afghanistan.

Religious parties were reported to have initiated a vigorous recruitment drive to enlist young men to fight alongside the Taliban regime in Afghanistan.[30] News sources indicated that the Taliban had requested Deobandi groups in Pakistan to send in approximately 500,000 volunteers before the anticipated US ground campaign commenced. Long queues of potential recruits were witnessed at various madrassas in Pakistan. In Karachi, approximately a dozen mosques and madrassas, especially the Binori Town seminary, the largest Deobandi madrassa in Pakistan, were at the forefront of the enlistment drive. The clergy at the Binori Seminary, including Mufti Nizamuddin Shamzai, are considered very close to the Taliban Chief, Mullah Mohammed Omar. Shamzai was also the leader of a delegation, which the former Director General of the ISI, Lt. Gen. (Retd) Mahmud, took to Kandahar in an apparent attempt to impress upon Mullah Omar to hand over bin Laden to the US authorities. Maulana Masood Azhar, the Jaish-e-Mohammed (JeM) Chief also maintains close linkages with the Binori clergy. In fact, the first visuals of Azhar's release consequent to the terrorist-hostages swap at Kandahar were of his arrival at the Binori mosque. Mufti Nizamuddin Shamzai, on September 18, 2001, gave a call for Jehad to defend Afghanistan if the US launched attacks against the Taliban and Osama bin Laden. Shamzai said in his fatwa "If non-Muslim forces attack Afghanistan, it would be the religious duty of every Muslim to fight jihad side by side with their Afghan brothers." In a direct warning to Pakistan, he said Muslim countries that supported an attack against Afghanistan by non-Muslim forces would lose their authority under Islam.

Primarily, it is a version (or perversion) of the Deobandi creed that forms the religious and ideological base for both

JeM as also the Taliban. In fact, the Taliban movement was launched by students of the same network of JUI-run madrassas, which are the JeM's parent organisations. The leader of the JUI, Maulana Samiul Haq, a former member of the National Assembly and Senate and whose madrassa—Dar-ul-Uloom Haqqania—was an important training base for the Taliban leadership. According to Ahmed Rashid, "In 1999, at least eight Taliban cabinet ministers in Kabul were graduates of Haq's madrassa and dozens more served as Taliban governors in the provinces, military commanders, judges and bureaucrats." The intensity of the Haqqania madrassa enlistment is elucidated by Rashid: "In February 1999, the madrassa had a staggering 15,000 applicants for some 400 new places making it the most popular madrassa in northern Pakistan." Indeed, Rashid quotes Samiul Haq to indicate the Taliban-Madrassa nexus: "Before 1994, I did not know Mullah Omar because he had not studied in Pakistan, but those around him were all Haqqania students and came to see me frequently to discuss what to do. I advised them not to set up a party because the ISI was still trying to play one Mujaheddin party against the other in order to keep them divided. I told them to start a student movement. When the Taliban movement began I told the ISI, 'let the students take over Afghanistan'". Haq, according to Rashid, was in constant touch with Mullah Omar and assisted him in dealing with 'international relations' and also offered advice on important Sharia decisions. He was also the principal organiser for the recruitment of Pakistani students to fight for the Taliban. An instance of the deeper involvement is evident when "after the Taliban defeat in Mazar in 1997 he (Haq) received a telephone call from Omar asking for help. Haq shut down his madrassa and sent his entire student body to fight alongside the Taliban. And after the battle for Mazar in 1998, Haq organised a meeting between Taliban leaders and 12 madrassas in the NWFP to organise reinforcements for the Taliban army. All the madrassas agreed to shut down for one month and send 8,000 students to Afghanistan. The help the Taliban receive from Pakistan's Deobandi madrassas is an important level of support they can rely upon, quite apart from the government and the intelligence agencies." JUI's fate has been intricately linked to the presence or absence of a Taliban regime in Afghanistan. The Taliban rose from madrassas run by the JUI to capture a country bereft of a central authority. Consequently, they also revived JUI politically. The Islamist revanchist backlash, which became more pronounced after the US air strikes, assumed critical dimensions vis-à-vis the various liberal forces within Pakistan. Groupings that had strong linkages with the Taliban regime were in the lead in the demonstrations and riots that occurred in various parts of Pakistan after '9/11'.

The danger in Pakistan has gradually escalated over the past decade, as it becomes increasingly uncertain whether its leadership is "master or victim" of the militant fundamentalism it fuelled for its campaign against the Russian presence in Afghanistan through the 1980s, and continues to stoke in pursuit of its strategic ambitions in Kashmir, despite recent and cosmetic changes under US pressure. Ahmed Rashid notes the devastating potential of Pakistan's flirtations with 'fundamentalist' mass mobilization:

In the late 1990s the repercussions were much more pervasive, undermining all the institutions of the state... law and order broke down as Islamic militants enacted their own laws and a new breed of anti-Shia Islamic radicals, who were given sanctuary by the Taliban, killed hundreds of Pakistani Shias between 1996 and 1999. This sectarian bloodshed is now fuelling a much wider rift between Pakistan's Sunni majority and Shia minority and undermining relations between Pakistan and Iran. At the same time, over 80,000 Pakistani Islamic militants have trained and fought with the Taliban since 1994. They form a hardcore of Islamic activists, ever ready to carry out a similar Taliban-style Islamic revolution in Pakistan.

Pakistan's entire posture has been based on 'deniability' of its support to terrorism. Thus, their public posture proclaims their firm opposition to terrorism, even as they fund, support and encourage it with unprecedented vigour. This duplicity has been possible because the Western nations have found it expedient, for their own misconceived strategic goals, to pretend that there was insufficient 'evidence' of Pakistan's involvement in the past. In fact, this posture is very similar to what the Taliban did with the Americans: proclaiming loudly that there was no evidence, or no sufficient evidence to act against bin Laden. Interestingly, after the Pakistan leadership publicly accepted—under mounting US pressure—that there was, in fact, sufficient prima facie evidence against bin Laden, the Taliban stand shifted, and they asserted that, even if evidence was given, bin Laden could not be handed over to the US. The demand for evidence, here, is no more than an obstructive device, unrelated to any principled quest for the truth or for the protection of rights. This, precisely, has been the Western position in the past, where the reality—for instance of the proxy war in J&K—that had been documented and acknowledged by the intelligence agencies of these countries, was deliberately ignored since it was erroneously believed to constitute no direct threat to Western interests. The Black Tuesday attacks in New York and Washington changed this in significant measure.

Pakistan is currently in an extremely difficult situation, and there is a process of violent internal churning that is being built up. Given the history of that country, it is possible that it will seek to cope with these internal pressures by trying to focus attention elsewhere—by provoking greater violence in Kashmir and other parts of India. There are, of course, grave risks involved in such adventurism, far greater than ever before. In order to maintain deniability, Pakistan may, in fact, increasingly direct its covert war away from Kashmir, and into other parts of India, especially the metropolii and various areas where it has already penetrated and established cells.

The Assembly Lines of Jehad

South Asia comprises the largest concentration of Muslims in the world, with over 395 million people professing Islam as their Faith. Indeed, India has the second largest population of Muslims—after Indonesia—for any country in the world: nearly 142 million.

As a region, South Asia has a long history, both of communal confrontation and violence, on the one hand, and of co-existence within an eclectic culture that has accepted differences, on the other. This dualism is ingrained in the unique and diverse set of practices and beliefs that particularly comprise Indian Islam—and at some point of time, also comprised sub-continental Islam. There is, consequently, a clear note of caution that must be sounded here. There has been a long and widely acknowledged process of the demonisation of Islam over the years—indeed, perhaps over the centuries. John Esposito rightly warns against "the temptation to view Islam through the prism of religious extremism and terrorism," and identifies the "demonisation of a great religious tradition due to the perverted actions of a minority of dissident and distorted voices" as "the real threat."

The total strength of extremist Islamist terrorists in India would number a few thousand in a population of 142 million.

The number of those who sympathise with their cause would certainly be many times greater, and those who are ambivalent in their responses could be a significant proportion of the total population. The fact, however, remains that even the sum of all these would only be a very small fraction of those who seek to live in peace, within the culture of coexistence that has become the essence of the Indian Weltanschauung.

This is not the case with India alone. Even in Pakistan, the country marked by the most rabid and widespread extremism in this region, the constituency of militant Islam is small in proportion to the total population, and this has repeatedly been borne out in the occasional elections that have been held in that country between its extended periods of military rule. Despite decades of military patronage, a continuous flow of governmental and international funding, and a political discourse dominated by Islam, the electoral performance of religious 'fundamentalist' political parties, the Jamaat-e-Islami (JEI), the Jamaat-e-Ulema-e-Islam (JUI) and the Jamaat-e-Ulema Pakistan (JUP), has been dismal. In 1988, they won 11 seats out of 207 in the National Assembly, claiming a mere 6.6 per cent of the vote. In 1990, they slipped down to 10 seats, with 5.4 per cent of the vote. In 1993, the Pakistan Islamic Front (PIF), headed by the JEI, bagged 3 seats, and electoral support for all religious parties was a bleak 3 per cent. The JEI and the JUP boycotted the 1997 elections, and two seats were returned in the National Assembly to the JUI (Fazlur Rahman faction) that participated.

This said, it must also be emphasized in the strongest terms possible that moderate Islam is, today, under deep, penetrating and sustained attack in every concentration of Muslim populations throughout South Asia, and there is a 'hardening' of beliefs that may lend itself to the extremist jehad in an uncertain future. The demonisation of Islam is loudly protested, both by neutral scholars and by the apologists for extremist Islam. But, there is a neglect of an even more vicious process of the demonization of all other Faiths and nations among the people of Islam—and this goes beyond the 'Great Satan', America, or the 'Brahminical conspiracy' of 'Hindustan', or the visceral anti-Semitism of the Arabs, to embrace all Kafirs or non-Muslims, and also all Muslims who do not conform to the perverse vision of extremist Islam. There is a profound ideology of hatred that is being fervently propagated through the institutions of Islam, particularly the madrassas or religious schools and seminaries that are proliferating rapidly across South Asia and is winning many ardent converts. As stated before, these are still a minority among South Asia's Muslims; but this is a vocal, armed, well-supported, extremely violent and growing minority. The majority, by contrast, has tended to passivity and conciliation, and there is little present evidence of the courage of conviction or of the will for any moderate Islamist resistance to the rampage of extremist Islam.

What Pakistan achieved in Afghanistan was, indeed, extraordinary. The 'tactic of a thousand cuts' produced such an unbearable 'haemorrhaging of men and money', that the wounded Soviet superpower eventually withdrew before what the world had thought of as a rag-tag army of 'the lunatics of Allah'. The billions of dollars and the unlimited supplies of arms and ammunition that were pumped in by an unlikely coalition of backers, the unrelated unravelling of a corrupt Soviet system, and the fact that it was the Afghans themselves who did most of the fighting, cannot detract from the triumph of the Pakistani architects of the 'jihad' in Afghanistan.

This is the second tainted triumph that has brought inconceivable misfortune upon Pakistan. The first occurred when it was forged as a separate nation out of a philosophy of hatred and exclusion, an ideology that denied the possibility of the coexistence of communities with any significant differences of culture, belief or values under a single political order. Less than three per cent of the population of Pakistan now comprises non-Muslims, and the proportion declines each year. But, the intolerance and the rage that created the nation must constantly find new enemies. It was this bigotry that resulted in its first dismemberment and the creation of Bangladesh. It is the same malevolence that seeks out new victims among subgroups of the Muslims themselves—such as the Ahmadiyas and the Shias. Today, as sectarian divisions inevitably compound themselves, every regional and cultural group in Pakistan—the Punjabis, the Sindhis, the Pashtuns, the Baluchis and the Mohajirs—sees the other as an enemy.

This is the fractious milieu within which General Zia-ul-Haq created the Taliban, and to which they victoriously returned after establishing their 'control' over most of Afghanistan. Olivier Roy succinctly defined the Frankenstienian dilemma that confronts Pakistan:

The apparent victor, Pakistan, could pay dearly for its success. The triumph of the Taliban has virtually eliminated the border between Pakistan and Afghanistan. On both sides, Pashtun tribes are slipping towards fundamentalism and becoming increasingly implicated in drug trafficking. They are gaining autonomy, already small fundamentalist tribal emirates are appearing on Pakistani soil. The de facto absorption of Afghanistan will accentuate centrifugal tendencies within Pakistan.

At the heart of the crisis is the network of increasingly powerful marakiz (centres) and madrassas that has now established itself as the source, not only of international 'pan-Islamic' terrorism, but of an overwhelming proportion of internal strife as well. Its roots can be traced back to General Zia-ul-Haq's vigorous use of Islam as a tool of regime legitimization, a trend that was first introduced by Zulfiqar Ali Bhutto in 1971, and that has been variously reinforced by every succeeding regime. The growth of these madrassas is, indeed, an accurate index of Pakistan's mounting difficulties. In 1947, there were 137 madrassas in the entire country. By 1971, this number had grown to 900. But, with Zia's policy of generously funding "madrassas of all sectarian persuasions.... by the end of the Zia era in 1988, there were 8,000 madrassas and 25,000 unregistered ones, educating over half a million students. As Pakistan's state-run educational system steadily collapsed, these madrassas became the only avenue for boys from poor families to receive the semblance of an education." Sources indicate that by the middle of the year 2000, the number of madrassas had grown to nearly 9,500, and some commentators in Pakistan estimate the current number of unregistered madrassas at between 40,000 and 50,000.

The mind-blunting curriculum of most of these madrassas entirely neglects all branches of secular instruction, including the basics of mathematics and science, and comprises 16 long years of purely theological education, recitation of the Quran, Fiqah (interpretation of the Sharia), and indoctrination for jihad. The inevitable consequence of such an education has been the chronic "inability to produce reality-based theories of change", extraordinarily narrow and exclusionary perspectives, and deepening sectarian divisions that spill over into increasing violence. With an estimated 60 per cent of funding emanating from abroad, these schisms are magnified further by the ideological and strategic contests of foreign funding agencies and states. Afzaal Mahmood, for instance, notes that, "By allowing Iran and Saudi Arabia to fund, influence and use some sectarian organisations of their liking, we have virtually encouraged Teheran and Riyadh to fight a proxy war on the soil of Pakistan, with serious consequences for sectarian harmony and law and order in the country." Funds have also come from Libya, Iraq and several other Gulf countries, creating an intricately nuanced web of conflict. Shia and Sunni madrassas have spawned rival terrorist forces that visit gratuitous slaughter on sectarian rivals - most prominently, the Sunni outfit Sipah-e-Sahaba Pakistan (SSP); and the Shia outfits Tehreek-e-Jafaria Pakistan (TJP) and Sipah-e-Muhammad Pakistan (SMP). There is also a deep schism between Sunni Deobandi and Barelvi madrassas, and a large number of Ahle Hadis madrassas have also emerged recently in Baluchistan, Sindh and the North West Frontier Province (NWFP). Most sectarian bombings and shootouts originate from or occur at mosques housing these schools, and significant proportions of those killed are madrassa students. Patterns of international rivalry are also visible in the some retaliatory killings. Thus, Iranian diplomat, Sadiq Ganji, was gunned down in Lahore following the assassination of SSP founder Haq Nawaz Jhangvi in March 1990. Similarly, the 1997 assassination of Jhangvi's successor, Zia-ur-Rehman Farooqi and 26 others in a bomb blast at the Lahore Sessions Court, saw the alleged revenge killing of Iranian diplomat Muhammad Ali Rahimi and six others in an attack on the Iranian Cultural Center at Multan.

Sectarian violence is, however, a relatively minor consequence of the proliferation of madrassas. Their primary output has been the export of international extremist Islamist terrorism, and this has created enormous internal concentrations of armed, trained and indoctrinated irregular (terrorist) forces who, at some point of time or the other, may have been supported by the government through the Inter Services Intelligence (ISI) that oversaw the Afghan campaign, and that currently guides the export of terror into Jammu & Kashmir and other theatres across the world, but who do not acknowledge the power of the government to define their long-term goals and objectives. Their allegiance is commanded by the various 'spiritual leaders' who run madrassas that have acquired extraordinary notoriety over the past years, both as hotbeds of terrorism and as the spawning ground of the Afghani Taliban. It is here that a 'theology of rage' is taught, and the Talib (student) exhorted to practice a 'sacred violence' that is his greatest duty in Islam. These institutions include most prominently the Dar-ul-Uloom Haqqani at Akora Khattak; the Markaz-ad-Da'awa-wal-Irshad (MDI) at Muridke; the Jamiat-ul-Uloom Islamia Madrassa in Karachi; the Dar-ul-Uloom, Pashtoonabad; the Dar-ul-Iftah-ul-Irshad, Nazimabad; and the Ahle-Sunnat-wal Jamaat madrassa at Rawalpindi. Many of these institutions run a multiplicity of schools across the country - the Markaz-ad-Da'awa-wal-Irshad, for instance, had 137 madrassas by late 2000. These, however, are only a sampling, the visible tip of the iceberg, and there are hundreds of less known 'Jihad factories' - the 'supply line for jihad' - that indoctrinate their students and give them 'military' training, both for the sectarian war, and for international terrorism.

The apparatus of training for terrorism reflects the same curious dualism and principal-agent conflict that characterises the growth of the madrassas. A number of training camps, especially those that fuel the terrorist movement in J&K, have long been run by the Army and the ISI; most, however, function with various degrees of autonomy under the charge of quasi-independent extremist Islamist institutions and groupings; and even where active state support is lacking, their activities are fully tolerated on Pakistani soil. Occasional difficulties did, of course, crop up - and the Taliban in Afghanistan had willingly provided sanctuary and space to armed groups whose sectarian activities may have passed beyond Islamabad's levels of declared tolerance, and whose sectarian orientation was in conformity with their own. This may have been a highly collusive and convenient arrangement, and Pakistan had, at least on occasion, found it opportune to relocate specific training camps in Afghanistan when international pressure becomes excessive. This, for instance, happened in 1992-93, when Pakistan feared that the US would declare it a state sponsor of terrorism for its activities in J&K. In response, Pakistan simply moved most of its Kashmiri militant groups to bases in eastern Afghanistan, and by 'privatising' its support to the Kashmiri mujaheddin, made the Islamic parties responsible for their training and funding. The shift was temporary, and while a number of camps continued to function in Afghanistan till the US campaign commenced, there was a proliferation within Pakistan as well, and one estimate in late 2000 placed the number of existing terrorist training camps in Pakistan at 128. This is, however, a fluctuating figure, and the location of many of these camps is frequently changed. Various sources and agencies have identified a significant number of such camps over the years, and they extended from Pakistan occupied Kashmir (PoK), through Pakistan, to Afghanistan.

The 'privatisation' of these camps and of the jehadi armies, however, had disastrous consequences, and there was mounting evidence of a loss of control as the autonomous religious groups challenged, not only their Army and ISI handlers, but the government itself. No clear division now exists between various social, political, religious and terrorist organisations; and most groups that have actively participated in street violence and acts of terrorism, both within Pakistan and abroad, are also openly active on Pakistan's political landscape. There has, moreover, been increasing penetration by extremist Islamist elements into Pakistan's Army, and elements of 'Islamisation' have been introduced into the Army's training programs at various levels. In 1992, the then Prime Minister appointed a well-known Tablighi (congregationist), Lieutenant General Javed Nasir, as the Director General of the all-powerful ISI. General Pervez Musharraf's military regime, moreover, lacks the capabilities and support to contain the extremist elements and has, on more than one occasion, been forced to back off on policies and reforms in the face of Islamist opposition. The cumulative impact of nearly two and a half decades of 'Islamisation' has now put in doubt the Army's ability—indeed, will—to suppress the extremist Islamist forces in case of an open confrontation with government, and it is apparent that at least some sections within the Army would side with the extremists if such an eventuality emerged.

Such a confrontation now appears increasingly probable. The madrassas and the mujahiddeen are committed to the establishment of a 'Taliban style' government for Pakistan, and some of the groups recently put Pervez Musharraf's military regime on notice to establish 'Islamic rule' in the country, or to face the consequences. Maulana Samiul Haq, the chief of his own faction of the JUI, speaking at the Jamia Ashrafia at Peshawar in January 2001, declared that both the so-called democratic and martial law regimes had been tested and had failed to deliver, and that, consequently, only the Islamic Sharia could 'solve the problems faced by the masses.' Maulana Jalil Jan, the provincial leader of the JUI (F) added that, if the government failed to implement Islamic Sharia, the 'religious students will resort to the use of force to do the same'.

Lieutenant General Hamid Gul, who headed the ISI through critical periods of the Agency's campaign in Afghanistan, shares the vision of the Islamist fundamentalists and argues that "Pakistan will go through its own version of an Islamic revolution.... The army is the last hope. And if the army fails - and it probably will—then people will realise they will have to do it themselves, revolt against the system... Because everything else in this country has failed, Islam will have to lead the way."

It seems clear that, unless current trends are radically and immediately reversed, it is only a matter of time before Pakistan is sucked into the turmoil of an Afghanistan-like anarchy.

The Web of Terror: Erosion & Encirclement

Among the primary targets of the armies of mujahiddeen, and their suicidal hard core, the fidayeen, who pour out of the madrassas and Pakistani terrorist training camps, is the Indian State of Jammu & Kashmir (J&K), though recent events may gradually induce a shift in strategy, with increasing terrorist incidents in various metropolitan areas in India. It is significant, in this context, that the leadership of the terrorist movement in J&K passed out of the hands of local militants, into groups created by and based in Pakistan as far back as in 1993, when the most powerful terrorist group indigenous to the State, the Jammu & Kashmir Liberation Front (JKLF) chose to give up arms and seek a 'political solution' to its grievances. The JKLF still demands Kashmiri 'Independence', but is strongly opposed to any amalgamation with Pakistan. The Pakistan-based groups, quite naturally, are far more amenable to a merger with that country.

Terrorist groupings enjoyed substantial mass support, particularly in the Kashmir Valley, as long as the movement for secession remained indigenous. Progressively, however, a process of disillusionment with the activities of Pakistan sponsored militants has combined with exhaustion to diminish this base, and terrorism is now sustained purely on inputs - ideologies, material, and increasing numbers of men - from across the border. The terrorist groups currently most active in the State are each headquartered in Pakistan, and include the Hizb-ul-Mujahiddeen (HM), linked to the JuI in Pakistan; Lashkar-e-Toiba (LeT), the armed wing of the Markaz-ad-Da'awa-wal-Irshad; the Harkat-ul-Jehad-e-Islami (HuJI) and the Harkat-ul-Mujahiddeen (formerly the Harkat-ul-Ansar), linked to the JUI, the Pakistan Tablighi Jamaat and to the Hizb-e-Islami of Afghanistan; Al Badr; and the Jaish-e-Muhammad (JeM). There are another score of minor and dormant groupings, also located in Pakistan. The umbrella Muttahida Jehad Council co-ordinates the activities of 13 of the most prominent terrorist factions.

The years 1997, 1998 and the first half of 1999 had seen a gradual decline in violence and fatalities in J&K, but there was a radical escalation after the Kargil War of May-July 1999. The trends underwent a further deterioration after two cease-fires—the first announced unilaterally by the Hizb-ul-Mujahiddeen in July 2000, and the second, again unilaterally, by the Indian Prime Minister, A B Vajpayee, in November 2000—as the possibility of an emerging peace process threatened the entrenched interests and ideological ambitions of the extremist Islamist groups in Pakistan, and of their official sponsors there. A total of 30,275 persons had died in this conflict between 1988 and 2001. These include 11,377 civilians, 15,246 terrorists, and 4,102 security force (SF) personnel. Among the civilian fatalities, 8,712 (nearly 85 per cent) have been Muslims. [Graphs 1, 2 & 3]

Significantly, the proportion of foreign mercenaries and mujahiddeen involved in the militancy in the State has been steadily rising, from a mere 6 per cent in 1992 to an estimated 55 per cent today. A majority of these are drawn from Pakistan and Pakistan occupied Kashmir (PoK). There is also a limited engagement of the 'Afghan Alumni', and terrorists

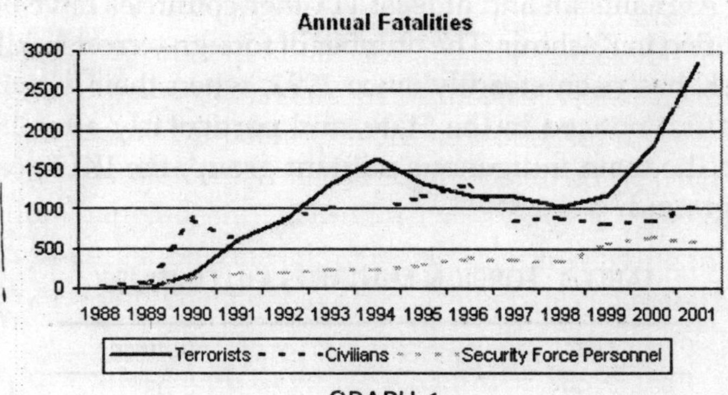

GRAPH 1

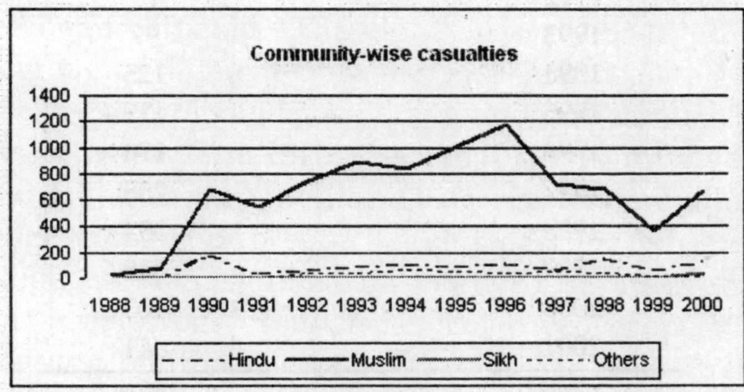

GRAPH 2

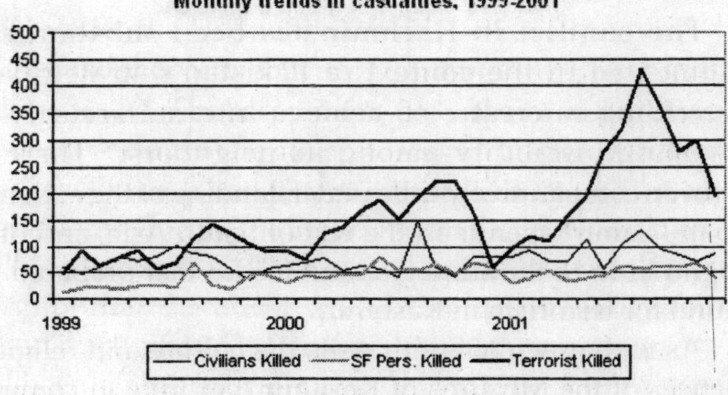

GRAPH 3

from Afghanistan and at least 11 other countries have been identified in Kashmir. The number of foreign terrorists killed in J&K has risen steadily since 1991, when their activities were first noticed in the State, and particularly after 1993, when the main indigenous militant group, the JKLF, came overground:

TABLE 1: FOREIGN MILITANTS KILLED IN J&K

Year	*Number*
1991	03
1992	19
1993	97
1994	125
1995	119
1996	194
1997	258
1998	394
1999	348
2000	403
2001	541
Total	2501

Source: Institute for Conflict Management.

The conflict in Kashmir has been substantially documented in the context of Pakistan's strategy and "overriding interest... to achieve internal security by provoking instability among its neighbors." There is, however, comparatively little understanding of the extremist or pan-Islamist agenda in the rest of South Asia, and of its integral links to the strategies and tactics that prepared the ground for terrorism in Kashmir.

As with much of South Asia, the culture and religious practices of the Muslims of Kashmir had little in common with the rigid and distorted version of Wahabbi Islam—with its ideological source in Saudi Arabia—that is the dominant ideological force among contemporary extremist Islamists. Kashmiri Islam was seeped with the mysticism and values of the devotional Sufi order, and the Kashmir Valley was, indeed, held up as a unique and inspirational example of secular values at the time of Partition and Independence, and in the decades that followed. The emergence of terrorism in the State was preceded by decades of religious mobilisation and reorientation centred primarily in the mosques in the Valley. When terror broke out in the late 1980s, it was the mosques and the madrassas that provided the motivation, the moral sanction, and the initial impetus, not only to the violence, but to the near complete ethnic cleansing of the Valley of its Kashmiri Pandit minority. It is interesting that, among the priority targets of the terrorists was the network of secular school, most of which were shut down under threat, especially in rural areas. This progressively forced the children into the only surviving 'educational' institution—the madrassa—the 'schools of hate' that created new 'supply lines' for jihad.

There is today, a sustained effort—with mixed results—to replicate these processes of religious mobilisation and an extremist Islamist reorientation throughout South Asia. In India, while there have been several political factors and events contributing to higher levels of communal polarisation, general communal conflict—expressed in the incidence of communal riots—has been on a decline. Political parties are yet to abandon the electoral strategy of exploiting religious sentiments and insecurities, but the mass base and credibility of those who seek to do so has suffered steady erosion. Nevertheless, the intent and strategy of Pakistan's covert agencies and extremist religious groupings is increasingly apparent in a wide range of activities intended to provoke communal confrontations, engineer terrorist incidents, and recruit soldiers for a pan-Islamist jihad in pockets of Muslim populations across India. A process of 'encirclement' and massive demographic shifts that deepen the danger compound these initiatives, particularly along India's eastern borders.

During a three-day annual congregation of the members of the Markaz-ad-Da'awa-wal-Irshad at Muridke near Lahore on February 6, 2000, the Amir (Chief) of the Markaz, Hafiz Mohammad Saeed, declared that Kashmir was a 'gateway to capture India' and that it was the aim of the Markaz and its military wing, the Lashkar-e-Toiba, to engineer India's disintegration. Saeed added that his organisation's campaign in Hyderabad (Andhra Pradesh) and Junagadh (Gujarat) were among the highest priorities. Abdul Rahman Makki, the LeT's ideologue, expanded on this theme, proclaiming that the group had opened a new unit in Hyderabad to liberate the Indian city from "un-Islamic Indian rule". These declarations are, at once, an expression of the pan-Islamist ambitions shared by all extremist Islamist groups operating in the region, and a reiteration of Pakistan's larger strategy of destabilisation beyond the scope of the supposed 'core issue' of Kashmir.

Within this larger design was a series of 13 bomb blasts in various churches in Andhra Pradesh, Karnataka and Goa between May and July 2000, executed by an obscure Islamist sect created in 1924, the Deendar Anjuman. The Anjuman is headed by Zia-ul-Hassan—the son of the Anjuman's founder—who is based in Peshawar, Pakistan, where the sect goes by the name Anjuman Hizbullah. Hassan is also said to have floated a militant organisation, the Jamat-e-Hizb-ul-Mujahiddeen in Pakistan, in order to 'capture India and spread Islam'. Intelligence sources indicate that Hassan is bankrolled by the ISI, and the Indian Union Home Minister stated in Parliament that investigators had established linkages between the Deendar Anjuman and Pakistan's covert intelligence agency. Investigations have exposed a network of the Anjuman's subversive activities extending across several small towns and urban centres, including Nuzvid, Atmakur, Kurukunda, Palem, Vijayawada, Khammam and Nandyal in Andhra Pradesh; and Batakurki, Ramdurg and Hubli in Karnataka.

Another series of 19 explosions had earlier, on February 14, 1998, left over 50 dead and more than 200 injured in the Coimbatore district of Tamil Nadu. While the Al Umma group, founded by S A Basha, was blamed, investigations and subsequent arrests exposed the involvement of a wide network of extremist Islamist organisations across South India. These included the Indian Muslim Mohammadi Mujahideen, the Tanzim Islahul Muslimeen, the Jihad Committee in Tamil Nadu; and the Islamic Sevak Sangh, subsequently banned and revived as the People's Democratic Party (PDP), headed by Abdul Nasser Madani, in Kerala. ISI agents involved, included Azam Ghauri (who was subsequently killed in an encounter with the police at Jagityal, Karimnagar District, Andhra Pradesh, on April 6, 2000), Saleem Junaid, Farooq Ahmed and Mohammad Mansoor.

The first major bomb blast in Tamil Nadu occurred in 1993 when the RSS office was blown up in Chennai. It was reported that Islamist fundamentalist groups, which had been proliferating, had masterminded the blast. The immediate causal factor for the proliferation is traced to the demolition of the Babri mosque in 1992. The Tamil Nadu police stumbled on an important lead when they arrested a person, Imam Ali, in the Mettupalayam forests in 1994. Imam Ali was found to be imparting training in explosives to four youths. He reportedly confessed that he had been training Islamist fundamentalists. According to intelligence sources in Coimbatore, Kashmiri militants may also have trained Imam Ali. Certain letters recovered from him pointed towards linkages in Bangladesh. Three bomb blasts were subsequently reported on different trains in Tamil Nadu and Kerala on December 6, 1997, and pamphlets recovered from the incident site pointed to the involvement of the Islamic Defence Force (IDF). Ten members of two Islamist fundamentalist groups were chargesheeted on October 5, 1998, for a bomb blast on a Coimbatore-bound train on December 6, 1997. The IDF also claimed responsibility for a bomb blast that occurred under the Anna flyover in Chennai on January 10, 1998. This was followed by another blast in a rice mill at Thanjavur on February 8, 1998. Police investigations revealed that Abdul Khader, son of the mill owner, Abdul Hameed, was connected to Muslim fundamentalist organisations.

The professed objective of such Islamist outfits, aided by Pakistan, vis-à-vis India is to 'liberate' the Muslims, not only of Jammu and Kashmir, but the rest of India, from 'Hindu control', and to establish 'two more independent homelands' for the Muslims of the sub-continent—one in North India and the other in the South. After Tamil Nadu and Kerala, their focus shifted to comprehend Andhra Pradesh as well. There has also been a considerable flow of funds to the Al Ummah of Tamil Nadu and its allied organisations in Kerala from Pakistan-based Islamist terror groups, possibly through the Gulf.

The then Kerala Chief Minister E K Nayanar admitted in June 1998 that certain terrorist groups had been operating in his State. These included radical Islamist outfits such as the National Development Front (NDF), the Jamiyathul Ehsaniya, the Students Islamic Movement of India (SIMI), the Islamic Movement and the Al-Umma, whose base of operations covers Kozhikode, Malappuram and Thrissur districts. The arrest of the Peoples Democratic Party Chairman, Abdul Nasser Madani, for allegedly harbouring Al-Umma militants involved in the Coimbatore bomb blasts indicated a nexus between the PDP and the extremist outfits. Though Al-Umma has been active in Kerala, its roots and theatre of operations lie in Tamil Nadu. The free movement of people between these two states has helped Al-Umma activists to slip across and blend with the Muslim population of Malapuram.

13 NDF activists were arrested on September 6, 2001, while undergoing arms training at a college in Palakkad. Recent intelligence reports have reportedly indicated that the State is fast emerging as a haven for fundamentalist and subversive forces. Central intelligence agencies had reportedly apprised the State government regarding the Mumbai Mafia's role in training NDF activists in areas such as Malapuram and Kasarkode.

By far the most dramatic serial blasts engineered by the ISI took place in Bombay on March 12, 1993, and these revealed a unique pattern of operation that has gradually consolidated itself over the years—the use of organised criminal networks to execute terrorist strikes. Nearly 1,800 kilograms of RDX, and a large number of detonators and small arms, had been smuggled through the West Coast of India prior to these blasts, which killed over 300 persons and targeted critical commercial infrastructure, including the country's largest stock exchange at Dalal Street. The explosions were executed by the notorious D-Company headed by Dawood Ibrahim. Ibrahim now lives under state protection in Karachi, and runs India's largest criminal empire through aides located outside India, and primarily in the Middle East.

Gujarat has currently become a significant centre for subversive activities by various Islamist fundamentalist organisations and Pakistan-sponsored terrorist outfits. Since 1992, the State's borders with Pakistan, including the 1600 kilometre long coastline, has been subjected to incessant subversive activity by these outfits who utilise the State as a launch pad for various terrorist operations in the rest of India. Particularly, the Kutch region, Saurashtra and Junagadh have witnessed growing incidents of smuggling of arms and ammunition, as also narcotics and fake currency. The marshy area of the Rann of Kutch - the 512-kilometre border with Pakistan comprising several hundred smaller channels that merge into three large creeks (Sir Creek, Kori and Mainwari) - renders it uniquely vulnerable to smuggling with the help of small fishing boats called hodas. Smugglers and gunrunners from Mumbai and Dubai frequent this area. In the aftermath of the demolition of the Babri mosque in 1992, the smuggling of RDX and other explosives began to be routed increasingly through the Gujarat coast to Porbander in the Saurashtra region. Indeed, a large cache that arrived through the border, passed through Bulsar in south Gujarat, and was subsequently trans-shipped to Mumbai, where it was used to engineer the serial blasts that killed more than 300 people and left thousands injured.

In August 1995, security force personnel arrested 10 Pakistani nationals in the Kutch region. Six AK-47 rifles were also seized from their possession. The ISI has been able to set up well-organised bases in the State. For example, Abdul Ghani alias Assadullah, a Kashmiri terrorist collected RDX from Nepal and set up bases in Ahmedabad. He also supplied RDX for the Delhi and Dausa blasts of May 1996. The Gujarat police later arrested him in June 1996. On May 24, 1996, the State police arrested four Jammu and Kashmir-based terrorists who subsequently confessed that they had been sent by 'Colonel Farooq' of the ISI to set up a base in Ahmedabad. They also revealed that they had been asked to recruit youth in Gujarat and Maharashra for terrorist training in Pakistan. In March 1998, police killed six criminals allegedly belonging to the Dawood Ibrahim gang in the walled area of Ahmedabad, and seized a huge cache of arms and ammunition, including 10 kilograms of RDX. On March 24, 1998 a huge cache of arms and ammunition was recovered from the Gandhinagar and Daryapur areas of Ahmedabad. The weapons were reportedly supplied by the ISI. In July 1999, six terrorists arrested in Ahmedabad confessed during their interrogation that the ISI had trained them in explosives handling in Pakistan. In the same month, two suspected ISI agents were arrested in Bhuj and 24 kg of RDX and two Chinese-made pistols were seized from their possession.

On July 24, 2000, five suspected ISI agents were arrested in Sarwej. 25 Chinese-made pistols, five magazines, 200 rounds of ammunition and six kg of heroin and six AK-47 rifles were recovered from their possession. On April 2001, seven persons, including four arms-dealers allegedly having links with the ISI were arrested from various parts of the capital city, Ahmedabad. On May 27, 2001, a Lashkar-e-Toiba terrorist was arrested with an AK-56 rifle at the Hajipir area of Rann of Kutch. During the course of interrogation, he is reported to have said that he had acquired training in terrorist activities at Muzaffarabad in Pakistan occupied Kashmir (PoK), and had 'sneaked into India for a special task'. This was the third case since March 2001 when the ISI sent armed terrorists into the Kutch region.

The ISI is also trying to create communal tension with the help of fundamentalist outfits such as the recently proscribed SIMI. There has also been a proliferation of madrassas (religious seminaries) in the border areas. These madrassas are reportedly securing funds from Saudi Arabia, Pakistan as also from certain other Gulf countries. Available evidence suggests that the ISI is using the Gujarat border in its attempts to revive terrorism in Punjab. Official sources have indicated that the ISI had reportedly asked the Babbar Khalsa International (BKI) terrorists Wadhawa Singh and Mehal Singh, both located in Pakistan, to revive terrorism in Punjab. In January 2000, five terrorists of the BKI, with alleged links to the ISI, who were planning to launch major countrywide terrorist activities by making Gujarat their base, were arrested from the Narol area of Ahmedabad. Criminal underground networks have also been mobilised in this endeavour. Reports indicate that outfits like the Khalistan Zindabad Force (Punjwar faction), based in Sialkot, have also been instructed by the ISI to exploit the porous Gujarat border. In August 1999, Chhota Shakil of the Karachi-based Dawood Ibrahim gang is reported to have visited Kabul twice in order to place orders for arms and ammunition, as also to meet Osama bin Laden. As a result, a red-alert was sounded in the border areas, especially in the Rann of Kutch, which is considered to be a critical route for the Dawood gang's arms traffickers. The carriers come from Karachi, cross the Kutch border into Gujarat and make their way to Ahmedabad, Dawood's biggest base in India after Mumbai, from where their deadly contraband is distributed throughout the country.

The ISI is also involved in circulating fake Indian currency across the Gujarat border. The Agency has set up a printing press at Sukkur where fake Indian currency notes are printed, and brought into the country via Shahgarh Budge near Jaisalmer in Rajasthan through Gujarat. In a single seizure on November 3, 1998, police recovered Rs. 2,749,700 worth of counterfeit currency from an aircraft coming from Sharjah to Jamnagar.

The operational ISI units at Sialkot and Karachi have been co-ordinating the attempts of various terrorist outfits—Khalistani and Kashmiri—to breach the western coast of the country. At least three Islamist extremist / fundamentalist organisations—Lashkar-e-Toiba, Ahl-e-Hadis and Tablighi Jamat—are active in Kutch. Of late, the activities of the Jamaat-e-Islami's student wing have also been increasing in this thinly populated district.

India's Northeast is another interesting area of emerging Islamist militancy, and here it combines with major demographic shifts that hold significant dangers for the future stability of the region. Illegal migration on a large scale across the border from Bangladesh is the most potent single factor in the destabilisation of the Northeast. In November 1998, the Governor of Assam, Lt. Gen. (Retd.) S K Sinha, submitted a report to the Indian President, which estimated the total volume of this infiltration at six million people. Most of this increase was concentrated in a few areas, with a dramatic impact on the local demography and, hence, electoral politics. According to the report, four districts of Assam—Dhubri, Goalpara, Barpeta and Hailakandi—had been transformed into Muslim majority districts by 1991 as a result of this mass infiltration. Another two districts—Nagaon and Karimganj—would have had a Muslim majority since 1998 and yet another district, Morigaon, was fast approaching this position. This demographic destabilisation, combined with the widespread violence and political instability in the region, has created a unique recruiting ground for the Islamists, and there has been a veritable efflorescence of Muslim terrorist groups operating along India's borders with Bangladesh in the Northeast. In Assam alone, there are over 15 terrorist groups operating under an Islamist banner, and the ISI's role in funding and arming these groups has now been fairly well documented.

Reports in October 2001 indicated that, inspired by the activities of Osama bin Laden, a new militant group, the Islamic Security Force of India (ISFI) had intensified its activities in various Muslim-dominated areas of Assam. The militant group, which was constituted in Mumbai in the year 2000, reportedly with the active support of Al Qaeda, commenced recruiting Muslim youth to launch a jehad against what it perceived as the repression and suppression of the Muslim community. Official sources have indicated that the ISFI's activities came to light after recovery of vital documents distributed in the remote areas of Darrang district. From the seized documents it was found that the ISFI has close links with the Hizb-ul-Mujahideen (HM), the Lashkar-e-Toiba (LeT) and the Jammu and Kashmir Liberation Front (JKLF). ISFI is also reportedly associated with Al-Umar, which has been providing financial help and arms and ammunition to the militant group.

In Nagaon and Marigaon districts, there is a section of active supporters of extremist and proscribed groups such as the Muslim United Liberation Tigers of Assam (MULTA), Muslim United Liberation Front of Assam (MULFA) and SIMI, who have been propagating the idea of a separate Islamic State, comprising several districts of Assam. There was also a spurt in pro-bin Laden mobilisation along and across the Bangladesh border and, according to B P Rao, Inspector General of Police (Law and Order), "We have reliable intelligence inputs that efforts are being made to export a group of highly-motivated Muslim fundamentalists, carrying photographs of Laden, into Assam. They have plans to cross over through the Indo-Bangla border in Karimganj district of Assam." He also added that some processions had been taken out by bin Laden supporters in certain areas of the trouble-torn Nalbari district. Rao also pointed out that there had been a 'madrassa boom' in Assam in recent years: "Compared to other states, construction of madrassas during the last couple of years has been much more in Assam. As many as 350 of these, located in minority pockets, are not registered—moreover, we have reports that some of these are being used for propaganda against the majority community and the government." The Jamiat Ulema-e-Hind President, Maulana Syed Asad Madani, has been reported to have called on Muslims in the State to unite for jehad in view of the US attacks on Afghanistan.

In the wake of the Kargil war, Maj. Gen. B P Bopanna had stated that "some madrassas in the North-east have become the harbourers of ISI agents of Pakistan." The Union Home Ministry has also been particularly concerned about the mushrooming of madrassas in the border areas, with extensive funds from the Gulf countries. According to a report, 236 mosques and 157 madrassas had recently come up in Assam, 194 mosques and 72 madrassas in Tripura, 17 mosques and two madrassas in Meghalaya, along their borders with Bangladesh.

The State Government of Assam admitted in the Legislative Assembly on November 6, 2000, that some top militants belonging to Muslim extremist outfits "had been connected with the activities of madrassas" but hastened to add that this should "not to malign all the madrassas in a sweep." The State government also spoke of taking legal action against the offending madrassas. Documents with the Assam Police indicate that the Nurani madrassa near Dhaka is being used as transit camp by Harkat-ul-Mujahideen (HuM) cadres for their trans-border movement to India. The Garijam madrassa in the Kamrup district is under watch on suspicion that it is being misused by the ISI.

The recent elections in Bangladesh, which brought to power a regime that is relatively hostile to India, have led to an increased vigil by the security establishment in the Northeast. The militant and pro-Pakistan Jamaat-e-Islami had 16 members elected to the Bangladesh Parliament. Furthermore, the ruling Bangladesh Nationalist Party (BNP) also has strong linkages—including shared business activities —with terrorist groups active in the Northeast, most prominently, the ULFA. Since the BNP came to power, there has been a sudden escalation in atrocities against minorities in Bangladesh, leading to increased distress migration into Tripura. The Indian Home Ministry apprehends a similar influx of refugees in the Karimganj district of Assam, and there are suspicions that some pro-Taliban elements from Bangladesh may enter Assam along with the refugees to create disturbances in the State.

In West Bengal, the State Government ascertained, in March 1999, that there were at least three new groups active in the State, which had been receiving monetary and other support from Osama bin Laden. The three groups whose names were not immediately disclosed reportedly planned a conclave in mid-March at a mosque at the small town of Dhulian in Murshidabad district bordering Bangladesh. The bin Laden connection to certain Islamist fundamentalist groups in the State was discovered when police arrested a person from Lalgola, also a Murshidabad town adjacent to the Bangladesh border, in the early part of year 1999. The man from Lalgola was recruited as an ISI agent in New Delhi, where his uncle lived. For several months, he carried letters to Rajshahi, the neighbouring Bangladeshi town. Then he was given the job of despatching a consignment of explosives to a location in Haryana. The explosives were said to have been used in terrorist actions in J&K. Other than Calcutta, the government has identified Murshidabad, and Shiliguri, as well as Kishangunj in Bihar, as the corridors frequented by ISI agents operating in the State. While Murshidabad and Kishangunj offer easy access from Bangladesh, Nepal agents use the Shiliguri corridor into north Bengal.

More than 15 million illegal immigrants are reported to have entered India over the last five decades from

Bangladesh, an intrusion that has completely changed the demography of large parts of Assam, Meghalaya, West Bengal, Tripura and Bihar. This has been observed in a 135-page report of the Group of Ministers (GoM) headed by Union Home Minister L K Advani and submitted to the Government recently. The report notes: "Today, we have 15 Million Bangladeshi, 2.2 Million Nepalese, 70,000 Sri Lankan Tamils and about one lakh Tibetan migrants living in India. Demographic changes have been brought about in the border belts of West Bengal, several districts in Assam, Bihar, Tripura and Meghalaya as a result of large-scale illegal migration. Even states like Delhi, Maharashtra and Rajasthan have been affected."The GoM Report observed that smuggling of different consumer and intermediate goods, trafficking in drugs and narcotics etc., flourish through large parts of India. The ISI is also reportedly involved in encouraging these activities. Drug couriers are allowed passage on condition of collecting and reporting trans-border intelligence. Trained saboteurs and terrorists are prevailed upon to carry drugs for sustenance and to recover operational expenses from the sale proceeds. Passage to couriers of contraband is often conditional to carrying and delivering arms and ammunition.

The Union government recently decided to proscribe SIMI under the Unlawful Activities (Prevention) Act 1967. A large number of its activists including its national president were arrested. The ban came in the wake of strong demands made by various State governments including Maharashtra, Madhya Pradesh and Uttar Pradesh. The Chief Ministers of these States, during the annual conference of police chiefs in Delhi on September 5, 2001, had recommended a ban on SIMI, alleging that the outfit was indulging in subversive and terrorist activities. SIMI is said to have links with the ISI and has been acting in support of the Taliban and Osama bin

Laden. It has also been supporting secessionists and advocating violence in order to establish an 'international Islamic order'. On July 31, 2001, police, during a nation wide crackdown, arrested 23 persons belonging to the SIMI and Hizb-ul-Mujahideen from Jalgaon, Kanpur, Hyderabad and Delhi. These arrests revealed that the Kashmiri terrorist groups had recruited many youth into terrorist activity with SIMI's assistance. In July 2001 the police also arrested the office secretary of SIMI, Mohammed Waqar-ul-Hasan on the charge of conspiring with Hizb terrorists who had caused a bomb blast in Nagpur in May 2001. The Uttar Pradesh government has also reportedly been able to establish SIMI's links with terrorist outfits in West Asia, including the Hamas and the Hezbollah of Lebanon. The Union government and State intelligence agencies have maintained that SIMI, over the years, had developed fairly extensive contacts in the Islamic world. The outfit is closely associated with the Riyadh-based World Assembly of Muslim Youth (WAMY) and the International Islamic Federation of Students' Organisation in Kuwait. The group also has extensive links with the students' wings of the Jamaat-e-Islami units in Pakistan, Bangladesh and Nepal. The Chicago-based Anti-India Consultative Committee of Indian Muslims was also in touch with SIMI. Jamayyatul Ansar, an organisation of SIMI activists comprising expatriate Indian Muslims, reportedly operates from Saudi Arabia.

The Union Home Secretary, on September 28, 2001, stated that the government had evidence linking the SIMI with Al Qaeda. He said SIMI's links with terrorist outfits were exposed during investigations into 14 terrorist acts causing 15 deaths and injuries to 80 persons in Uttar Pradesh and Delhi in 2000-2001. The inter-linked triad of concepts—Ummah, Khilafat and Jehad—provides the rationale for SIMI's postures and activities. SIMI cadres regard Osama bin Laden as an outstanding example of a true Mujahid, one who has undertaken Jihad on behalf of the Ummah. SIMI's General Secretary, Safdar Nagauri, while addressing a Press conference in Lucknow on October 10, 2001, alleged that declaring bin Laden as an international terrorist was part of an 'evil design of America'. He admitted that cassettes of bin Laden's speeches were distributed during a SIMI meeting in Kanpur a few months earlier.

Serial bombings and overt terrorist movements, however, cannot be a measure of the penetration that has been achieved by the extremist Islamists and their state sponsors. Acts of terror—especially on a large scale—represent the culmination of years of preparation that are reflected in motivation, mobilisation and organisational development. Evidence of these processes is mounting throughout India, and is reflected in the number, both of fundamentalist and of subversive groups in existence, and the geographical spread of their activities. The most prominent of these include the Jamaat-e-Islami Hind (JEI Hind), the All India Milli Council (AIMC), All India Jihad Committee (AIJC), the People's Democratic Party (PDP, formerly the Islamic Sewak Sangh), All India Muslim Federation (AIMF), Muslim United Front (MUF), Tamil Nadu Muslim Munnetra Kazhagam (TNMMK), National Development Front (Kerala), Tabligh Jamaat, Students Islamic Movement of India (SIMI), Students Islamic Organisations (SIO), Al Umma, Al Jihad, and the Muslim Sena Sanghathan, Ikhwan-ul-Muslameen, Islami Inqalabi Mahaz, Tanzim Isla-ul-Muslameen, and the Minorities United Front, among others.

Each of these organisations runs one or more 'non-governmental organisations' (NGO), many of which have offices abroad. Substantial funds are received, and ranges of interactions, including frequent 'Tablighi conferences' with foreign delegations, are organised. The flow of funds is primarily through what are known as hawala (illegal) channels and, while Pakistan largely defines the patterns of use and the beneficiaries, the preponderance of such transfers originate in Saudi Arabia, Kuwait, United Arab Emirates, Qatar and Oman. Thus, very substantial transfers of foreign funds generated under the pretext of providing relief to the Coimbatore riot victims were diverted for use in executing the Coimbatore blasts.

The range, volume and the persistence of such subversive activity throughout the country is more a measure of Pakistan's tenacity and the intensity of the extremist Islamist vision, than it is of the present impact these activities have had on the larger Muslim community in India. The tragic loss of life, wasted human and developmental resources and the atmosphere of fear and suspicion that sporadic incidents of terrorism generate notwithstanding, India has the flexibility, the resilience and the political space to absorb a level of subversive and extremist Islamist activities significantly higher than the present. Nevertheless, the sheer lethality of weaponry and explosives, the possibility of an escalation to a new generation of Chemical and Biological Weapons, and the inherent uncertainty of the politics of a complex society characterised by immense religious and cultural diversity, make the existing risks and levels of activity unacceptable.

These risks are even greater and less acceptable in countries where such space is wanting, where political instability is at higher levels, and where the roots of democracy are yet to take firm hold of the soil. Islamist subversion threatens peace and regime stability more immediately in neighbouring Bangladesh, where religious extremism has emerged as a major threat to the prevailing political order and to internal security. There are grave and immediate dangers to peace and stability in Bangladesh: the revival of the activities of the Jamaat-e-Islami, the return to Bangladesh and its politics of Pakistan-backed elements who collaborated closely with the genocidal campaign of 1971 in what was then East Pakistan, the rising rhetoric of Islamic hukumat (rule), and the deepening linkages between militant Bangladeshi groups and the extremist Islamists in Pakistan, Afghanistan and West Asia. Here again, the pattern of funding, subversion and mobilisation through the mosque and the madrassa is clearly in evidence. Prior to Independence, there were 1,467 madrassas in Bangladesh. Their number has currently risen to over 6,500, with more than 90,000 teachers and about 1.8 million students. A large number of these institutions have been established as a result of massive foreign aid, primarily from Gulf countries, and largely unmediated by official channels. Bangladesh's madrassas are the chief recruiting ground for Islamist militant groups, including several that are linked to Pakistan and also to Osama bin Laden's Al Qaeda. The latter category.

According to sources, subsequent to the '9/11' incidents in USA, and the increasing pressure on Pakistan—and directly on the ISI to curb subversive activities in the region—the situation in the Bangladesh ISI unit became somewhat confused. There has, however, been no brief for a withdrawal of activities, though a low profile is currently being maintained. The new regime is expected to provide a more favourable context for the operation of extremist forces in the country. Many BNP MPs, leaders and officials have direct business linkages, including partnerships, with corporations and financial operations that are run by or co-owned with leaders of terrorist groups operating in India's Northeast and in Bangladesh.

Despite a temporary lull in militant activities—partially because of the international pressure on Islamist extremist groupings after the September 2001 attacks, and partially because the imperatives of anti-state violence have declined because of a sympathetic incumbent regime—terrorist and subversive activities of religious extremists and pan Islamist terrorist outfits remain the most serious threat to internal security in Bangladesh. During Begum Khaleda Zia's last tenure, Bangladesh had encouraged and allowed a large number of volunteers to fight in Afghanistan against the former Soviet Union and subsequently in Jammu and Kashmir. A large number of these mujahideen are now present in the country and are spearheading the Islamist fundamentalist movement in Bangladesh with their extensive connections with the international Islamic jihad movement.

Available evidence prior to the October elections suggested increasing involvement of Islamist fundamentalist organisations in terrorist and subversive activities in Bangladesh. There were a number of bomb blasts in the country in the year 2001. On January 20, there were two separate bomb blasts in Dhaka in which an estimated six persons were killed and 50 others injured. The then Home Minister Mohammad Nasim held Jamaat-e-Islami and its associated organisations responsible for the blasts. On April 14, 2001, at least eight persons were killed in a bomb blast at a Bengali New Year cultural function in Dhaka. On June 8, 2001, police arrested four persons including Maulana Mohammad Akbar Hossain, Vice Principal of Siddirganj Madrassah, for their alleged involvement in the blast. Ten persons were killed and 25 others injured in a bomb blast at a Catholic Church mission church at Baniachar, Gopalganj district, on June 3. Again on June 15, an estimated 21 persons were killed and over 100 injured in a bomb blast at the Awami League party office at Narayanganj town. The then Foreign Minister had stated that the unholy nexus of extreme religious zealots and fundamentalist elements with organised international terrorist groups was responsible for the blast. On June 29, 2001, police arrested an activist of the Islami Chhatra Shibir (ICS), the student wing of the Jamaat-e-Islami, for his alleged involvement in the Narayanganj blast.

Earlier, an alliance of Islamist fundamentalist groups, the Islamic Okiya Jote (IOJ), a member of the new ruling alliance led by the Bangladesh Nationalist Party (BNP), had intensified its campaign against the December 2000 High Court verdict banning two fatwas (religious edicts). The alliance declared the two judges, Golam Rabbani and Nazmun Ara Sultana, who had delivered the verdict, as murtad (enemies of Islam) and pronounced 'death sentences' on them. The IOJ had also declared a jehad against the United Forum of Citizens, a group of NGOs which supported the High Court's action of banning the fatwas. At the time of the High Court Order, a series of protest strikes had been organised by the BNP alliance and, following the murder of a policeman, who was dragged inside a mosque and killed on February 3, 2001, the police launched a major crackdown. Top leaders of the alliance, including its Chief, Shaikhul Hadith Maulana Azizul Huq, who is also the Chief of the Ulema Mashaek organisation; the Secretary-General Mufti Fazlul Haq Amini, who is also the Convenor of the 'Committee for Implementation of Islamic Laws' and also the Secretary-General of the radical Islamic Unity Alliance, and several activists were arrested under the Public Safety Act on charges of threatening to kill the two High Court judges and damaging public and private properties. A madrassa, run by IOJ leaders was raided and a large number of weapons were seized. The township of Brahmanbaria, the stronghold of the Jamaat-e-Islami, which borders the Indian state of Tripura, witnessed several violent protests against the crackdown in which seven persons were killed and an estimated 100 injured during clashes between Islamist fundamentalists and security force personnel.

Islamist extremism in Bangladesh also has widespread foreign connections. On January 9, 1999, police in Chittagong arrested Syed Muhammad Nurul Afsar, a man with a 'Libyan connection', on charges of smuggling firearms and explosives into the country. Police said Afsar had travelled to Libya several times to be trained in the use of explosives. He had visited Czechoslovakia in June 1998 to purchase weapons and explosives, which were then shipped to Bangladesh. Police described Afsar as a 'high ranking terrorist' belonging to an obscure group called Freedom in Bangladesh, dedicated to turning the country into an Islamic theocracy. In January 1999, Delhi Police picked up Bangladeshi Sayed Abu Nasir and charged him with planning bomb attacks on the US consulates in Chennai and Calcutta. Two kilograms of RDX explosive was seized from him. The police claimed Nasir was a member of the Lashkar-e-Toiba and that he entered India in October 1998 along with six others. Three of his Indian contacts were picked up from Shiliguri near the Bangladesh border, but the others, believed to be four Egyptians, a Sudanese and a Myanmar national, escaped. In the latter half of January 1999, police in Bangladesh arrested five people suspected of plotting the January 18, 1999 assassination attempt on the life of celebrated poet Shamsur Rahman. All belonged to Harkat-ul-Jehad-al-Islami (HUJI), which has been building up its operations in the country since early 1990s. In the next few days, police picked up an interesting melange of people, who included apart from two more Bangladeshis, an Afghan, a Pakistani and two South Africans. Police said interrogation of this lot revealed a plan to assassinate 28 Bangladeshi intellectuals, who had been dubbed 'atheists and enemies of Islam.' These included National Professor Kabir Choudhury, writer Taslima Nasreen and the Director General of the Islamic Foundation,

Maulana Abdul Awal.

Intellectuals, cultural organisations and sects of Islam, which are regarded as 'deviant' by the fundamentalists, have also been preferred targets of violence. On March 7, 1999, six persons were killed and more than 100 injured when two bombs planted by suspected religious extremists exploded at a cultural function in Bangladesh's western Jessore district. The function was organised by Udichi Shilpi Gosthi—a Dhaka-based pro-liberation and left-oriented organisation of cultural activists. On October 8, 1999, seven people were killed and about 40 injured when a bomb exploded during Friday prayers, at the Kadiani Mosque of the Ahamadiya sect of Muslims in Khulna. Police suspicions for this bombing focused on religious extremists who had earlier demanded a ban on the activities of the Ahamadiyas, who are regarded by orthodox Muslims as a blasphemous non-Muslim sect. The same day, powerful explosive devices were recovered from a mosque of the Ahamadiya sect and the office of a Bengali language daily, Janakantha, in Dhaka.

On July 21, 2000, an assassination plot to kill the then Bangladesh Prime Minister, Sheikh Hasina Wajed, was unearthed. Investigations revealed the main suspect in the plot to be Mufti Abdul Hannan, a Pakistan-trained leader of the Harkat-ul-Jehad-al-Islami (HUJI), who had manufactured the explosives at a soap factory, Sonar Bangla Chemical Industries Limited, near Gopalganj. While Hannan evaded the Bangladesh police, many of his associates including his brother Motiar Rehman were arrested. According to Mohammed Jashimuddin, then Superintendent of Police of Gopalganj, Hannan had recieved training in Peshawar before taking part in the Afghan war. A central committee member of HUJI, he returned to Bangladesh in 1998 and had been training madrassa students to use fire arms and manufacture explosives.

A number of transnational Islamist terrorist groups, including the Al Qaeda of Osama bin Laden, have established a presence in Bangladesh in alliance with the various fundamentalist organisations in the country. Indian Intelligence discovered in early 2001 that bin Laden was generously donating funds to the Pakistan-based extremist outfit Harkat-ul-Mujahideen (HUM), which had contacts with the Dhaka-based Bangladesh Harkat-ul-Jihad-e-Islami (HUJI). The HUJI was, in fact, established with Osama bin Laden's aid in 1992, under the leadership of Shawkat Osman alias Sheikh Farid, and with Imtiaz Quddus as its 'General Secretary'. It has an estimated strength of about 15,000 and strong connections with the ISI.

HUJI was assigned the task of recruiting Bangladeshi and Indian Muslims to fight in Kashmir under the command of the Harkat-ul-Mujahideen. Reports in 1999 said that HUJI planned to recruit 5,000 mujahids from madrassas in Bangladesh. Another 10,000 were to be recruited from among the Muslim refugees at Rohingya, who fled the Arakan province of Myanmar and were staying at Cox's Bazar, Bangladesh. HUJI terrorists have been active against secular politicians and intellectuals in Bangladesh. The professed objective of this Islamist radical group is to turn Bangladesh into a Dar-ul-Islam or a land of believers. The previous Awami League-led government of Sheikh Hasina Wajed had tried to curb the activities of the group, and arrested a number of its activists.

HUJI is also said to maintain six terrorist camps in the Chittagong Hill Tracts (CHT) of Bangladesh, where the cadres are imparted arms training. Several hundred recruits have also been trained in Afghanistan. HUJI activists frequently cross over to India for terrorist activities. The cadres of the outfit who style themselves as the 'Bangladeshi Taliban' are alleged to infiltrate regularly into India's eastern corridor and maintain contacts with terrorist and subversive outfits of the region.

The Osama bin Laden and Al Qaeda connection in Bangladesh came to light during the visit of the then United States President, Bill Clinton, to Bangladesh in March 2000. President Clinton's scheduled visit to Joypura village and the national memorial at Savan were reportedly cancelled due to alleged threats that emanated from Al Qaeda.

The ISI is deeply involved with the Islamist terrorist outfits operating in Bangladesh. On June 2000, an Indian intelligence agency intercepted a radiogram, which revealed that the ISI had set up a strong base in Kurigram and Rangpur areas of Bangladesh near the Coochbihar border. There was also direct evidence that a section of officials and personnel of the Bangladesh Rifles were colluding with the ISI. Indian intelligence also believes that the ISI, in collusion with the HUJI, was training militants in the use of sophisticated arms and explosives at camps set up at Rangmari, Sundermari, Masaldanga and other villages. This area is one of the epicentres of the ISI's operations, from where it exports terror into India.

Rising extremist Islamist activity, despite the fact that Muslims constitute a bare three per cent of the population is also challenging the security agencies of the infant democracy of Nepal. Such activity is, presently, primarily directed against India, but its linkages with organised criminal operations and the destabilisation of pockets of Muslim concentrations in the Terai region bordering India are a cause of increasing concern for Kathmandu. A succession of recent reports has documented rising activities of the ISI and by the Pakistan Embassy at Kathmandu, involving strong organised criminal networks and prominent political leaders in a range of activities targeting India and reinforcing the Islamist agenda within Nepal. The Muslim pockets of the

Terai, especially Bardiya, Banke, Rupendehi and the Parsa-Morang belt have seen increasing 'tablighi' activities, and the construction of mosques and madrassas with financial flows from Pakistan—often directly from the Embassy at Kathmandu—from Saudi Arabia and from a range of pan-Islamist organisations. Over the past two decades, more than 275 mosques and madrassas have been built in just the four districts of Rupandehi, Banke, Kapilvastu and Bardiya. There are some 15 major tablighi/fundamentalist organisations in Nepal, and at least five of these are well within the ambit of Pakistan's influence and control. These include the Jamaat-e-Millat-e-Islamia; the Nepal Islamic Yuba Sangh; the Nepal Muslim League; the Nepal Muslim Ekta Sangh; and the Democratic Muslim Welfare Association. Nepal is, consequently, emerging as an important 'staging post' for Pakistan's strategy of erosion and encirclement against India, and is increasingly the preferred route for terrorists' movements to various areas of low-intensity conflict in J&K and the Northeast.

In Sri Lanka, the Muslim community and emerging fundamentalist forces have generally aligned themselves with the interests of the government. The Island nation's Muslim population is mainly Tamil, but has been driven out of the ethnically cleansed northern areas controlled by the Liberation Tigers of Tamil Eelam (LTTE), and is now concentrated along the eastern coast, the north-west coast, Kandy and suburban Colombo. Islamist fundamentalist mobilisation in Sri Lanka began after a succession of attacks on the Muslims by the LTTE in the early 1990s, after which the government decided to arm the Muslim youth for self-defence. The conflict between Hindu and Muslim Tamils resulted in the polarisation of mindsets on the issue of religious identity. There are, today, nearly a dozen Muslim fundamentalist organisations in Sri Lanka who are funded by foreign countries, primarily Saudi Arabia, with at least two political parties drawing significant support from Iran.

The Extremist Islamist Internationale

The threat of extremist Islamist terror in South Asia must be estimated, not just in terms of visible violence and subversion, but the unique and lethal mix of a virulent and vigorously propagated ideology; international and state support and sponsorship; the movement of experienced cadres across theatres that span the entire world; and the access to and destructive potential of contemporary weapons and information technologies. Pakistan's experience and the Afghan war have given rise to "a kind of Islamic 'internationale' through the recruitment of volunteers throughout the Muslim world" and "a global network of radical Muslim terrorists." Among these are the experienced and ideologically motivated Arab Afghans, with their roots in West Asia. South Asia is, moreover, awash with small arms and lethal explosives. The recovery of gas masks from bunkers held by Pakistani forces and irregulars during the Kargil War, and recent reports regarding Osama bin Laden's intent to use chemical weapons suggest that extremist Islamist forces and their state sponsors are, at least, evaluating the possibility and impact of the use of weapons of mass destruction (WMD) in their low-intensity wars in various countries. Indeed, when asked by Time in 1998 about reports that he was trying to acquire nuclear and chemical weapons, bin Laden replied, "If I seek to acquire these weapons, I am carrying out a duty. It would be a sin for Muslims not to try to possess the weapons that would prevent the infidels from inflicting harm on Muslims." Laden in a recorded interview released by the Qatar-based Al Jazira in the aftermath of the September 11,2001, attacks, said that "we supported the Pakistani people and congratulated them when God was gracious enough to enable them to acquire the nuclear weapon. We regard this as one of our rights, our Muslim rights...it is the duty of the Muslims to possess them...we believe that the right to self-defence is to be enjoyed by all people. Israel is stockpiling hundreds of nuclear warheads and bombs and the Christian West is largely in possession of such weapons. Hence we regard this as a right." On or about May 29, 1998, bin Laden had also issued a statement entitled "The Nuclear Bomb of Islam" under the banner of the "International Islamic front for Fighting the Jews and Crusaders" in which he stated that "it is the duty of Muslims to prepare as much force as possible to terrorise the enemies of God."

It is not necessary to belabour the obvious point that there are 'many Islams', and that the adherents of the murderous mix of religion and terror are only a small fraction of Muslims in the world. There is, however, a difficulty that needs to be confronted: that of the separation of legitimate religious, educational and charitable activity engaged in by Islamist religious institutions, including the madrassas, from overt or covert support to terrorism and a militant Islamist agenda. This difficulty is enormously compounded by the ideological continuity among those who currently propagate the dogmas of Islamist extremism from the fringes of Europe and through Asia and Africa, as also by the continuity of sources of finance and support through every theatre of Islamist terrorism and 'fundamentalist' subversion in the world. In the absence of enormous co-operation in documentation and sharing of intelligence, and the containment of terrorist funding, movement and activities, between nations who have a stake in defeating terrorism and across all traditional borders of suspicion and narrow 'interests of state', it is not clear how this challenge can be met.

References

1. Ashton Carter, John Deutch and Philip Zelikow, "Catastrophic Terrorism", Foreign Affairs, Washington, November/December 1998.
2. Ely Karmon, Osama bin Laden: Speculations on Possible State Sponsorship, The International Policy Institute for Counter-terrorism, September 17, 2001, Herzliya, Israel.
3. Ambassador Michael A Sheehan, Coordinator for Counterterrorism, US Department of State, Statement for the Record Before the House International Relations Committee July 12, 2000, http://www.usinfo.state.gov/topical/pol/terror/00071702.htm. Ambassador Sheehan was echoing Secretary of State Madeline Albright's earlier statement (of May 1, 2000) that there had been an "eastward shift in terrorism's center of gravity" towards South Asia.
4. Total Fatalities: 1990 - 1177; 1991 - 1393; 1992 - 1909; 1993 - 2567; 1994 - 2899; 1995 - 2796; 1996 - 2903; 1997 - 2372; 1998 - 2261; 1999 - 2538; 2000 - 3288; 2001 - 4499. Source: South Asia Terrorism Portal; Countries; India; J&K; Data Sheets; Annual Casualties; www.satp.org.
5. Altaf Gauhar, The Challenge of Islam, London: Islamic Council of Europe, 1978, p. 309.
6. Allah Buksh K. Brohi, "Preface", in S K Malik, The Quranic Concept of War, New Delhi: Himalayan Books, 1986, pp. xix-xx
7. See Patterns of Global Terrorism 2000, US State Department, www.state.gov/s/ct/rls/pgtrpt/2000/index.cfm?docid=2432
8. Ibid.
9. There is significant evidence of progressive shifts in the US position on this count since this paper was presented, but the general observations remain valid for the context within which they are made. The evolving US position, moreover, is not entirely unambiguous, and is subject to possible and subsequent dilution or reversal.
10. "Terrorism: New option backed", Dawn, Karachi, May 10,

2001. Also available at www.dawn.com/2001/05/10/top15.htm

11. The anthrax attacks are now believed to have been unrelated to Islamist terrorist groups, but the early discourse on them was based on a presumption that their source was the same as the 9/11 operations.
12. Cited in Lisa Beyer, "Osama's Endgame," Time, October 15, 2001, Vol. 158, No. 17. http://www.time.com/time/magazine/printout/0,8816,178412,00.html
13. The imagery of this description is based on private conversations with some Indian Islamist fundamentalists and their assessments of the rising 'crisis of morality' and the 'disintegration of the social and political order' in the world.
14. See "Bin Laden: No 'security or safety' for U.S.", http://asia.cnn.com/2001/WORLD/asiapcf/central/10/07/bin.laden.statement/
15. The humiliating defeat of the Taliban and dishonourable flight of the leaders of the Al Qaeda has, however, diminished American vulnerabilities to such a process. The '9/11' aftermath weakened the world image of the US. The collapse of the Taliban-Al Qaeda has strengthened it immensely. Future attacks in America, unless they exceeded a certain improbable scale and frequency, would, in fact contribute to a consolidation of counter-terrorism measures and a deepening legitimacy for the American cause, as against the growing delegitimisation of Islamist extremist violence. Here it is significant to understand the role of success in consolidating terrorism as a strategy. As Fareed Zakaria has noted in another context, "Military victory is indeed essential. Radical political Islam is an 'armed doctrine,' in Edmund Burke's phrase. Like other armed doctrines before it—fascism, for example—it can be discredited only by first being defeated." Fareed Zakaria, "How to Save the Arab World", Newsweek, December 24, 2001, p. 23. (Author's note).
16. S K Malik, The Quranic Concept of War, p. 59.
17. See "Iraqi clerics declare jihad vs US-led war on Afghanistan", http://www.inq7.net/brk/2001/oct/17/brkafp_17-1.htm

18. An interesting assessment of the power (or absence thereof) of the Muslim 'Ummah' has been given by General Pervez Musharraf in his address to a gathering of Ulema on June 5, 2001, http://www.pak.gov.pk/public/chief/CE_Seert_Conf.htm
19. Quoted in Pakistan-based Urdu paper, Ausaf, December 27, 2000. See www.armyinkashmir.org/articles/jihad_machine.html.
20. Three senior army personnel including the ISI Chief Gen. Ahmad were removed on October 8, 2001.
21. "Sidelining of Islamist generals puts Musharraf on safer ground",
22. See "About Turn", www.rediff.com/news/2001/oct/17spec.htm
23. 'Ibid.
24. "Jihad enrolment drive gathers momentum: JI", Dawn, Karachi, October 21, 2001. Also see "Pakistan's tribals decide to fight beside Taliban", www.thenewspapertoday.com/world/inside.phtml?NEWS_ID=27926
25. "Peshawar: Drive for recruiting volunteers continues in NWFP, Fata", Dawn, October 21, 2001. Also at www.dawn.com/2001/10/21/local18.htm
26. Ibid.
27. Ibid.
28. Ibid.
29. "The choice between jehad and jirga", The News, Islamabad, October 21, 2001. Also at www.jang.com.pk/thenews/oct2001-weekly/nos-14-10-2001/spr.htm
30. "Fundos boast thousands of jehadis for Taliban cause", The Friday Times, Lahore, October 19-25, 2001. Ibid.
31. Ibid
32. "Scholar calls for Jihad", Dawn, September 19, 2001. Also at www.dawn.com/2001/09/19/nat23.htm.
33. "Scholar calls for Jihad", Dawn, September 19, 2001. Also at www.dawn.com/2001/09/19/nat23.htm.
34. The Dar-ul-Uloom seminary at Deoband has, however, repeatedly repudiated all connections with the ideologies and

terrorists that claim their inspiration from the teachings of this influential centre of traditional Islamic learning. See, for instance, Sankarshan Thakur, "What Taliban have done is horrifying, un-Islamic but you need to ask why", The Indian Express, New Delhi, March 14, 2001.

35. Ahmed Rashid, Taliban: Islam, Oil and the New Great Game in Central Asia, London: I B Tauris, 2001, p. 90. Haqqania is in Akhora Khatak, in the North West Frontier Province.
36. Ibid.
37. Ibid, pp. 90-1.
38. See "Master or Victim: Pakistan's Afghan War", in Ahmed Rashid, Taliban: Islam, Oil and the New Great Game in Central Asia, pp. 183-195. Jessica Stern refers to this as a typical "principal-agent" problem, observing that the interests of the state (principal) and those of the militant groups (the agent) are not fully aligned. See, Pakistan's Jihad Culture, Foreign Affairs, November-December, 2000 at http://www.foreignaffairs.org/issues/0011/stern.html
39. Ibid., p. 194.
40. John L. Esposito, The Islamic Threat: Myth or Reality, New York: Oxford University Press, 1999, p. xiii.
41. Mohammad Yousaf and Mark Adkin, The Bear Trap: Afghanistan's Untold Story, Lahore: Jang Publishers, 1992, p. 3.
42. See John Cooley, Unholy Wars: Afghanistan, America and International Terrorism, London: Pluto, 1999; Also see, Vijendra Singh Jafa, "India & Pakistan in a Quagmire: Superpower Games and Human Tragedies", Faultlines: Writings on Conflict & Resolution, New Delhi, Vol. 6, August 2000, New Delhi: ICM-Bulwark Books, pp. 109-110.
43. K P S. Gill and Ajai Sahni, eds., Terror & Containment: Perspectives on India's Internal Security, New Delhi: Gyan Publishing House, 2001, pp. 13-15.
44. Olivier Roy, Middle East Report, Winter 1997, cited in Ahmed Rashid, Taliban, p. 187.
45. Ahmed Rashid, Taliban, p. 89.
46. Jessica Stern, "Pakistan's Jihad Culture," Foreign Affairs,

November/December 2000, http://www.foreignaffairs.org/issues/0011/stern.html.

47. Ahmed Rashid, Taliban, p. 87.
48. Afzaal Mahmood, "What price Jihad culture," Dawn, January 15, 2001. Also at http://www.dawn.com/2001/01/15/op.htm
49. In April 1995, for instance, the Benazir Bhutto government released a list of 38 foreign funded madrassas and sectarian organizations that possessed arms and imparted weapons training to local and foreign students. Saudi Arabia, Iran, Iraq, Libya, UAE and Kuwait were identified as the sources of funding and support to these organizations. Shafiq Awam, "Foreign-funded madaris list provided to govts," The Nation, Lahore, April 16, 1995.
50. See South Asia Terrorism Portal; Countries; Pakistan; Backgrounder; www.satp.org
51. Ibid
52. "Jihad culture spreading world over, says Lashkar chief,", News, December 3, 2000. Also at http://www.jang.com.pk/thenews/dec2000-daily/03-12-2000/metro/k2.htm.
53. An expression used by Mujibur Rehman Inqalabi, the SSP's 'second in command' to describe the madrassas. See Jessica Stern, "Pakistan's Jihad Culture."
54. In 1988, after hundreds of Shia had been massacred by the SSP, their leaders fled to Kabul where they were offered sanctuary. See Ahmed Rashid, Taliban, p. 92.
55. Ibid, p. 186.
56. Robin Wright, "The Chilling Goal of Islam's New Warriors", Los Angeles Times, December 28, 2000. Also at http://www.latimes.com/news/nation/20001228/t000123583.html.
57. For instance, 127 Islamic organizations addressed a joint Press Conference on April 29, 2000, protesting against the Musharraf government's bid to bring peripheral amendments to Pakistan's blasphemy law. The government backed off on the 7th of May, and on May 16, 2000, Musharraf himself told the Press that "there would be no change in the blasphemy

law whatsoever in view of the pressing demand from the public, including the Ulema and the Mashaikh." The attempt to reserve seats for women in local bodies was similarly abandoned when the Islamists argued that this was a move intended 'to spread vulgarity' among the people. The March 1, 2000, ban on the public display of firearms is also held in open contempt by most of the major militant Islamic groupings.

58. Hasan Khan, "Harkat chief for military training at Madaris", www.afghanradio.com/news/2000/october/oct23k2000.htm
59. Robin Wright, "The Chilling Goal of Islam's New Warriors."
60. The State of J&K comprises a total area of 152,298 square kilometers, with a population of 6,815,000. It is divided into three regions: the Muslim majority Kashmir region (HQ Srinagar), with an area of 15, 898 square kilometers and a population of 3,977,000; the Hindu majority Jammu region (HQ Jammu), with an area of 26,293 square kilometers and a population of 2,538,000; and the Buddhist majority Ladakh region (HQ Leh), with a population of 300,000. Cf. www.jammukashmir.nic.in.
61. The Hizb has recently reduced its operation, first after its own unilateral cease-fire of July 2000, and subsequently after the Indian Prime Minister's declaration of cease-fire. The Hizb is the largest terrorist group in J&K, and is dominated by 'local' cadres. The other groups are primarily drawn from Pakistani and other foreign elements.
62. Data and analysis on Kashmir are primarily based on research and documentation at the Institute for Conflict Management and the South Asia Terrorism Portal, www.satp.org.
63. Till December 31, 2001. The data is based on the South Asia Terrorism Portal's compilations from official and media sources in India. www.satp.org.
64. The proportion of foreigners among the active militants would be higher—upto 75 percent—since the Hizb reduced its operations.
65. Shaul Shay and Yoram Schweitzer, "The 'Afghan Alumni'

Terrorism: Islamic Militants against the Rest of the World", ICT Papers, The International Policy Institute for Counter-Terrorism, Herzilya, Israel, September 2000, Vol. 6.

66. Mark Huband, Warriors of the Prophet: The Struggle for Islam, Colorado: Westview Press, 1999, p. 9. Also see Manoj Joshi, The Lost Rebellion: Kashmir in the Nineties, New Delhi: Penguin Books, 1999; Tavleen Singh, Kashmir: A Tragedy of Errors, New Delhi: Penguin Books, 1996.
67. Over 400,000 Kashmiri Pandits—out of an original population in the Kashmir Valley of 425,000 prior to 1989—continue to be displaced. Official records indicate that some 216,820 of them live as migrants in makeshift camps at Jammu, another 143,000 at Delhi and thousands of others are now dispersed across the country. Many of those registered at the camps have also been dispersed according to the exigencies of employment and opportunities for education, trade or business. There has been little effort to facilitate their return to the Valley in recent years. Earlier attempts were neutralized by brutal campaigns of selective murder, including the killing of seven Pandits at Sangrama in Budgam district in March 1997, three at Gul in Udhampur district in June 1997, 26 in the massacre at Wandhama in Srinagar district in January 1998, and 26 at Prankote in Udhampur district in April 1998. The possibility of reversing the terrorists' ethnic cleansing of the Valley remains remote, and there are now reports of a hidden migration from some of the border areas in the Jammu region where the Hindus are a minority. www.satp.org.
68. Jessica Stern, "Pakistan's Jihad Culture."
69. Praveen Swami, "The 'liberation' of Hyderabad," Frontline, Chennai, Vol. 17, No. 10, May 13-26, 2000, www.frontline.com/fl/1710/17100390.htm.
70. "Church blast cases busted; 15 arrested," indiainfo.com, July 17, 2000, http://news.indiainfo.com/2000/07/17/blast.html.
71. "Centre may consider ban on ISI-backed Deendar Anjuman," Indian Express, August 4, 2000.
72. "30 killed as serial blasts rock Coimbatore." http://www.indiaserver.com/thehindu/1998/02/15/

front.htm#Story1; "Panic Following Blasts," http://www.indiaserver.com/thehindu/1998/02/15/thb02.htm#Story2; "Union Home Ministry reviews situation,"http://www.indiaserver.com/thehindu/1998/02/16/thb01.htm#Story5; "Six extremists die in Coimbatore blasts, toll 44," http://www.indiaserver.com/thehindu/1998/02/16/thb02.htm#Story1; "Arrests throughout the state" http://www.indiaserver.com/thehindu/1998/02/16/thb02.htm#Story2

73. "30 killed as serial blasts rock Coimbatore." http://www.indiaserver.com/thehindu/1998/02/15/front.htm#Story1; "Panic Following Blasts," http://www.indiaserver.com/thehindu/1998/02/15/thb02.htm#Story2; "Union Home Ministry reviews situation," http://www.indiaserver.com/thehindu/1998/02/16/thb01.htm#Story5; "Six extremists die in Coimbatore blasts, toll 44," http://www.indiaserver.com/thehindu/1998/02/16/thb02.htm#Story1; "Arrests throughout the state" http://www.indiaserver.com/thehindu/1998/02/16/thb02.htm#Story2
74. "Weapons of anarchy", The Week, Cochin, March 8, 1998.
75. Ibid. Blasts occurred on the Cheran Express, Pandyan Express and Alleppey Express trains on December 6, 1997, the anniversary of the Babri mosque demolition. Official sources indicated that the Islamic Defence Force of Kerala, a shadowy outfit, was behind these explosions, which killed nine persons.
76. "Ten charged in train blasts case", Tribune, Chandigarh, October 6, 1998. Also at www.tribuneindia.com/98oct06/head4.htm. Among those chargesheeted was Erwadi Kasim, President of the IDF.
77. See "Messages from the States", Frontline, Vol. 15, No. 6, March 21-April 3, 1998. Ibid
78. See "The fundamentalist underworld", www.rediff.com/news/1998/jun/26isi.htm. Also see "7 `terrorist' groups identified in Kerala", www.kerala.org/news/online/1997/march/news/news38.html.
79. Ibid

80. Ibid. The organisation's suspected links with the perpetrators of the Coimbatore blasts surfaced with the arrest of NDF office bearer Zubair on the grounds that he had harboured Al-Umma activists Ommai Babu, prime accused in the blasts case.
81. "Kerala a haven for subversive forces", The Hindustan Times, New Delhi, September 7, 2001
82. See Ghulam Hasnain, At Home in Exile, Outlook, New Delhi, November 20, 2000 (also at www.outlookindia.com), pp. 30-38.
83. See "Extending terror", Frontline, Vol. 16, No. 6, March 13 - 26, 1999.
84. See South Asia Terrorism Portal; Terror Tuesday; International Linkages of Islamist Terrorist outfits; Gujarat; www.satp.org
85. Ibid.
86. Ibid.
87. Ibid.
88. Ibid.
89. Ibid.
90. Ibid.
91. Ibid.
92. See "Militants held", www.indian-express.com/ie/daily/20000121/ina21083.html
93. See "IB suspects Dawood-Osama tie-up for terror campaign", www.hvk.org/articles/0899/29.html
94. See South Asia Terrorism Portal; Terror Tuesday; International Linkages of Islamist Terrorist outfits; Gujarat; www.satp.org.
95. "Report on Illegal Migration into Assam submitted to the President of India by the Governor of Assam, November 8, 1998," See South Asia Terrorism Portal; India; Documents; Assam; www.satp.org.
96. South Asia Terrorism Portal; India; Assam; Terrorist outfits; www.satp.org
97. "ISI Activities in Assam: Statement laid on the table of the house of Assam Legislative Assembly under item No. 12

dated 6.4.2000 by Shri Prafulla Kumar Mahanta, Chief Minister, Assam," See South Asia Terrorism Portal; India; Documents; Assam; www.satp.org.

98. "ISI Activities in Assam: Statement laid on the table of the house of Assam Legislative Assembly under item no. 12 dated 6.4.2000 by Shri Prafulla Kumar Mahanta, Chief Minister, Assam," See South Asia Terrorism Portal; India; Documents; Assam; www.satp.org.
99. "Laden aides in Nagaon, Govt asks police to keep strict vigil", The Sentinel, Guwahati, October 16, 2001.
100. "Laden aides in Nagaon, Govt asks police to keep strict vigil", The Sentinel, Guwahati, October 16, 2001.
101. See "Army's wake-up call behind arrest of ISI operatives", www.mumbai-central.com/nukkad/aug1999/msg00050.html. Maj. Gen. Bopanna was General-officer-Commanding, 21 Mountain Division.
102. "Monitor madrasas: Centre to NE", Sentinel, October 7, 2001
103. ibid.
104. ibid.
105. ibid.
106. http:/www.satp.org

Chapter 5

TERRORISM IN AFGHANISTAN AND CENTRAL ASIA

Dr. R.B. Singh

The Taliban, led by Mulla Mohammad Omar, its Amir, and the Hizb-e-Islami (HEI), led by Gulbuddin Heckmatyar, continue to be active not only in the Pashtun belt in the Afghan territory across Pakistan's border with Afghanistan, but also in and around Kabul. A terrorist strike in Kabul before the Presidential elections of October, 2004, directed at the personnel of a private American company, which provides physical security to President Hamid Karzai, proved that their reach extends even to Kabul. They apparently have pockets of support even there.

However, the widely-expressed apprehensions that they might be able to disrupt the Presidential elections were belied. In the months preceding the elections, they indulged in sporadic terrorist strikes in the provinces, which used to be the stronghold of the Taliban before the US-led coalition intervened in Afghanistan from October 7, 2001, but they did not disrupt the elections and a surprisingly large number of voters exercised their franchise, without letting themselves be intimidated.

However, it would be incorrect to infer from the successful conduct of the elections that the Taliban and the HEI are now a declining force and hence do not pose a major threat to Afghanistan's security. Reliable sources in Pakistan indicate that the absence of major acts of terrorism on the eve of and during the elections is a testimony not to the declining capability of the terrorist elements, but to their continuing amenability to Pakistani control and influence.

According to these sources, during President Pervez Musharraf's talks with President George Bush and other American leaders in New York in September, 2004, they stressed upon him the importance of Pakistan ensuring that the Taliban and the HEI did not disrupt the Presidential elections. In the weeks preceding the US Presidential elections, there were two major demands on Pakistan from the officials of the Bush Administration. The first related to the capture of Osama bin Laden and his No. 2 in Al Qaeda, Ayman al-Zawahiri, and the second to ensuring that the Taliban and the HEI did not disrupt the Afghan elections.

While Musharraf did not deliver bin Laden and/or al-Zawahiri to the US, he ensured that there was no disruption of the Afghan Presidential elections and that the Pashtun refugees from Afghanistan still staying in Pakistani territory participated in the elections in large numbers. It would be difficult to have a correct idea of the extent of the popular support enjoyed by Karzai inside Afghanistan without an assessment of how many votes he got from the Pashtuns , who were amenable to pressure from Pakistan's Inter-Services Intelligence (ISI) Directorate. It is doubtful whether Karzai would have won in the first round itself with more than a 50 per cent majority, without the Pashtun votes on both sides of the Pakistan-Afghanistan border, including the votes of the refugees, mobilised my Musharraf and his ISI. A reward for this promptly came from President Bush in the form of a new military package for Pakistan worth about US $ 1.3 billion. Whereas the previous post 9/11 military packages for Musharraf from the US consisted essentially of counter-terrorism items such as helicopter gun ships, communication and interception equipment etc, the latest package contains items which Pakistan would need only for possible use against India and not against the terrorists.

The terrorist infrastructure of the Taliban and the HEI in Pakistani territory is intact under the protection of the ISI. While helping the US to put an end to the Taliban's rule in Afghanistan post-9/11, the ISI has ensured that the Taliban's organisational capability and terrorist infrastructure remained undecimated so that Pakistan could use them to protect its strategic interests in the future. The Amir of the Taliban, Gulbuddin and many of their senior colleagues and jihadi cadres have been given sanctuary in Pakistan's North-West Frontier Province (NWFP) and Balochistan.

Not only the provincial Governments of the NWFP, which is run by the fundamentalist coalition called the Muttahida Majlis-e-Amal (MMA), and of Balochistan, in which the MMA is an active partner in a coalition with the Pakistan Muslim League (Qaide Azam), the surrogate political party of Musharraf, but even the Pakistani military-intelligence establishment has been providing funds, protection and sanctuaries to the dregs of the Taliban and the HEI in Pakistani territory.

The active involvement of the Pakistani military-intelligence establishment in keeping the Taliban and the HEI alive and active is not only attested to by independent reports coming from the NWFP and Balochistan, but is also corroborated by reports in the Pakistani media itself as well as by periodic statements from Hamid Karzai and his officials, the US diplomats in Kabul and writings by well-known Pakistani experts on Afghanistan such as Ahmed Rashid.

The US, with its large intelligence presence in Pakistan and large military and intelligence presence in Afghanistan, cannot be unaware of the continuing Pakistani complicity with the dregs of the Taliban and the HEI, but yet, prefers to close its eyes to it so long as the Musharraf Government is co-operating with it in the hunt for bin Laden, Al-Zawahiri and the other surviving senior operatives of Al Qaeda.

There is a difference in the US perceptions of Al Qaeda and the Taliban. It looks upon Al Qaeda as continuing to pose a threat to US homeland security. Is therefore, determined not to relent in its war against it, till bin Laden, al-Zawahiri and its other senior operatives are captured or killed. While it perceives the surviving Taliban as posing a threat to peace and security in Afghanistan, it does not view it as a threat to US homeland security. Its pre and post-9/11 anger against the Taliban was due to its action in giving shelter to Al Qaeda and its terrorist infrastructure in Afghan territory.

This dichotomy in the US perceptions of Al Qaeda and the Taliban should explain its tolerance of the continuing Pakistani complicity with the Taliban. Musharraf continues to make a distinction between the bad and the not-so-bad elements in the Taliban. The not-so-bad elements are projected as no longer having any nexus with Al Qaeda and its largely Arab terrorists. They are also projected as elements who, if properly handled, could be made to strengthen the rule of Karzai.

Barring sporadic incidents such as the recent terrorist strike in Kabul, possibly involving a suicide bomber, against the personnel of the American company, the Taliban and the HEI have not come to notice for any targeted attacks on the

US troops. There have been clashes resulting in small American casualties, but these would appear to have taken place when US troops intercepted Taliban and HEI terrorist groups when they were going from Pakistani territory to attack a non-US target or returning to Pakistani territory after launching an attack.

The dregs of the Taliban and the HEI operating from Pakistani sanctuaries have been mainly concentrating their attacks on Afghan Government servants loyal to Karzai and workers of foreign non-governmental organisations. There have been some incidents inside Afghan territory, where individual Arabs, mainly Yemenis or Yemeni-Balochis (of mixed blood), were suspected to have operated with the Taliban and HEI elements. Apart from these, there are no reports of any large-scale involvement of Arabs, either from Al Qaeda or from any other organisation, with the Taliban and HEI groups operating in Afghan territory.

Even though the US and Pakistan continue to claim that bin Laden, al-Zawahiri and other surviving senior operatives of Al Qaeda have taken shelter in the tribal areas across the Pakistan-Afghanistan border, independent reports from Pakistan do not speak of any large presence of Arab terrorists in the tribal areas—either in Afghanistan or in Pakistan. After intensive operations in the South Waziristan area of the Federally-Administered Tribal Areas (FATA) since March, 2004, the Pakistani authorities are now reluctantly admitting that bin Laden, al-Zawahiri and others are probably not in this area. Since March, 2002, all major arrests of senior Al Qaeda operatives were made in the big urban cities of Pakistan such as Faislabad and Gujrat in Pakistani Punjab, Karachi and Rawalpindi and not in the tribal areas.

Independent reports indicate that while bin Laden and other senior Al Qaeda survivors of the Tora Bora battle of November-December, 2001, continue to live in Pakistan with the protection of their benefactors in the fundamentalist parties, the ISI and in the community of retired intelligence officers, many of their Arab cadres have moved over to Iraq via Iran or Saudi Arabia and have been helping the Iraqi resistance fighters there. There is no credible evidence of the Taliban and Al Qaeda operating in tandem in Afghanistan. Statements emanating from Mulla Omar and other Taliban leaders, including the latest one from Omar issued on the occasion of the third anniversary of the collapse of the Taliban Government in Kabul and the end of the fasting period, hardly have any references to Al Qaeda or bin Laden.

It is significant to note that there have been very few incidents of suicide terrorism in Afghanistan as compared to the large number taking place almost every day in Iraq and that there has been hardly any involvement of Afghan nationals in the various post-9/11 terrorist incidents attributed to Al Qaeda in various parts of the world. As against this, there have been innumerable instances of the involvement of Pakistani nationals, not only in Pakistan itself, but also in other countries of the world.

From time to time, there have been reports of a split in the Taliban due to differences over the leadership of Mulla Omar and his amenability to the influence and control exercised by the Pakistani military-intelligence establishment, but these have not been confirmed. A group calling itself the Jaish-e-Muslimeen (the Army of Muslims), headed by one Mullah Sabir Momin, has recently kidnapped three UN workers from Kabul—an Irish, a Filipino and the third from Kosovo—and has been demanding an end to the UN operations in Afghanistan and the release of 26 Taliban members captured by the US-led coalition. Some of them are stated to be held in custody in Afghanistan and some in the US detention camp in Guantanamo Bay. It is not clear whether this group has any links with the Taliban. However, it has to be mentioned that one does not find in Afghanistan what one has been witnessing in Iraq—namely, innumerable groups operating autonomously without any central command and control under different names. (Comments: The hostages have since been released)

Despite the action taken by many countries under the UN Security Council Resolution No. 1373 to freeze bank accounts, which are suspected to be used for funding terrorism, the Taliban, Al Qaeda and the International Islamic Front (IIF) have not been short of funds. The production of heroin has again emerged as an important source of funds for the terrorist organisations operating from the Afghanistan-Pakistan region. There has been a steep increase in the production of opium and heroin in Southern and Eastern Afghanistan. In their hunt for the dregs of Al Qaeda and the Taliban, the US security forces have been using Afghan warlords of the pre-1992 vintage and narcotics smugglers because of their good knowledge of the topography of the area. It has been alleged that at the request of the US intelligence agencies and security forces, many narcotics barons, undergoing imprisonment in Pakistan, were got released in order to use their services; and that action against opium producers and heroin smugglers was given low priority.

South Waziristan: Mini Iraq

Pitted against the Pakistan Army in the current fighting in South Waziristan, which has already cost the lives of about 190 Pakistani troops, including some commissioned officers, is a mixed force of Chechens, Uzbeks, Uighurs from Xinjiang as well as the Uighur diaspora in the Central Asian Republics, mainly Kazakhstan and Kyrgystan, and some Arabs. These were all members of the Uighur and Uzbek components of bin Laden's International Islamic Front (IIF), but not of Al

Qaeda. They support bin Laden's pan-Islamic ideology and advocate the division of the Islamic world into independent regional caliphates, including one encompassing Central Asia, Afghanistan and Xinjiang. At the same time, they have maintained their separate ethnic identities and have not allowed themselves to be subsumed in Al Qaeda.

They enjoy the support of the local Pashtun tribals, who have provided them with sanctuaries. Many of the members of this mixed force have married local Pashtun women, acquired landed property and had been indulging in farming until they took to arms following the military operations launched by the Pakistan Army in October last year under US pressure because of the American suspicion that they are helping the Taliban in its operations in Afghan territory and have given shelter to bin Laden and other senior operatives of Al Qaeda, who had fled from Tora Bora in end-2001.

There are no reliable reports of the number of Uzbeks, Chechens and Uighurs in South Waziristan. Some Pakistani journalists, who had visited the South Waziristan area in March-April, 2004, had estimated the total number of foreigners, who had been given shelter there by the local tribals, as about 600, about 200 of them Uzbeks and the remaining Chechens, Uighurs, Arabs and others. Other reports place the number of Uighurs at about 100. The presence of Uzbeks, Chechens and Uighurs in the Taliban and in Gulbuddin Heckmatyar's HEI now operating in Afghanistan has also been reported. Their number is not known.

The Pakistan Army has claimed to have killed a large number of these dregs. In a recent statement by the military commanders operating in the area, it has been claimed that nearly 500 members of this force have been killed or captured since March, 2004, and that only about a hundred are still active. These claims have to be treated with considerable reserve. Like the American military commanders in Iraq, the Pakistani commanders in South Waziristan have been making highly exaggerated claims of the successes scored by them in the form of arrests and killings of terrorists without being able to produce those arrested or the dead bodies of those killed before the media. Last week, they claimed to have killed 40 terrorists, but admitted that they could find only six dead bodies. They often assert that their claims and estimates are based on electronic intercepts and not physical body counts.

Despite their claims of continuing success, the terrorists in the South Waziristan area of the FATA have retained their ability to organise surprise ambushes, attacks with improvised explosive devices and land-mines and mortar attacks. There have also been instances of Pakistani military gunships, given by the US, being brought down by terrorist fire from the ground.

While there has been no involvement of US ground troops in the counter-terrorism operations in this area, the Pakistan Army units operating in this area have been in receipt of back-up support from the intelligence collection teams of the USA's Central Intelligence Agency (CIA) and the National Security Agency (NSA). The results produced by this intelligence support have been meagre and have not led to any significant improvement in the ground situation.

In fact, it would not be an exaggeration to say that since March, 2004, the FATA in general and South Waziristan in particular have gradually been becoming Pakistan's mini-Iraq—with almost daily terrorist strikes by small groups of Pashtuns, Uzbeks, Chechens, Uighurs and Arabs operating autonomously from different pockets.

The dregs of the IIF from Afghanistan have not been able to replicate in the Pakistani territory in this region the extensive training infrastructure which Al Qaeda and the IIF used to have in Taliban-controlled Afghanistan pre-9/11. However, a limited training infrastructure is already in place in the areas under the control of the terrorists in South Waziristan, with Chechen and Uzbek instructors providing training to local tribal recruits as well as to recruits from other parts of Pakistan, Xinjiang and the Central Asian Republics. It has been reported that some of the members of the Jundullah (the Army of Allah), a new organisation which was allegedly involved in an unsuccessful attempt to kill the Pakistani Army Corps Commander in Karachi in June,2004, had been trained in these new camps by Uzbek instructors.

Reliable reports from the area indicate that this mixed force consists of surviving dregs of the jihad of the 1980s against the Soviet troops as well as those of the post-9/11 jihad against the US troops in Afghanistan. Towards the end of the Soviet involvement in Afghanistan in the 1980s, Moscow started increasingly depending on its Muslim soldiers recruited in the Caucassus and the Central Asian Republics for dealing with the large number of Arab mercenaries, who were trained, armed and inducted into Afghanistan by the CIA and the ISI.

In successful Psywar operations, the Afghan Mujahideen and the Arabs were able to brainwash many of them and turn them against Moscow. They came to Afghanistan from the USSR as communists not believing in God. In Afghanistan, they became born-again Muslims. Some of them deserted and joined the Mujahideen, while many others went back to their country, deserted from the Soviet/Russian Army and started a jihad against their respective Governments in the Caucassus and the Central Asian Republics. The Taliban's fight against the Northern Alliance post-1994 also attracted a number of Uzbeks, Chechens and Uighurs and those among them, who survived the post-9/11 US military operations, have crossed over into the FATA.

They have succeeded in re-motivating the Uzbek, Chechen and Uighur dregs of the anti-Soviet jihad of the 1980s, who had married locally and settled down in the FATA after the collapse of the Najibulla Government in Kabul in April, 1992, to take to jihad again by joining them—this time against the US.

What role do these dregs play in the on-going jihadi terrorism in the Central Asian Republics and in Chechnya? How many of the Uzbeks are Afghan nationals from the Mazar-e-Sharif area and how many are from Uzbekistan? Do recruits from the CARs manage to come to South Waziristan via Afghanistan despite the US presence for being trained there? How do they manage to go back to the CARs after their training—via Afghanistan or via Saudi Arabia/ Iran/Turkey? Is there a networking between this mixed force and those operating in the CARs and Chechnya and is there a common command and control? If not, are those operating in the CARs, particularly in Uzbekistan, doing so autonomously? It is difficult to give categorical answers to these questions on the basis of the evidence available till now. However, attention needs to be drawn to the history of the evolution of jihadi terrorism in Uzbekistan. This could help in a better understanding of the situation.

Uzbekistan

The first signs of Islamic fundamentalism appeared in Uzbekistan in December 1991, when some unemployed Muslim youth seized the Communist Party headquarters in the eastern city of Namangan, to protest against the refusal of the local Mayor to permit the construction of a mosque. The protest was organised by Tohir Abdouhalilovitch Yuldeshev, a 24-year-old college drop-out, who had become a Mulla, and Jumaboi Ahmadzhanovitch Khojaev, a former Soviet paratrooper who had served in Afghanistan and returned from there totally converted to Wahabism.

Yuldeshev and Khojaev, who later adopted the alias Juma Namangani, after his hometown, became members of the Uzbekistan branch of the Islamic Renaissance Party (IRP). Following the IRP's reported refusal to support their demand for the establishment of an Islamic State in Uzbekistan, they formed their own party called the Adolat (Justice) Party, which was banned by President Islam Karimov. They then fled to Tajikistan. While Namangani fought in the local civil war, Yuldeshev went to Chechnya to participate in the jihad there. In 1995, he went to Pakistan, where the jihadi organisations gave him shelter in Peshawar. From there, he re-named the Adolat Party as the IMU and was allegedly in receipt of funds from the intelligence agencies of Pakistan, Saudi Arabia and Turkey. After Osama bin Laden shifted to Jalalabad from Khartoum in Sudan in 1996, he crossed over into Afghanistan.

After the end of the civil war in Tajikistan, Namangani settled down for a while as a road transport operator. He was also allegedly involved in heroin smuggling from Afghanistan. Subsequently, he too crossed over into Afghanistan and joined the IMU and became its leader. The IMU allegedly earns a major part of its revenue from heroin smuggling.

After the Taliban captured Kabul in September, 1996, Namangani and Yuldeshev held a Press conference at Kabul at which they announced the formation of the IMU with Namangani as the Amir and Yuldeshev as its military commander. In 1998, the IMU joined the International Islamic Front (IIF). bin Laden was reportedly greatly interested in the IMU because he was hoping to use it for getting nuclear material and know-how from Russia and other constituent States of the erstwhile USSR.

The IMU's initial goal was described as the overthrow

of Uzbek President Islam Karimov and the establishment of an Islamic State in Uzbekistan. It reportedly changed its name to the Islamic Party of Turkestan (IPT) in June 2001, and called for the establishment of an Islamic Caliphate in Central Asia consisting of Kazakhstan, Kyrgyzstan, Tajikistan, Turkmenistan, Uzbekistan, and China's Xinxiang province. It has been recruiting members from all these areas, including Uighurs from Xinjiang. Initially, its recruits were trained by the Arab instructors of Al Qaeda in the training camps in Afghan territory and after 9/11 by Chechen and Pashtun instructors of the Taliban in the South Waziristan area of Pakistan. Despite its 2001 change of name as IPT, it continues to be known in Uzbekistan as the IMU. The name IPT is not widely known.

After the reported death of Namangani in a US air strike in Afghanistan post-9/11, Yuldeshev took over the leadership of the IMU and crossed over with the surviving members of the IMU into South Waziristan where he and his Uzbek/Chechen instructors were reported to have set up a training camp for training jihadi terrorists. In an operation launched by the Pakistani security forces in South Waziristan in March-April, 2004, to smoke out the dregs of Al Qaeda, Yuldeshev was reported to have been injured, but he managed to escape. His present whereabouts are not known. It is not even known whether he is alive or succumbed to the injuries subsequently.

There are also reports about the presence of many Uzbek women in South Waziristan. Many of them are the wives of local Pashtuns, Chechens and Arabs. It is not known how and when they came there. Some reports allege that in addition to heroin smuggling, the IMU also indulges in human trafficking, particularly of women.

Jihadi terrorism made its first major appearance in Uzbekistan on February 16, 1999, when there were six car bomb explosions in Tashkent, the capital, killing, according to official accounts, 16 persons and injuring 130 others. The explosions took place near the headquarters of the Council of Ministers where President Islam Karimov was to preside over a Cabinet meeting, outside a nearby cinema hall, near the office of the Interior Ministry, outside the Traffic Police headquarters and a building owned by the national bank.

While no organisation claimed responsibility for the explosions, the Uzbek authorities, including President Karimov himself, projected the explosions as an abortive attempt by Islamic extremist elements to assassinate the President. However, Russian experts, including Dr. Sergei Abashin, an expert on Uzbekistan at the Anthropology and Ethnology Institute of the Russian Academy of Sciences, while not ruling out the involvement of Islamic fanatics, drew attention also to the possibility of the political opponents of Karimov hiring local mafia groups to eliminate the President due to personal and political grudge.

There were three explosions outside the US and Israeli embassies and the local Prosecutor's office in Tashkent on July 30, 2004. Two private security guards employed by the Israeli Embassy were killed. An injured police officer, who was on duty outside the US Embassy, died subsequently. Seven people were injured outside the Prosecutor's office.

The local authorities attributed all the three explosions to suicide bombers. Uzbekistan had been periodically witnessing incidents of violence, including acts of terrorism, by Islamic fundamentalist elements since 1999. There were, however, no acts of suicide terrorism till March-April, 2004, when 42 people were killed in different incidents in Tashkent, Bukhara and other places. The incidents involved use of explosive devices and attacks with hand-held weapons. For the first time since 1999, the local authorities blamed suicide bombers for some of those incidents and depicted them as

Wahabis. According to them, two of the suicide bombers were women.

The incidents of July 30, 2004, took place four days after the start of the trial of 15 persons, who had been accused by the local police of involvement in the incidents of March-April, 2004. The Prosecutor's Office, outside which one of the explosions took place, has been handling the prosecution of the case.

The explosion outside the US Embassy was attributed to resentment over the use by the US of an airbase in Uzbekistan for its operations against the dregs of Al Qaeda and the Taliban in Afghanistan and over the role allegedly played by the US Special Forces in assisting the Pakistan Army in its operations in South Waziristan. Anger over the continued US occupation of Iraq also seems to have been one of the factors.

The explosion outside the Israeli Embassy was attributed to its alleged suppression of the Palestinians and its alleged assistance to the intelligence and security agencies of Uzbekistan in their operations against the jihadi terrorist elements.

As against this, the terrorist incidents of March-April, 2004, were largely motivated by anger over the repressive policies of the Islam Karimov regime and its co-operation with the US in its so-called war against terrorism.

The needle of suspicion in respect of the incidents of this year points towards the Islamic Movement of Uzbekistan (IMU) and the Hizbut Tahrir. An Islamic website claimed responsibility in respect of the July 30 blasts on behalf of these two organisations, but the organisations themselves remained silent. The reliability of the web site is not known.

There is so far no evidence to show that the suicide bombers of July 30 might have gone to Tashkent from South Waziristan. If it is established that they belonged to the IMU, they might have been recruited locally by the local cells and need not have necessarily come from South Waziristan. This would show that despite the strong measures taken by the Karimov regime, secret cells of the IMU have managed to survive in Uzbek territory and that their motivation and capability for action remain unimpaired.

The Hizbut Tahrir of Uzbekistan, led by Vahid Omran, is estimated to have more local support than the IMU. It denies involvement in acts of terrorism. Like the IMU, it advocates the establishment of an Islamic Caliphate in Central Asia, including Xinjiang, but claims that it wants to achieve its objective through political means and not by resorting to terrorism.

Like the Hizbut Tahrir of Pakistan, its Central Asian counterpart is also a highly clandestine organisation, which seeks to achieve its objective not through overt acts of violence, but through covert penetration of the security forces and the intelligence agencies. In the long term, it could be even more dangerous than the IMU.

A third organisation calling itself the Islamic Jihad group of Uzbekistan also claimed responsibility for the incidents of March-April as well as of July 30, but one does not even know whether such an organisation exists and, if so, what is its background and who are its leaders.

Of the five Pakistani jihadi organisations, which are members of the IIF, the Harkat-ul-Mujahideen (HUM) and the Harkat-ul-Jihad-al-Islami (HUJI) have a long history of involvement in the jihad in Uzbekistan, Tajikistan and Chechnya. While the HUM operates in Chechnya, the HUJI operates in Uzbekistan and Tajikistan.

The Uighurs

This year has also seen Chinese engineers and other experts working in Afghanistan and Pakistan being targeted by suspected terrorist elements. Uighurs allegedly trained by the IMU were suspected of involvement in the explosion in Gwadar in Balochistan on May 3 last in which three Chinese engineers were killed and in the explosions on July 31, 2004, at the same town in which no casualties were reported.

These incidents were followed by the kidnapping of two Chinese engineers working in an irrigation project in South Waziristan by a group of pro-bin Laden jihadi terrorists in the beginning of October, 2004, and the death of one of them on October 13, 2004, during a rescue operation mounted by the US-trained Special Services Group, the parent Army unit of Gen. Pervez Musharraf.

Talking to a group of senior Pakistani newspaper editors after a visit to China last year, Musharraf was reported to have stated that he was shocked by the strong language used by the Chinese leaders while talking of the activities of the Uighur jihadi terrorists from Pakistani territory. Since then, the Pakistan Army and its ISI have mounted special operations to smoke out the Chechens, the Uzbeks and the Uighurs operating from the FATA in co-operation with each other. Apart from killing or capturing a few Uzbek and Chechen terrorists and killing an Uighur terrorist, these operations have not produced any significant results. In the meanwhile, the Hizbut Tehrir, which has a strong presence in Pakistan and the CARs, has started wooing the Uighurs in an attempt to set up sleeper cells in Xinjiang. Amongst the major successes claimed by the Pakistani authorities since March last are the killing of Hassan Mahsun of the East Turkestan Islamic Movement and of Nek Muhammad, a local Pakistani tribal leader, who was allegedly assisting the Al Qaeda and the Taliban remnants and causing serious injuries to Yuldeshev.

Following the Gwadar explosion of May, a number of

Chinese intelligence officers from its Ministries of State (external) and Public (internal) Security have reportedly been deployed in Balochistan and South Waziristan to assist the Pakistani authorities in their investigation and in their hunt for the Uighur jihadi terrorists.

According to some sources, the jihadi organisations suspect that many of the Chinese intelligence operatives inducted into Balochistan and the FATA after the explosion of May last work under the cover of members of the staff of Chinese construction companies, which have been helping Pakistan in its various projects in these areas.

The Pakistani military authorities have projected Abdullah Mahsud, a former Taliban commander who was released by the US authorities from detention in their Guantanamo Bay detention camp in March last, as the mastermind of the kidnap and have admitted that apart from some local tribal followers of Abdullah Mahsud, three Uzbeks were also involved. They have claimed that the apparent objective of the kidnappers was to secure the release of some foreign terrorists arrested in the area recently. They have played down the possibility of any specific anti-Chinese motive.

Afghanistan also saw a terrorist strike directed against the Chinese on June 10, 2004, when 11 Chinese road construction workers in the Kunduz area in the North-East were gunned down by unidentified elements. Though the Afghan authorities claimed to have made some arrests, it is not clear as to who was responsible for this incident and what was their motive.

Chapter 6

NON-TRADITIONAL THREATS
Maritime Terrorism in South Asia and its Impact on India's Security

*Dr. Abhaya Kumar Singh**

Introduction

The security environment in South Asia is being challenged from several directions. The region is plagued with piracy, and has also witnessed maritime terrorism-related activities, drug smuggling, gun running and illegal migration. Some of these have the potential to disrupt and destroy maritime enterprise. Efforts have been made by regional countries to address these problems and there has been an encouraging response to their efforts to combat disorder at sea. Nevertheless, concerns with threats of maritime terrorism in the region remains high primarily due

* Associate Professor, Dept. of Defence & Strategic Studies, K. S. Saket Post Graduate College, (Dr. R. M.L. Awadh University) Ayodhya, Faizabad.

to the rise of Islamic fundamentalism in the region, presence of al Qaeda - linked groups like Jamaah Islamiyah (JI), and the importance of the strategic choke points comprising the Malacca, Sunda and Lombok Straits. Besides, there is also a noticeable link between threats of terrorism with the increasing incidents of sea robbery attacks on maritime shipping in the Straits.

Maritime Geography and Geo-strategic Importance of Indian Ocean

South Asia is primarily a maritime area. Most of its countries have long coastlines. Besides, the region is home to strategic maritime choke points like the Malacca, Sunda and Lombok straits that have direct impact on the economic and social well being of all the Asia Pacific countries. Among these, the Strait of Malacca is the main waterway that connects the Indian Ocean and the Pacific Ocean. The strait is 600 nautical miles long, varying in width from 300 nautical miles in the west to three nautical miles in its most constricted point. It is relatively shallow and vessels of up to 65 feet draught are permitted passage.[1] Every year, more than 60,000 ships pass through the Strait of Malacca carrying a variety of cargo like oil, gas, raw materials and finished goods. The traffic is about three times the number of ships that transit through the Panama Canal and more than double the number that sail through the Suez Canal.

Admiral Mahan said in 1890: "Whoever controls the Indian Ocean will dominate Asia…in the 21st century, the destiny of the world would be decided on its waters".[2] The Indian Ocean has seen intense maritime activity for the past 600 years, primarily for trade. Centuries ago, the motivation was for silk and spices. Today, it is for oil, the primary energy source powering the economic-industrial sectors of major states which, therefore, becomes the principal strategic determinant. West Asia contains 65 per cent of the world's proven reserves[3] and accounts for more than half of the world's oil exports and almost all of Asia-Pacific's imports. The demand for oil imports is expected to grow and despite efforts to diversify sources, disruption of supplies is bound to impact severely, as in the case of past oil shocks, on national economies leading to inflation and widespread unemployment. Exports to the West through the Indian Ocean also include large quantities of agricultural products such as tea, coffee, rubber and sesame. Not only this the Indian Ocean holds 65 per cent of strategic raw minerals and 31 per cent of gas, comprises 30 per cent of the world population and is characterised by fast-growing economies and a large consumer market.[4] This necessitates a collective desire for security and stability in the region.

One-third of the world's trade and almost all of East Asia's oil pass through the Eastern Straits, Malacca, Sunda and Lombok-Makasser. Of the 14 states constituting East and Southeast Asia, 12 are highly dependent on West Asian oil.[5] In a sense, the sea-route extending from the North Arabian Sea to the Sea of Japan through the Indian Ocean is akin to the 'New Silk Route'[6] and its protection becomes a convergent strategic priority for many states. Japan's thirst for energy—acute and vital for its national interests—compelled it to venture right till India's doorstep to seek cooperation with India.[7] China has vital trading interests transit through the Indian Ocean. It is also poised to become the second largest oil importing country; surpassing Japan.[8] Consequently, emergence of an inimical Indian Ocean power may adversely affect its trade and energy flow. Straddling this new silk route, India's interests are linked to its maritime trade—95 per cent in volume. It is currently the world's seventh largest oil consumer and is expected to become the fifth largest by 2020.[9] Importing 65% of its energy requirements from West Asia (expected to rise to 81% by 2011-12),[10] the oil sea-route originating from the region will continue to be valued by India despite improvements in indigenous production, diversification and recourse to nuclear/non-conventional sources. The importance of energy to the 'demand heartland' (India, China and Japan) is extensive. These countries view Sea Lines of Communication (SLOCs) as their very lifelines. At current levels of consumption, the oil import dependence of India is expected to reach 82.2% by 2010 and 91.6% by 2020. In the case of it will be 61% and 76.9%, while for rest of Asia, it will be 95.1% respectively.[11] For India, with nearly 89% of its oil imports arriving by sea, it is imperative that the SLOCs be secure. This security angle is enhanced many fold, since most of oil originates in West Asia, and the SLOCs pass through areas under the influence of India's adversary, Pakistan. Added to this is the political turbulence of areas in West Asia that often holds hostage the supply of oil from the region. In the past, supplies from this region have been disrupted on at several occasions, all of which were due to political causes and were not market driven.

Geographically, India lays astride the major SLOCs in the Indian Ocean—providing it with considerable strategic importance and potential. The vast proportion of our foreign trade—97% in volume and 76% in value terms—is sea-borne. According to World Bank estimates, in 1999 the world seaborne trade was pegged at 21,480 billion ton-miles, it is expected to reach 35,000 billion ton-miles in 2010 and 41.800 billion ton-miles in 2014.[12] The United Nations Conference on Trade and Development (UNCTAD) Report, "Review of Maritime Transport 2000", notes that world sea-based trade recorded its fourteenth consecutive annual increase, and Asia's share of import and export was 26.1% and 18.8% respectively. Thus, the prospects for sea-borne trade are set to raise dramatically.[13]

It is imperative, therefore, that maritime security issues are perceived in a holistic, not a compartmentalised, manner. India's "Look-East" policy has resulted in increased economic, strategic and other engagement with South Asian countries. A bigger share of India's trade passes through the Malacca Strait, making the waterway a crucial security concern for India in view of the threat of piracy and maritime terrorism. Unfortunately, along with this rise in traffic, the variety and intensity of threats, including, maritime terrorism, drug trafficking, gunrunning, piracy, natural disasters and inter-state conflicts, are also expected to show a proportional rise.

MARITIME SECURITY THREATS

Maritime Terrorism

In the wake of the tragic events of September 11, 2001 in the United States, the maritime community had concluded that there was an urgent need to review measures to combat violence and crime at sea. The 7 took the lead and called for a resolution for reviewing the existing international legal and technical measures and procedures to prevent acts that threaten the security of ships at sea and ports was also adopted. It was agreed to adopt new regulations and mandatory statutory instruments to enhance maritime security by preventing and suppressing acts of terrorism against shipping and make sea-lanes safe for international commerce.[14] Since the 1970s, perhaps due to turmoil in the Middle East, the phenomenon of terrorism has been gathering momentum. Today one finds a large number of terrorist groups located all over the world, and some even are transnational in their activities and linkages. What is perhaps the most disturbing aspect of the rise in the number of such groups is that they have pervaded every facet of human activity, be it politics, governance, economics, trade and even religion. Interestingly, some groups are so ideologically driven that their primary agenda is to preserve their religious faith.

It is true that most of the terrorist activities take place on land than at sea. But the threat of maritime terrorism is not a new phenomenon. In the past there have been several instances when ships have been taken over by insurgents or attacked by terrorists.[15] The takeover of a Portuguese passenger lines Santa Maria in 1961 ushered in the modern age of maritime terrorism.[16] In 1988, City of Poros, a Greek cruise ferry carrying 500 tourists, was attacked by terrorists.[17] But it was the Achille Lauro incident that caught the attention of the international community with regard to the menace of terrorism at sea and the formulation of an international convention under the United Nations. On 8 October 1988, a group of Palestine Guerillas hijacked the Italian cruise vessel Achille Lauro. Similarly, on November 03, 1988, two trawlers carrying 150 PLOTE (People's Liberation Tamil Tigers Elam) mercenaries landed in the Maldives.[18] The mercenaries quickly overpowered the Maldivian militia using rockets and machine guns and attacked the President's residence. A 'panicked' Maldivian Government sent out calls asking for assistance to both Colombo and New Delhi and India responded. Operation Cactus was launched and a large contingent of paratroopers made an unopposed landing at Male. The island was secured within thirty minutes after the arrival of forces.[19] The attacks on USS Cole[20] on 12th October 2000 at Aden and soon after that there was an attack on the French supertanker, MT Limburg off Yemen's coast in October 2002 awakened the world to the realities of such a threat.

The Council for Security Cooperation in the Asia Pacific (CSCAP) Working Group has offered an extensive definition for maritime terrorism: [21]

"...the undertaking of terrorist acts and activities within the maritime environment, using or against vessels or fixed platforms at sea or in port, or against any one of their passengers or personnel, against coastal facilities or settlements, including tourist resorts, port areas and port towns or cities."

This definition, however, does not define what terrorism is and whether it would only include maritime attacks against civilian (merchant) vessels or also attacks against military crafts. According to Akiva J. Lorenz, "the maritime terrorism is the use or threat of violence against a ship (civilian as well as military), its passengers or sailors, cargo, a port facility, or if the purpose is solely a platform for political ends."[22] The definition can be expanded to include the use of the maritime transportation system to smuggle terrorists or terrorist materials into the targeted country. Maritime terrorism is motivated by political goals beyond the immediate act of attacking a maritime target.

Given these definitions, the grey area are cases of kidnap-for-ransom incidents, such as the May 2001 abduction of three American citizens and 17 Filipinos at the Dos Palmas resort on Palauan by Abu Sayyaff Group (ASG), an Al Qaeda affiliate.[23] Motivated by the need to finance their political aims, ASG repeatedly perpetrated such acts of piracy. Their actions are an example of the blurring of the distinction between terrorism and piracy.

A high degree of threat is being predicted from maritime terrorism to sea-lines and hub ports enclosed within the Hormuz and the Southeast Asian straits.[24] Insurgencies and terrorist activities with maritime traditions abound in the later sub-region, viz, several terrorist organisations in and around the Indian Ocean are known to possess to merchant fleets of various types like—the Free Ache Movement, the Moro Islamic Liberation Front, the Abu Sayyaff and LTTE. The established links of these regional groups with global terrorist groups like Jamaah Islamiyah (JI) and Al Qaeda, security concerns for the Indian Ocean littoral states will be high. While the spillover effects of South Asian secessionism to the Bay of Bengal is a distinct possibility, the LTTE's activities equally pose a threat to littoral states as far away as in South Asia, given the Sri Lankan separatist group's claims that the Sea Tigers be recognized as a 'navy' in the region. The LTTE is known to indulge in piracy for its funding and material assets and hence, cannot claim insurgent/ belligerent rights under international law, nor the status of a navy for the 'Sea Tigers'.[21]The LTTEs have an entire flotilla engaged in dubious maritime trade. The level of the threat posed by it, was exemplified by the incident in which it captured Maldives and the Indian forces were send their. Most of these are registered under Flag of Convenience (FOC) countries known as "pan-ho-lib," i.e. Panama, Honduras and Liberia,[25] and are difficult to track as they routinely change names and registry. Lloyds of London lists 11 merchant ships belonging to Asian front companies that are in reality managed by Kumaran Pathmanathan of the LTTE. [26]

Thus, Flag of Convenience (FOC) pose another major challenge to maritime security. Flying the flag of a state other than the country of ownership enables the owners to avoid high registration fees and taxes, and to employ cheap labour operating under sub-standard conditions. It is estimated that there are about 30 such registries (some in private hands operating on behalf of states) mainly run by small island or impoverished nations.[27] Since the checks and balances introduced by these registries are undeniably lax, there is no guarantee as to the type of crew or the type of cargo that these ships carry. Such ships are considered the safest bet for carrying out terrorist-related activities.

If a small explosive-ridden dinghy could cripple a state-of-the-art warship such as the Cole, replete with 'aegis' of 'various calibers', a similar attack on a defenceless cruise-liner or oil tanker would spell disaster. Limburg and Cole were both 'combatant vessels' involved in the 'War on Terror', but with the terrorists' aim of disrupting valuable and vulnerable sea-borne trade being evident, the threat to commercial ships, SLOCs and ports can be easily extrapolated. What emerges is the high probability of sinking an oil tanker in one of the vital choke points such as in the Malacca Straits or cruise a LNG carrier into a hub-port on a suicide mission.[28]

The Indian Ocean and its contiguous waters have always had a major share of global pirate attacks and armed robbery in territorial waters due to dense shipping, frail maritime policing and favourable hide-to-vanish environs. According to the 2003 IMB Report, the Indonesian waters were declared the world's most dangerous, followed by Bangladesh, Nigeria and India.[29] While such attacks declined worldwide by 22 per cent in the first six months of 2004, the Malacca Straits, however, recorded a 33 per cent increase.[30] Links between terrorism and piracy having being uncovered lately[31] and the distinct possibility of WMDs falling in the hands of terrorists due to theft of vessels ferrying such material, further add to the threat.

Besides, one cannot ignore water as the medium to convey instruments of terror. Being the most inexpensive means of transportation, over 80 per cent of the world's trade involves ocean transit. Containerisation of sea-borne trade and resort to Flags of Convenience (FOC) shipping by non-state elements, compound the threat. Al Qaeda is known to maintain a secret shipping fleet flying such flags, allowing it to conceal ownership and covertly transport arms, drugs, recruits and maybe, even WMD material.[32] Indian Navy thus cannot ignore this part. Indian Navy had in the past (like in 2001) provided escort to American warships travelling through the Strait of Malacca (to take part in Operation Enduring Freedom). Also the increasing commercial activities in the Gulf of Mannar make it the most preferred destination for pirates and terrorist elements like LTTE, Al Qaeda, LeT and other groups that have a series of incidents of using the sea route to attack targets. Maritime security has assumed a new dimension after horrific Mumbai attacks. Following the attacks, the possibility of maritime terrorism is of increasing concern. The Mumbai incident has only reiterated the urgency for the Navy not only to work during wars but in these proxy wars too.

Drug Trafficking and Gunrunning

An important adjunct to maritime terrorism is drug trafficking. With profit margins running into hundreds of per cent, drug trafficking is by far the most lucrative means of generating funds to fuel ever-growing terrorist activities and insurgencies around the Indian Ocean region. The terrorist groups often work hand-in-hand with drug cartels. While this symbiotic relationship provides established routes for drug and arms smuggling, it also provides terrorists with the logistical infrastructure to move people, arms and material according to their desires.[33] Considering the geo-political setup of the Indian Ocean region, Pakistan, Iran and Afghanistan form a major portion of the drug-infested "Golden Crescent," while Myanmar (Burma), Thailand and Laos constitute the majority of the "Golden Triangle," notorious for its illegal drug production. It is natural that narco-terrorism is a major security concern for littoral states like India, which has seen its own emergence as a transit point for a majority of the drugs that emanate from these two areas. Drug trafficking leads to money laundering and funds from the sale of drugs are used to fuel gunrunning, insurgent and terrorist activities. Added to these is the transnational security concern linked to human smuggling that has multiple effects, ranging from fuelling terrorism to illegal immigration causing socio-political instability.

The symbiotic relationship between gunrunning and drug trafficking is well known. It is extremely difficult to control one without controlling the other. Gunrunning by sea is by far the safest means for transferring arms and ammunition around the world, while drug trafficking is most lucrative. The LTTE has a vast and well-established network for gunrunning, with its reach extending as far as Japan. Their arms mostly originate in Cambodia, and are later loaded into small fishing trawlers from the port of Ranong in southern Thailand. This arms cargo is then transferred to bigger ships (often in mid-ocean), which transport the consignment to Sri Lanka. The seizure in a boat yard in Singapore of an incomplete submersible bound for the LTTE displays the extent of arms that are being transported illegally.

Bangladesh's capture of several small fishing craft laden with arms during the last few years has led to the conclusion that a lot of these arms also make their way from Thailand to the Cox Bazaar in Bangladesh. Similarly, the Royal Thai Navy's seizure of arms meant for the People's Liberation Army (Manipur) off the port of Ranong clearly demonstrates the close nexus between arms trafficking and insurgent groups. The other major pipeline for Cambodian weapons is through Southern Thailand and from there across the Malacca Straits to Aceh.[34]

There are clear links between the narcotics and illegal light weapons trade that include shared supply and transit routes, the use of weapons for protection amongst drug traffickers themselves, and funding of gunrunning through drug trade and vice versa.

Piracy

According to article 101 of the 1982 United Nations Convention on the Law of the Sea (UNCLOS) is defined as:[35]

1. "Any illegal acts of violence or detention, or any act of depredation, committed for private ends by the crew or the passengers of a private ship or a private aircraft, and directed: (i) on the high seas, against another ship or aircraft, or against persons or property on board such ship or aircraft; (ii) against a ship, aircraft, persons or property in a place outside the jurisdiction of any State;
2. Any act of voluntary participation in the operation of a ship or of an aircraft with knowledge of facts making it a pirate ship or aircraft;
3. Any act inciting or of intentionally facilitating an act described in sub-paragraph (a) or (b)."

Thus, according to international law, any illegal acts of violence and detention which are committed within State's territorial waters are not defined as piracy. However, according to the IMB, nearby all illegal acts in Southeast Asia occur within territorial waters and thus would not fall under the definition of piracy. Technically, if an attack occurs within the territorial jurisdiction of a state, the event is only classified as piracy if that nation's penal code criminalizes it as such. Moreover, the IMO defines any unlawful act of violence or detention or any act of depredation at anchor, off ports or when underway through a coastal State's territorial waters as armed robbery against ships.[36]

In order to overcome the distinctions between high seas and territorial waters, the IMB defines piracy as: "an act of boarding (or attempted boarding) with the intent to commit theft or any other crime and with the intent or capability to use force in furtherance of that act."[37]

Today, Piracy has become the bane of the modern seafarer. The numerous cases of reported and unreported piracy have led to considerable concern and multinational efforts to control this violent menace. According to the International Maritime Organization Annual Report 2002,[38] the Malacca Straits, South China Sea and Indian Ocean are the areas that have been most affected by piracy. Piracy not amounting to terrorism has been on the increase. Piracy against the world's shipping increased by 37 per cent in the first half of 2003 from the same period in the previous year with a record 234 attack reported. Waters off Indonesia were the most dangerous with 64 attacks; 15 attacks occurred in the Malacca Straits while other attacks were reported near Malaysia, the Philippines and Vietnam (ICC Commercial Crime Services, 2003a). During 2002, Indonesia again experienced the highest number of attacks, with 103 reported incidents. Piracy attacks in Bangladesh ranked the second highest with 32 and India was the third with 18 attacks. Peter Chalk, a terrorism-risk analyst at the Rand Corporation, said in a report on piracy and terrorism in June, 2008, that "there has been a modest yet highly discernable spike in high-profile terrorist incidents at sea over the past six years."[39] Heavily armed Somalia gunmen have seized more than 30 vessels in this year, making the busy shipping lanes through the Gulf of Aden the most dangerous in the world.[40] In September 2008, the Somali gunmen hijacked a Japanese ship MT Stolt Valor and a Japanese cargo ship was also seized by pirates of the coast of Somalia on 15th November, 2008. Soon after the release of the MT Stolt Valor's crew on 16th November, 2008, the pirates seized a Saudi super tanker carrying crude oil worth US$100 million and they also captured three more ships in the Gulf of Aden.[41] Somali pirates on 17th December, 2008, seized four ships in Gulf of Aden. A Kenyan maritime group said pirates had hijacked an Indonesian Tugboat, a Turkish cargo ship, a Chinese fishing vessel and a yacht on Tuesday 16th December, 2008.[42]

This heavy infestation of piracy has a lot to do with the geography of the area, but economic conditions and the mindset of the coastal people in the hundreds of minor islands that lace the Malacca Straits and South China Sea are also a significant factor. Recently, piracy-related incidents seem to have spilled over from these two areas into the Bay of Bengal and the Arabian Sea. Indeed, the center of gravity of piracy may shift to the waters around India.

There also seems to be a distinct change in the type of piracy that is occurring. Earlier acts were of the type termed 'Asian Piracy' that often involved mere stealing of valuables from ships with a negligible amount of associated violence. However, recent cases in the region have displayed a dramatic increase in brazen violence, and the methodology has made them akin to the South American or West African type of piracy.[43] In addition, the involvement of organized crime in hijacking ships was evident from the MV Alondra Rainbow case, from pirates in the Arabian Sea in late 1999 by the Navy and the Coast Guard. This case is also a modern example of various enforcement agencies acting together to fight piracy.[44] Unless law enforcement agencies of various states co-operate to bring piracy under control, this phenomenon will not only increase dramatically but may spin out of control. The portents of this problem lie in the fact that Asian operatives have become exceptionally well organized, with entrenched gangs and, at times, under state sponsorship. Their link with other form of "maritime disorder and terrorism," such as norco-terrorism and human smuggling, is well-established and organic extensions of one another. Thus, India is seriously concerned about the maritime challenges posed by terrorism, trafficking of narcotics, arms human smuggling and piracy being in the Indian Ocean region, where it has the vital stakes in the security and stability of the region.

SUGGESTIONS

1. Strengthening the Regulatory Mechanisms

The regulatory mechanisms in India's maritime zones need to be strengthened by the enactment of new legislation and enforced by setting up mechanisms for implementation. To deal with such a situation, a formal mechanism for coordination among the multiple users of the sea is urgently required. In this respect, the Group of Ministers' report has recommended the formation of "an apex body for management of maritime affairs". Addressing the 14th annual meeting of the ASEAN Regional Forum (ARF)[45] at Manila on August 2, 2007, Pranab Mukherjee, India's Minister for External Affairs, underlined the continued importance attached by 'India to the Look East Dimension' of its maritime security policy. He said: "India will design and conduct a training module on maritime security especially for the ARF member-states, with themes of anti-piracy, search and rescue missions, off-shore and port security, anti-smuggling and narcotics control and anti-poaching operations. The nucleus of the module would be capacity-building for these and related aspects of maritime security."[46] Apart from this the UN Security Council adopted a resolution for the first time authorizing international land operations against audacious, armed pirates sheltering in Somalia. The UN resolution 1851 authorizes the states to "take all necessary measures that are appropriate in Somalia" to suppress "acts of piracy and armed robbery at sea."[47]

2. Promoting Regional Co-operation

There should also be a concerted focus on maritime security in India's diplomatic bilateral/multilateral relationships. This could take the form of a regular maritime security dialogue with countries of the Indian Ocean Rim (IOR) to ensure the stability of sea lines of communication in the area which accounts for over half the world's merchant fleet, by tonnage. Beside this regional states should also develop marine technology and a joint strategy to ensure the safety of ports and harbors.

3. Strengthening the Maritime Security Capability

There is a need to induct certain capabilities which are necessary to ensure maritime security of our nation. First, the entire area should be kept under surveillance; all contacts in all dimensions in this area need to be tracked. Secondly, the Navy must have the capability to meet threats ranging from maritime terrorism to high-end intensive warfare in a force structure that would be networked throughout. It must have reach, staying power and adequate sea-lift capacity. It must be balanced in these capabilities in all the three dimensions. Integral air, anti-submarine and anti missile defence must be built in with strong underwater defence and offensive capability.

4. Resuscitate Counter Maritime Terrorism Mechanism

The threat of maritime terrorism to the global maritime system is likely to increase and the system of management in the Indian Ocean will have to improve to face these challenges. Three areas of activities need to be given greater attention. First, the internal system of ocean management should be refined within the maritime nations by setting up Ocean Commissions. Secondly, greater maritime cooperation is a must between maritime nations. And finally, the global maritime environment should be made more disciplined by replacing the system of Flags of Convenience with a more secure system to face the growing challenges of maritime terrorism.[48]

In short, the effective maritime counter-terrorism, like effective counter-terrorism on land, is dependent on the following:

1. A good intelligence collection capability in respect of human (HUMINT) as well as technical (TECHINT) intelligence.
2. Effective physical security.
3. A good crisis management capability if the terrorists manage to carry out an act of maritime terrorism.
4. Regional and international co-operation in the form of intelligence sharing, mutual operational assistance, mutual legal assistance and effective enforcement of internationally-agreed measures to thwart maritime terrorism.

CONCLUSION

Technological forces are directly impacting on international and regional security at a time when the world is still in transition from the cold war security order to a post-cold war security order. In the face of technological change at an unprecedented rate, the ability to keep pace with rapid change may distinguish the successful cultures from the not-so-successful cultures. In the last five decades, the world has amassed more scientific knowledge than was generated in the previous 5,000 years. The swiftest advances in technology, however, have been occurring since the late 1980s with the advent of the Information Age, with scientific information now increasing two-fold about every five years. It is imperative for us to stay abreast with technological developments to safeguard our security and decision-making autonomy. Particular attention needs to be paid to the maritime dimensions of national security as they are linked to India's political stability and economic prosperity. To maximize our interests at sea and to effectively manage the fast-paced technological developments, we need to formulate a sophisticated proactive multi-pronged, long-term strategy.

No nation can aspire to be great if it does not have adequate maritime strength. India is already a great maritime nation. Now it must show that it has the capacity and the will to manage effectively the ocean area of vital national interests. This can only be done if the Indian Navy is developed to meet these tasks in a balanced manner. Time has come for us to appreciate the challenges to our maritime security. Maritime security issues are of both a military and a non-military nature. It is, therefore, necessary to take both these components into account for a proper understanding of their collective impact on national security. In this context, ports, shipping and imports of energy resources, for example, should be seen as critical dimensions of maritime security.

References

1. Henry J. Kenny, An Analysis of Possible Threats to Shipping in Key South East Asian Sea Lanes, Center for Naval Analyses, Alexandria, Virginia, 1996, p. 4.

2. A.T. Mahan, The Influence of Sea Power upon History 1660-1783, 1890, Scrivener; New York.
3. http://www.greekshares.com/global_energy.asp
4. K.K., Kohli, Maritime Power in Peace and War: An Indian View, African Security Review, 1996, p. 5.
5. K. Hashimoto, Excluding Myanmar and land-locked Laos, Asia's Energy Security and Role of Japan, PHP Research Institute, May 2000 at http://www.rice.edu/projects/baker/Pubs/workingpapers/jescgem /aesrj11/aesrj.html
6. C., Uday Bhaskar, Regional Naval Cooperation, Strategic Analysis, November 1992, p. 736.
7. C. Raja Mohan, "After China, Fernandes Warms up to Japan", The Hindu, April 30, 2003 at http://www.worldpolicy.org/journal/articles/wpj03-2/menon.html
8. China People's Daily, November 20, 2003.
9. After US, China, Japan and Germany, See Oil & Gas Journal, January 20, 2004.
10. B.K., Singh, India's Energy Security, The Hindu, June 9, 2003.
11. P.K.Ghose, "The Maritime Dimension", in "Oil and Gas in India's Security" ed. Jasjit Singh, Knowledge World, New Delhi, July 2001.
12. http://community.middlebury.edu/docs/ghose
13. http://community.middlebury.edu/docs/ghose
14. Vijay Sakhuja, Maritime Terrorism and Piracy: Security Challenges in South East Asia, SSPC Paper 3, p. 4, 2005.
15. Between 1857 and 1876, there were at least eight recorded cases of acts of terrorism committed on board ships. See, Samuel Pyeatt Menifee, "Piracy, Terrorism and Insurgent Passenger" in Natoline Ronzitte, Maritime Terrorism and International Law, Maritnus Nijoff, London, 1991, pp.43 - 55.
16. Ibid, pp. 56-58.
17. "Danish Newspaper Explains City of Poros Slaughter", www.washingtonreport. org/backissues/1088/8810039.htm
18. "Operation Cactus", at <http://www.bharatrakshak.com/CONFLICTS/Operationcactus.htm
19. Ibid.
20. On October 12, 2000, the USS Cole, an Arleigh Burke class

destroyer, was attacked by a small craft loaded with 270 kg of C-4 explosives while making a routine refill stop in the port of Aden, Yemen. Steered by two Saudi suicide 20 Ibid,11 terrorists, Hassan al Khamri and Ibrahim al-Thawar, the small craft exploded alongside the USS Cole 47 minutes after the refuelling was initiated, killing 17 U. S. servicemen and injuring 37 more. The attack caused $250 million in damage to the warship taking 14 months to repair, http://www.cargolaw.com/2000nightmare_cole.

21. http://www.maritimeterrorism/definition/SSPC Paper 3
22. Akiva L. Lorenz, Al Qaeda's Maritime Threat, first published at http://www.ict.org.il/apage/11847.phpapri15,2007
23. ICT Profile of ASG at http://fighel.com/organizations/org_frame.cfm?orgid=3
24. Holt, Andrew, Plugging the Holes in Maritime Security, Terrorism Monitor, May 6, 2004.
25. According to C. Fenwick, "...where a de facto political organization had been set up ...and conducting military and naval operations in accordance with laws of war..., the situation must be recognized as one of public war (justifying it belligerent rights)." See, K.R. Singh, "Maritime Violence and Non-state Actors". Dialogue, Apr-Jun 2003, at http://www.asthabharati.org/Dia_Apr03/krs.htm
26. "Killing of Sea Bird Not A Big Blow to LTTE Shipping Operations", The Sunday Times, February 1996.
27. "Killing of Sea Bird Not A Big Blow to LTTE Shipping Operations", The Sunday Times, February 1996.
28. "What are FOCs: A brief guide to flags of convenience", www.itf.org.uk/seafarers/foc/Body_foc.html
29. G.S.Khurana, Maritime Security in the Indian Ocean: Convergence plus Cooperation Equals Resonance, Strategic Analysis, Vol. 28, No. 3, Jul-Sep 2004, p. 415.
30. http://news.scotsman.com/latest.cfm?id=2461349
31. http://www.alertnet.org/thenews/newsdesk/KLR2992.htm
32. Terrorists are known to indulge in piracy to obtain funds. Other links have also come to light, as in case of hijacking of

the Indonesian tanker, Dewi Madrim off Indonesia in March 2003. Ten armed men seized the ship for learning how to steer it, may be equivalent to terrorists who took flying lessons at Florida flight school and a precursor to a 'maritime 9/11' at http://www.iags.org/n0524042.htm

33. http://www.military.com/content/morecontent/1, 12044, FL_ports_103001, 00.html
34. For a detailed treatment see B. Raman, "Control of Transnational Crime and war against Terrorism", Indian Defence Review, Apr- Jun 2002, vol. 17(2).
35. Capie David, "Small Arms Production and Transfers in South East Asia," Canberra Papers on Strategy and Defence, No. 146, 2002, p. 20.
36. United Nations Convention on the Law of the Sea at: http://www.un.org/Depts/los/convention_agreements/texts/unclos/closindx.htm
37. Ibid.
38. International Maritime Organisation, "Reports on Acts of Piracy and Armed Robbery against Ships—Annual Report 2002," dated 17 April 2003, available in pdf at http//www.imi.org
39. Herald Tribune, November 25, 2008.
40. The Times of India, November 17, 2008.
41. The Times of India, November 20, 2008.
42. The Times of India, December 16, 2008.
43. http://community.middlebury.edu/docs/ghose
44. MV Alondra Rainbow, a 7,000-ton Panama-registered vessel belonging to Japanese owners was hijacked. The vessel was en route from Kuala Tan Jung, Indonesia to Milke in Japan. The Piracy Reporting Center of the International Maritime Bureau had announced through a worldwide broadcast that pirates had captured the vessel. After a high-speed chase and drama it was finally captured by Indian Naval ship (INS Prahar).
45. The ARF comprises the United States, China, Russia, Japan, India and the European Union, besides the 10-member Association of Southeast Asian Nations (ASEAN). It also has

among other countries Australia, Pakistan, Bangladesh, and Sri Lanka.

46. The Hindu, August 3, 2007.
47. The Times of India, December 18, 2008.
48. Tribuneindia.com, Sunday, December, 4, 2005.

Chapter 7

NUCLEAR HOLOCAUST
A Threat to All

*Dr. S.K. Mishra**

Introduction

Science and technological progress makes it possible to ensure a life of plenty on earth, to create the material conditions for the flourishing of mankind. Yet these very products of man's brain and hand are being turned against him due to selfish class-inspired ambitions and in pursuit of enrichment by the capitalist world's ruling elite. Naturally, science and technology by themselves do not threaten peace. The threat comes from international reaction, and notably, US imperialism, using scientific and technological advances for aggressive ends. The unprecedented imperialist-instigated arms race, primarily the nuclear arms race, is a grave crime against humanity.

* Reader, Department of Defence Studies, Government P.G. College, Hisar.

We live in a world of new and involving threats, threats that could not have been anticipated. Destruction of the natural environment continues on all continents. Tropical forests, the most important source of atmospheric oxygen, are being destroyed intensively. More and more toxic substances pollute the air, soil and water. The uncontrolled use of chemicals affects the quality of farm produce. The upper fertile layer of soil is being destroyed. The growing carbon dioxide content in the atmosphere threatens with adverse climatic changes. The time has come forward off threat of nuclear war, halt the arms race and safeguard and strengthen universal peace. Preventing the spread and use of nuclear, biological and chemical weapons is essential if we are to have a more secure world.

NUMBER OF NUCLEAR WEAPONS AND NUCLEAR TEST

Country	*Nuclear Weapons*	*Nuclear Test*
Russia	14,000	715
U.S.A.	10,656	10302
China	400	50
France	350	210
Israel	200	-
Britain	185	45
India	70	6
Pakistan	50	6
North Korea	40	2

Through sustained efforts, the world community has achieved numerous agreements aimed at reducing nuclear arsenal, excluding their deployment from certain regions and environments (e.g., outer space, ocean floor), limiting their proliferation and ending testing. Despite these achievements, nuclear weapons and their proliferation remain a major threat to peace and a major challenge to the international community. Issues of concern in this area include in particular the need for reduction in weapons of mass destruction (WMD), upholding the viability of the nuclear non-proliferation regime, and preventing the development and proliferation of ballistic missile and missile defence system (M.D.S.). While international efforts to contain nuclear weapons continue in different forums, it has been generally understood that the nuclear-weapon powers hold special responsibility for maintaining a stable international security environment.

DATE OF FIRST NUCLEAR POWER PLANT

Country	*Year*
U.K.	1956
France	1959
United States	1960
West Germany	1961
Canada	1962
Italy	1963
Japan	1963
India	1969
Pakistan	1971
China	1991

Humanity has reached a point that requires maximum responsibility from all people especially from the leaders of power processing nuclear arms. Nuclear tests are not necessarily conducted for military purposes. For 62 years humanity has lived without a new Hiroshima. But the ongoing production of nuclear weapons is fraught with the danger of a global disaster. Nuclear tests are conducted to develop new type of nuclear weapons, improve existing system, and check stockpiles for their potential reliability in possible military conflicts. The race is testing, therefore, fuels the race in arms, and this in turn requires new experiments. How can this vicious circle be broken? The answer is obvious. It is necessary to stop and bass test immediately, before it is too late. As we know that if a nuclear war begins, it will not bypass a single continent, a single region. The struggle to eliminate nuclear weapons is a struggle for mankind's survival.

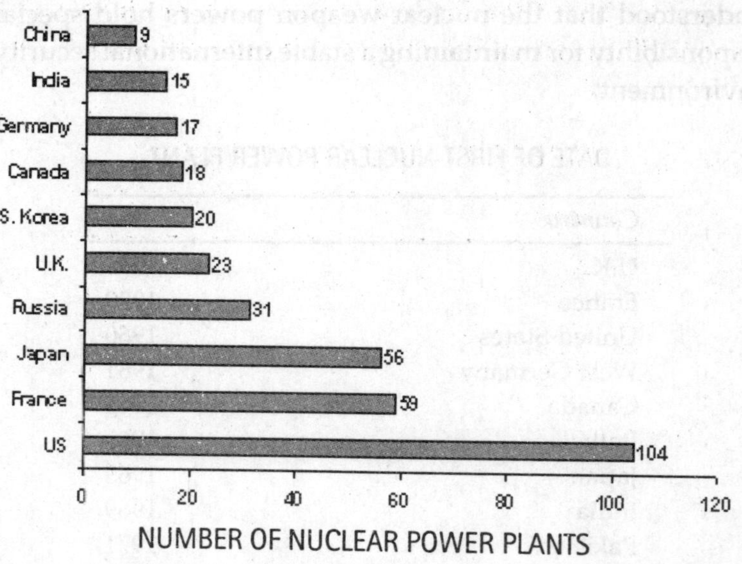

Now that the world has huge nuclear stockpiles and the only thing experts argue about is how many times or dozen of times humanity can be destroyed. No task is more important today than that of preserving peace and eliminating the threat of nuclear or weapons of mass destruction. Mankind is at turning point in its history. Nuclear weapons threaten to destroy not only every thing that our civilization has created over the ages but life on earth as well. The unprecedented Imperialist-instigated arms race, primarily the nuclear arms race, is a grave crime against humanity. In essence, human security means safety for people from both violent and non-violent threats. It is absolutely necessary to make a break without dated political mentality. People must come to realise that arms race and nuclear cannot be won. When they realize this, they will see that no country can be secure if there is no universal security.

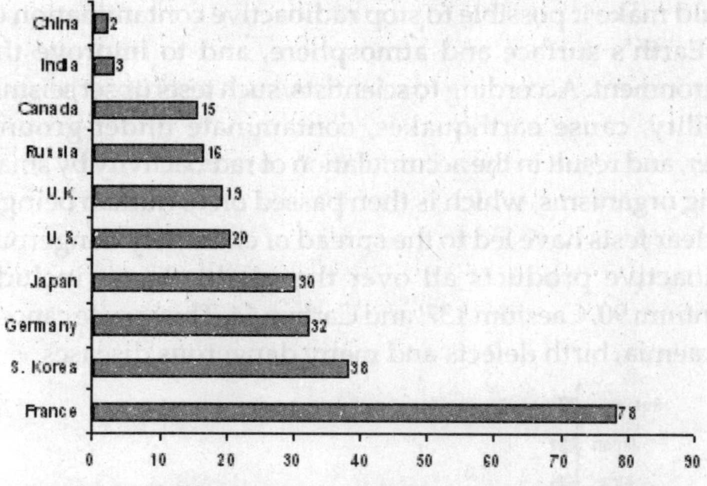

SHARE OF ELECTRICITY GENERATED BY NUCLEAR POWER

The world has long recognised that nuclear weapons pose greatest danger to human kind and therefore it is essential for it to take urgent step towards their complete elimination. First, an end to nuclear test is the best way to stop to nuclear arms race and prevent an arm race in space. A halt to nuclear test would put an end to the development of new types of nuclear arms and the perfection of existing stockpiles. Second, an end to nuclear testing could lead to the scrapping of stockpiled nuclear system without testing and modernisation, nuclear arms would become obsolete and eventually useless. Undoubtedly, this would create an extremely reliable guarantee against nuclear disaster.

Third, an end to nuclear tests would promote nuclear non-proliferation. Countries bent on acquiring nuclear weapons would be unable to conduct tests that are—let us stress this point—essential to their development. Fourth, an end to nuclear explosions, which involve huge expenditure, would release tremendous funds measured in the thousands of millions, for the economic and social needs of development. And fifth, an end to nuclear weapon tests would make it possible to stop radioactive contamination of the Earth's surface and atmosphere, and to improve the environment. According to scientists, such tests upset seismic stability, cause earthquakes, contaminate under-ground water, and result in the accumulation of radioactivity by small living organisms, which is then passed on to human beings. Nuclear tests have led to the spread of extremely dangerous radioactive products all over the world. These include strontium 90, Caesium 137, and Carbon 14. They cause cancer, leukaemia, birth defects and many dangerous diseases.

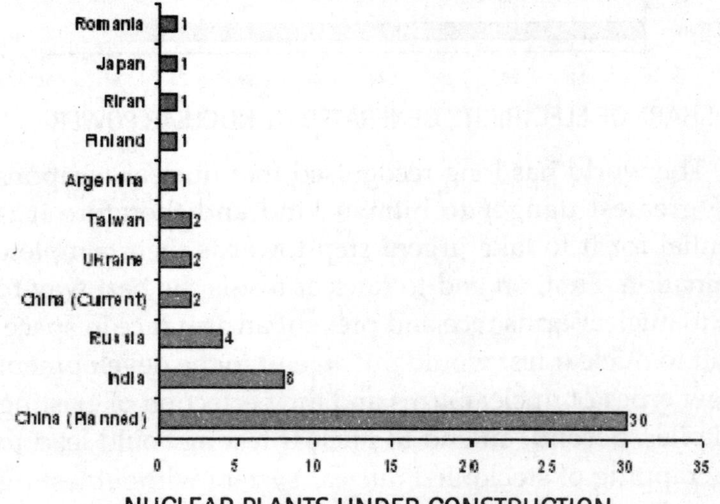

NUCLEAR PLANTS UNDER CONSTRUCTION

Nuclear plants emit no carbon. Nuclear power is emerging as a way of saving the earth from the global warming, but the twin spectres of nuclear waste and proliferation—nuclear material getting into the wrong hands—cast doubt on whether nuclear power can fulfil this promise. When the uranium fuel of a nuclear power plant is 'spent', what's left is a mixture of radioactive substances, or which 1 per cent is plutonium—a highly toxic material used to make nuclear weapons. Because plutonium stays radioactive for tens of thousands of years, it must be kept in a facility that lasts a long time. Building such facilities is politically fraught. The proposed Yucca Mountain repository in Nevada is a legal and technical mess after decades of research and $ 9 billion in expenditures. France's repository program is also in deep trouble, and Germany's ground to a halt in the 1990s. Meanwhile, nuclear waste keeps pilling up- and the odds of its falling into the wrong hands increases. The world's spent nuclear fuel already contains enough plutonium to make about 200,000 nuclear bombs. To mitigate the waste problem, the nuclear establishment is advocating 'reprocessing'—in which plutonium is separated out and recycled as nuclear fuel. Ninety-nine per cent of what remains might be easier to dispose of, but the 1 per cent that remains is pure (bomb-grade) plutonium. The world's most powerful countries should be careful of heading down a path that could lead to a nightmare.

There is now no more important task than to put an end to the nuclear arms race on earth, to prevent its spread to outer space, and to abolish all nuclear and other mass annihilation weaponry. Do not fear your enemies—the worst they can do is kill you. Do not fear your friends—they worst they can do is betray you. Fear the indifferent—they neither kill nor betray, but only with their silent consent to betrayal and murder exist on earth.

It should be added that in difference to such an important issue as the prevention of war, whether a big or a small war, a nuclear or a non-nuclear war, will lead to murder, to the annihilation of whole countries and nations. Only we those living on the earth, can ensure the survival of the present and future generations and the preservation and flourishing of human civilisation because planet earth is our common home.

The past year saw a series of devastating natural disasters, continuing terror attacks and conflict, and the threat of virulent new diseases. These issues effect enemy one of us with no respect for political or geographical borders; they are perhaps an integral aspect of globalisation. But most effective search for solutions to these global problems stairs with a focus on our immediate, individual realities.

Disarmament education with this deeper goal can play an important role in moving us from a culture of war—of conflict and confrontation—to a culture of peace based on cooperation and creative coexistence. We must fully integrate disarmament education in every way possible and develop activities to this and throughout civil society. The arms race has always been a result of abnormal relations between states. Today it is increasingly becoming the main cause of such relations, because the build-up and modernization of armaments gives rise to fear and suspicion, increases distinct and poisons political relations. This undoubtedly concerns all states including developing ones. We repeat that the danger of the nuclear self destruction of our planet is today greater than ever before. It is no exaggeration to say that this obliges every person who cherishes peace to double his efforts in the struggle against the nuclear threat and against the nuclear and mass destruction weapons race.

Suggestions

Preventing the spread and use of nuclear, biological and chemical weapons is essential if we are to have a secure world. To that end the following measures are suggested—

- Doing better at reducing demand for these weapons, and curbing the supply of materials. Which means living up to existing treaty commitments, including for negotiations towards disarmament and enforcing international agreements.

- Strengthening the non-proliferation regime by creating incentives for states to forego the development of domestic uranium enrichment and reprocessing facilities, and call for a voluntary time-limited moratorium on the construction of any such facilities.
- Negotiations for a new arrangement which would enable the International Atomic Energy Agency (IAEA) to act as a guarantor for the supply of fissile material to civilian nuclear users at market rates.
- The International Atomic Energy Agency should adopt the 'additional protocol' as the Agency standard for inspections.

People must come to realise that the arms race and nuclear, biological, chemical and vacuum bomb (Father of the Bombs) war can not be won when they realise this, they will see that no country can be secure if there is no universal security. In today's world, a threat to one is threat to all. The issue of war and peace have moved to the foreground of international life. This is quite understandable, for never before has the world faced so serious a danger. Now that the world has huge nuclear stock-piles and the only thing experts argue about is how many times or dozens of times humanity can be destroyed. Nuclear weapons threaten to destroy not only every thing that our civilization has created over the ages but life on earth. The world seems to be possessed by an inescapable dilemma. The time has come for the save world from nuclear holocaust.

- Let us have deeds, not words.
- Let us have life, not death.

- Let us have peace, not war.
- Let us have policy, not dilemma.
- Let us have prove, not promise.
- Let us have security, not ruin.
- Let us have bread, not bomb.
- Let us have survival, not elimination.
- Let us have new clear concept, not nuclear development.

It can be done, if the people of the world unite to do it.

A more secure world is our shared responsibility. Hazards to our security must be countered where they emerge. Today, the world's focus is on economics. Since the planet's resources are limited, and our lives are driven by the engine of economics, war is inevitable. Unless subtler aspect of life becomes important, peace remains a dream. Our greatest priority should be changing people's mind-set and behaviour so that they are grounded in a culture of peace.

Notes and References

1. Whence the Threat to Peace, Forth Edition, Military Publishing House, Moscow, 1987.
2. Planet Earth: Our Common Home, Novasti Press Agency Publishing House, Moscow, 1984.
3. Stop Nuclear Explosions, Novasti Press Agency Publishing House, Moscow, 1984.
4. A More Secure World: Our Shared Responsibility—U.S.I. Journal, Oct-Dec, 2004.
5. Adler J. Mortimer (1995). How to think about war and peace, New York.
6. Bok-Sissela (1989). A strategy for peace: Human values and the threat of war, New York.
7. Pauly V. Parakal. Stop Reagan: Save our world from nuclear holocaust. CPI Publication, Delhi.

8. Alexie Khaborov and Alegjander Snegin—Nuclear war, NawYug Press, New Delhi.
9. George Kim. Peace and Security for Asia, Allied Publication, New Delhi.
10. Fred Guterl: Another Nuclear Dawn, News Week, Feb. 6, 2006.

Chapter 8

G-8 AND GLOBAL WARMING ISSUE

*Dr. S.K. Mishra**

Global warming is a problem that cuts across national boundaries; it has to be dealt with by the international community working together. Despite growing scientific evidence our present patterns of consumption and production are leading to a massive disruption of the planet's life support systems, particularly of our climate and essential resources such as water, the most governments continue to hide their respective heads in the sand. Global warming threatens the very survival of the planet just as the possibility of a nuclear holocaust did in the cold war years. Yet is remarkable how the G-8 continues to waffle on the subject. The G-8 summit at Heiligendamm, Germany, got nowhere near agreeing to German Chancellor Angela Merkel's proposal that world emissions be halved by 2050. If that seemed too ambitious to G-8 leaders, and US in particular, they might as well have declared that they did not want to

* Reader, Department of Defence Studies, Government P.G. College, Hisar.

deal with the problem even as the doomsday clock ticked away. No doubt the world may have crossed the tipping point, or the stage after which climate change will become irreversible. Considering the already unfolding consequences of the climate change, what are the world leaders waiting for.

The G-8 is the world's economic top table, without those economies, the world would be in an even greater state of the poverty than it already is, with one-third of humanity surviving on less that $ per day. All of us are dependent on the G-8 for our present and future prosperity. The G-8's staple diet should be economic issues, but the greatest long term threat to life on this planet goes further. G-8 or rich countries are too broke to save the world, they have money for weapons and research on ribbed condoms. But not for fighting global warming. They have money for everything which keeps the engines of economy running, but not for making the world safe for living with clean air and water. Climate change affects us all. Therefore, it is only a truly global effort that can save the world.

The G-8 leaders to agree to seek 'substantial' cut in green houses, gas emissions and to give 'serious consideration' to the goal of halving such emission by 2050. First of all we must understand that what is the Group-8 or G-8. The G-8 or Group of Eight, comprises seven of the world's leading industrialised countries—America, Britain, France, Germany, Italy, Japan, Canada and Russia. It is an informal but exclusive body with no headquarters, budget or staff. The leaders of the eight countries meet annually to discuss economic and trade matters and more recently, its agenda has expanded to include issues like terrorism, HIV/AIDS and global warming.

G-8 members can agree on policies and can set objectives, but compliance with these is voluntary. The G-8 has considerably clout in other world bodies due to the economic and political leverage of its members. The member countries take turns in assuming presidency of the group. The country that holds the presidency sets the group's annual agenda and hosts the summit for that year. Germany holding the presidency for this year hosted the 33rd G-8 in Heiligendamm from June 6-8. The concept of G-8 emerged during the 1973 oil crisis when the Arab countries decided to hike oil prices to punish countries that supported Israel in its war against Syria and Egypt. During the economic recession that followed, the America created an informal group, the Library Group, of senior financial officers from the America, the Britain, West Germany and Japan.

In the following year in 1975, the French President invited the heads of state of the America, the Britain, West Germany, Italy and Japan to a summit in Rambouillet. Thus, G-6 was formed with its members agreeing to a revolving presidency and an annual meeting. The next year, Canada joined the group and it became G-7. Since 1977, the president of the European Union too has been represented at the summit. Russia became a full-fledged member only in 1998, making it G-8. Though it became a G-8 member, Russia, which has the smallest economy amongst the G-8 countries, does not participate in financial and economic discussions, which are conducted by the G-7.

Eight countries (G-8) comprising just 14% of the world population and representing 65% of the world's economy, discuss macroeconomic management, international trade, and relations with developing countries. From this, the agenda has now been broadened to include microeconomic issues such as employment and the information highway, transnational issues such as the environment, crime and drugs, human rights and HIV/AIDS. At every summit, G8 countries make certain commitments to various issues like health, education, energy security, climate change and so on.

A study on the compliance level of the various G8 countries to the commitments they have made show that general compliance levels have gone down. Compliance happens when a government alters its behaviour to meet a summit commitment such as budgetary allocation and new legislations or programmes. Commitments to the health and education sectors have the worst compliance record while that towards energy security shows relative success. Russia shows the best compliance record compared to most other G-8 countries along with Germany and America, which also show better performance.

Group eight countries have become as much a site for unique and creative protests, colourful street demonstrations and even terrorist bomb-attacks as a meeting of world leaders. Critics of G-8 have accused it of being an elite group of industrialised nations that push their own interests to the disadvantage of the rest of the larger less developed parts of the world. G-8 is held responsible for poverty in countries in the grip of debt crises, unfair trading policy, global warming, the medicine patent regime making drugs unavailable to the poor and so on. Hence, G-8 leaders are expected to take responsibility to combat problems they are accused of creating. The group has no African or Latin American members or any member for the developing world.

And the fastest growing economies with the largest populations, India and China are not represented. G-8 pushing the agenda of globalisation has provoked much resentment resulting in riots and anti-globalisation demonstrations at summit venues, most notably in Genoa, Italy in 2001 where the protest turned violent resulting in the death of a protester. G-8 summits have become high profile meetings held under fortess-like security outside major cities since then. Though G-8 has launched drives to counter diseases like HIV/AIDS and announced debt-relief schemes, critics are not impressed as they feel the spending is inadequate.

The G-8's staple diet should be economic issue, but the greatest long-term threat to life on this planet goes further. Only we, those living on the Earth, can ensure the survival of the present and future generations and the preservation and flourishing of human civilization because planet Earth is our common home. The present threat of warming of the surface temperature of the Earth is resulting from an increase of green house gases in the atmosphere. Second week of June 2007, the G-8 talking heads decided to cut the green house gas emissions by 50% by 2050. But the greens are not happy. They say the world is running out of time and the rich world must slash emission at least by 80% in just over four decades to avoid death and destruction in the poor world. But the leaders of the rich club refuse to see these points. They are not ready to spend money on efforts to check global warming. The poor world, including India and China, needs more than $50 billion every year to adapt to climate change. Some 80% of this money has to come from the G-8 pockets: 44% from the America, 13% from Japan, 7% from Germany, 5% from the Britain, and 4% to 5% each from Italy, France and Canada. But, they seem to be dragging their feet on this issue. Their point is: There is no urgency and there is not enough money to tackle the problem. Is it true?

Not quite, there is enough scientific evidence now to show that if the rise in global warming is not kept below two degrees Celsius and if a reduction in greenhouse gases doesn't begin by 2015, we will have catastrophic consequences- floods, droughts, famine, deaths and wars—within the lifetime of the present generation. Some 150,000 people are already dying every year as a result of the Earth getting hotter. The First World has money for everything else but the problem which, with soaring temperatures and rising sea levels, is not going to spare anyone. Last year, rich countries gave just $ 103 billion in aid to poor and developing nations. This was much less than the money people in cities spent on bottled water around the world and less than one-tenth of the total money spent by the world on defence and wars.

Since there is no business like war business, the leaders always find money for guns, tank, missile, rocket, fighters' aircraft and other killing machines. Last year, the world spent $ 1.1 trillion—2.5% of world GDP or an average spending of $ 173 per capita—on military pursuits. In the past ten years, global military expenditure has risen by 35%. Despite hundreds of body bags going home from Iraq every month, the America is spending $ 200 million a day or $ 6 billion every month in the devastated country. So far, the America has spent $ 400 billion on its military operations in Iraq. Following the Americans, governments in Central Asia, North Africa and South Asia, including India and Pakistan, have hiked their military budgets and the increase is disproportionate to their means.

According to the Stockholm International Peace Research Institute, the real military spending is far higher than the numbers reflected in official government data on budgeted expenditures. And since national security is a holy cow, any amount of money can be spent on it without raising any eyebrows. President Bush, who is always at the forefront of scuttling any sensible move to check global warming, allotted 21% of the total American federal budget ($3 trillion) to defence. This figure is three times the GDP of India.

Green house effect on the earth is identified by the difference between the effective radiating temperature of the planet and its surface temperature. Naturally occurring green house gases (GHGs) such as water vapour, carbondioxide

(CO2), tropospheric ozone (O3), oxide of nitrogen (NOx) and methane (CH4) bring about the green house effect through the property that they strongly absorb the radiation emitted by the Earth in the infrared region of the spectrum. Almost every kind of economic activity spews out these greenhouse gases that trap heat, raising the global temperature. But the most importanltly, unlike other greenhouse gases, carbon dioxide has a longer life in the atmosphere.

It can last for almost 50-200 years accumulating in the air above and adding to the green house effect. The sudden increase in carbon-dioxide concentration in the atmosphere began with the industrial revolution in what are today called the developed countries, like the America and Europe, when the consumption of energy leapfrogged. Economists have concluded that there is a direct correlation between economic growth and emission of greenhouse gases, at least if the world follows the current pattern of economic development.

CUMULATIVE EMISSIONS (1950-2003)

Rank	*Country*	*$MtCO_2$*	*World total*	*Tons CO_2 per person*	*Ranking**
1	USA	230,200.80	26.37%	7916	2
2	EU (25)	187,773.90	21.51%	4116	24
3	China	83,515.60	9.57%	64.8	91
4	Russian federation	81,779.50	9.37%	56.56	11
5	Germany	49,946.20	5.72%	605.1	8
6	Japan	41,05730	4.70%	321.8	35
7	UK	31,415.70	3.60%	5273	12
8	India	22,098.00	2.53%	20.8	124
9	Ukraine	21,722.20	2.49%	4543	18
10	France	19,854.90	2.27%	330.8	33

WORLD CHG EMISSIONS

Sector	*End use/activity (%)*
Energy	64.8
Road	9.9
Air	1.6
Rail, ship and other transport	2.3
Residential buildings	9.9
Commercial buildings	5.4
Unallocated fuel combustion	3.5
Iron & Steel	3.2
Chemicals	4.8
Cement	3.8
Other industry	5
T & D Losses	1.9
Coal mining	1.4
OPI/gas extraction, refining & processing	6.3

EMISSION IN 2003 ALONE

Country	*Tons CO2 per person*	*Rank**
Qatar	44.5	1
Kuwait	26	2
UAE	23.9	3
Luxembourg	22.8	4
Bahrain	22.6	5
USA	19.9	6
Trinidad & Tobago	19.5	7
Brunet*	183	8
Canada	17.2	9
Australia	17.2	10
India	11	120

*Per capitals emissions

The following major results have emerged about anthropogenic global warming and its major impacts:

- CO_2 emissions alone account for 64% of global warming.
- Snow cover has decreased by 10% since 1950s.
- Frequency of extreme events like floods, and droughts is expected to increase.
- This is very serious threat that sea level has risen by 10-20 cm in 20th century and will further rise in the 21st century.

As we know that it was not safe and many people are seriously sick or dying because they inhaled toxic air six years ago. But he had lied because he wanted to keep Wall Street operating. Such lies are now battling the realities of global warming. Unfortunately, for governments, people are statistics.

That the G-8 had invited leading developing countries—India, Brazil, China, Mexico and South Africa—asoutreach partners to its recent summit had a message. Clearly, the G-8 is gradually losing its ability to meet the challenges faced on its own. It can no longer afford to ignore the emerging nations, which have an increasing role to play in the international political economy. The joint declaration signed at the conclusion of the summit, and the launch of the Heiligendamm Process indicating the need for close and continuous cooperation between the two groups, is indicative of this. Nevertheless, that there was a glass ceiling that separated the two groups was evident from the reluctance of the G-8 to expand to incorporate any other country. As an alternative, Brazil has suggested that the emerging powers form a group—G-5. However, Prime Minister Dr. Manmohan Singh has expressed his reluctance to form such a forum. A G-5 forum of developing nations is not an answer to a restricted G-8. It is very much in the interest of the G-8 countries to include the large emerging powers in a comprehensive decision-making process.

The five—and Russia, a late entrant into the G-8 and still very much an outsider—account for a substantial share of the world's growth and output. In terms of the evolving global system, the choices and associations that the group makes are more likely to determine the future course of world affairs. While G-8 represents only 13 per cent of the world's population, the five invitees to their show represent a much greater proportion. These countries are market driven economies. Brazil, China, India and Russia are likely to be among the largest economies in the world by 2050.

These fast developing nations are some of the largest producers and consumers of energy, and hence are crucial in charting global energy security. If the G-8 is indeed serious about influencing world affairs effectively, it has to transform itself from being a closed club or rich countries. No feasible solution can be found for major global issues without engaging the newly powerful nations thoroughly in the decision-making process.

We should always remember that do not fear your enemies the worst they can do is kill you. Do not fear your friends—the worst they can do is betray you. Fear the indifferent—they neither kill nor betray, but only with their silent consent do betrayal and murder exist on earth. All peoples, every inhabitant of our planet must become aware of the impending danger, become aware of it in order to pool their efforts in the struggle for existence. Group eight countries must remember that leadership comes with the price of responsibility and the weight of expectation.

Chapter 9

INDIA'S STRATEGY TO COUNTER THE DYNAMICS OF NUCLEARISATION OF SOUTH ASIA

*Col. P.N. Verma**

"Whoever thinks earnestly and objectively the question of a general disarmament and considers it in its remotest contingencies, must come to the conviction that it is a question which cannot be solved so long as men are men, and states are states."

— *Theobold Von*

Introduction

Post 9/11, the South Asian Region's volatile security scenario took a backseat due to preoccupation of the world at large with Iraq and Afghanistan. The complexity of the Region's politics and strategic compulsions make it very difficult for the leaders to resolve the disputes to the mutual satisfaction of the conflicting parties. Of particular concern

---

* Army officer

is the nuclearisation of the two old warring States, i.e., India and Pakistan. Add to it is the Nuclear Weapon State (NWS) of China and its long outstanding border dispute with India.

The nuclearisation of India and Pakistan with the latter's inability to control its proliferation is a grave matter that requires deft and careful handling and a very calculated approach both in political and military terms for India to adopt to ensure that nuclear weapons remain a deterrent and steps are taken to minimise risks of nuclear war and aim to ultimately go from arms control towards total disarmament. The inherent nature of the belligerent regime in Islamabad with possibility of loose nukes has the world worried, particularly India and the USA, and in this regard steps ought to be taken to reduce the risk of the Pakistan's nukes falling into wrong hands. The necessary political and military response by India has to be measured against the geo strategic and the regional environment in view and also keeping in mind the domestic factors, economy and security aspirations of India.

It is, therefore, imperative to analyse the security situation in South Asia considering the now declared nuclear weapons programme of India and Pakistan and China's NWS status and recommend India's political and military strategic response to it.

Security Concerns in South Asia

Nuclear deterrence worked during the cold war era in the case of USA and the then USSR, but it did not prevent India and Pakistan from going to limited war at Kargil in 1999 and almost an all out war during OP PRAKARAM in 2002. Does it imply that nuclearisation of the two countries cannot prevent war between the estranged neighbours? In the case of India and Pakistan, it does appear that conventional war with a nuclear backdrop, which may escalate to a nuclear war, is quite possible. This makes the region a nuclear flash point and in the words of former USA President Bill Clinton, "the most dangerous place on earth right now," where an Indo-Pakistan crisis if not managed properly could lead to a nuclear exchange. This is an issue that cannot be brushed under the carpet and we owe to find ways and means to ensure that we are not bled profusely in the event of a nuclear conflagration in the region. There seems to be no let up on the part of India and Pakistan in developing the nuclear weapons delivery systems particularly medium to long range missiles and sea based launchers. The standoff and the consequent arms race would neither benefit India nor China or Pakistan and, therefore, there is a necessity to understand the environment in which the nuclearisation took place and assess the situation and focus on India's political and military strategies to be followed in order to keep India's security concerns addressed and not be caught wanting as we have been for centuries against foreign aggression.

Global Security Scenario

Global security situation is as dynamic as the political realignments in the world dictated by a myriad of factors. India is located in a region where the global and particularly the US security and strategic interests lie. These interests include energy, nuclear proliferation and the threat from terror networks with bases and strong roots in the region. In the uni-polar world today, the security focus remains that of USA's involvement in Iraq, Afghanistan and other strongholds of Al Qaeda network. It also remains preoccupied with future trouble spots like North Korea, Iran and Syria to name a few.

The global security situation changed dramatically since 9/11. The focus of USA remains in Iraq and Afghanistan and due to the latter; Pakistan became a necessity for USA in its bid to decimate the Al Qaeda and Taliban. As a sequel to Afghan war and spill over of Taliban into Pakistan territory, the latter not only relented and agreed to abandon Taliban, but actively involved militarily alongside US Forces to eradicate the menace. Prior to 9/11, during the Clinton era, Pakistan was not figuring in the strategic calculations of the USA and India had cosied up to the USA and it seemed to be finding favour as a long term strategic partner. However, 9/11 changed all that and Pakistan came into focus again. As a result, USA once again started propping Pakistan up as a frontline state in its war against terror, ignoring India's security concerns. Though USA still needs to maintain strong ties with India due to its geo strategic compulsions, but it cannot be at the cost of jettisoning Pakistan at this stage when its war against terror in the region is continuing.

For India, USSR and the cold war rivalry does not exist and Russia is no more a prop against China and China itself remains Pakistan's strategic ally and elusive to India's overtures in resolving the border dispute. China's possession of nuclear weapons, its ranges and recognition as NWS are known and a major concern for India. China by itself is emerging as a global power with its economy surging. Though China's focus at the moment is not the border dispute, but this could well become the spark should China perceive India to be a threat in the future as a growing power in the Asian Region. Hence, in the global matrix of security dynamics, India will have to furrow its own path and find ways and means to ensure that its security concerns are not overlooked or compromised by the fast changing security related developments in this world.

South Asia Security Scenario

South Asia has become the global 'Centre of Gravity' and is likely to witness increased presence and engagement by all major players, on numerous counts, i.e., presence of the world's fastest growing economies; epicentre of international terrorism; embroilment of most of the countries with external and internal security challenges; presence of maximum numbers of nuclear states; home to world's largest armies; highest defence spending and transportation of 70% of oil through the Indian Ocean, besides having the maximum density of population. India, therefore, has its hands full, as far as problems of political, economic, social and military nature are concerned. All the nations in the region fall into the 'developing nations' category and are still engaged in national cohesion and cementing an identity for themselves. In such a situation, balanced perspective as far as economic and security strategies are concerned, do not always materialise in a logical flow. Countries get tended to be carried away by rhetoric, a skewed sense of national pride and influenced by socio - cultural compulsions. All countries face the problem of fiscal management due to limited resource mobilisation and populist and quasi-patriotic financial irresponsibility.

Years of strained relations derived from history, religion and colonial era, further complicate the perceived security threats from one another. The bonding, the combined strength that would have made the region prosper remains absent. These inadequacies lead to a faulty security policy and strategies or an utter lack of it particularly in India. Pakistan, on the other hand has a security and strategic culture, ironically, due to long years of military dictatorships under the power hungry Generals. Smaller nations in the region continue to view India with suspicion and are unwilling to shed the misperception of India being a hegemonic state. Though, countries of South Asia other than Pakistan, do not pose a serious military threat to India, the differences with them on various issues is a cause of concern in terms of regional stability and political alignments. India also needs to look beyond South Asia in the immediate neighbourhood like Myanmar, South East Asian Region and the Central Asian Republics and strengthen political, economic and security ties with them. This would help propel our economy and enhance India's strength in dealing with various inter and intra regional disputes.

INDIA'S SECURITY CONCERNS

India's Security Concerns in South Asia

India remains a major entity in the South Asian Region being a country having boundaries with all its South Asian neighbours, unlike the other countries in the region which do not have borders with one another. Its political relationships with each of the countries in the region would dictate India's security concerns. For a stable environment in which all countries could focus on economic development of their countries, it is important to have good relations which are free from tensions or security concerns. However, it is not so for a variety of reasons mainly intrinsic and some extrinsic shaped by history.

Indo-Pak Relationship

Efforts to normalize relations between India and Pakistan over a period of time have proved futile and this alone remains a major stumbling block in the full exploitation of the potential of SAARC as the two biggest and economically strong states have historical animosity that defies logic as well as solution in the short and medium term. Belligerent Pakistan's leaders have often made policy statements of the nature that suggest that the problem with India is a never ending one and relates to religion, self identity distinct from India's and the perception that India has designs of an 'Akhand Bharat' which would ultimately gobble up Pakistan. This has largely contributed to the volatile security environment in the region. Pakistan has perennial problems arising out of historical disputes ranging from partition, Indus waters, Sir Creek and the major issue of Kashmir. Even if all of these are resolved, Pakistan would still find it difficult to live peacefully with India as it has still not come to terms with its own identity which it indirectly links with India while directly steadfastly making efforts to delink itself from our common past.

Much is known about it and it would be beyond the scope of this paper to dwell any further than to lay bare the essential facts. Jammu and Kashmir remains the major problem which Pakistan claims should have gone to it on the basis of religious composition, the basis of partition in 1947 of the undivided India then. For Pakistan it remains the unfinished agenda of partition. No amount of logic or legal factual detail wherein its accession to India was carried out can convince Pakistan to change its mind or give up its claim. The numbers of wars fought over this have made the security situation far worse than it was at the beginning of each of these wars culminating in the declared nuclear weaponisation status in 1998 by both countries. Pakistan utilises most of its resources, efforts and energy to destabilize India. Besides proxy war in J & K, it has well orchestrated designs like propagating religious fundamentalism by exploiting Indian Muslims, resorting to terror attacks and blasts in other parts of India, drug trafficking, narco-terrorism and pumping in the fake Indian currency to keep India bleeding. Pakistan, suffice to say, remains a major security concern for India in the near future.

India's Relations with other South Asian Countries

No country in South Asia other than Pakistan, poses a direct serious military threat to India but the relationships with these countries need to be stable for India to have no security concerns. Though relations with Sri Lanka remain matured, it still has its ethnic Tamil problem which India has a stake. Any major turbulence there would affect the State of Tamil Nadu and induce India into this region. Bangladesh continues to be hostile towards India and provides unabated support to the ISI of Pakistan and separatist groups of North East Region. The situation in Nepal is in a state of flux and is likely to remain volatile in the foreseeable future, as the process of national reconciliation and reconstruction is predicated to be protracted. Spill over of Maoist's / Madhesi's activity and alongside Nepal's palpable shift towards China are matter of concern. Bhutan and Maldives are the only countries in South Asia which do not have serious areas of dispute that can cause any security imbalance in the region.

The geo-strategic importance of India, arising out of its geographic centrality, big size, advanced democratic institutions, comparative economic and military might perhaps contribute, among India's neighbours, to a sense of insecurity, a feeling of being dwarfed which in turn manifests in perceptions that lead to a conflict situation, disproportionately larger than it actually is. The nuclearisation of India and Pakistan has made the situation more dangerous and complex which needs from India and Pakistan a politically correct and de-escalatory approach.

Security Concerns Related to China

China has resolved its boundary dispute with all her neighbours except India and Bhutan. China never accepted the McMohan Line as this was signed by the Government in

Lhasa and not in Beijing. Even though China has made concessions in the case of Sikkim, it remains steadfast in its territorial dispute with India in Arunachal Pradesh. China perceives India being propped up by the USA to counter its progress as a world power. She also views India as a potential rising power which could be inimical to its domination in Asia. In the long term, relations between the two countries will, therefore, depend upon the changing geo-strategic environment, clash of economic interest and resolution of the boundary issue. The evolving geo- strategic environment and the requirements of the burgeoning economies of both China and India may lead to the relationship between the two gradually transforming itself from cooperation to competition and on to rivalry. This could result in a short duration, high intensity conflict involving high-end technology and state of art weapons and systems with the potential for further escalation. India, therefore, needs to have in place a force structure that can effectively act as a deterrent against any possible Chinese designs even though there is a bit of a thaw in the relationships at the present moment.

Other Security Concerns

India is strategically located in South Asia whereby it dominates the main Sea Lines of Communication (SLOC) of the Indian Ocean. It has access to the 'South East Asian Economies' and dominates the access to the Malacca Straits to the East. To the West, India is poised to plug the routes of ingress and egress to the oil rich Middle East. USA has global and regional interests related to energy security and its current war against terror. Therefore, it remains the focus of other powers in the world notably USA, EU, Japan and Australia.

ENVIRONMENT AND ORIGINS OF NUCLEARISATION OF SOUTH ASIA

The environment of South Asia, particularly, the hostile nature of relationship between India and Pakistan and the influence of the major powers of the world namely USA, China and Russia have had an overbearing impact on the nuclearisation of South Asia over the years culminating in the nuclear tests of May 1998 and the declaration of the overt policy of possessing nuclear weapons by both India and Pakistan.

In India, however, a number of factors other than above have contributed to nuclearisation as against the single most important factor of security concern. The political landscape in the country and across the world, the nuclear technology itself, the personality of the political leaders and nuclear scientists, "Oppositional Nationalism" of the BJP, China and Pakistan factors, pressures of the Nuclear Proliferation Treaty (NPT) and the Comprehensive Test Ban Treaty (CTBT) and the national prestige involved pushed India towards nuclearisation and it conducted its second series of nuclear tests and declared the policy of arming itself with nuclear weapons in 1998.

Pakistan on the other hand had only India specific nuclear programme and its policy has therefore been a reaction or follow up of the progress India kept making in this field. Its nuclearisation and security concerns can thus be summarized as a reaction of the steps initiated by India in conventional and nuclear fields. Pakistan did outpace India at one stage in the eighties of the last century, in coming close to covertly developing the nuclear bomb thus prompting India to hasten up its own weaponisation programme.

In order to comprehensively understand the nuclear

security environment in South Asia, it is thus important to understand the chronological sequence of events and the political and other compulsions that led to a situation where the world considers the South Asian Region as the "most dangerous place on the earth". The development and nuclearisation of India and consequently of Pakistan took place over three distinct periods of time i.e. from 1947 to 1974 till "The Buddha is Smiling" PNE (Peaceful Nuclear Explosion); thereafter 1975 till the five tests of 11 and 13 May 1998 and the last period from May 98 till date. Some western Nuclear analysts like George Perkovich have analysed the development of India's nuclear programme in four phases i.e. broken Phase II into two; 1974 to 1996 till the time when India under PV Narasimha Rao almost went ahead with the testing but were forced to back out under pressure from the USA and from 1996 to 98 till the BJP Government came to power and went ahead with the now well documented five nuclear tests in May 98.

Development of India's Nuclear Programme—Phase I: 1947-74

Nuclear Policy under Nehru: Nehru as the first Prime Minister of independent India was keen to develop nuclear technology for purely peaceful means in order to harness it for electricity and meet the growing demand of power for the country. He was of an era in India's post independence history that followed the righteous and a morally correct path. Yet Nehru was keen to establish India's position as a major world leader. In 1948 India established the Atomic Energy Commission (AEC) which oversaw the complete gamut of nuclear power, peaceful or otherwise. Nehru also understood the international power and recognition that India would gain if it went nuclear and hence he and Dr Homi Bhabha declared in 1958 that India could become a nuclear power in three to four years time if it chose to do so. Under Homi Bhabha, Chairman of the AEC, India did go in for reprocessing of spent fuel to make weapon grade plutonium in 1964. This ambiguous stand taken under Nehru conveyed the message that India did indeed have the technology to become a nuclear power yet it steered clear of it for moralistic reasons.

Role of Homi Bhabha and Raja Ramanna: Dr. Homi Bhabha was a charismatic personality, respected scientist and his statements were taken seriously by all leaders. So when he said that India could build bombs in three to four years at a reasonably low cost, hardliners from the erstwhile Jan Sangh and Socialists, after the 1962 defeat to China, quoted him and sought from the Government assurances of developing nuclear weapons. Bhabha had quoted in 1964 that the cost of exploding a nuclear device would be $350,000 to $600,000 depending upon the yield which was not prohibitive. This was far from true as some USA officials had calculated the cost at about 30 to 40 million dollars . But it did manage to convince the leaders at that time to go nuclear as economic considerations permitted it. Shastri who had by then taken over as Prime Minister after Nehru's death in 1964 finally agreed that "no bomb" approach was subject to change. In November 1964 he declared that AEC would pursue development of PNE and this major policy shift laid the foundation of the Pokharan explosion of May 1974. This policy shift had much to do with Bhabha as Shastri who was under immense political pressure, had consulted Bhaba on the day of the announcement and had invoked his name and rationale which offset all political criticism of Shastri. This suited Bhabha as there was hardly any technical difference between PNE and a nuclear bomb. Bhabha would have the bomb and Shastri PNE which would not go against India's moralistic stand or affect its international prestige. The surprise death of Bhabha in an air crash in Jan 1966 brought Vikram Sarabhai at the head of AEC who had moralistic objections to Nuclear bomb, and soon after taking over, he ordered closure of all work related to bomb design under Dr Raja Ramanna. Ramanna continued to secretly pursue the design of the nuclear weapons along with R Chidambaram and other scientists of AEC and DRDO (Defence Research and Development Organisation) in single minded pursuit of technological advancement and without concern to the security environment in the region at that time.

Technological Capacity and Status: The growth of India's nuclear technology had much to do with the decision to go nuclear. Undoubtedly, one cannot become a nuclear power if the technology does not exist or a country is unable to buy or smuggle it as some nations such as Pakistan, North Korea and Iran have done. As the world saw the emergence of nuclear weapons, India too sought to study its efficacy and development. India's defeat by China in 1962 war and China's first nuclear testing at Lop Nor in 1964 further hastened the technological development as a result of the political alignments as prevailing then. No doubt the possession of the nuclear technology has generated perceptions of external threats way beyond the normal realms. Thus India's nuclear capabilities arose from an unusual mix of autonomous scientific growth and the personalities at the helm of the scientific community particularly Homi Bhabha and Raja Ramanna who relentlessly pursued the nuclear programme to push India to the forefront of nuclear technology.

Sino-Indian War 1962 and China's Nuclear Explosion of 1964: The humiliating defeat at the hands of the Chinese in 1962 was no doubt a major reason to push India ahead in developing the nuclear technology related to its weaponisation. On 29 Dec 1962, the Jana Sangh became the first party in India to declare that India must go nuclear as part of its long term security threats. China carried out its first nuclear test on 16 October 1964 at Lop Nor and this created a new development. India felt China was racing ahead in international prestige and recognition, besides being able to threaten India's security interests. Intensified debates on the issue followed and with the events described above Shastri did come under pressure and gave a go ahead for PNE in 1964. China perhaps has been the single most important factor in shaping India's nuclear philosophy during the sixties and the seventies not so much because of security necessity but also to match the growing prestige, status and clout of the Chinese enjoyed in the international arena.

Indo-Pakistan War 1971 and its Aftermath: Indo-Pakistan war of December 1971 also lent weight to the development of the nuclear programme. During the conflict, China had issued ultimatum to India to dismantle its bases on the "Chinese" side of the border. In addition the sailing of the 7th Fleet of US with its nuclear powered carrier USS Enterprise to flex its muscles in the Bay of Bengal put additional pressure on the Indian leadership to respond notwithstanding USSR's support to India. India then had no answer to meet the challenge on its own. Given this situation many analysts were of the opinion that India needed deterrence to this kind of threat and this alone could be provided by the policy of acquiring nuclear weapons technology. This incident is still quoted by some as a major reason for Indira Gandhi to authorise the PNE in 1974. In addition, however, domestic political and economic problems also forced Mrs Gandhi to give a go ahead to the tests in order to divert public attention and pressure off her for some time.

PNE of 1974 at Pokharan, Rajasthan: In Sep 1972 Mrs

Gandhi gave a go ahead to Homi Sethna, then Chairman of AEC after the death of Sarabhai, to build a nuclear explosive device. Further talks continued in 1973 and after many deliberations amongst the hawks like Ramanna and anti nuclear advisers like Haksar she relented and said to Ramanna "Let's have it". The PNE of 20 May 1974 at Pokharan in Rajasthan brought joy and euphoria in the country both to the scientists and the public at large. The yield of the nuclear device that exploded was 12 KT roughly the same as dropped in Hiroshima in 1945. India did join a select nuclear club but preferred not to go in for acquiring nuclear weapons and stated that the PNE was indeed for peaceful purposes only knowing fully well that the option to weaponise could be exercised in a relatively short period of time. This marked the end of a tumultuous phase of nuclearisation of India in which many actors and events played a role in achieving the goal of taking India to the threshold of becoming a nuclear weapon power.

Development of India's Nuclear Programme-Phase II: 1974 - 98

Policy of Self Restraint: Strangely, defying all logic, India chose a policy of self restraint during the next 24 years after the first PNE of 1974, and conducted no more atomic tests nor went in for weaponisation programme. It was not that as if the security situation had so dramatically altered so as not to warrant any more tests or weapons programme. Neither was India lacking in technology and nor was it in any position from where it could not withstand international pressure. The decision not to go nuclear was not without reason and many factors contributed to it. Primarily, the domestic political compulsions of the Governments of the day and the personalities of the Prime Ministers concerned dictated the terms and showed the path for the nuclear programme post 1974. Mrs Gandhi had declared emergency in 1975, following a court verdict against her that led to widespread agitation against her government. This turmoil continued till 1977 when the Congress was defeated and Morarji Desai came to power heading the Janata Party Government which also had the hard line and pro bomb party—Jana Sangh as part of it. Desai was an eccentric man with an aversion to nuclear weapons and he declared India would never make a bomb and at the same time stood against the NPT as he was morally convinced that it was discriminatory in nature. The relatively unstable governments that followed suit kept the issue in the background as most of the leaders were involved in either saving or cobbling up a coalition government. Following 1980 elections and return to power of Mrs Gandhi, Indian scientists again pressed for another nuclear test and weaponisation but she was reluctant to accede to their demands as she saw no good coming out of it and remained focused in the internal political situation prevailing in the country. After her assassination in 1984, her successor son Rajiv Gandhi also was wary of according permission for development of nuclear weapons. He was a pacifist by nature and was influenced by Mikhail Gorbachev who was then emerging as the leading proponent of global disarmament. India's restraint also owed much to its desire to grow technologically which was not possible without help from the USA and this would not be forthcoming if India had decided to go nuclear. Hence, throughout the rest of seventies and eighties and early nineties India kept away from further development in the nuclear field even though it was aware of the clandestine development of nuclear technology of Pakistan.

Pakistan's Development of Nuclear Technology: In the eighties, China faded to the background of India's security concerns and it became aware of the nuclear programme being followed by Pakistan clandestinely with the help of the Chinese under a secret agreement in June 1976. Many believe that Pakistan was indeed ready with a nuclear device as early as 1983 and it was perhaps tested as well. While Pakistan scientists continued to develop and head towards a simple robust design with a view to definitely go nuclear some day, Indian scientists were as yet nowhere near this stage though they were continuously upgrading the designs and sophistication. In 1987 in an interview to the Indian journalist Kuldip Nayyar, the Father of the Pakistan Bomb, A.Q. Khan made the startling statement that Pakistan had an atomic bomb and it could possibly use it if India threatened its sovereignty or territorial integrity. It was the American intelligence that discovered in 1990 that Pakistan was actually quite close to assembling a nuclear bomb and India was quite unaware of this . USA was then involved in Afghanistan with Pakistan's help and tended to downplay the situation.

India's Compulsions to go Nuclear. Having been jolted by the developments in Pakistan and the pace of the Chinese in the nuclear technology field, pressure on the Indian government grew from the scientists for attaining an overt nuclear power status. Ironically, while in Pakistan the control of the nuclear policy, weapons and its possible use rested with the army, in India the military brass was generally excluded from the policy formulation and decision making. Meanwhile, globally the push towards nuclear disarmament was growing and with the signing of the NPT by 179 countries, and the pressure mounting on India to relent, the policy makers felt that outside pressure may limit India's nuclear programme. At the same time the growing demand of the scientists, the military and most importantly the ever strong BJP forced the Narasimha Rao Government in 1995 to accede to conduct nuclear tests. While preparations were on, the Clinton Administration intelligence tipped him and pressure was brought upon India to once again desist from going ahead with the tests.

Phase III: 1998 till Date

The Advent of BJP to Power: The BJP Government came back to power in 1998 and soon thereafter, decided to go ahead with the tests. Once again the decision to go nuclear was taken by a select few i.e., the Prime Minister, Jaswant Singh, then Deputy Chairman of the Planning Commission, R Chidambaram, Chairman AEC, Abdul Kalam who was then the Head of the DRDO and Brajesh Mishra, the Principal Secretary to the Prime Minister . This decision was in keeping with the hard line stand of the BJP in its election manifesto even though no strategic evaluation of the aftermath was thought out or discussed for formulation of any security doctrine. In addition to the threat from China and Pakistan, the decision to go nuclear also stemmed from the political need of the time for the BJP to consolidate its hold over the domestic political environment where it was then heading a coalition government. China was indeed a motivating factor but less for the security threat it posed and more for catching up with it in gaining international prestige and stature. The Indian nuclear scientists no doubt kept pushing the government towards nuclearisation but that was purely to prove their scientific and technological abilities rather than any desire emanating from security considerations. The go ahead was taken and the world and indeed the Indian military were taken by surprise with the pace of the events that followed.

Nuclear Tests of May 1998: On May 11, 1998, at 3.45 PM, the nuclear tests began in the remote desert of Pokharan in Rajasthan. After 24 years of self restraint and dithering, India had finally gone nuclear. Three devices, a fission bomb, a sub kiloton explosive and a thermo nuclear device (hydrogen bomb) were exploded in a matter of five seconds totalling 60 kilotons. On 13 May 1998, two more sub kiloton devices were exploded that marked the end of the nuclear testing phase. Many statement were made by the political leaders trying to justify the blasts but none more apt than what Mr. Jaswant Singh said, "All that we have done is given ourselves a degree of strategic autonomy by acquiring those symbols of power which have universal currency" .

The Indo-U.S. Nuclear Agreement. A key development in recent years has been the Indo-U.S. Nuclear Cooperation Agreement which was first unveiled in July 2005. The agreement process went through a number of steps, i.e., passage of the Hyde Act by the U.S. Congress in December 2006 to authorize the US Government to negotiate a bilateral nuclear agreement with India; adoption of a bilateral '123' Agreement in August 2007; approval of a safeguards agreement between India and the International Atomic Energy Agency (IAEA) in August 2008; and approval by the Nuclear Suppliers Group (NSG) for Indian participation in nuclear trade in September 2008. Subsequently, in October 2008, the bilateral nuclear cooperation agreement was approved by the US Congress and signed into law by the then President George W. Bush. In March 2009, the IAEA formally approved the Additional Protocol (AP) to the Indian safeguards agreement , followed by ratification of the India Specific Safeguards Agreement (ISSA) in April 2009. This cooperative framework has allowed India to engage in international nuclear trade while New Delhi would allow safeguards on a select number of nuclear facilities that would be classified as 'civilian.' The remaining facilities will come under the military side of the program and off-limits to international inspectors.

Nuclear Force Architecture: India's nuclear deterrent is

centered on a dyad consisting of a small number of land-based bombers and land-based short- and medium-range ballistic missiles. However, in the long term, the Indian government envisions a "minimum deterrent" based on a triad of land-, air-, and sea-based nuclear forces. At present, Prithvi-1 (150 km range/ 1,000 kg payload) and Prithvi-2 (250 km range/ 500 kg payload) are the only ballistic missiles in service with the Indian Army and Air Force. However, the Prithvi suffers from several limitations such as its short-range, liquid-fueled engines, which not only add to the logistics burden and fuel toxicity but increases the difficulties in handling the weapon system under field conditions. Hence, Prithvi missiles will be replaced in future by the new solid-fueled Agni ballistic missiles with short range (700-800 km range/1 000 kg payload), medium range (2,000-2,500 km range/ 1,000 kg payload) and the intermediate range (3,500-4,000 km range/ 1,000kg payload) variants. In early 2008, India has also tested the K-15/ Sagarika, a submarine-launched ballistic missile for Indian Navy. India, however, appears to have stopped short of building an intercontinental ballistic missile (ICBM), named Surya, probably as a result of a conscious political choice to avoid threatening or challenging the legally recognised members of the nuclear club, with the exception of China, which India regards as a potential long-term threat to its security. Moreover, it is likely that the negotiations over the Indo-U.S. nuclear agreement have been a key factor in restraining the range of India's missiles. As part of a programme to develop a secure, sea-based, second-strike capability, India has finally developed a nuclear powered submarine, named Arihant. India is also developing several variants of the BrahMos cruise missile, a joint Indo-Russian project. The missile has already been deployed with the army and the air force, and variants for the submarine fleet are under development.

Nuclear-Use Doctrine: India's primary goal is to achieve "economic, political, social, scientific, and technological development" and autonomy in domestic and strategic decision making in an environment free of coercion from either the threat or use of nuclear, chemical, or biological weapons. With these objectives in view, the Indian government has adopted a nuclear "no-first-use" or doctrine of "retaliation only". The doctrine's central goal is to deter the threat of nuclear (subsequently revised to include chemical and biological) weapons use by any state or entity against India or its armed forces. In the event of deterrence failure, the doctrine states that India will resort to punitive strikes to inflict unacceptable losses on the adversary state or entity. However, India will not resort to the threat of use or use of nuclear weapons against states that do not possess nuclear (subsequently revised to include chemical and biological) weapons, or are not aligned with states that possess such capabilities.

India and the Nonproliferation Regime: India remains steadfastly opposed to the NPT. Since the late 1960s, a consensus has emerged in India that the NPT is an inequitable instrument that divides the world into "nuclear haves" and "have nots," and the solution to the problem of nuclear proliferation is comprehensive global nuclear disarmament. The Indian government, even while remaining steadfastly opposed to the NPT, has reiterated its resolve to undertake nuclear disarmament as part of a time bound and comprehensive worldwide effort in that direction. Although India was initially one of the most enthusiastic supporters of the CTBT when that treaty was first proposed in the 1950s and among the first to sign the Partial Test Ban Treaty (PTBT) in 1963, the Indian government's position has changed radically since then. By the early 1990s, when negotiations on the CTBT rapidly moved towards a resolution, Indian elites came to regard the CTBT not as an instrument of controlling the nuclear arms race, its original goal when it was first proposed, but rather as an instrument of nonproliferation that sought to freeze countries along the nuclear learning curve.

Having seen the historical perspective and the many tumultuous and difficult periods of time before India went nuclear, it is perhaps important to understand the security situation in the region that always remained a major factor for India's decision to go nuclear notwithstanding the catalytic political and scientific reasons. Once that is understood the political and military strategic response would flow more logically. In the days after the tests, India has come a long way in framing these strategies but still more refinement is required and an ongoing debate still goes on with regard to this. India lives in a dangerous neighbourhood and hence it is important that it guards against this danger to ensure its security; the decision to go nuclear was, therefore, perhaps a right one at the right time. The future of the South Asian Region remains volatile in terms of the security situation. Pakistan remains as unstable and unpredictable as it always has been. The rising power of the fundamentalists and the ever present danger of coups in that country which could possibly catapult to power a hardliner, poses a serious threat to the security environment in the region. USA's growing military involvement with high stakes in Pakistan and Afghanistan is also matter of concern to India. A war with Pakistan over Jammu and Kashmir that could escalate to nuclear dimension cannot be ruled out. It is for such reasons it is felt that this is indeed the most dangerous place on the earth right now. The following will substantiate this statement.

PROLIFERATION OF NUCLEAR WEAPONS IN ASIA

Nuclear Environment in the Region. India has a stated nuclear doctrine, which has been well documented, debated and accepted by the Governments and strategists all over the world as to be workable and in the best interests of India's security concerns. Pakistan, on the other hand, has made no such announcement and has left it deliberately open ended which implies that it would not hesitate to make a preemptive use of nuclear weapons should India cross its so called threshold of tolerance. Such ambiguity on issues of nuclear strategy is deliberate for the simple reason that Pakistan wants to deter India from launching an all out conventional war and if India does so, then limiting it to levels below those that could trigger a nuclear war in Asia. While India's stated nuclear doctrine has had no deterrence effect on Pakistan but on the contrary the unstated nuclear doctrine of Pakistan has had some effect on the thinking of Indian planners and military hierarchy that seems worried by the possible use of nuclear weapons by Pakistan. No one is sure what the threshold levels are; whether these are the population centres, the Pakistan army mobile reserves, or its economic potential. In the South Asia Region, possession of nuclear weapons does not deter a conventional war (Kargil/ Op Vijay) nor state sponsored terrorism or a possible use of conventional force (OP PARAKARAM). Lessons of the Cold War cannot be applied in our context. The historical enmity, the security concerns, the deep rooted political differences over Jammu and Kashmir or otherwise and the irrationality of the approach to nuclear conflagration and its disastrous consequences will not deter either India or Pakistan for going nuclear in the event of a war.

Pakistan's Nuclear Programme. From Dec 1990 onward it

was never in doubt that Pakistan was in possession of a Nuclear Bomb. For the next eight years it focused on developing its missile programme including the Ghauri missile which it tested on 6 April 1998. The liquid-fueled Ghauri is basically a North Korean No Dong missile, itself a Scud derivative. A two-stage Ghauri-2 was tested on April 14, 1999, three days after the Indian Agni-2 test flight. A third version of the Ghauri, with an unconfirmed range of 2,500-3,000 km, is under development and was test launched on August 15, 2000. Besides, its possession of F16 aircraft capable of carrying nuclear missiles, there is no doubt that Pakistan can launch nuclear warheads deep into the country hitting cities like New Delhi and Mumbai with ease. With these missile delivery systems tipped with nuclear warheads, the complete Indian Subcontinent would be in the range of the Pakistan missiles. Taking into account the Pakistani nuclear programme and delivery systems and assessment of its nuclear capability, it would reveal the possession of up to 240 kgs of Highly Enriched Uranium (enrichment levels of 95%) and 125 to 230 kgs of Plutonium. It requires 15-25 kgs of enriched uranium or 4-5 kgs of plutonium to make a nuclear bomb, Pakistan would possibly have up to 24 to 48 nuclear devices in a ready state and up to 20 - 25 untested nuclear bombs, a 'Screw Driver' turn away. The most reliable estimate is that Pakistan has produced enough fissile material for 30-52 nuclear weapons .

Evaluation of Pakistan's Nuclear Threat: Pakistan has and will remain a major threat and a problem that cannot be resolved easily. Its inner contradictions and deep rooted historical animosity towards India and a sense of irrational approach to relations with India makes it a potent nuclear adversary. Pakistan could launch a conventional war or resort to a pre-emptive nuclear strike against India for reasons which may vary from a perceived threat of its dismemberment or economic collapse or to counterbalance internal inimical forces to the regime of the day. Pakistan has long outstanding dispute with India and it has not forgotten the humiliating defeat and subsequent dismemberment of East Pakistan in 1971. It possesses the nuclear know-how and resources to produce a nuclear bomb and possesses delivery systems in terms of strike aircraft and missiles. The six nuclear tests conducted by Pakistan on 28 May 1998 and the pace of development of its delivery systems, makes the Pakistani threat a diabolical reality.

Evaluation of China's Threat: India shares a 4060 km border with China. The Chinese Foreign Policy is backed by a clear defence strategy and a nuclear doctrine that is against no first use quite similar to our own. That is not to suggest that India faces no nuclear threat from China, as countries are known to change the course of the strategy as it suits their national interests. China has often flexed its muscles to achieve its national aim and objectives and it is known to be fond of teaching lessons to its neighbours. Relations between India and China thawed when Mr. Rajiv Gandhi visited China in 1988. This was followed by the visit of Mr. Narasimha Rao in 1993 and the signing of the treaty of "Maintenance of Peace and Tranquility along LAC". The Chinese Premier, Mr. Jiang Jemin visited India on 30 Nov 1996 and both countries have been involved in a series of Confidence Building Measures (CBM). The visit of our former Prime Minister Mr. Vajpayee in 2003 did lead to a mutual give and take in TAR (Tibet Autonomous Region) and Sikkim, but it has not been able to address the border and territorial dispute that remain. Thus by and large it can be said that relations between the two countries though stabilising, differences at the strategic level remain not only on account of the border dispute but due to China's close proximity and assistance to Pakistan, its growing relations with Myanmar and that it perceives a challenge from India in its desire to dominate the political and economic affairs in Asian region..

China's Nuclear Threat: Under China's recently adopted modernisation policy, nuclear weapons have the highest priority over all military programmes. China possesses a triad of nuclear delivery means and this is well accepted and well known. China operates approximately 120 ballistic missiles of four types: the DF-3A, DF-4, DF-5/5A, and DF-21A . Older DF-5s are being replaced with longer-range DF-5As, an upgraded version that may be completed around soon. A new missile, of 8000 km range, DF-31, is under development. China is also developing a modified version of the DF-31, the DF-31A, with an extended range of up to 12,000 km. China's submarine programme consists of a single Xia-class submarine, the Xia. China is expected to deploy the (Julang-I) medium-range SLBM aboard the Xia SSBN. The Xia carries 12 single-warhead Julang- I SLBMs, which have an estimated range of 1,700 kilometers. Indian metropolises of Delhi, Calcutta, Madras and Bombay thus become easy targets. China has begun work on a new SSBN called Project 094. This is expected to carry 16 three-stage Julang- II SLBMs, a variant of the DF-31 missile, with an estimated range of up to 8,000 km. China's strategic bomber force consists of 100-120 Hong-6 (H-6; NATO designation B-6) medium-range bombers based on the 1950s Soviet Tu-16 Badger. China also possesses approximately 150 tactical nuclear warheads with yields ranging from 10KT-20KT. China may possess Multi Independent Re Entry Vehicle (MIRV) warheads. Intelligence reports indicate the deployment of 70 MRBMs and 20 IRBMs in Nagchu (Tibet) approximately 320 km Northeast of Lhasa. This is a direct indication of India being the potential target of China. Its vast nuclear arsenal has a reach that can target all major cities in India.

Other Nuclear Proliferators in the Region: There are other nuclear proliferators in the region like Iran, Israel and North Korea. Though these countries have no major differences with or pose any serious threat to India, but the fact that these countries are located in the region is a cause of concern. USA, a nuclear power with global reach, seems to be digging down for a long time in our neighbourhood, is also a cause for concern for us. It is unlikely to leave bases in Pakistan even if Osama et el are killed or captured. It has paramount geo-strategic interests in Afghanistan and Central Asian Republics (CARs) and its willing ally Pakistan would continue to provide bases to it unless the domestic opposition grows far more than what it is today. USA also maintains its naval bases in Diego Garcia and its global reach and nuclear arsenal can hit any part of the country. The USA's military presence in our neighbourhood is a long term concern which needs to be factored before evolving a security strategy for India.

NUCLEARISATION OF SOUTH ASIA: INDIA'S POLITICAL STRATEGY

National Consensus: Having seen the security threats and own progress in the development of nuclear capability, it now remains to be seen the strategy that India should pursue in dealing with the situation arising out of the nuclearisation of South Asia and role of other global nuclear players in the region. India has always been a matured democracy and it has always taken a political consensus regarding matters dealing with its security and by and large politicisation of security matters has been minimal. This approach must continue in matters of nuclear strategy since it decides the long term approach of nuclear arming and doctrines besides reflecting the nation's support to it.

Arms Control to Disarmament: Mr. Rajiv Gandhi had proposed a nuclear free world by 2010 in an address to the United Nations in May 1988 which was largely ignored by the leading powers then. In the long term perspective, elimination of nuclear weapons from the surface of the globe is the ultimate guarantor of survival; however, till this happens, India needs to maintain a balanced stockpile as per the strategic requirements. The provisions of the NPT being discriminatory in favour of the NWS, must not be accepted by India under any circumstances. Ultimately the country should go in for an international forum or opinion that favours total disarmament as an international goal that is universal in its execution and not discriminatory. However, that is not likely in the foreseeable future and therefore a calculated approach to global and particularly regional arms control must be professed as a national nuclear strategy. This would send the right political signals to all including our smaller neighbours about our minimum needs, our peaceful intentions and desire to promote peace and economic development in the region. In this regard it is important for India to continuously monitor the developments and progress that the countries are making in the field of nuclear weapons particularly Pakistan and China and then initiate and progress the dialogue further.

Gujral Doctrine: Problems with normalisation of relations with Pakistan would continue and would perhaps take a long time to resolve. India must look for good relations with its smaller neighbours. This despite the open hostility towards us from Nepal and Bangladesh would have to be followed to prevent strong opposition to India's nuclearisation which may in the long run invite international attention and consequent disadvantages.

Building Nuclear Diplomatic Finesse: In the wake of series of nuclear blasts in May 1998, there was a lot of chest thumping and threats given out by leaders of the day which did send wrong signals to the nations around the globe particularly to China, Pakistan and the smaller nations of the region. This could and did do considerable harm to India's interests. The needlessly provocative statements from our leaders created a huge political opening for Pakistan to campaign against an 'aggressive India' and paint its own nuclear tests as "defensive reaction".

Display Strong Political Resolve. One of the major concerns of our polity and the political leaders is the lack of strong resolve to take tough decisions. For centuries we have been perceived as soft and divided. For the sake of deterring any adversary from using nuclear weapons we must have the capability, a strong will to use that and our adversary must be aware of the same. Constant buckling under pressure from sections of the public or the political parties must be avoided as it conveys a lack of strong will on the part of our leadership. For nuclear weapons to be effective as deterrent it is essential to show strong resolve for second strike to deter an aggressor.

Improving Relations with Nuclear Neighbours: To avoid a nuclear war, it is best to have good relations with potential adversaries and keep them engaged. This is particularly important against China. This issue was not handled well before especially when China was singled out as our long term threat by the then Defence Minister Mr. George Fernandes while speaking in a seminar on 03 May 1998 and a letter from the then Prime Minister Mr. A.B. Vajpayee to Mr. Bill Clinton, reasoning the China threat as a primary cause of India going nuclear. This conveyed a wrong view that India was now capable of taking all measures for its security primarily against China. This pushed USA and China even closer on their views of nuclear non-proliferation in South Asia and isolated India. Nonetheless, if China can have missiles deployed in Tibet targeted towards India, there is no way that anyone can deny India the legitimate right to go nuclear. This also does not prevent India and China from building bridges and mending their past differences as they have been doing recently. Likewise with Pakistan, India must take initiatives in resolving or at least reducing the tensions. President Musharraf's offer on Jammu and Kashmir in October 2004 in demilitarizing is a bold one and needs to be further refined and debated. Efforts to reduce tensions in the region would be a prudent political step.

Build Nuclear Awareness. In India and Pakistan, most people lack basic information about nuclear dangers. In India, a November 1999 post-election national opinion poll survey found just over half of the population had not even heard of the May 1998 nuclear tests. In the middle of the spring 2002 crisis, the BBC reported the level of awareness of the nuclear risk among the Pakistani public was "abysmally low". Even educated people seem unable to grasp basic nuclear realities. Some believe that a nuclear war would be the end of the world. Others think of nuclear weapons as just bigger bombs that guarantees peace. More and more people in India and Pakistan take it as a symbol of superiority over the other as a continuation of decades old rivalry. Previous crises have also seen such lack of fear about the threat and use of nuclear weapons. A key factor is the absence of an informed and organized public opinion able to keep political and military leaders in check and restrain them from brandishing nuclear weapons. Close government control over national television, especially in Pakistan, has ensured that critical discussion of nuclear weapons and nuclear war is not aired.

Allow Nuclear Dissent: There are a number of people in the country particularly the intelligentsia that is against the nuclear bombs, as a solution to India's security needs. They have a point in that the economic condition of both India and Pakistan does not allow for large amount of expenditure in developing the bombs and the infrastructure, the delivery means etc that go with it. Prominent personalities like Arundhati Roy have always opposed it and they should not be seen as enemy of the state. On the other hand their contribution to the education of the masses about the dangers of a nuclear war must be acknowledged in order to build a national consensus.

Looking Beyond to New Frontiers of Warfare: While the scientific and technological prowess of India deserves kudos for developing the nukes, the nuclearisation is neither the ultimate weapon of destruction of an enemy nor does it guarantee any degree of security from conventional or nuclear war in the South Asian region. Hence, India must look beyond and develop technologically more advanced non nuclear arsenals like the long range missiles, space based weapons, the IT related Information Warfare and the fast emerging applications of the nano-technology. Adequate funding for research must be made available for this.

Crisis Management: In case of a nuclear war or nuclear accident or sabotage with effects such as mass deaths, injuries and fires, it is essential to have a crisis management scheme in place to address the critical situation that is likely to develop. Of primary importance is the public health and safety. An effective crisis management organisation, which would be an essential part of the scheme, should be able to detect, monitor, continuously assess the radioactive levels and handle the mass destruction and catastrophic situation that is likely to develop. To meet such emergencies it would be essential to have an organisation across the country to handle such a situation and be equipped with it. The Department of Atomic Energy (DAE) has been identified as the nodal agency in the country in respect of man made radiological emergencies in the public domain. For this purpose, a Crisis Management Group (CMG) has been functioning since 1987 in DAE. In the event of any radiological or nuclear emergency in the public domain, the CMG is immediately activated and co-ordinates between the local authority in the affected area and the National Crisis Management Committee (NCMC). The CMG comprises senior officials drawn from various units of DAE like the Nuclear Power Corporation of India Ltd. (NPCIL), Bhabha Atomic Research Centre (BARC), Heavy Water Board (HWB) and the Directorate of Purchase and Stores (DP&S). It also includes a senior official from the regulatory authority, the Atomic Energy Regulatory Board (AERB). The role of the defence forces is not particularly spelt out for emergencies in the public domain. Most of the troops would be engaged in frontline duties and therefore it is essential for the civil administration to have an organisation in place without the defence forces to handle nuclear emergencies during war. However, in the event of the use of a tactical nuclear weapon against counter force targets, the army authorities in the field are to take necessary measures as obtaining in their standard operating procedures and drills for which they are trained. As regards major nuclear facilities of DAE like the nuclear power stations, they have an Exclusion Zone of 1.6 km surrounding the power station in which no habitation is permitted. The entire area is fenced or walled off and defines the boundary of the site. Beyond this is the public domain and an area of 16 km radius around the plant site is called the Off Site Emergency Planning Zone (EPZ). The local District Administration, the Crisis Management Group, DAE and the National Crisis Management Committee (NCMC) get involved in this last type of Emergency. To say the least in India we are not so well equipped for handling national emergencies other than the minimum stipulated by the International Atomic Energy Agency (IAEA). The provisioning of nuclear shelters, evacuation procedures, doctors and hospitals and fire fighting personnel would be most in demand. Unfortunately in India where millions are homeless, it is laughable to think of nuclear hardened shelters or even of the kind of medical and fire fighting facilities that needs to be provided in a nuclear war or accident. In case of a nuclear attack on Mumbai, there are likely to be 136,900 deaths and 224,600 injuries besides serious damage to properties. Mumbai can barely manage to handle such a situation notwithstanding the emergency schemes in place. Similar would be the case for other cities which are woefully inadequately prepared to handle a crisis of the magnitude arising due to a nuclear attack. The National Crisis Management Committee needs to do more on this important aspect of public safety and health. Suffice to say in India a lot more needs to be done to put the crisis management structure in place like it was in the USA in the wake of 9/11 strikes by terrorists in New York.

INDIA'S MILITARY NUCLEAR STRATEGY

The nuclear weapons in the Indian context are strictly political and would be used as political weapons only. While political strategy aims at higher goals of nation building and disarmament, military planners at the strategic level must continue to build a nuclear philosophy encompassing all aspects before arriving at a nuclear doctrine or a strategy. The need for continuous research, threat analysis, deployment of delivery means, command and control of nuclear weapon systems, operational and tactical requirements etc must remain primary consideration for a military nuclear strategist.

Assessment of India's Nuclear Doctrine: Continuous assessment of the nuclear doctrine must be done in relation to the threats and the regional and international situation that keeps changing. Accordingly the military nuclear strategists must continue to advise the political leadership on the need of any change. If for example, it is certain that an adversary is going to go nuclear and it may be strategically beneficial to go for a pre-emptive nuclear strike then this must be done.

Development of Delivery Means: The country must go in for multiple delivery means if we have to ensure a credible second-strike capability. Presently India has the Prithvi and the Agni series of missiles. While the Prithvi with ranges up to 250kms is already operationalised and inducted, efforts are required to induct the advanced variants of Agni series of missiles, as these have been successfully test fired since August 2004. Indian plans for an intercontinental ballistic missile (ICBM) programme, referred to as the Surya, must be followed through as most components needed for an ICBM are available from India's indigenous space programme. India should also push through with the naval systems like Sagarika and Dhanush, which should be equipped to carry nuclear warheads in the future.

Nuclear Targeting Philosophy: We have a professed second-strike nuclear doctrine; hence, it is neither immoral nor difficult to go in for counter value targets. These have to be continuously reviewed and prepared. It also has to be ensured that this is well documented and has the approval of the political leaders of the day.

Safety and Security of the Nuclear Arsenals: The nuclear arsenals are usually kept at multiple places and their deployment drills and methodology need to be streamlined. Adequate recourse and effort is required for deception to enhance security during transit and deployment to achieve surprise and ensure security. Procedural issues regarding safety in handling and storage need attention. Multiple agencies must be involved in handling and made responsible for the warhead, the launchers, the delivery means and the code settings. Being in the classified nature these aspects must be strictly made known only on need to know basis.

Command and Control Structure: There is a definite requirement of forming a Strategic Nuclear Command to ensure adequate safeguards against accidental or inadvertent use. The system should be able to respond rapidly and effectively under such situation and at the same time ensure it exercises adequate control at all times to avoid inadvertent and accidental use. Survivability, redundancy and duplication are a must for a robust command and control system. In the USA, authority is vested in the NCA (Nuclear Command Authority) comprising the President and the Secretary of Defence and their alternates and successors. Similar arrangement needs early formalisation and implementation in India as well. Once the Chief of Defence Staff post comes into being, he should be made operational commander of all nuclear arsenals under the National Command Authority comprising of the Cabinet Committee of Political Affairs.

Ballistic Missile Defence. The military leadership should also be looking for technology that would lead to the development of nuclear missile defence. It would not only include the anti ballistic missile but a complete structure of monitoring potential enemy's missile sites, the launch of missiles, its trajectory and likely interception points possibly outside own territory or over a point in space or atmosphere that would cause minimum casualties to own population. It is now believed that an Inter Service Committee has been set up for a detailed study on the technical and operational aspects of a missile defence cover for India as also the economic aspects. India is already in an advanced stage of negotiations with Israel in the Arrow missile defence systems and this must be pushed through and later India must acquire its own anti missile defence technology.

Conclusion

Nuclearisation of South Asia has thrown many challenges to India and has heightened her security concerns. This includes the omnipresent Chinese threat which has been further accentuated due to a long term, permanent presence of the USA in the region. India has come a long way and many factors can be attributed to India going nuclear. The Chinese nuclear programme, the need to have a deterrent against global powers to face the challenges of coercive diplomacy and the rapid nuclearisation of an inherently unstable and unfriendly Pakistan are some of the major factors that led to India's current status as a nuclear power. It is, therefore, important that India takes stock of the dangers of the nuclear war and prepares suitable political and military strategy to follow in the event of a war that may threaten escalation to nuclear dimension and be able to give a befitting and a measured response. Nuclear weapons are weapons of mass destruction and its results in terms of loss of lives and environment catastrophe can be enormous and hence it must remain as a political weapon and not a military solution to political problems.

References

Times of India, 11 March 2000. (www.timesofindia.com/today/11home2-htm).

Dixit JN: Security in South Asia—Trends and Directions. APH Publishing Corporation 2004. Ed. Vandana A & Ashok Shukla.

Chapman Graham P., The Geopolitics of South Asia. Ashgate Publishing Ltd. UK. 2003, p. 262.

Hymans, Jacques E.C., Why Do States Acquire Nuclear Weapons.

Nuclear India in the Twenty First Century. Eds DR Sardesai and Raju Thomas. Palgrave-McMillan. USA. 2002, p. 144.

Perkovich, George. What Makes the Indian Bomb Tick. Nuclear India in the Twenty First Century. Ed DR Sardesai and Raju GC Thomas . Palgrave - McMillan, England. 2002, p. 26.

Ibid., pp. 27.

Ibid.

Lavoy, Peter ; The Cost of Nuclear Weapons in South Asia. Nuclear India in the Twenty First Century. Ed DR Sardesai and Raju GC Thomas . Palgrave - McMillan, England. 2002, p. 261.

Subramayam K, India and the International Nuclear Order. Nuclear India in the Twenty First Century. Ed D R Sardesai and Raju Thomas, Palgrave-McMillan, New York, 2002, pp. 74-75.

Perkovich, *op. cit.*, p. 39.

Perkovich, *op.cit.*, p. 46.

Jaswant Singh, Foreign Minister of India, after India carried out the nuclear tests at Pokharan, Rajasthan, in May 1998.

Rama Lakshmi & Glenn Kessler, "International Group Backs Nuclear Accord for U.S., India," The Washington Post, September 7, 2008, www.washingtonpost.com.

Siddharth Varadarajan, "India and the Additional Protocol," The Hindu, March 7, 2009, www.hindu.com/ 2009/ 03/ 07/ stories/ 2009030755691000.htm.

"India Working on Ratification Procedures," The Hindu, April 13, 2009, www.hindu.com/ 2009/ 04/ 13/ stories/ 2009041360 211100.htm. . www. The bulletin.org. Bulletin of Atomic Scientists Jan/Feb 2002, p. 71.

Spector, Leonard S. Spector, Nuclear Ambitions; Carnegie Endowment, Western Press; 1990, p 34. www. thebulletin.org. Bulletin of Atomic Scientists Jan/Feb 2002, p. 71 www. The bulletin.org. Bulletin of Atomic Scientists Nov/ Dec 2003, p. 77.

Perkovich, George, India's Nuclear Bomb. Oxford University Press. New Delhi. 2000, p. 298.

Dr Raja Mohan C, "A Nuclear Strategy for India". USI National Security Series 1999. Ed Basrur, Rajesh M.

Majumdar Anindyo J. Nuclear India into the New Millennium.

Lancer's Books, New Delhi, 2000, p. 178.

Joshi, Arun. Hindustan Times, 28 October 2004, New Delhi, p. 4.

Pervez Hoodbhoy and Zia Mian www. The India-Pakistan conflict— Towards the failure of nuclear deterrence. www.dae.gov.in

Abani. Dr MC. Nuclear Emergency: Preparedness and Response.NBC Defence Journal. June 2002. CME Pune, p. 3.

Nair, Brig Vijai K. Nuclear India. Lancer International, New Delhi. 1992, p. 67.www.indiadaily.com. 16 Oct 04.

Hindustan Times, New Delhi. 02 August 2004, p. 4.

Chapter 10

IMPACT OF TECHNOLOGICAL WORLD ON ENVIRONMENT

*Dr. S.K. Mishra**

Science and technological progress makes it possible to ensure a life of plenty on earth, to create the material conditions for the flourishing of mankind. Yet these very products of man's brain and hand are being turned against him due to selfish class-inspired ambitions and in pursuit of enrichment by the capitalist world's ruling elite. Naturally, science and technology by themselves do not threaten peace. The threat comes from international reaction, and notably, US imperialism, using scientific and technological advances for aggressive ends.

Environment is defined as the aggregate of all external conditions and influences that affect the life and development of organisms. Fortunately, the responsible world is aware of the effects of environment on survival of life on the planet.

---

* Reader, Department of Defence Studies, Government P.G. College, Adampur (Hisar).

There is focussed attention on major environmental issues. When localised, the issues are those that affect the territorial integrity or political stability of a nation such as disputes over scarce water resources, or rehabilitation of hapless refugees fleeing a degraded environment in search of a better life. National governments have to see the global impact of environment while managing environmental security.

Future climate and its impact could well trigger bloody wars fought over access to basic necessities like drinking water. The greenhouse effect is causing melting of glaciers that are precious reservoirs of clean water. Not only would the melt destroy the world's freshwater reservoirs, it is projected to cause floods and droughts, reduce the area of arable land, adversely impact fish and food stocks, erode coastlines as sea levels rise and trigger large movement of populations to safer areas. Climate refugees could face hostility from local residents and this could lead to conflict. Large-scale migration and competition for resources could become a serious security challenge.

Environment, in its natural state, has its complex physical, chemical and biotic factors that act upon an organism or an ecological community and ultimately determine its form and survival. Environmental security relies more on the protection and preservation of the environment to make it more potent for sustainable development and survival of life on earth than on response activities. Currently, environmental security, in its serious sense, is applicable to the three geophysical terrains—land, ocean and air space. It is yet to extend seriously to the no-geographical, though physical, outer space. There are already concerns of outer space becoming an overhead (Albert Einstein may not favour this expression) junkyard of space vehicles, burnt-out rockets, slipped-off screwdrivers and other knick-knacks. It may be a short gap before the world communities seriously take note of clean outer space contiguous to the air space. Outer space is the terrain through which the earth gets blasted every moment with harmful radiation. The ozone layer at the outer border of air space acts as an armour, protecting the planet from harmful rays. It is reported that ozone depleting gases have pierced the ozone layer creating a hole that is likely to expand, over the South Pole.

Challenges to environmental security

Ironically most of the challenges to environmental security originate from activities meant to improve standards of human life. Identified causes are:

- Rise in population and their insatiable need for resources
- Clash of developmental projects with the environment
- Overuse of renewable resources
- Wasteful use of resources
- Use of environment damaging resources including fuel
- Terrain abuse
- Inability to appreciate the interactive matrix of the geophysical terrains
- Disasters that cause permanent changes in environment
- War and military preparations
- Casualties, and acts of sabotage and terrorism
- Toxic wastes and hazardous materials
- Problems of legislation and enforcement
- Global warming and climate change

Population growth

Population growth induces pressure on the

environment, thereby making the policies and measures inadequate for its protection and regenerative preservation. Though there is a different school of thought advocating that population, if controlled and made supportive, is good for a nation. An oversized population increases demand for resources and energy.

Development and environment

Development work often encroaches into sustainable and life-supporting environmental areas. The result will be destruction of life-sustaining habitats.

Resource usage

Over consumption, exploitation and wastage of resources can leave a telltale effect on the world permanently.

Terrain abuse

Terrain abuse in developmental and habitation activities is far too common. Degradation of land, air and ocean is a much feared subject.

Lack of appreciation of the interactive matrix of geophysical terrains

The three geophysical terrains are environmentally interactive. Activity in one can cause collateral damage in another. This has to be understood.

Disasters

While a disaster-free world is hard to imagine, the beginning of a solution for environmental security is based on the principles of zero disaster policies.

War and military preparations

War and military preparations can cause serious

damage to the environment. It has an ancient beginning when the Romans destroyed the fields of Carthage by spreading salt. In the modern world, the United States experimented with chemical weapons and climate modifications in Vietnam. Environmental warfare techniques are quite seriously etched in the memories of the Vietnam War. In the Persian Gulf War of 1991, the retreating forces of Saddam Hussein intentionally set fire to oil wells causing unprecedented air and water pollution. The Environmental Modification Convention of 1997 forbids hostile use of environmental modification techniques having widespread, long-lasting or severe effects as the means of destruction, damage, or injury to any other state party. Wars can destroy environment. A nuclear winter may follow large-scale nuclear war. Outer space if used for military purposes could be contaminated, making Earth an unsafe habitat.

Causalties, and acts of sabotage and terrorism

An accident can cause serious environmental damage. The accident at the Chernobyl nuclear power station in the former Soviet Union on 25-26 April 1986 was the worst in history so far. Such causalties are bound to happen anywhere and at anytime when human slackness overpowers caution.

Toxic wastes

Currently, production, trade, use and release of synthetic chemicals and toxic wastes are widely recognised as a threat to human health and environment, but safe handling of these wastes is a neglected practice.

Legislation and enforcement

Legislation and enforcement calls for stringent laws without affecting the normal "traffic ad business" at national and international level. Such laws will also need the backup enforcement that includes a quick delivering judicial system.

Global warming and climate change

Global climate change is considered as one of the major issues that may affect environmental security. The starting point was the alarm caused by the discovery of a hole in the ozone layer over Antarctica in 1985. Chlorofluorocarbons are the principal cause of ozone depletion. According to author Paul Brown, large parts of the civilised world may not survive if global warming is not arrested. Small coastal and island nations are likely to disappear below the rising sea when the ice-caps melt. James A. McCarthy, an environmental scientist based in Harvard University, predicts that most of the earth's people will be on the losing side. There are also voices that say global warming is nothing new, but a cyclic process in which the world gets hot and cold periodically since it has not yet settled down.

Global warming is a problem that cuts across national boundaries; it has to be dealt with by the international community working together. Despite growing scientific evidence our present patterns of consumption and production are leading to a massive disruption of the planet's life support systems, particularly of our climate and essential resources such as water, the most governments continue to hide their respective heads in the sand. Global warming threatens the very survival of the planet just as the possibility of a nuclear holocaust did in the cold war years. Yet is remarkable how the G-8 continues to waffle on the subject. The G-8 summit at Heiligendamm, Germany, got nowhere near agreeing to German Chancellor Angela Merkel's proposal that world emissions be halved by 2050. If that seemed too ambitious to G-8 leaders, and US in particular, they might as well have declared that they did not want to deal with the problem even as the doomsday clock ticked away. No doubt the world may have crossed the tipping point, or the stage after which climate change will become irreversible. Considering the already unfolding consequences of the climate change, what are the world leaders waiting for.

The G-8 is the world's economic top table, without those economies, the world would be in an even greater state of the poverty than it already is, with one-third of humanity surviving on less that $ per day. All of us are dependent on the G-8 for our present and future prosperity. The G-8's staple diet should be economic issues, but the greatest long term threat to life on this planet goes further. G-8 or rich countries are too broke to save the world, they have money for weapons and research on ribbed condoms. But not for fighting global warming. They have money for everything which keeps the engines of economy running, but not for making the world safe for living with clean air and water. Climate change affects us all. Therefore, it is only a truly global effort that can save the world.

Developed countries should cut their carbon emissions at least by 80% by the year 2050, with 20-30% cuts by 2030, if the earth has to be saved from a complete environmental catastrophe, says the Human Development Report (HDR) 2007 released on Tuesday, Nov. 27, 2007. The report also calls for 20% cuts in carbon emissions by fast growing economies like India and China. These steps would stabilise CO2 equivalent concentration at 450 parts per million in the atmosphere (currently it is 379 process would be only 1.6% of global GDP upto 2030. To achieve these emission targets, the report proposes a set of policies which include carbon taxation, cap-and-trade programmes, reduction in emission quotas, encouraging renewable energy through economic incentives, stringent implementation of efficiency measures in industry, buildings and transport and support to breakthrough technologies for carbon capture and storage.

The United Nations Development Programme's annual report focuses on various aspects of human development like health, gender and poverty every year. The 2007 report makes a stronger case for action on climate change which it calls the 'defining human development issue of our generation. Drawing upon the scientific evidence revealed by the Intergovernmental Panel on Climate Change (IPCC), the UN report says that there is a small window of opportunity in this century for limiting the global temperature increase of 2 degrees Centigrade. If this is not done, humanity will face a series of climatic changes that will wreak havoc on the planet. These will include flooding of coastal areas crop failures, epidemics, severe water scarcity, and increase in natural disasters.

In perhaps the most severe indictment of the way governments have been handling the issue of climate change, last year's report says "the gap between scientific evidence and political response remains large." "The world's poor and future generations cannot afford the complacency and prevarication that continues to characterise international negotiations on climate change." It says, calling for a slew of measures to hasten global cooperation on the issue, world leaders are stated to meet in Bali, Indonesia, in December last year to discuss measures for controlling carbon emissions. The Kyoto Protocol which called for voluntary cuts in emissions is set to expire in 2012, but major emitters like the US and Australia have not signed it.

The world is in our hands. As we entered the third millennium, humanity is faced with a daunting challenge. The global economy is expanding amidst a global deterioration in the environment. In this articles argue, unless we arrest the current trends in the environment of planet earth, there will soon be an economic decline as well. We need a shift in paradigms to deal with shrinking forests,

GREENHOUSE GASES: MAJOR CULPRITS

Country	*CO_2 Emissions (Million Tons)*	*Growth rate (1990-2004)*	*CO_2 Emissions per capita (Tons)*
United States	6046	25	20.6
China	5007	109	3.8
Russia	1524	-23	10.6
India	1342	97	1.2
Japan	1257	17	9.9
Germany	808	-18	9.8
Canada	639	54	20.0
United Kingdom	587	1	9.8
Korea	465	93	9.7
Italy	450	15	7.8
World	28983	28	4.5

falling water tables, disappearing plants species and the changing climate. There is no time to lose. The balance of nature is being destroyed through sound, air and water pollution, causing danger to the lives of all living beings. It is time for us to wake-up and safe-guard our earth for today and tomorrow. The environmental challenges in India mirror those in the rest of the world. Here, people's movements to protect the environment and livelihoods are calling for a new model of development that provides benefits for all without stripping the environment and destroying livelihoods.

As the 21st century begins, several well-established environment trends are shaping the future of civilization like population growth, rising temperature, falling water tables, shrinking cropland per person, collapsing fisheries, shrinking forests and the loss of plant and animal species. Global average temperature has also risen during the last three decades—the period when carbon dioxide (CO_2) levels have been rising most rapidly. The rich countries are too broke to save the world, they have money for weapons and research.

But not for fighting global warming. They have money for everything which helps the engineers of economy running, but not making the world safe for living.

The time has come for the save world from global warming earth on fire.

- Let us have deeds, not words.
- Let us have life, not death.
- Let us have peace, not war.
- Let us have policy, not dilemma.
- Let us have prove, not promise.
- Let us have security, not ruin.
- Let us have bread, not bomb.
- Let us have survival, not elimination.
- Let us have new clear concept, not nuclear development.
- Let us work towards a clean, green and healthy atmosphere. For today and tomorrow.

It can be done, if the people of the world unite to do it. Start today, because tomorrow, we may not have a planet left to save.

A more secure world is our shared responsibility. Hazards to our security must be countered where they emerge. Today, the world's focus is on economics. Since the planet's resources are limited, and our lives are driven by the engine of economics, war is inevitable. Unless subtler aspect of life becomes important, peace remains a dream. Our greatest priority should be changing people's mind-set and behaviour so that they are grounded in a culture of peace.

We should always remember that do not fear your enemies—the worst they can do is kill you. Do not fear your friends—the worst they can do is betray you. Fear the indifferent—they neither kill nor betray, but only with their silent consent do betrayal and murder exist on earth. All peoples, every inhabitant of our planet must become aware of the impending danger, become aware of it in order to pool their efforts in the struggle for existence. In conclusion I would like to say that I believe green peace is likely not only to remain international in its scope and vision but will become increasingly global threat and opportunities. None than this, I believe it is clear that, due to the dominance of industrialism, the main difficulties we face—ecological and societal in the form of rethinking politics and its relation with environment, economics, science and technology—are found in very similar forms all over the world. It is time for us to wake-up and safeguard our earth for today and tomorrow.

References

1. Survey of the Environment—2000, The Hindu Publication.
2. Editorial: Times of India.
3. Global Warming, Subodh Verma, Times of India, Nov. 29, 2007.
4. National Security, Prabhakaran Paleri, New Delhi.
5. Environmental Education, R.L. Madan, New Delhi.
6. Whence the threat to peace, Military Publishing House, Moscow, 1987.
7. Global warming issue, Dr. S.K. Mishra.
8. Nuclear Holocaust: A Threat to all, S.K. Mishra.

Chapter 11

THE ENVIRONMENTAL CHALLENGES AND ITS SECURITY IMPLICATIONS FOR SOUTH ASIA

*Dr. Abhaya Kumar Singh**

Introduction

Armed conflicts are often caused by disputes over shared resources and struggles over these resources are often the result of population depletion, degradation, or unsustainable use. Environmental issues often have a direct impact on armed forces and national security as well. A number of scholars have recently asserted that large-scale human-induced environmental pressures may seriously affect national and international security. Unfortunately; the environment-security theme encompasses an almost unmanageable array of sub-issues, especially if we define

* Associate Professor, Dept. of Defence & Strategic Studies, K. S. Saket Post Graduate College, (Dr. R. M.L. Awadh University) Ayodhya, Faizabad.

"security" broadly to include human, physical, social, and economic well-being. Environmental change may contribute to conflicts as diverse as war, terrorism, or diplomatic and trade disputes. Furthermore, it may have different causal roles: in some cases, it may be a proximate and powerful cause; in others, it may only be a minor and distant player in a tangled story that involves many political, economic, and physical factors.

Environmental change is a serious and long term challenge that has the potential to affect each and every one of us. It is one of the biggest issues facing the world today—a regional and global threat, no nation can resolve alone. The South Asian region's volatile geological situation and high degree of mutual mistrust and the potential for environmental degradation to trigger events means environmental factors could become a major cause of instability and threat to South Asian security. This region comprises of seven adjacent countries—India, Pakistan, Sri Lanka, Bhutan, Nepal, Maldives and Bangladesh. The region has many inter-state rivers and common sea coastline extending from Pakistan in the West to Bangladesh in the East. Five of them share land borders with India except the island nations of Sri Lanka and Maldives. Bhutan and Nepal are land locked nation. This geographic contiguity is separated by geo-political rivalries and security concerns between the different political units, whose political system run from a well established and deeply rooted democracy in India to an inexperienced one in Bangladesh and uncertainty in Nepal through monarchy in Bhutan to military dictatorship in Pakistan. Internally, these nations are struggling with their own internal problems.

The attention demanded by increasing domestic problems and struggling political, economic and social interests between them confine environmental problems primarily to the realm of low politics. This is also because the complexity of environmental problems and the intricate linkages between development, population, poverty, ethnic conflict and mass migration to the natural environment are often indirect or difficult to understand. Yet, the fundamentals can not be ignored. There are four main interrelated social effects in South Asian region—population growth, reduced agricultural production, economic decline, population displacement, and disruption of regular and legitimized social relations. These social effects, in turn, may cause several specific types of conflict, including scarcity disputes between countries, clashes between ethnic groups, and civil strife and insurgency, each with potentially serious repercussions for the security interests of the South Asia.

ENVIRONMENTAL THREATS FOR SOUTH ASIA: AN OVERVIEW

1. Global Warming

Global warming is the increase in the average temperature of the earth and the oceans in the recent times and the likelihood of a continued increase in temperature in future. Gases like Carbon dioxide, Methane, Ozone, Nitrous oxide, Sulpher hexafluoride HFCs and PFCs as well as water vapour—called greenhouse gases—collect in the atmosphere like a blanket trapping the Sun's heat that is radiated off the earth's surface. These emissions of Carbon dioxide and other greenhouse gases into the atmosphere help trap heat and lead to global warming. The Fourth Assessment Report of the Intergovernmental Panel on Climate Change (IPCC) clearly established that warming of the climate system was 'unequivocal' and if the annual emission of Greenhouse gases remains are today's levels, by 2050 it will be 550 parts per million. This means a potentially catastrophic mean global temperature increase of 5 degree Celsius. That would imply seas rising and submerging half of Bangladesh. Glaciers would melt, leading first to floods and then droughts as river run dry. There would be more dengue, more malaria, and more diarrhoea.[1]

Global warming is sure to become one of the most pressing security issues of this century. Global warming could reverse decades of social and economic progress across South Asia, where food shortages loom and more than half the continent's 4 billion people live along vulnerable coasts, a new report issued by Oxfam and Greenpeace in its document "Asia-Up in Smoke." It reports on the growing scientific consensus that all of South Asia will warm during this century, and the result could be less predictable rainfall and monsoons affecting the food supply.[2] Most scientists agree that temperature will rise by between 2 to 6 degrees Celsius this century due to carbon emissions from burning fossil fuels for power and transport. They say this will cause melting at the polar ice caps and weather patterns to change bringing floods, famines and violent storms, putting billions of lives at risk.[3] A temperature rise of between 3 and 4 degree Celsius would displace 340 million people through flooding, droughts would diminish farm output, and retreating glaciers would cut drinking water from as many as 1.8 billion people.[4] It will reorder the political map by submerging some nations, flooding others, and creating refugees from rising waters. All of Maldives and large parts of Bangladesh are among the South Asian regions estimated to go under water.[5] The United Nations' Intergovernmental Panel on Climate Change (IPCC) estimates that sea-level will rise 9 to 88 cm by the year of 2100 with a 50 per cent probability of sea-level rising to 45 cm.[6] The NASA scientists are projecting that the Arctic sea ice was melting so rapidly that it could be disappear entirely by the summer of 2040.[7] A NASA scientist Jay Zwally said that if the melting of Arctic ice is so rapidly the Arctic Ocean could be nearly ice-free at the end of summer by 2012 much faster than previous prediction.[8]

In the monsoon season one-third of the Bangladesh's land is submerged in water. This would mean a significant displacement of Bangladeshi people internally and externally. India could face severe problems in case of large scale migration if such a situation arises, complicating its already worse security situation. The global warming may also worsen the crisis in agricultural production. While a two-to-three degree Celsius mean global warming might not seem too significant for agricultural production, it may produce a large increase in crop-devastating droughts, floods, heat waves, and storms.[9]

2. Population Growth and Its Impact on South Asia

One of the main drivers behind environmental scarcity in South Asia is population growth. The region is among the most densely populated in the world. Population growth and increasing population density represent demographic forms of social change. Population growth may lead to geographic expansion of a society, military conflicts, and the intermingling of cultures. Increasing population density may stimulate technological innovations, which in turn may increase the division of labour, social differentiation, commercialization, and urbanization. On the other hand, population growth may contribute to economic stagnation and increasing poverty, as may be witnessed in several South Asian countries today.

In South Asian region three countries—India, Pakistan and Bangladesh are among the world's 10 most populous countries. India's current population is 1.10 billion and by 2050 it is predicted to overtake China, Pakistan's current population of 159 million will reach 295 by 2050 and Bangladesh with a population of 141 million will have twice that number by 2050.[10] High population growth rates lead to more intense use of resources, exacerbating existing scarcities and over exploitation.[11] The region's population growth will have a direct bearing on its renewable resource system such as forest, land and water as well as on energy demand. The renewable resources are being subjected to significant pressures. Some important factors like deforestation, land degradation and water crisis indicates a high level of stress on the South Asia region's renewable ecosystem.

On account of industrial and agricultural expansion as well as trade in forestry products, deforestation remains a major concern in South Asia. Bangladesh and Pakistan are the countries with the highest rates of deforestation. In Nepal too, over 75% of population depends on fuel wood for energy needs, which puts tremendous pressure on the country's forest resources. Landslides and soil erosion increase the sediment loads in rivers and cause sedimentation and flooding downstream.[12]

Areas with most extensive degradation, already, include the cultivated Himalayan belt in India and Nepal, the Western Ghats of India and watershed areas of Sri Lanka. According to the Food and Agriculture Organisation forest resources assessment 2005, the six countries of South Asia (India, Pakistan, Bangladesh, Nepal, Bhutan and Sri Lanka) together account for the loss of more than half a million hectares of forest annually between 1990 and 2000.[13] The FAO predicts that at existing rate of deforestation, Bangladesh and Pakistan will completely loose their forest by 2011 and 2015 respectively.[14] It is very alarming for the South Asian countries.

In the continuing struggle to provide food and other basic needs of the South Asian region's burgeoning populace, land degradation has emerged as an important issue. Soils suffer from varying degrees of degradation on account of rapid deforestation, poor irrigation and drainage practices, and overgrazing. The depletion of land resources through desertification and the loss of nutrient-rich topsoil through water and wind erosion threaten the livelihood of countless millions throughout the region. The per capita unit land resources are below the world average of 0.26 hectares in South Asian countries. Population increase and unsustainable agricultural practices are primary contributors to land shortage and land degradation. Another cause of land degradation common to the countries in the region is mining, which is typically unorganized and unscientific, without any defined environmental management and land reclamation plans. In some cases there are clear trans-boundary impacts. Poor mining practices in the dolomite mining areas of Bhutan, adjoining the state of West Bengal in India, have resulted in increased landslides and soil erosion. The Indian foothills have taken the burden of landslide debris.

Depletion of aquifers in many parts of the South Asian countries and growing demand for water will bring agricultural, industrial, and urban use of water into conflict. This shortage will force water-usage restrictions and will increase the cost of water consumption. Water could become the "energy crisis" of the early 2000. Conflicts over water will grow over the coming decades as growing populations demand more and climate change affects supply. With the overwhelming majority of the world's rivers shared by two or more nations, these challenges will test diplomats and political leaders worldwide.[15] Some South Asian countries are in water crisis. South Asian countries may fight over dwindling supplies of water and the effects of upstream pollution. The quantitative supply problems are increasing. It is estimated that India will enter the stress zone by 2025, where the per capita water availability fell from 6000 cubic meters in 1947 to 2300 cubic meters in 1998. Estimates for the year 2050 predict acute shortage of water in India,[16] Pakistan, Sri Lanka and Bangladesh shortly after 2025.[17] The rapid growth of both agriculture and urbanization has imposed growing pressure on the region's already strained water resources in terms of both quantity and quality. This is evident in the gradual decline in per capita availability of water throughout the region.

3. Population Displacement

Environmental crisis in the rural areas of developing countries has increasingly become an important cause of cross-border migration of population and South Asia is no exception of this phenomenon. Bulging populations and land stress may produce waves of environmental refugees,[18] that spill across borders with destabilizing effects on the recipient's domestic order and on regional stability. Large scale migration in South Asia has continued unabated for last five decades. This gravest problem has been faced by India from last twenty years. In 2003, India has about 20 million Bangladeshi migrants to neighbouring West Bengal and Assam and various parts of India,19 2.2 million Nepalese, 70,000 Sri Lankan Tamils and about 100 thousand Tibetans.[20] Presently, this migration is limited not only to Assam, Tripura and West Bengal but is to far-off states like Tamil Nadu, Maharashtra, Gujarat and Delhi.[21] This phenomenon has generated a host of destabilising political, social, economic, ethnic and communal tensions in many states and union territories of India.

Issues of migration or population displacement, refugee repatriation and alleged state support for insurgent groups have become a point of tension between India and Bangladesh. It is alleged that this migration has not only environmental base, instead they are induced to cause premeditated population imbalance on religion line. Subversive elements are being pushed by ISI in the garb of environmental migrants to implement its sinister design of 'Greater Bangladesh'.[22] It is a challenge for India to manage its borders. In this situation, it is the first and foremost duty of our leadership to take concrete action to secure our frontiers and sub-serve the best interests of the country.

4. Food Production

In South Asian countries, a sharp drop in food crop production could lead to internal strife across urban-rural and nomadic-sedentary cleavages.[23] If environmental degradation makes food supplies increasingly tight, exporters may be tempted to use food as a weapon.[24] The region's economy is heavily reliant on climate-sensitive sectors such as agriculture and forestry. The impacts of climatic change on potential rice production, as studied by the International Rice Research Institute indicate that increasing temperatures may decrease rice potential yield up to 7.4 per cent per degree increase in temperature,[25] while wheat production could fall by 32% by 2050.[26] The changes in rainfall pattern and distribution owing to climatic change can lead to shifting of agricultural lands and may also force intensive cultivation of marginal lands which in turn will exacerbate deforestation in future. Environmental change could ultimately cause the gradual impoverishment of societies in this region, which could aggravate class and ethnic cleavages, undermine liberal regimes, and spawn insurgencies.[27]

5. Agricultural Land and Agricultural Production

Land constitutes the most important natural resource of South Asia and agriculture is the most important activity using this resource. For South Asian countries, cropland grew at just 0.26 per cent during the 1980s, less than half the rate of the 1970s. More importantly, in these countries per capita arable land dropped by 1.9 per cent a year.[28] In the absence of a major increase in arable land in South Asian countries, experts expect that the per capita world average of 0.28 hectares of cropland will decline to 0.17 hectares by the year 2025, given the current rate of world population growth,[29] 73 per cent of all rural households in developing countries are either landless or nearly landless. In the case of Bangladesh and Bhutan, per capita unit land resources are well below the world average of 0.26 hectares. Population increase and unsustainable agricultural practices are primarily contributors to land shortage and land degradation. For example, In India, the intensive agriculture has degraded 125 million hectares of land owing to monoculture, salinity and water logging with a result many fertile lands are now wastelands.[30] Large tracts are being lost each year to urban encroachment, developmental projects, and environmental degradation—erosion, nutrient depletion, salinization, water logging, acidification, and compacting. The geographer Vaclav Smil, who is generally very conservative in his assessments of environmental damage, estimates that two to three million hectares of cropland are lost annually to erosion; perhaps twice as much land goes to urbanization, and at least one million hectares are abandoned because of excessive salinity.[31]

Decreased agricultural production is often mentioned as potentially the most worrisome consequence of environmental change. The effects of this change causing greenhouse warming and climate change which affect the agricultural production. Coastal cropland in countries such as Bangladesh is extremely vulnerable to storm surges. Such events could become more common and devastating, because global warming will cause sea levels to rise and might intensify storms. The greenhouse effect will also change precipitation patterns and soil moisture; while this may benefit some agricultural regions, others will suffer. Many plants grow faster and larger in a warm environment rich in carbon dioxide, and they often use water more efficiently.[32] Thus, the scarcity of productive agricultural land and decline in agricultural production seem to be two important reasons for inducing cross border migration in South Asia. One study suggests that the number of people crossing over to India increases during periods of environmental disaster.[33] If these situations continue unabated, the volume of migration from affected countries will increase in the future and sheer dictates of history, geography and economy will encourage their movements to India and other countries.

Thus, it is a matter of great concern that the seriousness of the environmental crisis as a threat to security escapes the attention of the policy makers of the region. The governments of the region should come forward to check the menace before it becomes too late.

Preventive Measures to Control the Environmental Challenges

The prevention is for cheaper than cure in every one of these instances—whether it's curbing adaptive reinforcement of structures in disaster-prone areas. The cost of such prevention is usually a fraction, often less than 1% of GNP, while the gains from such action are multiple of that. The social calculus would seem to be obvious-it pays to take care of South Asian countries and the planet's conditions. Then why the South Asian nation's governments do not take the needed protective measures? A primary reason is that no single South Asian country has enough motivation or the political will to comfort global problems alone. That's because only a part of the benefits accrue to those taking action, while others can have a free ride, a dilemma compounded by competitive pressures. Equally important, even when the gains from actions are local, they accrue over a time frame that stretches beyond the tenure of most politicians.

This split between what is good for society and what drives private interest can only is addressed by concerted action by regional governments. But for that to happen there needs to be a change in the mindset of the policy governments to feature the environment in growth policies as well as in the measures of economic success—

1. Deep Cuts in Carbon Emissions

It must lead to deep cuts in Carbon emissions by developed and South Asian countries. South Asian countries need to arrest or slow down deforestation, which accounts for a filth of all Greenhouse gas emissions, more than from all of transportation. The policy shift needs to stop encouraging the waste of natural resources, hard as it is politically. The world spends a quarter of a trillion dollars a year on energy subsidies, draining the public purse, promoting energy waste and locking the polluting infrastructure for decades. In many South Asian countries, ware for agriculture is undervalued, while globally, the overuse of freshwater is estimated at 5-25%. Even when intended for the poor, these energy and water subsidies are not well-targeted anyway, be in it South Asia.

2. Population Control

Unabated population growth, as at present, not only adds to the economic burden for all developmental activities, but also reduces the impact of economic growth on our society. Therefore, for the success of our planning, population control becomes the most urgent necessity. A comprehensive programme, with strong political backing and appropriate socio-economic measures, fully utilizing the available scientific know how, simultaneously making efforts for developing new methodologies, and supported by modern communication technology and managerial and organizational skills, is essential for success in this most difficult area. Population control should be a national mission for the next decade.

3. Strengthening of Institutions and Legislation

Recent years have witnessed the emergence of a number of national and local responses to environmental problems in countries of the Indian subcontinent. These initiatives have taken the form of development of national environmental action plans, environmental regulation, and some effort to seek market-based remedies. In some countries, intervention has taken the form of decentralization and devolution of power to local/provincial governments for environment planning and management, as well as increased support for grass-roots organizations such as associations of water-users in the design and implementation of solutions.

Among the institutional mechanisms for regional cooperation on the environment, the most significant one is SACEP (South Asia Cooperative Environment Programme), established in 1982 under the aegis of the United Nations. Its membership consists of nine countries: seven member nations of SAARC (South Asian Association for Regional Cooperation), Afghanistan, and Iran. SACEP's Council, consisting of the ministers of environment and forests in member countries, meets once in two years. Its secretariat is in Colombo, Sri Lanka. The organization implements projects funded by the UN and other multilateral or bilateral agencies. Given the gravity of common concerns in the region, there is an urgent need for an agenda to implement remedial action among countries of the region. The establishment of SACEP and efforts within the framework of SAARC are clear steps in the right direction. In view of extensive loss of life and colossal damage to property as a result of earthquake and tsunami and other natural disasters in South Asia, the Heads of State underscored the urgency to put in place a permanent regional response mechanism dedicated to disaster preparedness, emergency relief and rehabilitation to ensure immediate response. They underlined the need for collaborating action in the area of environment to promote sustainable development. They decided to proclaim the year 2007 as the "Year of Green South Asia," devoted to a region-wise aforestation campaign.[34] However, translating broad principles into concrete action will need the coordinated efforts of many institutions within governments, public sector organizations, and private institutions. While efforts within SACEP and SAARC may take some time before they lead to any action, there are other avenues for regional cooperation to be explored.[35]

It will require strengthening of existing institutions at different levels. It will need a close linkage among the compartmentalized sectors which have been historically dealt with by separate organizations. It will call for a change in the institutional mechanism for enlisting public participation. It will necessitate quick decision making on development projects based on assessment of their potential of rendering long term sustainable benefits to the society at large, particularly vulnerable sections. It will also require effective implementation of laws and regulations for environmental protection through strengthening of and closer interaction among the regulatory bodies and administrative machinery. Existing laws and enforcement mechanisms should be subjected to periodic review to evaluate their adequacy and efficacy in the light of changed circumstances and experience.

4. Training and Orientation Programmes in Environmental Management

Formal education and training programme in specialized areas of pollution control and environmental management will be a continuing need. For this purpose, intensive programmes for education and training will need to be introduced in the Universities, Indian Institute of Technologies and other professional institutions. Environmental education at the school level including training of teachers shall be an important component of educational programmes.

5. Promoting Environmental Awareness

The mass media ranging from local folklores to electronic media should serve as a vital role to raise public awareness and involvement in environmental activities. The development of environmental education resource material and use of traditional and modem media of communication need to be strengthened to raise the public awareness on environmental issues and to promote people's participation in environmental activities and conservation of natural resources. We believe a combined and sustained effort by the corporate and media can make a major contribution towards making environmental change a national priority.

6. Rehabilitation of Project Ousters

While implementing the projects in various sectors, conscious efforts should be made to avoid displacement of local people. Where it is unavoidable, necessary measures should be taken to ensure their rehabilitation by providing suitable facilities.

7. Strong Political wills of Regional Governments

Above all, it requires a strong political will on the part of regional governments. The political environment of South Asian nations is not very much encouraging. The political initiative obligatory to implement the suggestions is not coming forth. Governments of the region should come forward and should take concrete action to comprehend the emerging threats of the environmental mismanagement.

Conclusion

It is only through such initiatives the contours of which have been highlighted in preceding paragraphs, we will be in a position to resolve the conflicts which often arise between the environmental concerns and developmental pursuits that have a direct bearing on the very fabric of our society and life styles. The task before us would be daunting if it were not for the many positive factors that are emerging: people's movements to conserve their own environment, greater public and media concern for environmental issues and spread of environmental awareness among children and youth. It is up to us, as nations and their citizens, to undertake development process in keeping with our heritage and the traditional conservation ethos and in harmony with the environmental imperatives of this land. South Asian Countries experiencing chronic internal conflict because of environmental stress will probably either fragment or become more authoritarian. Fragmenting countries will be the source of large out-migrations, and they will be unable to effectively negotiate or implement international agreements on security, trade and environmental protection. Authoritarian regimes may be inclined to launch attacks against other countries to divert popular attention from internal stresses. Any of these outcomes could seriously disrupt South Asian security. The social impacts of environmental scarcity therefore deserve concerted attention from security scholars. Effective implementation of necessary measures, as outlined in this paper, will be facilitated by a partnership role of South Asian nation's Governments. Many environmental problems assume regional significance. Hence, the policies and programmes at the regional level should be drawn up keeping in view overall national policy considerations.

The recent frenzy in the debate on climate change at Bali-Indonesia, and some commitments to act, are timely and welcome. But any real impact will hinge on how regional and international leaders and their governments of the economy chart growth policies. For tangible results, they must greatly elevate the priority for the environment—without which the drive for growth will be self defeating, mired in its own devastation.

Above all it can be said that "Either we act quickly, or prepare to join the dinosaurs. Alternatively, find another planet."

References

1. The Times of India, December 10, 2007.
2. The Times of India, November 20, 2007.
3. The Times of India, January 5, 2007.
4. The Times of India, November 20, 2007.
5. The Times of India, February 5, 2007
6. Uttam K. Sinha, Environmental Stresses and their Security Implications for South Asia, Strategic Analysis, Vol. 30, No. 3, Jul-Sep.2006, p. 604).
7. The Times of India, December 13, 2007.
8. Ibid.
9. WRI, et al., World Resources 1990-91, p. 111.
10. Population Reference Bureau, 2004, World Population Data

Sheet, p. 1. quoted by Uttam K. Sinha, Environmental Stresses and their Security Implications for South Asia, Strategic Analysis, Vol. 30, No. 3, Jul-Sep.2006, pp. 601-60.

11. http://www.un.org/popin/fao/centasia/faotext 1.htm
12. http://static.teriin.org/energy/envsec.htm#water
13. http://www.un.org/popin/cenasia/faotex3.htm
14. Ibid.
15. http://www.pacinst.org/topics/environment and security
16. http://static.teriin.org/energy/envsec.htm#water
17. Uttam K. Sinha, Environmental Stresses and their Security Implications for South Asia, Strategic Analysis, Vol. 30, No. 3, Jul-Sep. 2006, p. 603.
18. Jodi Jacobson, Environmental Refugees: A Yardstick of Habitability, World Watch Paper No. 86 (Washington, D.C.: World Watch Institute, 1988.
19. The Hindustan Times, January 3, 2003.
20. Uttam K. Sinha, Environmental Stresses and their Security Implications for South Asia, Strategic Analysis, Vol. 30, No. 3, Jul-Sep. 2006, pp. 609.
21. http://www.thesouthasian.org/archives/000113.html
22. Dr. Nand Kishore, 'Bangladeshi Ghuspaith ka Nihitarth', Sanatan Prabhat (monthly) Goa, December, 2005.
23. Peter Wallensteen, "Food Crops as a Factor in Strategic Policy and Action," Westing, Global Resources, pp. 151-155.
24. Ibid. p. 146-151.
25. www.epa.com and www.fao.com
26. The Times of India, November 20, 2007.
27. Ted Gurr, "On the Political Consequences of Scarcity and Economic Decline," International Studies Quarterly, Vol. 29, No. 1 (March 1985), pp. 51-75.
28. Nafis Sadik, The State of the World Population 1990, (New York: United Nations Population Fund, 1990), p. 8.
29. WRI, et al., World Resources 1990-91, p. 87.
30. Uttam K. Sinha, op.cit., p. 603.
31. Thomas F Homer-Dixon, "On Threshold: Environmental Changes as causes of Acute Conflict," International Security, Vol. 16, No. 2, 1991, p. 109.

32. R.A. Warrick, R.M. Gifford, and M.L. Parry, "CO_2, Climatic Change and Agriculture: Assessing the Response of Food Crops to the Direct Effects of Increased CO_2 and Climatic Change," in Bert Bolin, et al, (ed). The Greenhouse Effect, Climatic Change, and Ecosystems, SCOPE No. 29 (New York: Wiley, 1986), pp. 393-474.
33. Sarfaraj Alam, Environmentally Induced Migration from Bangladesh to India, Strategic Analysis, Vol. 27, No. 3, Jul-Sep. 2003, p. 433.
34. Strategic Digest, Vol. 35, No. 12, December 2005, pp. 1613-14.
35. Environmental Security in South Asia, Romir Chatterjee, at http://static.teriin.org/energy/envsec.htm#response

Chapter 12

THE DYNAMICS OF SOCIAL AND ECONOMICAL CHALLENGES FOR SUSTAINABLE ENVIRONMENT IN SOUTH ASIA

*Dr. Sarvesh Gautam**

Environmental protection and social rights are major fields for the subject of Sustainability. Sustainability is the concept derived from a discussion about the recognition of global ecological problems and globally increasing Social Problems of poverty as a result of Economic Development process. It represents the extension of the Social concept responsibility in relation to the Global Development conditions of humanity and as based on the assumption that ecological, economical and social problems have to be solved by means of new integrated strategies involving guiding actions. Our species has a special gift, the ability to recall the past and foresee the future. Once we have a vision of the future, every decision

* UGC Research Fellow, Defence & Strategic St., University of Allahabad.

becomes a moral judgment. Those who understand what is happening to mother earth the only mother earth the only home for us and other species will not shrink from the responsibility to help make the transition to a Sustainable Society.

With the growth of technology and industries the modernists believed that they could not only tap the basic secrets of nature but also establish a society in which these would be greater rationality and greater justice. Hence it was urged that the inculcation and development of what is known as scientific temper in the field not only of science but of human relations and social conduct was what was needed most urgently. But today, the worst problem we face is the various crises of the environment that have arisen as by product of scientific development. It is alleged by the environmentalists that tremendous growth of science and technology has led to endangering the very equilibrium of the ecosystem. The 1970's and 1980's were periods of intense academic and popular interest in environmental issues. The ecological movement started during the period focuses its attention on the kind of relation between human life and its natural environment.

The environmental impact of Socio-Economic activities in the past was small enough for the natural environment to recover and regenerate on its own. However, since the Industrial Revolution the environmental impact has grown rapidly and steadily to a point where our Socio-Economic activities have far exceeded the regenerative capacities of Earth's eco-system resulting in degradation of Environment. To pass on the valuable Global Environment to future generation's people need to recognize that they are all part of nature and should strictly limit their economic activities to a level that are within the regenerative capacities of Ecosystem. In order to overcome the most serious threat to our own existence due to emerging environmental degradation. We need to face it with great indepth understanding and innovative approach for enhanced material and energy effectivity in production and usage, with structural economic change in our planning to less resources intense sectors for achieving Sustainable Development.

Global unsustainability is due to two basic trends that have now reached critical thresholds:[1]

- The worldwide growth of the human population and its increasing use of the planet's physical resources and biological life-support system.
- The accelerating depletion of many of the planet's physical resources and impairment of its biological life-support systems.

In a very precise statement, the connection of population and environment has been explained right on target thus "As human population increases and globalization proceeds. Key policy questions are, how to use available resources of land and water to produce food for all, how to promote economic development and end poverty so that all can afford to eat and in doing so how to address the human and environmental consequences of industrialization and concerns like global warming, climate change and loss of biological diversity."[2] The size of the human population, multiplied by the amount of resources it uses and the waste and pollution it generates. Specifies the load placed on the planet's physical resources and biological systems. The problem of unsustainability arises because global resources are in finite supply and its biological life support systems are progressively impaired. Given the continuation of these trends, the demand and supply curves will intercept. Humanity's demand will exceed the planet's readily accessible supplies and effective regenerative capacities that will threaten the survival of the human population, most immediately its poorest, economically and politically weakest segments. The above are long-term trends, but previously, they have not posed an acute survival threat. It was only in the middle of the 19th century that the human population reached the level of one billion, but by today the population grew to more than 6.6 billion. Although this is a large number, in purely quantitative terms it is not critical humankind still constitute only 0.14% of the quantitative growth of human population, but because of its per capita resource use.[3] In the past 50 years humankind has used more of the planet's resources than in all of the preceding millennia put together. At present global resource use exceeds the level of Sustainability.

Climate change is the most important Global Environmental Challenge facing humanity with implications for food production, natural ecosystems, fresh water supply and health. The rising temperature of earth is responsible for this. It is rising steadily. The Intergovernmental Panel on Climate Change (IPCC) an international body of over 3000 experts, projects that the global mean temperature may increase between 1.8 to 4°C per decade, almost double the annual increase over the last 50 years, is projected for the next two decades. The IPCC predictions have become increasingly worse over the past 15 years and their attribution to human influence has become more certain. Such temperature increases have worst effect will be on poorer countries even though the problem has been created by the rich.[4] Even if the process of global warming cannot be reversed, the rate at which the earth's temperature is rising can be checked by measures that both rich and poor countries can adopt not. For the growing economy of India and China such measures are urgent as the negative impacts of climate changed could adversely affect their rate of growth. The unprecedented increase is expected to have severe impacts on the Global Hydrological System, ecosystem, sea level, crop production and related process.

Earlier in the early 1970's, drawing on experiments by persons such as the Indian Sir Jagdish Chandra Bose, two authors conducted experiments on plants explaining the unknown force in the vegetable kingdom.(Peter Tompkins and Christopher) Birds. The Secret Life of Plants (Middlesex: Penguin Book, 1973). The proved that synthetic chemicalisation is harmful to the soil. Nature way through organic farming is the best solution. The test case of human communication with plants still exists at find harm in Scotland as the find Horn Foundation. Here, after World War-II Squadron leader Peter Caddy settled in a Wasteland to turn it into a green patch. Much to the surprise of agricultural experts.[5]

The comprehensive security is the object that needs to include human and environmental security. Water is one of the most important environmental resources that entail the concept of security origination from the human actor. Water resources are facing or about to face serious stress. They are falling short, leading to disputes over sharing. Some of these stresses that need to be understood are:[6]

a) Drop in per capita figure due to population increase.
b) Provision of safe drinking water.
c) Conflicting priorities over water use among the agriculture, industrial and domestic sectors.
d) Problems in urban water supply and planning.
e) Depletion of ground water resources.
f) Water-logging and salination.
g) Floods.
h) Soil erosion.
i) Pollution of rivers, coastal areas and oceans due to anthropogenic reasons like Chemicalisation of

agriculture and effluents and waste from industries.

j) Disputes between states over sharing of river water.

Industrialization has provided livelihood and opportunities to million in urban worlds. However, it has also brought in its wake problem of waste disposal, contamination of environmental-air, soil, surface water bodies and ground water aquifer etc., which have resulted in contamination hazard imperiling human beings, livestock and plant life. Lack of proper planning in siting of industrial units, inadequate development of infrastructure, and lack of waste management facility etc., has precipitated this debacle, turning most of them into environmental flash points. Urgent measures for amelioration, waste management, recycling waste minimizations, punitive action against defaulters etc, would facilitate halting of damage to ensure recovery.

A special analysis for Indian metropolitan cities which are facing these problems is explored below:[7]

Based on this analysis it was found that Hyderabad metropolitan region had changed drastically. While in 1971, agriculture was dominant accounting for 62.6% area with open scrub, settlement and water bodies accounting for 15, 5.7 and 5.6% respectively. However, by March 2007 Agriculture had lost its preeminence to Urbanization and built-up area accounted for 43% of the study area. There was a corresponding decrease in area under open scrub (4.2%) and water bodies (2%) and the number of water bodies' decrease from 1271 to 960 during the corresponding period. Besides these catchments of major water bodies in the region, viz. Himayat Sagar, Osman Sagar and Hussain Sagar were severely encroached upon adversely affecting inflow and decreasing dilution potential.

Similarly, Bangalore metropolitan region witnessed tremendous change in land use and land cover owing to Urbanization and Industrialization, while Agriculture was predominant in 1971 (64.82%), wasteland built-up area and water bodies occupied 11.8, 5.4 and 3.6% of the study area respectively. By March 2007 built-up area increased to 13.3% of the study area while wasteland and water bodies shrank to 8.6% and 4.1% respectively.

In Delhi region, watershed of Kirtinagar and Okhla were studied. While Okhla faces contamination hazard from pharmaceutical units, Kirtinagar is being contaminated by Dye industry. The other two industrial areas which threaten the Delhi environment are Gurgoan and Sonepat. There has been a massive population explosion in Delhi during this period. It increased from 4 million in 1970 and more than 15 million in 2007, which was accompanied with massive growth in industrial activities. However due to absence of any zoning regulation or a comprehensive plan for urban development, most industries were located haphazardly leading to overcoming traffic bottlenecks and unhealthy living conditions as many industries were located in residential areas.

In Chennai region, watersheds of Thiruvallur, Avadi, Ennore, Mandi, Kandipuram, Alture, Maraimalainagar, Nandambakkam, Pallavaram and Sriperumbudur are endangered owing to contamination. However the situation is grave at Avadi and Ennore in Thruvallur district. Chennai, population density increase tremendously during the corresponding period. In 1971 Agriculture was dominant with 57.4% of the study area while open scrub, built-up land and water bodies occupied 7.2, 10.1 and 12.8%. However by March 2007 agriculture was restricted to 43.5% while built-up area increased to 20.6%. There was a decline in area under open scrub, water body, reserved forest and mud flats along the coastline.

The "Incredible India" campaign to promote tourism in India urges people to experience the emerald islands of

Andaman and Nicobar and coastal area Goa etc. but tourism disturbing equilibrium of ecosystem, and create problem to tribes of that area. The World does not need to choose between averting climate change and promoting growth and development. Changes in energy technologies and in the structure of economies have created opportunities to decoupled growth from greenhouse gas emissions. Indeed, ignoring climate change will eventually damage economic growth. Tackling climate change is the pro-growth strategy for the longer term, and it can be done in a way that does not cap the aspirations for growth of rich or poor countries.[8]

The average atmospheric water vapour content has increased since at least the 1980s over land and ocean as well as in the upper troposphere. The increase is broadly consistent with the extra water vapour that warmer air can hold. Lake Chad and Kilimanjaro are even trickier. Lake Chad has lost 90% of its water but dams and overgrazing will have aggravated any fall in precipitation. Kilimanjaro glacier, because they mostly sublimate (turn from ice directly into vapour) rather than melt are unusual in comparisons with most mountain glaciers. The massive militarization in the eco sensitive Himalayas after he became independent has not been of our choosing. It has been thrust upon us by our adversarial neighbours due to geopolitical reasons. From a long term perspective, we may find that in us myopic vision of realism we may be fighting amongst ourselves as the Titanic prepares to sink. In that case, we all are destined to perish. This call for a new approach to peace and security like maritime security and the health of the India Ocean the Himalayan ecology is a multidisciplinary and international affair.[9]

The change perceptive and intense comparison of national, ecological and human security concerns in the region of Siachen Glacier is showing as a bar chart.[10] The

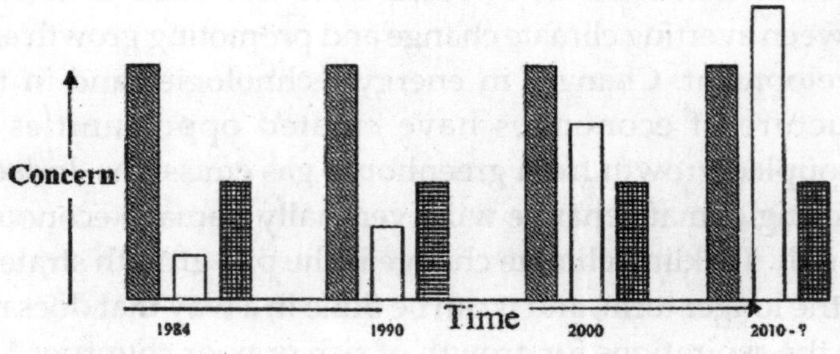

Note: ▩ National security concerns do not change
☐ Ecological security concerns keep increasing
▦ Human security of troop morale remains unchanged due to changeover of units and professionalism of both armies.

Himalayan region has the largest concentration of glaciers outside the polar caps. With glacier coverage of 33,000 sq km, the region is aptly called the "Water Tower of Asia", as it provides around 86,000,000 cubic meters of water annually. These Himalayan glaciers feed seven of Asia's great rivers. They ensure a year-round water supply to about one billion people. But the change in climate variability has led to a rapid retreat of mountain glacier systems. Satellite data show that rate of retreat in the last three decades has been more than three times the rate during the earlier 200 years or so. The pictorial plot [Fig. (A)] based on historical evidences and recent satellite data on the Gangotri glacier by Jeff Kargel of the U.S. Geological Survey illustrates the increased rate of retreat of the Gangotri.[11]

Government allocates large sums of money to their military sectors with the stated purpose of providing security for their citizens. The rationale that underlies this is based

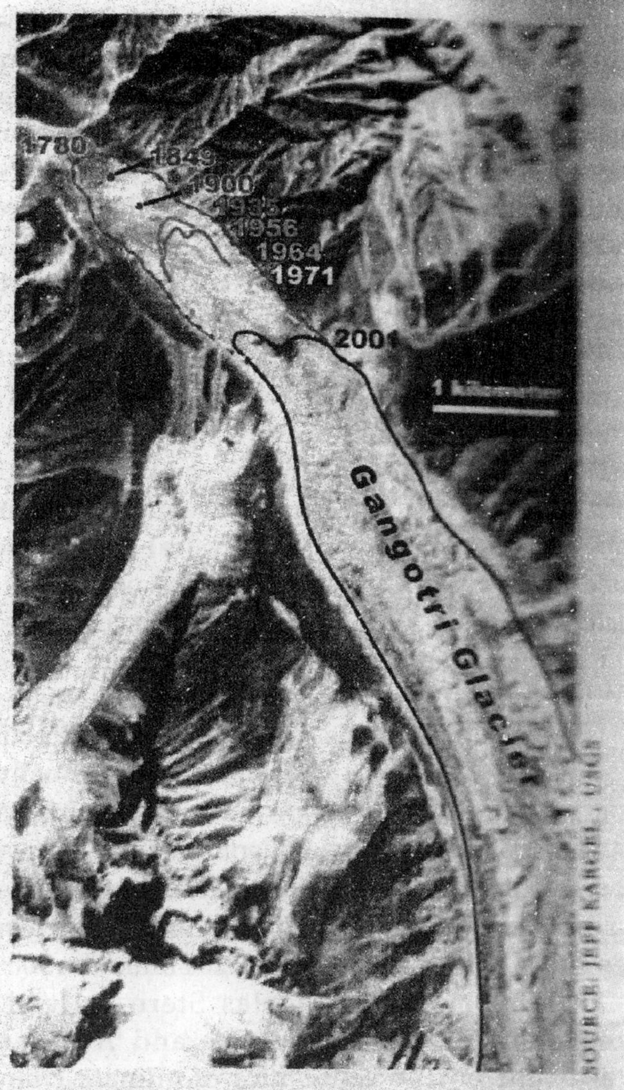

Retreat of the Gangotri glacier during the last 220 years

FIG. (A) RETREAT OF THE GANGOTRI GLACIER DURING THE LAST 220 YEARS.

on a narrow traditional concept of security that links it to the risk of organized violence. Recent security analyses taking different and broader definition of security call into question how far military measures can go towards providing security. They recognize a range of non-traditional security risks that cannot be addressed by military means. The field of public health offers many examples of areas where non-military spending could be far more cost-effective as a means to provide security of human lives. According to reports by the world health organization (WHO), among the 10 leading global risk factors identified for developing countries with high mortality rates, four are related to hunger and two are related to the physical environment—unsafe water, sanitation and hygiene, and indoor smoke. Both of these are in turn linked to poverty. Thus, preventive interventions to reduce hunger, improved the physical environment and reduce poverty are important means of improving the security of human lives. Furthermore, in comparison with military expenditure, the prevention strategies developed for the WHO and other parts of the United Nations to reduce the risks to human lives are highly cost-effective. For example, 8 million lives could be saved annually for an annual investment of $57 billion in basic health interventions, and the cost of attaining the Millennium Development Goals has been estimated at $135 billion. These levels of investment are small compares with the level of world military expenditure, which amounts to $1204 billion in 2006.[12]

The report of Sir Nicolas Stern,[13] Head of the Government Economics Service and Adviser to the Government on the economics of climate change and development.[14] This Review has assessed a wide range of evidence on the impacts of climate change and on the economic costs, and has used a number of different techniques to assess costs and risk. From all of these perspectives, the evidence gathered by the review leads to a simple conclusion: the benefits of strong and early action far outweigh the economic costs of not acting. Climate change will affect the basic elements of life for people around the world to water, food production, health, and the environment. Hundreds of millions of people could suffer hunger, water shortages and coastal flooding as the world warms. Using the results from formal economic models, the Review estimates that if we don't act, the overall costs and risks of climate change will be equivalent to losing at least 5% of global GDP each year, now and forever. If a wider range of risks and impacts is taken into account, the estimates of damage could rise to 20% of GDP or more. In contrast, the costs of action reducing greenhouse gas emissions to avoid the worst impacts of climate change can be limited to around 1% of global GDP each year. The investment that takes place in the next 10-20 years will have a profound effect on the climate in the second half of this century and in the next. Our actions now and over the coming decades could create risks of major disruption to economic and social activity, on a scale similar to those associated with the great wars and the economic depression of the first half of the 20th century. And it will be difficult or impossible to reverse these changes.

If no action is taken to reduce emissions, the concentration of greenhouse gases in the atmosphere could reach double its pre-industrial level as early as 2035, virtually committing us to a global average temperature rise of over 2°C. In the longer term, there would be very dangerous indeed; it is equivalent to the change in average temperatures from the last ice age to today. Such a radical change in the physical geography of the world must lead to major changes in the human geography— where people live and how they live their lives.

So, there are significant overlaps between the risk

factors for environment and for social and economical development, which suggests that there is an overlap in the agendas for 'freedom from want' and 'freedom from fear'. This has implications for different type of security strategy. In particular, it means that in addressing one type of security threat, others can also be considered. While economic scarcity and competition for resources are potential sources of conflict and violence, using the world's resources constructively to address hunger, environmental factors and poverty—including by transfers from the richer countries to the high-mortality developing countries—is likely both to improve human survival directly and strengthen international security indirectly. The concept of Sustainable Environment is closely linked to the carrying of ecosystem, as depicted in Fig. (B)[14]

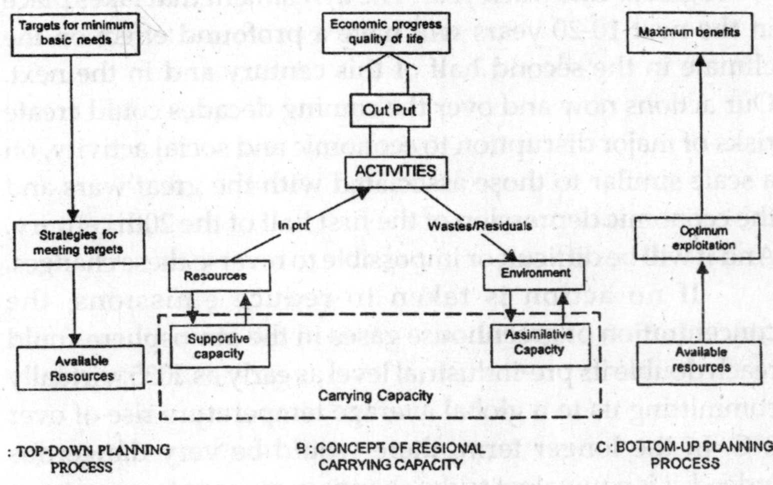

FIG. (B) THE PLANNING PROCESS-TRADITIONAL AND PROCESS

Accordingly, the underlying correlation between population, poverty and pollution must be analyzed against the backdrop of an ecosystem's capacity to provide supportive capacity for development and assimilative capacity for maintenance of an acceptable quality of environment. With these predictions, the following agenda for sustainable environment are to be incorporated in planning:[15]

- Regional Carrying-capacity-based development planning process.
- Prevention environmental policy including technology assessment.
- Structural change in economy
- Environmental impact assessment

Development planning in most countries has been traditionally based on the concept of meeting certain basic minimum needs of the poorest sections of population. This approach has led to greater inequality in the societies of developing countries as it overlooks the basic requirement of availability of the resources that form the building blocks in the development planning process based on regional carrying capacity takes cognizance of the fact that the environment, with it biotic and abiotic components, provides the basic resources that support production-consumption activities and assimilates the residues produced during the course of theses activities. Sustainable environment calls for trade-off between the desired production-consumption levels through the exploitation of supportive capacity and environmental quality within the assimilative capacity of regional ecosystems. The utilization of carrying capacity thus requires a series of adjustment to reconcile competing aspirations in the development process. This shift in the analytical models could be used to answer technical questions whereas value judgments must be made in societal and political domains for devising pragmatic development and environment strategies. Ecosystem carrying capacity provides the physical limits to economic development and may be defined as the maximum rate of resources consumption waste discharge that can be sustained indefinitely in a defined planning region without progressive bio-productivity and ecological integrity. While recognizing societal dependence on many ecological resources and functions for its survival, carrying capacity is ultimately determined by the single vital resources or functions in least supply. Working within the limits of carrying capacity does not, however, preclude some unavoidable environment damage in the course of development.

To understand the Ecological interdependence we need to become ecologically literate or Eco-literacy. Eco-literacy must be as an essential subject of school and college curricula. Universities being centers for excellence and higher learning, they have a special responsibility to transfer pertinent knowledge on various emerging global, regional and local environmental problems to young generation, so that they can develop wisdom to work for sustainable development. Nation-wide orientation classes should be arranged for adults as well as for students encouraging a symbiotic attitude on the part of humans towards all entities of the ecosystem. Allowing all entities the freedom to unfold in their own way unhindered by human domination should be the most effective force in that it can exert pressure on the authorities concerned who are often at the mercy of political pressure from various interest groups and consequently remain lethargic in developing proper technologies to face the ill effects of development.

A remarkable book combining the ecological, political, ethical, philosophical and cultural factors was Earth in the Balance (1992) written by Democrat Al Gore, the Vice President of the USA during the Clinton Administration and Peace Nobel Winner 2007. The Book deserving to be classical in its own right by a serving political emphasizes a greater role for the USA in solving the climate and environmental problem. Gore prescribed five strategic goals to save the environment. The goals identified are:

1. Stabilizing the world population.
2. Rapid creation and development of environmentally appropriate technologies.
3. Comprehensive and ubiquitous change in the economic rules of the road by which we measure the impact of our decisions on environment.
4. Negotiation and approval of a new generation of international agreements.
5. Establishment of a cooperative plan for educating the world's citizens about our global environment.

Every individual needs to have an ecological awareness, i.e. an awareness of his environment which includes the forces of nature, plants and animals around him. We should be well aware of the present dilemma that along with the great benefits conferred on us by science and technology, dreadful side effects are also unleashed. If we treat the problem as light, then human species has to take on an additional itself by developing its own high-tech methods of extinction. For solving interrelated problems of poverty, environmental degradation and population growth, it requires development based on the Mahatma Gandhi's concept of Antyodaya putting the poor and their environment first, not last. More beneficial and sustainable economic development can be achieved by:

- Leaning where and how people are living sustainably, and not disrupting such cultures.
- Involving local residents including women and private NonGovernmental Organization (NGOs) in the planning and executions of all projects like our

water user associations'\Janma Bhoomi programmers.

- Making use of local wisdom, skills, and resources: the poor generally know far more about poverty, survival, environmental sustainability, local needs and what will work locally than do outside bureaucrats or experts.

The three scientific laws governing matter and energy changes indicate that the best long term solution to our environmental and resource problems is to shift from a society based on maximizing matter and energy flow to a sustainable low waste society. Using these lessons from nature the following guidelines are suggested for achieving sustainable development,

1. Reduce the input of matter and energy resources to prevent excessive depletion and degradation of planetary sources.
2. Use energy more effectively and not use high quality energy for tasks that require only moderate quality energy.
3. Shift from exhaustible and potentially fossil and nuclear fuels to less harmful renewable energy obtained directly or indirectly from the sun.
4. Use potentially renewable resources, and use them no faster than the rate at which they are regenerated.
5. Not waste nonrenewable resources, and use them no faster than the rate at which a renewable resource used sustainably can be substituted.
6. Recycle and reuse at least 60% of the matter now discarded as trash.
7. Reduce use and waste of matter resource making things that last longer and are easier to recycle, reuse and repair.

8. Add wastes and pollutants to environment sinks no faster than the rate at which they can be recycled, reused, absorbed or rendered harmless to us and other species by natural processes.
9. Emphasize pollution and waste reduction instead of pollution clean up and waste management.
10. Slow (and eventually halt) human population growth to help reduce stress on global life support.
11. Greatly reduce poverty which degrades humans and the environment by forcing people to use resources, unsustainably to stay alive.

So, In order to over come the most serious threat to our own existence due to emerging environmental degradation, we need to face it with great in depth understanding and innovative approach for enhance material and energy effectivity in production and usage, with structural economic changes social awareness in our planning to less resources intense sectors for achieving sustainable environment. Global ecological marshal plants are necessary to re-structure the present critical imbalances between human life and activities and physical and biological resources of planet Earth.

References

1. Gwendolyn Burke & Ben Ramnarine Singh, Louis Theodore New Delhi. A United Service Institution of India Project. D.S. Kothari Chair, p .1.
2. John Wiley & Sons "Environmental Management: Issues and Solutions" Wiley Inter Science. John Wiley & Sons, Inc. Hoboken, New Jersey, 2005, p. 13.
3. Down to earth, June 15, 2000, p. 55
4. The Hindu, "Survey of Environment", 2006, p. .45.
5. P.D. Sharma "Environmental Biology and Toxicology" Rastogi Publications, Meerut 2002, p. 83.

6. Log on http:// www.aaas.org/ news/press_room/ climate_change/media/4th_spm2feb07.pdf
7. Log on www.cag.org.in.
8. The Hindu, "Survey of Environment", 2006, p. 28
9. The Hindu, Editorial, 13 Oct. 2007
10. P.K.Gautam, "Environmental Security". Knowledge World New Delhi, 2003, p. 65.
11. The Hindu, "Survey of Environment", 2007, p. 21.
12. Elisabeth Skons (Sweden) "Analyzing risks to human lives" SIPRI Military Expenditure and Arms Production Projects.
13. The Hindu, "Survey of Environment", 2007, p. 141.
14. Prof. Y. Anjaneyulri "Introduction to Environmental Science", BS Publications, 2000, p. 508
15. U.S. EPA, Communications and Public Affairs (A-107), Preserving Our Future Today, 2115-1012, October 1991.

Chapter 13

THE ROLE OF UNITED NATIONS MILITARY OBSERVER GROUP OF INDIA AND PAKISTAN FOR CONFLICT RESOLUTION AND MANAGEMENT IN SOUTH ASIA

*Dr. Vijay Khare**

Historical Background

In South Asia Kashmir problem is one which is consuming a lot lives, time, money and resources of Indian and Pakistanis since Independence. Various wars have been fought on the issue, but still there is no solution to it in sight. The Kashmir issue is typically cast as a "territorial dispute" between two belligerent and well-armed powers in South Asia. But there is much more to the story than that. The Kashmir problem is a mixture of clash of religious ideology, terrorism, state violence, subversion and general horror that

* Reader, Department of Defence & Strategic Studies, University of Pune.

rests upon several layers of history. There are at least five different dimensions of the Kashmir problem, each with its own origins, and each with its own consequences:

1. British Policy

Kashmir originally came into dispute because of a British failure of will when they divided and quit India in 1947. The mechanism by which the princely states were sorted out was inadequate. Each prince or ruler was to decide whether he would accede to India or Pakistan, presumably taking into account the makeup and interests of his population; but there was no adequate mechanism for ensuring that each ruler would make a fair or reasonable decision, or to ensure that the "third option," independence, would not be a temptation.

2. Identity Crisis

The leadership in both countries compounded the original problem when they turned Kashmir into a badge of their respective national identities. For Pakistan, which defined itself as a "homeland" for Indian Muslims, the existence of a Muslim majority area under "Hindu" Indian rule was grating; the purpose of creating Pakistan was to free Muslims from the tyranny of majority rule for Indians, their state had to include such predominately Muslim regions to demonstrate the secular nature of the new Indian state; since neither India nor Pakistan, so-defined, could be complete without Kashmir. This raised enormously the stakes involved for both.

3. Weapon for Domestic Politics

Kashmir came to play a role in the respective domestic politics of both states but especially Pakistan. For Pakistani leaders, both civilian and military, Kashmir was a useful rallying cry and a diversion from the daunting task of building a nation out of disparate parts. Further, there were and are powerful Kashmiri dominated constituencies in all of the major Pakistani cities; on the Indian side, the small, but influential Kashmiri Hindu community was over-represented in the higher reaches of the Indian government.

4. Strategic and Geopolitics Relevance

After nuclear test conducted by India and Pakistan in 1998 Kashmir became dangerous nuclear flash point in world. In the process of economic globalization and revolution in military affairs Kashmir acquired strategic and geopolitical relevance in South Asia.

5. Self-determination

There is a contemporary dimension to Kashmir: the stirrings of a national self-determination movement among Kashmiri Muslims. Encouraged by neither India nor Pakistan, it burst into full view in late 1989, and threatens the integrity of both states. There are two or three new generations of Valley Muslims, educated and trained in India, but with a window open to a wider world. Angry and resentful at their treatment by New Delhi, and not attracted to even a democratic Pakistan, they look to Afghanistan, Iran, the Middle East, and Eastern Europe for models, and to émigrés in America, Britain, and Canada for material support. Further, in an era when the international economy is fast changing and the prospect of the direct linkage of Central Asia to Kashmir, the old argument that Kashmir is not economically self-sufficient unless it is attached to a major state has lost credibility.

PAKISTAN STRATEGIC STAND ON KASHMIR

More than five decades after independence, Pakistan is no closer to a resolution with India of the dispute over Kashmir. Pakistan and India have fought three wars, two of them over the status of Kashmir. They have been on the brink of war on several other occasions, including in Siachen in 1987 and in Kargil in 1999. From December 2001 to October 2002, the nuclear-armed protagonists came close to war once again when India mobilized along its international border with Pakistan following the terrorist attack on the parliament in New Delhi. Intense diplomatic and political pressure by the U.S., in coordination with other G-8 countries, averted what could have been a catastrophic clash. The agreed ceasefire at the Line of Control (LOC) produced by Pakistan's unilateral announcement on 23 November 2003 and India's acceptance the following day, and confidence-building measures (CBMs) proposed by India in October 2003, have raised hopes of an improved environment for negotiations. Nevertheless, the potential for yet another Kashmir crisis that could result in armed conflict looms large, since mutual distrust and hostility remain high, and both countries' substantive positions are rigid. Meanwhile the Kashmiri people are caught in the crossfire between the militants and Indian security forces. Islamabad is under military and diplomatic pressure from India and the international community to stop the infiltration of militants across the LOC into Indian-controlled Kashmir. Stressing that his government has lived up to its pledges to prevent cross-border incursions, former President Musharraf has asked India to reciprocate by engaging in a substantive dialogue on the Kashmir dispute, which, his government believes, India has thus far avoided. In the perceptions of influential international actors as well as India, however,

Pakistan has yet to curb all cross-border infiltration across the LOC. Pakistani governments have depicted the Kashmir conflict as a clash of the same competing national identities that lay behind the creation of two separate states, India and Pakistan, out of British India. Pakistan insists that India has no legal or moral right to Muslim majority Kashmir and rejects its attempts to gain international acceptance of the territorial status quo. Pakistan's policy towards Kashmir is shaped by perceptions of an Indian threat and a history of war but also by the wider question of its relations with India. It is also influenced by domestic imperatives. The conflict is placed on the backburner when relations improve. Some governments have used the Kashmir conflict to reinforce Pakistani nationalism and others to strengthen pan-Islamism. Pakistani governments have also used the dispute to acquire domestic legitimacy or to ensure regime survival. Pakistan governments would prefer the implementation of UN Security Council resolutions that envisaged the Kashmiri people determining in a plebiscite, under UN auspices, whether to accede to Pakistan or India. Conscious that a plebiscite is unacceptable to India, Pakistan is also exploring, albeit unofficially, other solutions, including the possibility of restructuring the current LOC in a way that would best promote Pakistan's strategic and political interests. Any progress towards a negotiated settlement of the dispute with India, however, depends on a Pakistani reassessment of the internal and external costs of the confrontation, including the growth of sectarian violence, a by-product of Islamabad's support for religious extremists in Kashmir. Above all, the military would have to abandon the belief that the insurgency in Kashmir benefits Pakistan by undermining India, politically, economically and militarily. While sympathy and support for the Kashmiri people is fairly widespread in Pakistan, the politically dominant military and the religious parties are the strongest proponents of claims to the state. Previous attempts by elected governments, headed by centre-left or centre-right parties, to normalize relations with India have been derailed by the military. The international role could be crucial. The Security Council's aversion to mediating the Kashmir dispute notwithstanding, influential actors, particularly the U.S., have been pro-active in reducing tensions between Pakistan and India, given the risk of nuclear war. U.S. facilitation could help to create an enabling environment for negotiations on the Kashmir dispute. The ultimate responsibility for resolving the dispute will depend, however, on reciprocal willingness by the two parties to bridge the wide gap in their positions.

INDIAN STRATEGIC STAND ON KASHMIR

For half a century Kashmir has been the major issue of contention between India and Pakistan. In India's view, the conflict in the state of Jammu and Kashmir constitutes a major internal security threat and is driven by Pakistani interference. No solution is possible, according to the Indian leadership, until Pakistan ceases its support for militants there. The ceasefire at the Line of Control (LOC) established by India's acceptance on 24 November of Pakistan's announcement the previous day of a unilateral measure and confidence building measures (CBMs) proposed by India in October 2003 have raised hopes of an improved environment for negotiations. Nevertheless, the potential for yet another Kashmir crisis that could result in armed conflict looms large, since mutual distrust and hostility remain high, and both countries' substantive positions are rigid. Meanwhile the Kashmiri people are caught in the crossfire between the militants and Indian security forces. Internal constraints in resolving the Kashmir conflict extend beyond the conservative political parties to encompass an array of rightist forces. Within Kashmir, despite divisions between hardliners and moderates, the All Parties Hurriyat Conference still represents Kashmiri separatism. Kashmiri and non-Kashmiri militants pose formidable hurdles to conflict resolution. Any movement forward on Kashmir is made even more difficult by the lack of a national consensus on how the conflict within Kashmir and with Pakistan should be addressed. In general, public opinion is not set against an agreement and is supportive of peace initiatives since Kashmir, for most Indians, is not the most pressing of the country's major problems. However, popular sentiment hardens during crises, influenced by official and media rhetoric. There is then a tendency to move away from support for a negotiated settlement to preference for a military solution in dealing with Pakistan and the militants. India's bottom line on Kashmir has remained unchanged over the decades: the state of Jammu and Kashmir is an integral part of the Indian Union, and any settlement of the crisis there must be effected within the confines of the Indian Constitution. However, differences abound within Indian policy circles on the future shape of a possible solution, from support for incorporating into India all of Jammu and Kashmir, including territories presently under Pakistani and Chinese control, to the territorial status quo, to the increasingly apparent shift in official policy for recognition of the Line of Control (LOC) as the international border. Indian perspectives are moving in the following direction: that a holistic solution must include recognition that it is impractical at this late date to conduct a plebiscite; that New Delhi cannot avoid providing maximum autonomy to Srinagar; and that converting the LOC into an international border is necessary on pragmatic grounds. The Indian government remains publicly opposed to any international involvement in the dispute although it has urged the United

States to press Pakistan to end support for militants. Statements by Indian officials on all these matters are split. Most accept in private that a solution is possible along the basic lines just described. However, few have yet acknowledged this in public.

Role of United Nations for conflict resolution and management in South Asia

The United Nations has played an important role in maintaining peace and order in Jammu and Kashmir since the transfer of Power to India and independence to Pakistan in 1947. Immediately after the freedom a dispute erupted between India and the successor nation-state of Pakistan on the question of the very basis of accession of Jammu and Kashmir by the ruler. New Delhi took this matter to the United Nations and the Security Council passed resolution 39 (1948) and established the United Nations Commission for India and Pakistan (UNCIP) to investigate and mediate the issue. The United Nations Military Observer Group in India and Pakistan (UNMOGIP) was deployed in January 1949 to supervise, in the State of Jammu and Kashmir, the ceasefire between India and Pakistan. Following the 1972 India-Pakistan agreement defining a Line of Control in Kashmir, India took the position that the mandate of UNMOGIP had lapsed. Pakistan, however, did not accept this position. Given that disagreement, the Secretary-General's position has been that UNMOGIP can be terminated only by a decision of the Security Council. In the absence of such a decision, UNMOGIP has been maintained with the same mandate and functions. On January 1, 1948, India brought the matter before the UN Security Council, claiming that Pakistan was assisting and participating in the invasion of Kashmir and thus threatening international peace. Pakistan denied the charges and countered that Kashmir's accession to India was illegal and that the question should be decided in a plebiscite, held under UN supervision. From 1947 to till date Pakistan firm on Kashmir stand.

The Role of UN MOGIP for Conflict Resolution and Management in South Asia

After termination of United Nations Commission on India Pakistan Commission in March 1950 the Security Council decided to divorce the responsibility of UNMOGIP from the political duties of the representative. As the initial UNMOGIP mandate was both vague and indirect, its real duties were spelled out in the Karachi Agreement, a bilateral instrument between India and Pakistan. The agreement and subsequent elaboration on it established the UNMOGIP functions as being Observation of the cease-fire line, Investigation of alleged breaches, Adjudication of conflicting claims, Recording the nature and dispositions of the forces. These have been and still are the functions of UNMOGIP, derived not from a UN mandate but from bilateral national agreements. It was not until March 1951 that the Security Council formally "authorized" UNMOGIP when it decided that the military observer group shall continue to supervise the cease-fire in the state, such decision have been made periodically since.

Funding

UNMOGIP has been funded from the UN's regular budget under the heading "special Missions and Inquires" it has not generated much controversy, although on occasion the Soviet Union has objected to UNMOGIP expenditure on the ground that they were decided by the Secretary General contrary to the UN Charter. Since its inception UNMOGIP has been receiving money from UN budget.

Conclusion

The United Nations Military Observer Group in India and Pakistan is over five decades old, established in 1949 and still in operation. Its original purpose was to oversee a cease-fire between India and Pakistan in the disputed state of Kashmir where the two countries had been at war. In this, UNMOGIP was initially very successful. Today in the era of globalization and technology revolution change the concept of peace and security and strategic relation to each other hence it is necessary to reshape strategic partnership through confidence building measures and follow the top down to bottom down approach for resolving the Kashmir issue . To considering present international politics and issues between India and Pakistan there is very less chances to resolve Kashmir issue through UNMOGIP. In some extent UNMOGIP has successfully fulfilled its original task of observing the cease fire spelled out in the Karachi Agreement. UN presence in the South Asian region seems that Kashmir dispute alive international issues. India has sought to define Kashmir as an integral matter, arguing that the territory is an integral part of India. For resolving Kashmir issue the role of United Nations will not work out due to historical and ideological conflict between India and Pakistan. Presence of United Nations in South Asian region it means the presence of US and other P-5 states of Security Council of United Nations. From beginning India has taken stand that Kashmir issue can be resolved only through bilateral relation and not through any third party mediation or intervention by global actor. Hence it is necessary to review the role of UNMOGIP in present changing international security environment. After five decades of love and hate relation yet there is no shortage of solutions partition, plebiscite, referendum, UN trusteeship, revolutionary warfare, depopulation and repopulation, patience, good government, a revival of "human values," third party mediation, and doing nothing have all had their advocates. The Kashmir issue needs an outside perspective because Indian and Pakistani strategists are locked in a mindless competition over tactical advantage and scoring diplomatic points. To maintain peace and stability in South Asia and resolve Kashmir issue would third party has any important role for conflict resolution and management in Kashmir. Should the United States take the lead? Or should there be a joint U.S.-Russian, US-UK, China-US effort. In coming days there is no possibility to success third party mediation in Kashmir conflict. Confidence building measures are not solutions to any particular problem, but address the difficulty of getting both sides to meet and talk. CBMs build confidence, not solutions. Presence of UNMOGIP will not help to South Asian region for conflict resolution and management due to changing nature of global politics and market economy changing the concept of security. Today concept of security is no longer to only manage the border or weapons of mass destruction or military capability. Hence it is necessary to understand the role of UN for maintaining international peace and security. There is urgent need to restructure the Security Council and participation of developing world for maintaining international peace and security.

References

Primary Sources

www.un.org

United Nations Documents S/628, January 2, 1948

United Nations Document S/646, January 15, 1948

United Nations Documents S/2017 March 30, 1951

Secondary sources

1. Stephen P. Cohen, Sergei Kamenev, Vladimir Moskalenko and Leo Rose, Afghanistan and Kashmir (New York: The Asia Society, and Moscow: The Russian Oriental Institute, 1993).
2. Devin Hagerty, "The Powers of Suggestion: Opaque Proliferation, Existential Deterrence, and the South Asian Nuclear Arms Competition," Security Studies, 2:3/4, Spring/Summer, 1993, 256-283.
3. Raju Thomas, ed., Perspectives on Kashmir: The Roots of Conflict in South Asia (Boulder: Westview Press, 1992),
4. Sumit Ganguly and Kanti Bajpai, "India and the Crisis in Kashmir," Asian Survey, Vol. 34, No. 5, May 1994.
5. Vijay Khare 'Dr. B.R. Ambedkar and India's National Security', Kilasoo Books, New Delhi-2005.
6. Michael Krepon, Mishi Farugues, eds., Conflict Prevention and Confidence Building Measures in South Asia: The 1990 Crisis. The Henry L. Stimson Center, Occasional Paper No. 17, April 1994.

Chapter 14

US INTERESTS IN SOUTH ASIA AND RELEVANCE OF PAKISTAN

*Dr. Arun Patwari**

American strategic interests in the Southern Asian Region during the period of 1945-1990 the containment of communism. After 1990 American long term interests in Southern Asia Region with in the geo strategic context oil rich Gulf area. Consolidating the American interest opening up of the resource rich petrol products control Action republic. U.S. Defence Department reiterated that Kuwait war, Fragrant, we believe that Iran constitute both a serious immediate and long -term threat to security of Gulf Area. From perceived as a threats to the wider region and to prevent other regime from challenging our interests in the area. America developed the strategy of dual containment.

Central Asia is important to America because of its large mineral resources, the nuclear weapons and its strategic

* M.Sc., Ph.D., D.Sc. Scholar, ISODARCO, Fellow (Itly) Associated Professor Defence Studies/Research Director Research Centre for Defence Science, Hindu College, Moradabad.

location in the heart of the Eurasian Land mass. Control Asia/ Caspian sea is a giant field with reserves of petroleum, are viable for extraction. The entire region is estimated to be sitting on 20 billion barrels of proven oil reserves and seven trillion Cubic metres of natural gas.

American now attain strategic strategy that of economic dynamission, resources potential and other along the nuclear non proliferation. So the American interests in Asia go beyond the economic realm. There is a fundamental political interest to prevent the nations of Asia.

Pakistan now emerges as a useful country along both strategic strands and front line status by American. Pakistan utility for realising larger American strategic goods. Gen Musharraf focus Pakistan as a moderate democratic Islamic country 140 milion people can play. And the fact is that is strategically located at the tri-junction of South Asia, Central Asia, and the Gulf region of both political and economic opportunity.

The access to the central Asian region, Iran within the frame work of American influence must perforce pass through Pakistan and such parts of Afghanistan. Some steps are being taken to exploit the natural resources of the central Asia, an agreement was signed. Turkmenistan to consider building a pipeline to transport gas and oil from Tur Kmuntan to Karachi through Afghanistan. The deeper question of the ability of Pakistan to serve as a reliable facilitator of larger American interests.

The America as the single hegemony power and the other major powers in the region i.e. Russia, China and India have different strategic interests that will be shaped by the dominant American posture. Mackinder theory of Heart laud formulation on Pakistan strategic position. But Pakistan does not as an independent Centre of Power. India is one of the power. Who formulate the mackinder theory of Heart laud.

Mackinder theory making necessary changes due to technological context of war. Afghanistan - America war was shows the Electronic warfare Technology. America, Russia, China, Japan and India will engage in consolidating their respective advantages.

The current situation Pakistan of larger American objectives the containment of Iran amongst other goals, Iran-China Axis may see the need for American containment. So the relevance of Pakistan as a crucial state in a American design. Pakistan in order to get American support and to reach its aims and objectives in Afghanistan, Kashmir and Central Asia, has involved itself in a rift with China, India, Iran and wants to convert itself into front line state of America. American interests in Pakistan was its army. and avoid including Kashmir Terrorism and Economic issue, domestic policies etc.

Implication & for India

India - America relations from 1947 - 1991 the two largest democracies have remained estranged since disagreed on national security issue and fundamental importance to each other. Now they are coming never after "International Terrorism war".

History has show that the supply of new weapons to Pakistan resulted in its military indulging and adventurism against India. Once again American supply of military aid to Pakistan has tumbled the strategic Partnership. India and American relation while the need for a greater interaction between the America and India in the relevant strategic prism.

Now central Asian countries is a complex tussle between the major and other powers. China need a oil pipe line from central Asia Petrol. India out Russia also keen interest on petrol issues. American interest is already clear in above.

Pakistan have an alliance with America to protect its borders and cut down on its defence spending Pakistan cannot afford its military expenditure. The question of Pakistan having a military force that has a sustained offensive capability is simply not possible. The need is to have friendly relationship with other countries which should keep India at bay. If Pakistan continue to spend 30 or 40 per cent of our Budget on defence and neglect our social sectors we are doomed. Pakistan's total population was about 140 million. Today Pakistan have 100 million illiterate people out of total population of about 140 million. In the social sector Pakistan performance has been dismal. Pakistan are at the both of the countries like Afghanistan or Nepal.

Those who talk about dignity and being look at Germany. They were defeated. They went to war and fought hard. Ultimately because of the greater industrial power of the Americans they were defeated. Germany were totally humiliated and devasted. But what did they do ? After the war, the American laid down the rules. The German accepted the rules and beat them 50 years down the road when Germany out Japan have become economic super powers. Today their relations with America are their own wishes.

Today a country like China can throw out the western countries can we do that ? They can tell the American, we do not like your way of living. Can we do that ? Why ? Pakistan should be an economically vibrant Islamic country comparable to the best in the world. Obviously there is some thing lacking.

Pakistan make up his mind and reduced its budget out. This expenditure has to be in proportion to reach a point where you will not even be able to pay to do some infrastructure development.

The Indo-Pak Military Balance and Limited War

American determination to wage an all out attack on terrorism was welcomed in India, with saw itself as a lonely fighter against terrorism in the region. Beginning in the 1980s terrorist violence has taken thousand of lives in India. Pakistan has provided sanctuary and aid to separatist movements in the Indian Punjab, Jammu and Kashimir regions. In the 1990s thousands of Pakistanis entered Kashmir in the name of supporting a freedom struggle or fighting a jihad.

Some of the groups that the terrorist belong to Har Kat Ul Mujahideen had links with Taliban. Besides routine little support from the world community. Pakistan support of terrorist activity in India not only in the name of Kashmir, but as a larger effort of aiding and fomenting movements that could lead to a breakup of India and make it move manageable from Pakistan point of view. From its experience during the war with soviets army in Afghanistan, Pakistan learned that a Proxy war or low intensity conflict (LIC) was a convenient means of bleeding a bigger and better armed country without provoking a response. Its public posture has been that it provides only moral, political and diplomatic support to the Kashmir struggle against Indian repression.

Indian policy has been to get international support especially from the America to chastise Pakistan. The attack on America persuded India to up the ante in its already improving relation with the America. Through not unsympathic to India, the America has its own priorities. America prevent the out break of an all outconflict between India and Pakistan which could not only prevent the first tank from being completed but also degenerate into a nuclear conflict. So even while the America itself did not hesitate to act against these who sponsored terrorism. Its message to India has been to restrain itself and seek a peaceful solution.

When four terrorists attacked India's Parliament House on Dec. 13, 2001, there were calls for immediate retaliate. India mobilised its Army for war and demanded that Pakistan end cross border terrorism, dismantle the infrastructure it had created to back this activity, and deport twenty top terrorists on its wanted list.

Pakistan angrily declined, but the pressure from India and the world community compelled Pakistan's President Pervez Musharraf who also the commander in chief of the Army to declare that Pakistan would not allow its territory to be used for terrorist activity anywhere in the world.

Gen. Musharraf response to the Indian action was merely tactical designed to prevent India relation and deflect international pressure. Pakistan threatened India with nuclear retaliation. Pakistan declarations ending cross border terrorism. Indian Govt. decided to pull back their forces from the border.

Today some of these characterization are not openly articulated at the official level. But Pakistan has encouraged its intelligence agencies and Islamic fundamentalist groups to intervene in India's domestic discords. In the 1980 they provided shelter to Sikh militants and since the 1990s they have been supporting Kashmiri Militants and insurgents in India, troubled Northeastern region.

The Geo-strategic reality has been that while Pakistan is disadvantaged vis India. It has never been size location and terrain. Pakistani generals doctrine of offensive defence. The two periods of American - Pakistan alliance 1954-1960 and 1980-1990 conceded with Pakistan's decision to follow American strategic interest vis Russia. It can be argued that the first segment of Military aid attered Pakistan perspective towards India. The aid resulted in the form of supersonic jets, modern tanks, self propelled artillery and armoured personnel carriers into the south Asian region. Such technology may have been indulge Pakistan attitudes towards India.

Alliance with the America, Pakistan's alliance with China following the sino-Indian border war of 1962 was marked by a greater commonality of interest. Chinese ultimatum to India in 1965 may have been a crucial factor in causing India to end the Pakistan-initiated war at a point when the Pakistan Military's capability had been seriously degraded. The second peak occurred in the 1990s when the China supply of nuclear capable ballistic missiles ensured nuclear parity between India and Pakistan.

The Pakistan strategy since 1971 has been the development of nuclear weapons. Respite American pressure. Pakistan was able to fabricate its first nuclear device in 1986. The nature of China assistance to this program is contravene aid but there are no doubts that China played a major role in providing Pakistan with the delivery system in the form of M-11 and M-9 missiles Later the Pakistan added the North Korean No-Dong Medium range ballistic missile capable of carrying nuclear weapons and rechristened it the Ghauri with the nuclear weapons and the Ghauri whose range covers most of India. Now Pakistan at least secured strategic parity with India.

Expectations that nuclear parity would ease Pakistan Security concerns and then help reduce tension in South Asia have been disproven. Nuclear test may have made all out conventional war of the 1965 or 1971 type impossible in the region. But a nuclear deterrent has enabled Pakistan to pursue a proxy war in Jammu and Kashmir by a keep my a wider Indian response at boy. This appeared to be the message of the Kargil war initiated by Pakistan in the summer of 1999 a year after the nuclear tests.

In the Kargil war, India and Pakistan scrupulously upheld the sanctity of the 740 km have of control. Pakistan sent its Northern light Infantry to cross the line in the snowy Kargil heights and take up position overlooking a critical Indian road linking Srinagar with the Ladakh region. After a two month military campaign that cost over 500 lives and led to President Clinton's intervention, the Pakistan retreated to their side of the time of control.

The Kargil conflict that rocked the sub continent in the summer of 1999 was unusual. It took place in a situation where both countries had nuclear weapons and were apparently ready to use them. India saw this as a Pakistani effort to use their now overt nuclear capabilities to undertake high risk conventional conflict. But in the 1980 and 1990s. India was deterred from responding to Pakistan support or separatist terrorism because it feared that thin could trigger a wider conflict which in turn could escalate to a nuclear war. This in a Indian leaders began to speak of a new concept of limited war. Indian Defence Minister said that Pakistan was mistaken if it thought it could undertake limited war with India under the Nuclear umbrella. India was prepared to fight such a conflict and called for the armed forces to possess conventional capability of a sufficiently high level in order to left the conventional threshold as much as possible.

This there was pointed out in Indian expectation of stability which was assumed would follow after Pakistan nuclear weapons have neutralised Indian conventional superiority, have not been fulfilled. Nuclear weapon have instead encouraged Pakistan to take greater risks in the on going conflict in Jammu and Kashmir. In early 2002 Indian forces were mobilised and massed on the front for most of the year, resulting in expectation that they would strike, especially after the massacre of women and children of military personnel at Kaluchak cantonment near Jammu. Their expectation were not realised and barring episodic let up there has been no change in cross border support for insurgency in the states of Jammu and Kashmir. This implies that India remains deterred by Pakistan nuclear weapons and Pakistan appeared so far to have retained the ability to prosecute a proxy war below the nuclear or conventional threshold from 1980 onwards Pakistan moved along a three-pronged strategy which involved pursuit of nuclear weapons capability, building up conventional capability with the help of the America and China and supporting Indian separatist movements and terrorist activity in India. Pakistan's substantial defence planning has essentially revolved only around India which is seen as a powerful state with hegemonic appears to have the means, but not the will, to largely end cross border military permanently.

On the height of the India-Pakistan crisis, America had told both countries that war would not serve their interests. America applying pressure to both parties. Particularly President Musharraf. Mussharraf must stop the incursions across the time of control. He must do so.

Prox was the term here is used in the context of Pakistan assisting Islamic guerrillas and Kashmiri separatists to fight its war against India. Because it is a guerrilla war. It is also a low intensity conflict.

Since 1947 Pakistan made several attempts to seize Kashmir from India, as Kashmir's accession to India remained unacceptable to Pakistan. Pakistan tried to achieve its objective in 1947 by engineering a tribal invasion of Kashmir, which resulted in the Kashmir war of 1947-48. Pakistan tried to achieve the same objective through. Operation Gibralter in 1965 but failed to wrest Kashmir from India. In 1971 when decisive Indian Military International in the civil war between the two wings of Pakistan helped in the creation of Bangladesh. Pakistan again hoped was finally dumped from July 1972 onwards after the Simla Agreement, the Kashmir situation upto 1989 was peaceful except for the dismissal of the Kashmir government on the Indian side.

As Pakistan did not succeed in wresting Kashmir from India by the use of Military force during the three wars. In 1988 Pakistan launched a low intensity operation to create alienation of the valley from the rest of India. Pakistan abetted full scale subversion, terrorism and insurgency in Jammu and Kashmir. The proxy war by Pakistan was stepped up in 1990. Between 1990 and 1998, 5845 civiliaions were killed in Jammu and Kashmir while the figure for security forces killed is 1401. A large quantities of weapons were found in Jammu and Kashmir. These include 18378 A/c -47s and 2015 LMGS. The Pakistanis were convinced that such a form of unconventional war would help the discontent in the valley, lead it in the direction of Secession from India.

The involvement of Pakistan in the Kashmir valley, in the form of Proxy war has been a part of Pakistan's Policy to bleed India of its resource without having to get involved in open military confrontation. The most active militant group was the Jammu and Kashmir liberation front. J. K. L. F to be sidelined by Pakistan due to JKLF implying independence for Kashmiris. Over the years it became obvious that Pakistan was suffering a setback due to the fast declining Kashmiri support in the valley to Militancy, and things were fast approaching normalcy in Indian Kashmir by 1995-96. In fact Military activity gradually shifted to new areas such as Doda, Punch and Rajouri, as the Indian security forces came to have almost complete control of the security situation in the Kashmir valley. After 1995-96 the role and participation of foreign militants of Pakistani, Afghanistani and POK origins increased in the Kashmir valley. In recent years, the Harkatul Mujahideen Militants have been involved in fighting in Kashmir. The Harkatul Mujahideen is just a new front for the Harkatul Ansar which was declared a terrorist organisation by the US in 1994. The Harkatul Militants operate in Afghanistan and Kashmir, and have strong links with the Jamiat-Ul-Ulema-Islam, as well as the Sipphe Sahaba Pakistan (SSP) in Pakistan. The Laskar-e-Taiba another dominant militant group which sends its recruits to battle in Kashmir. The Hizbul Mujahideen operates in Kashmir and has strong links with the Jamaat-e-Islami.

India-Pakistan relations acquired an entirely new dimension with India conducting its nuclear tests on May 11 and 13 1998 and Pakistan responding with its own nuclear tests on may 28 and 30. In the midst of vigorous international criticism of both India and Pakistan and demands on both that further tests be abandoned and both countries sign the CTBT. Pakistan actively tried to link the nuclear tests with the Kashmir question by suggesting that Kashmir being an unresolved issue which has been the cause of frequent wars in the part is now the possibilities of a nuclear conflict in the sub continent. This has been projected by Pakistan as a good enough reason for third party mediation in the Kashmir dispute and Pakistan has been openly making a bid for intervention by the united States, U.K., China, Japan and other countries. India continues to take the position that Pakistan and India between themselves are capable of resolving this dispute bilaterally, also because this is the approach a greed upon by the two countries in the Simla Agreement. Former chief of Army staff (COAS) Aslam Beg stated in a seminar that in spite of the battle over Kashmir raging for the past many years, we have no fear of war, which has been possible because of the nuclear deterrence which exists today in the sub continent. The launching of the Proxy war in Kashmir in 1988 following the acquisition of the bomb and subsequent escalation of the Militancy in December 1989, proved this assessment. When both the countries went overtly nuclear in May 1998 Pakistan hoped that its nuclear weapons would deter India from responding to any act of aggression by it in Kashmir. However despite Pakistan's nuclear weapons, India took on the Pakistani challenge in Kargil and gave a befitting reply. In a sense the Pakistani bluff was called and India gave clear proof of its determination that it will not brook any violation of its borders, whether there are any nuclear weapons or not in the hands of the enemy.

It becomes important to take a look at the impact of the nuclear tests on the process of dialogue between the two countries. The dialogue process between India and Pakistan could not be resumed in June 1998 as the two could not agree on the modalities for talks. There was a difference in the interpretation of the June 23, 1997 agreement which was signed between the Foreign Secretaries of India and Pakistan in Islamabad. In July 1998 both Prime Minister Vajpayee and Prime Minister Nawaz Sharif stated that they would like to utilise the opportunity to hold a meeting on the margins of the summit to have a candid exchange of views on the post nuclear security situation and if possible agree on a frame work of official level talks in the near future. However the talks held between July 29 and July 30 ended in a stalemante. Meanwhile the intermittent firing exchanged between Indian and Pakistani troops across the line of control during July 1998.

The deadlock in Indo-Pakistan relations was finally broken when Vajpayee met Nawaz Sharif at New York on Sept. 23, 1998 during the UN General Assembly session. It was agreed that the two Foreign Secretaries would meet in Islamabad from October 15, 1998 to focus on Kashmir and peace and security, including confidence building measures. The talks at Foreign Secretary level held in October and November 1998 did not make concrete advances on major issues, yet the fact that talks took place held promise for future interaction.

Lahore Declaration

Both the Prime Ministers—recalling their agreement of 23rd September 1998 that an environment of peace and security is in the supreme national interest of both sides and that the resolution of all outstanding issues including Jammu and Kashmir, is essential for this purpose, have agreed that their respective Governments shall intensify their efforts to resolve all issues, including the issue of Jammu and Kashmir.... shall intensify their composite and integrated dialogue process for an early and positive outcome of the agreed bilateral agenda. The Irran stated that the Foreign Secretaries were, guided by the agreement between their Prime Ministers of 23rd September 1998 that an environment of peace and security is in the supreme national interest of both sides and that resolution of all outstanding issues, including Jammu and Kashmir is essential for this purpose. Pursuant to the directive given by their respective Prime Ministers in Lahore, to adopt measures for promoting a stable environment of peace, and security between the two countries, have on this day agreed to the following: the two sides shall engage in bilateral consultation on security concepts, and nuclear doctrines, with a view to developing measures for confidence building in the nuclear and conventional fields, aimed at avoidance of conflict.

Indo-Pakistan relations was normal when Indian Prime Minister Vajpayee's bus diplomacy, immediately after which these was tremendous good will between the two countries. Several issues were in the shape of the various agreements signed at that time. Pakistan's facade of friendliness was completely shattered when the Kargil war assured the complete breakdown of the high level of trust and good will created at Lahore. India's faith was completely lost in any future overture that may be made by Pakistan. India found its resilience being tested yet again as the Indian Airlines flight was hijacked and taken to Kandahar by Pakistan backed Harkatul Mujahideen. This contemptuous act was the final pushing Indo-Pak relations to their 1972 position. The talks became bogged down due to the usual accusation and counter accusation hurled by India and Pakistan towards each other. In some situation they were not able to move beyond their after stated position. Pakistan showed its tenacity in trying to bring in third party intervention into what should be bilaterally resolvable issue. However, the effort on both side to discuss a wide range of issues was itself commendable.

Indo-pak relation was the Indian Prime Minister Vajpayee's visit to Lahore on February 20-21 1999 on the inaugural run of the Delhi - Lahore bus service. The Lahore summit led to the signing of the Lahore Declaration by the Prime Ministers of Pakistan and India on February 21, 1999 referred to mutual adherence to the Principles of the UN charter, implementation of the Simla Agreement.

The contradiction in Indo-Pak relations became apparent again when Nawaz Shareef while visiting Rawalpindi stated that the Pakistan Army is fully greared and equipped to face any eventuality.

While the Lahore process was the culmination of Nawaz Shareef efforts towards taking Indo-Pak relations to a new high, it is known that the army in Pakistan was even then uncomfortable with this event, and had in the meanwhile been planning the Kargil adventure. It was reported in July 1999, that highly placed sources confirm that the decision to take over the Kargil Posts was taken in October last year and preparation started immediately after that. In an article Gen. Mirza Aslam Beg, the former chief of Army staff disclosed that the Mujahideen's operation was approved after briefings given to the Prime Minister at GHQ, and ISI Head Quarters as early as January 1999. It is generally accepted that Kargil was planned last year and its execution began in Feb. just about the time of the Lahore Declaration. Pakistan's aggression in Kargil marked an unanticipated downturn in Indo-Pakistan relations.

Kargil War

It became meaningful to examine the Kargil war on Indo-Pak relations. Kargil has to be seen in the context of the proxy war conducted by Pakistan. The purpose of the Pakistan Operation in Kargil is clear wanted to enlarge the conflict in Kashmir, and to bring to the focus of the international community, the danger of another Indo-Pak war, one in which nuclear weapons could be used. By fabricating this kind of danger Pakistan hoped for international intervention which would succeed in the Kashmir issue.

Pakistani strategy in the following manner.

1. Cut off the Srinagar - Leh road so that movement of supplies to Leh garrison and Siachen would become impossible.
2. It wanted to block Zojila pass and threaten Kashmir valley from the north, which would be a new direction to make in road.
3. It wished to have control over the Himalayan range so that it would have unopposed access for insurgent terrorists going into the Kashmir valley and Doda district of Jammu.
4. It wanted to outflank the Indian Army deployed on the LoC in north - western Kashmir and the Siachen glacier through Shyok valley. Pakistan assumed that India would not retaliate because of the threat of nuclear weapons but India fought and recovered its territony.

Pakistan wanted people to revolt in Kashmir due to terrorist activities, went for an elected government in 1996. Pakistan realising the hopelessness of the situation opted for military action in Kargil. Pakistan disregarded the peace initiative offered by India in Lahore. It deceived India by simultaneously planning the Kargil operations in great secrecy. The Kargil conflict was a great setback for the peace process and the confidence building measures initiated in the year preceding the Kargil intrusion. The Pakistani forces were found to be composed of Pakistan army units terrorist groups. Pakistani troops operating across the Loc were identified to be from the 2nd, 3rd, 4th and 6th Battalions of the Northern light Infantry, and Islamic militants trained by the Lashkar-e-Taiba and Harkatul-Ul-Mujahdeen, etc.

Indian stand received immense international support during the Clinton-Sharif meeting of July 4, 1999.

Nawaz Shareef agreed that concrete steps be taken for the restoration of the line of control in accordance with the Simla Agreement. Nawaz Shareef by agreeing with President Clinton on this point, admitted not only that Kargil constituted a violations of the Line of Control, but that it was in Pakistan's power to undo this violation. The implicit suggestion was that he would withdraw his forces from Indian Kashmir, to the position as it existed before Pakistani aggression in Kargil section across the Loc. Pakistani government accepted the sanctity of the Loc, there by approval on as forming a de facto boundary between India and Pakistan. Faced with a serious economic situation, Pakistan could not afford to antagonize America which could have withheld the 100 million dollar aid of the IMF loan due in July. The Gr. countries condemned the infiltration and demanded withdrawal of the intruder from the Indian side of the Loc. China stated that both India and Pakistan must exercise restraint and should solve the Kargil problem peacefully through negotiations. Severe provocation was widely appreciate by the International community.

Pakistan news magazine stated that—The Kargil adventure was ill-conceived, if not down right foolish, was becoming clear, albeit slowly, even to the congenitally blind. That consequently Pakistan, swallowing its pride and not a few of its brave and gallant words, would sooner or later have to mount a retreat was also becoming clear, especially after Ni 93 naik's secret visit to New Delhi. Which was a desperate bid to get India to agree to some kind of a deal which would provide a face saving way out for us.

Hijacking of Indian Plane

The hijacking of the Indian Airline plane became a way of subjecting the Indian population to terror tactics in continuation of the Kargil conflict. The Harkatul Mujahideen was involved, shows the backing of the Pakistani government. The complicity of the Pakistan army and the Taliban was further proved when there was no help in the release of the hostages and India had to concede the demands of the Hijackers. Pakistan seemed quite satisfied from the fact that India was forced to release the hard core militants who had been under detention in India because of their acts of terrorism.

Pakistan in the initial phase of the hijacking took the stance that it had extended all possible help in the safe landing of the hijacked airlines at Lahore airport and the Indian High Commissioner G. Parthasarthy was provided a special helicopter at his request for monitoring the ground situation. However, the Indian Airlines IC 814 plane took off from Lahore by the time he reached there. Gen. Pervez Musharraf on Dec. 28 emphasised that Pakistan had absolutely no involvement in the hijacking of the Indian Airlines. We do not really know the facts and the people as to who have hijacked the plane. He further stated that Pakistan had cooperated with India totally and we would like to cooperate with them totally. In a deal with the hijackers of the Indian Airlines plane could return home if his Pakistani identity was established. However the same news report went on to admit that Azhar had studied at Karachi's Jamia Uloom Islamia Binori Town. Azhar had links with the Harkatul Mujahideen. .

One of the terrorist group in Kashmir and that he was arrested in Kashmir in 1994. Another militant Mushtaq Ahmad Zargar, founder chief of Al-Umar Mujahideen, arrived in the POK capital late on Jan. 4 four days after he was released by the Indian government along with two other Kashmir freedom fighters in exchange for IST passengers of hijacked Indian Airlines plane on December 31. Other Mujahideens released were Maulana Masood Azhar and Ahmad Umar Saeed Sheikh, stated to be attributed with the Harkatul Mujahideen.

Pakistan's support for militant groups engaged in anti-India activities could no longer be hidden, as Maulana Masood Azhar, was allowed to address a Jamatul wida congregation at Jama Masjid Al-Sadiq in Bahawalpur, where he declared jihad against India, and urged the men in the congregation to sign up to fight against India rule in Kashmir. The hijacking further vitiated the atmosphere between India and Pakistan. This event which show cases of Pakistan's aggressive tendencies towards India. It becomes important to focus on Pakistan's attitude is a critical factor in the future of India - Pakistan relations means of deterrence but weapons of war which it would not hesitate to use. Gen. Musharraf talked of the possibility of use of nuclear power if Pakistan's security is threatened. Pakistan's security will never be compromised.

There is no negotiation, no talks with India unless the

Kashmir issue is discussed.

Pakistan Commerce Minister Abdul Razzak ruled out the possibility of trade with India in the existing regional and political situation, saying that a solution to the Kashmir issue tops the agenda of the present government.

Prospects for Indo-Pakistan Relations

Prospects for peace between India and Pakistan are bleak in the foreseeable future. In the short term there does not seems to be any hope for improvement in Indo-Pak relations. Any forward movement with Pakistan becomes difficult because of the ideological conflict between India and Pakistan. Pakistanis ideology is contradictory to that of India, and Pakistan's domestic opinion is steeped in that ideology. The Kashmir issue never fails to be a rallying point for governments in power in Pakistan when they want to divert attention from their internal problems. The Indian government has taken a clear stand that there can be no talks till Pakistan stops instigating terrorism across the border into India. This does not seem likely to happen. On the contrary, Pakistan has intensified its Jehad against India, and more specifically Kashmir. Gen. Musharraf's statement that hostility would continue even after resolution of the Kashmir issue, seemes to imply that the aim of the Pakistani establishment is not joint to get Kashmir, but the destabilization of the Indian state.

Both India and Pakistan view each other as adversaries and such images are transmitted not only through the medium of education but also through the print and electronic media. India and Pakistan share common problems. The two countries have not been able to exploit the existing potential for trade in a wide range of products which could be purchased at a lower cost and with a shorter delivery time.

While these are all examples of meaningful relations in the Indo-Pak context and what would be the ideal level of interaction between the two countries, only time will tell how much of this is advisable. Any forward movement will depend on maintaining a continuity in dialogue which is important for long term success in normalising relations between India and Pakistan.

References

1. Estranged Democracy : India and the United States—(N.D.U. Washington D.C 2003.)
2. The Origins of Pakistan's Political Economy of Defense - (Cambridge University from)
3. Military Balance - 2003.
4. SIPRI Year Book - 2003.

Chapter 15

INDIA AND US RELATIONS
Ground & Realities

*Dr. R.B. Singh**

The current era of India - US relations began with the election of AB Vajpayee in 1997and second term of President Clinton in US. Prior to that India - US relations can at best be described as satisfactory or reasonable. The latter state was predominantly caused by the Cold War hysteria in the West. India was dragged into it indirectly with US seeking regional allies to counter Soviet Union and found Pakistan as willing ally. US traded weapons for military bases. As a natural consequence, India maintained a neutral sort of foreign policy, which leaned more towards Soviet Union. The US and its media always poked fun at India and its development five year plans. The lowest point was in 1961-63, when promised help to set-up a large steel mill in Bokaro was withdrawn. The 1965 Indo-Pak war did not help. The

* Editor, Guest Lecturer, Department of Defence Studies, University of Lucknow.

subsequent 1971 Pakistani Army's blunder of military operation in Bangladesh and its subsequent defeat at the hands of India did not sit well with US Administrations. Subsequent decades were eventless for India -US relations. Although US wanted Indian support for an anti Soviet operation in Afghanistan, India disagreed with US on freely arming Afghan guerrillas and Pakistani Army. Badly mauled, Soviets left Afghanistan and later crumbled into an economic and political chaos. India suddenly had no friend left. The years leading to Vajpayee's election were of economic chaos and domestic political upheaval. A complete transformation of India - US relations immediately began then.

India Draws US and the World Attention to Itself

No amount of diplomatic moves or good fellow image, which India had projected from 1950 to 1996, could draw US and the West's attention to it. At best India was considered as a basket case. Something drastic needed to be done. Immediately upon becoming the Prime Minister, Vajpayee decided to explode the Indian Atom Bomb. This made US to sit up and take notice of India. Surprised, Clinton and his advisors ran with sanctions to block every possible avenue of technological trade with India. A month later, Pakistan followed it with its own Atom Bomb test. Clinton tried to prevent the latter but failed.

With the above one act, India became the focus of Clinton Administration. Diplomacy took the center stage. Clinton sent his ace foreign policy official, Strobe Talbot for diplomatic paw-paw with the Indians. Vajpayee sent his able Foreign Minister, Jaswant Singh to the diplomatic table.

India-US relations with one major act took a center stage. Pakistan on the other hand became the butt end of American ire.

Talbot - Jaswant Reconciliation talks

Over two years period these talks in seven countries concluded the following:

1. India will never give up the nuclear weapons, although further weapons development will severely be curtailed.
2. India wishes to further enhance economic ties with US. This will be mutually advantageous.
3. On the diplomatic front, India wishes to sit at the UNSC as a permanent member with all rights and privileges.
4. India offered and US partially accepted a strategic role for it in South Asia and Indian Ocean.

With the above issues under discussion, President Clinton decided to pay a visit to India and see for himself India and its potential. He came to India in 2000 and this visit transformed India - US economic relations.

Other Factors Drawing US and India Closer

China' economic progress, although made in USA with lavish FDI, is a cause for concern in America. It is a matter of time when China will challenge USA. Hence US is in search for a powerful nation in the region which can balance Chinese influence. India with its size and highly educated work force seemed to be an obvious choice. In addition US did not wish to put all its eggs in one basket. The manufacturing had been outsourced to China. US wished another nation to become a partner in service sector outsourcing. India with its skilled workforce and large presence in US, IT sector was again the obvious choice.

Strategically prior to 9/11, the Bush Jr. administration, considered India as a natural choice to police the Indian Ocean sea-lanes from Suez to Singapore. Enormous amount of trade flows through this route and safeguarding it on a long-term basis is not in the capacity of the US 7th fleet in the Pacific or 6th fleet in the Mediterranean. A local power is needed. India has the power and potential to do the job. The Vajpayee government in India liked the Idea and liked the importance it will give to India, hence welcomed it. In addition China's enormous military advantage on the mainland facing Taiwan could also be neutralized, if India kept the Chinese military reserve in central China somehow busy. Development of ICBMs by India is part of the plan. Although, US will not help yet it will not hurt the development of this strategic technology. These plans were under active consideration in US and India, when Osma Bin Laden struck on 9/11.

US - India Events, which are Drawing Apart

The events of 9/11 rudely interrupted the geopolitics in Asia underway. The US got defocused on its long-range objectives. Its policy suddenly became Middle East centric with an objective to remove the perpetrator of this crime from power in Afghanistan. It was an easy task. Overconfident, US went ahead and decided to remove Saddam Hussein in Iraq from power. It has succeeded but done very poorly with 1300 American soldiers dead and no end in sight. It is turning out to be America's Afghanistan with huge drain on resources and public opposition to it at home. In the process, it has befriended Pakistan and currently showering it with money, military hardware and diplomatic niceties.

The Cold War mentality in US State Department official is another factor, which is pulling US and India apart. India was previously lumped together with Soviet Union and today this attitude continues. These officials dominate the policymaking and place roadblocks in Indo - US relations.

American arms supply to Pakistan is currently

dominating the Indian mindset. The Indians are fixated on its negatives. US may have made an error in judgment on this issue. But for the greater good of the nation, Indian politicians have to find a way out of this situation. One way out is to get more economic aid and spend more money on defence as the economy grows. This will neutralize all the advantages Pakistan may have with new arms.

Net Impact of Pluses and Minuses on Indo - US relations

The net impact is that:

- China still gets $40 Billion a year of US money as FDI and India about $3 Billion. US have not encouraged industry to consider India for manufacturing outsourcing as an alternative.
- Pakistan is back in US good books and at the receiving end of cash grants and arms.
- India with its high IT skills, has been given the carte blanche to become service sector headquarter for the US economy.
- India has decided to develop its armed forces a bit further, with US not raising adversely on increased defense expenditures.
- India is seeking from US, strategic technology. This supply is bogged down in US State Department reviews. It may never materialize.

Above are good and bad. India is benefiting tremendously on IT and BPO outsourcing front. Unfortunately, AB Vajpayee government has been defeated on a host of domestic issues in spring 2004 elections. A left leaning government is leading India into a policy of silent disagreement and confrontation with US.

Current State of Geopolitics in Asia

China

While US is busy in Iraq and Afghanistan, China is quietly upgrading its economic presence in East Asia. Its manufacturing exports to this region have increased 70% in last three years alone. In a short while all the East Asian nations will economically become addendum to the Chinese economy. This again is happening mainly due to cheaper products coming from China. Mind it, Chinese products are cheaper not because nobody else knows how to make them as cheap as they do but due to almost free money, cheap labour and artificially low exchange rate of its currency. US knows about it but wishes to do nothing for two reasons. First, American businesses are reaping a bounty of profits and second all the money Chinese are earning is deposited back in US Treasury Bonds at low interest to help finance the ballooning US budget deficit.

South East Asia

Asian tigers of yesterday have become pussycats of today. The economic crisis of late nineties sobered them up. They are not building large manufacturing capacities to match China. They know that China is a favoured nation as compared to them. In a crisis situation geopolitics will dictate favouring China. Hence they wish to tie with China and maintain their somewhat lack luster economic ties with US. The recent ASEAN reconfirmed this thought. Over a period of next ten years, all of East Asian economies will be in the full clasp of the Chinese.

India

AB Vajpayee opened the economic window to the US and the West. The present government is keeping all the policies enacted by the former prime minister intact. Still, India is not receiving huge dose of FDI to invest in infrastructure, industry, trade and commerce. India is left to its own devices to upgrade all the forgoing. Still a healthy 6.5% to 8.5% growth rate has been achieved. Exports are slow to grow as no free money in large amounts has arrived still export growth is significant in last two years. One can easily say that India is doing better than it had done in last 50 years. It is now capable of facing up China.

Pakistan

It is a spoiler state with emphasis on Islam. It has a competent workforce but no emphasis on education, skill training, and modernization. It has done miserably in last 10 years economically. Only with the current infusion of cash by the Americans, the state has survived. Otherwise it would have completely failed. In last ten years, it allowed India to surge ahead of it economically. Its democratic institutions have failed. Mosques and Mullah are playing a greater role in national affairs as opposed to economists and politicians. It has no worthwhile exports other than sporting goods, cotton & textiles. Pakistan offers no economic advantage for FDI hence none is forthcoming. Militarily it is no threat. The Americans have compromised its nukes and the American withdrawal of spare parts and services can any time sabotage its military hardware.

Politics in India Affecting Indo - US relations

China is ruled by a Communist dictatorship, yet it has found a strategic advantage in US mindset to exploit and prosper. Initially, China was the back stabber of the Soviet Union, which US loved. Now it is the cost advantage of products made in China, which invites more and more FDI and prosperity. India is a democracy, but has no strategic advantages. Its location at the crossroads of major sea-lanes is the only advantage it has. Today, India is bypassed when companies in the West consider new location to set up manufacturing. Reasons for this are attributable to 50 years of left leaning politics in India and also to the American apathy.

The new phase of the evolution of the Indo-US ties started in 1998. This phase is now over. These ties have to be taken to next level. For this, it is India who has to take the initiative. Although Bush and Vajpayee with great fanfare announced the Next Step Strategic Process in 2004 yet it has yielded no results. US are leery of the current politicians in power in India and India sees US arming of Pakistan, a regressive step. US could not care less of India's objections.

Politics in India will have to be Re-formed to Encourage India - US Ties

The above can only be achieved with present UPA government distancing from its left leaning allies. The BJP should break free of its regional party support and dump communal politics. Then Congress and BJP could perhaps support each other on a few common policies for the welfare of the nation. This is not uncommon. Only recently, Prime Minister Arial Sharon in Israel dumped his party and joined hands with opposition Labor Party to push his Gaza withdrawal agenda. In USA Democrats and Republicans constantly vote for each other's initiated legislation.

What US has to do to prevent Indo - US relations Slide?

Slide in Indo-US relations could be prevented by US by:

- Rethink on the supply of arms to Pakistan. These arms will never catch Osma Bin Laden.

- Removing hurdles to export and import in both countries. US in turn should encourage investment in India.
- Not lumping India with Pakistan together in all policy decisions. India is in a different league and cannot be compared with Pakistan. Follow the same policy as US follows towards China and Taiwan. Each is dealt independent of the other.
- Discouraging negative media stereotype of India. Today, India is a highly skilled service economy. The old stereotype is to be dumped.
- US officials of cabinet level be paying more frequent visits to India. They will know more about India by their own visits than by media or embassy reports.

In the end, one can conclude that India and US are natural strategic partners. They have to work together to remove hurdles in the forward movement in their relations.

Chapter 16

INDO-PAKISTAN RELATION

*Dr. R.B. Singh**

Introduction

Indo-Pakistani relations are grounded in the political, geographic, cultural, and economic links between the Republic of India and the Islamic Republic of Pakistan two of the largest countries in South Asia. The two countries share much of their common geographic location, and religious demographics (most notably Hinduism, Islam, Sikhism, Buddhism); yet diplomatic relations between the two are defined by numerous military conflicts and territorial disputes. However, attempts to warm relations have been made.

Much of South Asia came under direct control of Great Britain in the late 18th century. The British Raj over the Indian subcontinent lasted for almost two centuries. 95% of the

* Editor, Guest Lecturer, Department of Defence Studies, University of Lucknow, Lucknow.

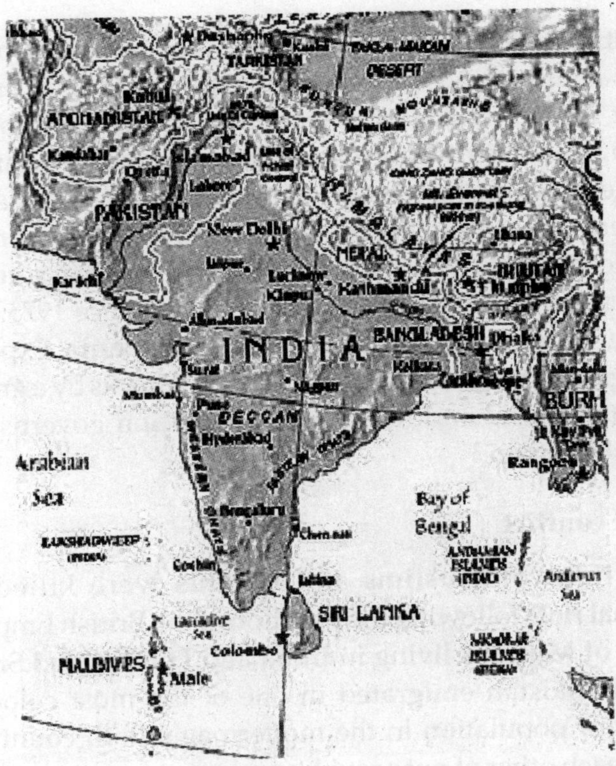

people living in South Asia practised either Hinduism and Islam or The Muslim League, headed by Jinnah, proposed the Two Nation Theory in the early 20th century. According to the theory, Muslims and others shared little in common, and British India should be divided into two separate countries, one for the Muslims and the other for the Hindu majority, which he feared would suppress the Muslim minority. The campaign gained momentum in early 1940s and by the end of World War II, British India's partition looked inevitable. The Partition of India in 1947 created two large countries independent from Britain: Pakistan as two wings in the East and West, separated by India in the middle. Soon after Independence, India and Pakistan established diplomatic relations. Subsequent years were marked by bitter periodic conflict, and the nations went to war four times. The war in 1971 ended in defeat and another partition of Pakistan. The eastern wing split off as a new country named Bangladesh, while the western wing continued as Pakistan.

There was some improvement in relations since the mid-2000s. Most notably, Pakistan released an Indian man accused of being a spy in 2008: he had been detained since 1975. But relations soured again after the 2007 Samjhauta Express bombings, and the 2008 Mumbai Terrorist Attacks by a group of Pakistani men,[1] and now mutual suspicion governs the relationship again.[2]

Seeds of conflict

Millions of Muslims and Hindus were killed in communal riots following the partition of the British Empire. Millions of Muslims living in India and Hindus and Sikhs living in Pakistan emigrated in one of the most colossal transfers of population in the modern age. Both countries accused each other of not providing adequate security to the minorities emigrating through their territory. This served to increase tensions between the newly-born countries.

According to the British plan for the partition of British India, all the 680 princely states were allowed to decide which of the two countries to join. With the exception of a few, most of the Muslim-majority princely-states acceded to Pakistan while most of the Hindu-majority princely states joined India. However, the decisions of some of the princely-states would shape the Pakistan-India relationship considerably, in the years to come.

Junagadh dispute

Junagadh is one of the modern districts of Saurashtra, Gujarat Junagadh was a state on the southwestern end of

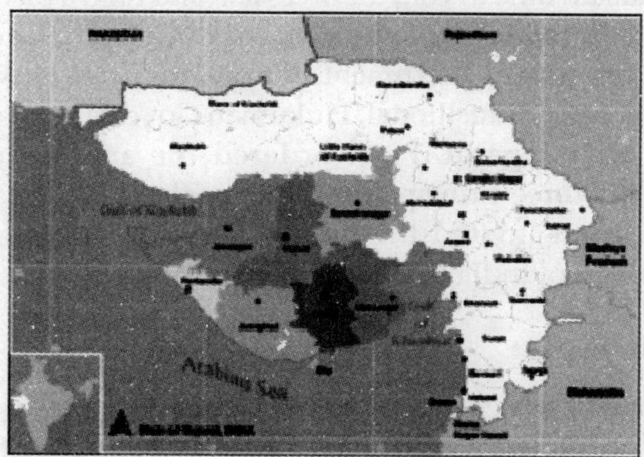

Gujarat, with the principalities of The Indian point of view was that since Junagadh was a state with a predominantly Hindu population it should be a part of India. Additionally, since the state was encircled by Indian territory it should have been a part of India. Indian politicians also stated that by giving Pakistan a predominantly Hindu region to govern, the basis of the two nation theory was contradicted.

The Pakistani point of view was that since Junagadh had a ruler and governing body who chose to accede to Pakistan, they should be allowed to do so. Junagadh, having a coastline, could have maintained maritime links with Pakistan. Additionally, Pakistani politicians stated that the two nation theory did not necessarily mean a clear division of land and absolute transfer of populations as the sheer magnitude of such a proceeding would wreak havoc upon millions.

Neither of the ten states were able to resolve this issue amicably and it only added fuel to an already charged environment.

Sardar Patel, India's then Home Minister, felt that if Junagadh was permitted to go to Pakistan, it would create communal unrest across Gujarat. The government of India gave Pakistan time to void the accession and hold a plebiscite in Junagadh to pre empt any violence in Gujarat. Samaldas Gandhi formed a government-in-exile, the Arzi Hukumat (in Urdu: Arzi: Transitional, Hukumat: Government) of the people of Junagadh. Patel ordered the annexation of Junagadh's three principalities. Junagadh, facing financial collapse, first invited the Arzi Hukumat, and later the Government of India to accept the reins of power.

Kashmir dispute

Kashmir was a princely state, ruled by a Hindu, Hari Singh. The Maharaja of Kashmir was equally hesitant to join either India—because he knew his Muslim subjects would not like to join a Hindu-based and Hindu-majority nation—or Pakistan—which as a Hindu he was personally averse to. Pakistan coveted the Himalayan kingdom, while Indian leader Mahatma Gandhi and Indian PM Jawaharlal Nehru hoped that the kingdom would join India. Hari Singh signed a Standstill Agreement (preserving status quo) with Pakistan, but did not make his decision by August 15, 1947.

Rumours spread in Pakistan that Hari Singh was trying to accede Kashmir to India. Alarmed by this threat, a team of Pakistani forces were dispatched into Kashmir, fearing an Indian invasion of the region. Backed by Pakistani paramilitary forces, Pashtuns invaded Kashmir in September 1947. Kashmir's security forces were too weak and ill-equipped to fight against Pakistan. Troubled by the deteriorating political pressure that was being applied to Hari Singh and his governance, the Maharaja asked for India's help. However, the Constitution of India barred the Indian Armed Forces' intervention since Kashmir did not come under India's jurisdiction. Desperate to get India's help and get Kashmir back in his own control, the Maharaja acceded Kashmir to India (which was against the will of the majority of Kashmiris), and signed the Instrument of Accession.[3] By this time the raiders were close to the capital, Srinagar. On October 27, 1947, the Indian Air Force airlifted Indian troops into Srinagar and made an intervention. The Indian troops managed to seize parts of Kashmir which included Jammu, Srinagar and the Kashmir valley itself, but the strong and intense fighting, flagged with the onset of winter, made much of the state impassable. After weeks of intense fighting between Pakistan and India, Pakistani leaders and the Indian Prime Minister Nehru declared a ceasefire and sought U.N. arbitration with the promise of a plebiscite. Sardar Patel had argued against both, describing Kashmir as a bilateral dispute and its accession as justified by international law. In 1957, north-western Kashmir was fully integrated into Pakistan, becoming Azad Kashmir (Pakistan-administered Kashmir), while the other portion was acceded to Indian control, and the state of Jammu and Kashmir (Indian-administered Kashmir) was created. In 1962, China occupied Aksai Chin, the northeastern region bordering Ladakh. In 1984, India launched Operation Meghdoot and captured more than 80% of the Siachen Glacier.

Pakistan maintains Kashmiris' rights to self-determination through a plebiscite in accordance with an earlier Indian statement and a UN resolution. Pakistan also points to India's failure of not understanding its own political logic and applying it to Kashmir, by taking their opinion on the case of the accession of Junagadh as an example (that the Hindu majority state should have gone to India even though it had a Muslim ruler), that Kashmir should also rightfully and legally have become a part of Pakistan since majority of the people were Muslim, even though they had a Hindu ruler. Pakistan also states that at the very least, the promised plebiscite should be allowed to decide the fate of the Kashmiri people.

India on the other hand asserts that the Maharaja's decision, which was the norm for every other princely state at the time of independence, and subsequent elections, for over 40 years, on Kashmir has made it an integral part of India. This opinion has often become controversial, as Pakistan asserts that the decision of the ruler of Junagadh also adhered to Pakistan. Due to all such political differences, this dispute has also been the subject of wars between the two countries in 1947 and 1965, and a limited conflict in 1999. The state/province remains divided between the two countries by the Line of Control (LoC), which demarcates the ceasefire line agreed upon in the 1947 conflict.

See also: Indo-Pakistani War of 1947, Indo-Pakistani War of 1965, and Kargil War

Other Territorial Disputes

Pakistan is locked in other territorial disputes with India such as the Siachen Glacier and Kori Creek. Pakistan is also currently having dialogue with India regarding the Baglihar Dam being built over the River Chenab in Jammu and Kashmir.

Bengal refugee crisis

In 1949, India recorded close to 1 million Hindu refugees, who flooded into West Bengal and other states from East Pakistan, owing to communal violence, intimidation and repression from authorities. The plight of the refugees outraged Hindus and Indian nationalists, and the refugee population drained the resources of Indian states, which were unable to absorb them. While not ruling out war, Prime Minister Nehru and Sardar Patel invited Liaquat Ali Khan for talks in Delhi. Although many Indians termed this appeasement, Nehru signed a pact with Liaquat Ali Khan that pledged both nations to the protection of minorities and creation of minority commissions. Although opposed to the principle, Patel decided to back this Pact for the sake of peace, and played a critical role in garnering support from West Bengal and across India, and enforcing the provisions of the Pact. Khan and Nehru also signed a trade agreement, and committed to resolving bilateral disputes through peaceful means. Steadily, hundreds of thousands of Hindus returned to East Pakistan, but the thaw in relations did not last long, primarily owing to the Kashmir dispute.

1971 Bangladesh Liberation War

Pakistan, since independence, was geo-politically divided into two major regions, West Pakistan and East Pakistan. East Pakistan was occupied mostly by Bengali people. In December 1971, following a political crisis in East Pakistan, the situation soon spiralled out of control in East Pakistan and India intervened in favour of the rebelling Bengali populace. The conflict, a brief but bloody war, resulted in an independence of East Pakistan. In the war, the Pakistani army swiftly fell to India, forcing the independence of East Pakistan, which separated and became Bangladesh. The Pakistani military, being a thousand miles from its base and surrounded by enemies, was forced to give in.

Simla Agreement

Since the 1971 war, Pakistan and India have made only slow progress towards the normalisation of relations. In July 1972, Indian Prime Minister Indira Gandhi and Pakistani President Zulfikar Ali Bhutto met in the Indian hill station of Simla. They signed the Simla Agreement, by which India would return all Pakistani personnel (over 90,000) and captured territory in the west, and the two countries would "settle their differences by peaceful means through bilateral negotiations." Diplomatic and trade relations were also re-established in 1976.

Afghanistan crisis

After the 1979 Soviet war in Afghanistan, new strains appeared in Indo-Pakistani relations. Pakistan actively supported the Afghan resistance against the Soviet Union, which was a close ally of India, which brought opposing political opinions.

The Taliban regime in Afghanistan was strongly supported by Pakistan—one of the few countries to do so—before the September 11 attacks and the start of the era of global terrorism. India, on the other hand, firmly opposed Taliban and criticised Pakistan for supporting it. Hatred for the Taliban grew amongst Hindu ultra-nationalists in India after they enforced laws on Afghan Hindus to "wear label"[4]

Agreements, talks, and confidence building measures

In the following eight years, India voiced increasing concern over Pakistani arms purchases, U.S. military aid to Pakistan, and a clandestine Pakistan's nuclear weapons programme. In an effort to curtail tensions, the two countries formed a joint commission to examine disputes. In December 1988, Prime Ministers Benazir Bhutto and Rajiv Gandhi concluded a pact not to attack each other's nuclear facilities. Agreements on cultural exchanges and civil aviation were also initiated.

In 1997, high-level Indo-Pakistan talks resumed after a three-year pause. The Prime Ministers of Pakistan and India met twice and the foreign secretaries conducted three rounds of talks. In June 1997, the foreign secretaries identified eight "outstanding issues" around which continuing talks would be focused. The dispute over the status of Kashmir (referred by India as Jammu and Kashmir), an issue since Independence, remains the major stumbling block in their dialogue. India maintains that the entire former princely state is an integral part of the Indian Union, while Pakistan insists that UN resolutions calling for self-determination of the people of the state/province must be taken into account. It however refuses to abide by the previous part of the resolution, which calls for it to vacate all territories occupied.

In September 1997, the talks broke down over the structure of how to deal with the issues of Kashmir, and peace and security. Pakistan advocated that the issues be treated by separate working groups. India responded that the two issues be taken up along with six others on a simultaneous basis. In May 1998 India, and then Pakistan, conducted nuclear tests.

2007 Samjhauta Express bombings

Main article: 2007 Samjhauta Express bombings

The 2007 Samjhauta Express bombings was a terrorist attack targeted on the Samjhauta Express train on the 18th of February.

2008 Mumbai attacks

The 2008 Mumbai attacks by ten terrorists killed over 173 and wounded 308. India blamed the Lashkar-e-Toiba, a Pakistan-based militant group, for planning and executing the attacks. Islamabad resisted the claims and demanded evidence. India provided evidence in the form of interrogations, weapons, candy wrappers, Pakistani Brand Milk Packets, and telephone sets.[5] Indian officials demanded Pakistan extradite suspects for trial. They also said that, given the sophistication of the attacks, the perpetrators "must have had the support of some official agencies in Pakistan".[6]

Terrorism in Jammu and Kashmir

Kashmiris Attacks on Jammu & Kashmir State Assembly: A car bomb exploded near the Jammu and Kashmir State Assembly on October 1, 2001, killing 27 people on an attack that was blamed on Kashmiri separatists. It was one of the most prominent attacks against India apart from on the Indian Parliament in December 2001. The dead bodies of the terrorists and the data recovered from them revealed that Pakistan was solely responsible for the activity.[7]

- 1997 Sangrampora massacre: On March 21, 1997, 7 Kashmiri Pandits were killed in Sangrampora village in the Budgam district.
- Wandhama Massacre: In January 1998, 24 Kashmiri Pandits living in the city of Wandhama were killed by Islamic terrorists.
- Qasim Nagar Attack: On July 13, 2003, armed men believed to be a part of the Lashkar-e-Toiba threw hand grenades at the Qasim Nagar market in Srinagar and then fired on civilians standing nearby killing twenty-seven and injuring many more.[8]
- Assassination of Abdul Ghani Lone: Abdul Ghani Lone, a prominent All Party Hurriyat Conference leader, was assassinated by an unidentified gunman during a memorial rally in Srinagar. The assassination resulted in wide-scale demonstrations against the Indian occupied-forces for failing to provide enough security cover for Mr. Lone.[9]
- July 20, 2005 Srinagar Bombing: A car bomb exploded near an armoured Indian Army vehicle in the famous Church Lane area in Srinagar killing four Indian Army personnel, one civilian and the suicide bomber. Terrorist group Hizbul Mujahideen, claimed responsibility for the attack.[10]
- Budshah Chowk attack: A terrorist attack on July 29, 2005 at Srinigar's city centre, Budshah Chowk, killed two and left more than 17 people injured. Most of those injured were media journalists.[11]

- Murder of Ghulam Nabi Lone: On October 18, 2005 suspected Army man killed Jammu and Kashmir's then Education Minister Ghulam Nabi Lone. No Terrorist group claimed responsibility for the attack.[12]

Terrorist activities elsewhere

The attack on the Indian Parliament was by far the most dramatic attack carried out by Pakistani terrorists. India blamed Pakistan for carrying out the attacks, an allegation which Pakistan strongly denied and one that brought both nations to the brink of a nuclear confrontation in 2001-02. However, international peace efforts ensured the cooling of tensions between the two nuclear-capable nations.

Apart from this, the most notable was the hijacking of Indian Airlines Flight IC 814 en route New Delhi from Kathmandu, Nepal. The plane was hijacked on December 24, 1999 approximately one hour after take off and was taken to Amritsar airport and then to Lahore in Pakistan. After refuelling the plane took off for Dubai and then finally landed in Kandahar, Afghanistan. Under intense media pressure, New Delhi complied with the hijackers' demand and freed Maulana Masood Azhar from its captivity in return for the freedom of the Indian passengers on the flight. The decision, however, cost New Delhi dearly. Maulana, who is believed to be hiding in Karachi, later became the leader of Jaish-e-Mohammed, an organisation which has carried out several terrorist acts against Indian Security Forces in Kashmir.[13]

On December 22, 2000, a group of terrorists belonging to the Lashkar-e-Toiba stormed the famous Red Fort in New Delhi. The Fort houses an Indian military unit and a high-security interrogation cell used both by the Central Bureau of Investigation and the Indian Army. The terrorists successfully breached the security cover around the Red Fort and opened fire at the Indian military personnel on duty killing two of them on spot. The attack was significant because it was carried out just two days after the declaration of the cease-fire between India and Pakistan.[14]

Two Kashmiri terrorists belonging to Jaish-e-Mohammed raided the Swami Narayan temple complex in Ahmedabad, Gujarat, killing 30 people, including 18 women and five children. The attack was carried out on September 25, 2002, just few days after state elections were held in Jammu and Kashmir. Two identical letters found on both the terrorists claimed that the attack was done in retaliation for the deaths of thousands of Muslims during the Gujarat riots.[15]

Two car bombs exploded in south Mumbai on August 25, 2003; one near the Gateway of India and the other at the famous Zaveri Bazaar, killing at least 48 and injuring 150 people. Though no terrorist group claimed responsibility for the attacks, Mumbai Police and RAW suspected Lashkar-e-Toiba's hand in the twin blasts.[16]

In an unsuccessful attempt, six terrorists belonging to Lashkar-e-Toiba, stormed the Ayodhya Ram Janambhoomi complex on July 5, 2005. Before the terrorists could reach the main disputed site, they were shot down by Indian security forces. One Hindu worshipper and two policemen were injured during the incident.[17]

Human rights violations

A report by the Human Rights Watch, stated two main reasons for the improving human rights condition in the region: First, sincere efforts were made by the new Jammu and Kashmir state government headed by Mufti Muhammad Sayeed to investigate cases of human rights abuses in the state and to punish those guilty including Indian soldiers. More than 15 Indian army soldiers were convicted by the Indian government in 2004 for carrying out human rights abuses in the state. Second, the decrease in cross-border infiltration into India by armed insurgents.[18]

Developments since 2004

Violent activities in the region declined in 2004. There are two main reasons for this: warming of relations between New Delhi and Islamabad which consequently lead to a ceasefire between the two countries in 2003 and the fencing of the LoC being carried out by the Indian Army. Moreover, coming under intense international pressure, Islamabad was compelled to take actions against the militant's training camps on its territory. In 2004, the two countries also agreed upon decreasing the number of troops present in the region.

Under pressure, Kashmiri militant organisations have made an offer for talks and negotiations with New Delhi, which India has welcomed.

India's Border Security Force blamed the Pakistani military for providing cover-fire for the terrorists whenever they infiltrated into Indian territory from Pakistan. Pakistan has in turn has also blamed India for providing support for terrorist groups inside Pakistan such as the MQM.

In 2005, Pakistan's Information Minister, Sheikh Rashid, was alleged to have run a terrorist training camp in 1990 in N.W. Frontier, Pakistan. The Pakistani government dismissed the charges against its minister as an attempt to hamper the ongoing peace process between the two neighbours.

Both India and Pakistan have launched several mutual confidence-building measures (CBMs) to ease tensions between the two. These include more high-level talks, easing visa restrictions, restarting of cricket matches between the two. The new bus service between Srinagar and Muzaffarabad has also helped bring the two sides closer. Pakistan and India have also decided to co-operate on economic fronts.

A major clash between Indian Security Forces and militants occurred when a group of insurgents tried to infiltrate into the Indian-administered Kashmir from Pakistan in July 2005. The same month, also saw Kashmiri militant attack on Ayodhya and Srinagar. However, these developments had little impact on the peace process.

Some improvements in the relations are seen with the re-opening of a series of transportation networks near the India-Pakistan border, with the most important being bus routes and railway lines.

An Indian man held in Pakistani prisons since 1975 as an accused spy walked across the border to freedom March 3, 2008, an unconditional release that Pakistan said was meant to reduce the deep-rooted enmity between the countries.[19]

Possible solutions to the Kashmir issue

Many consider that the best way to end present violence in Kashmir is negotiations between various Kashmiri-separatist groups, Pakistan and India. Here are a few possible solutions[20] to the Kashmir dispute[21]

The status quo	Currently a boundary—the Line of Control (LoC)—divides the region in two, with one part administered by India and one by Pakistan. India would like to formalize this status quo and make it the accepted international boundary. Factors Opposing—Pakistan rejects the plan partially as it will get lesser control over the region and wants greater. Kashmiri political parties too would oppose the plan as it violates the UN resolution for a referendum.
Kashmir becomes a part of Pakistan	Kashmir joining Pakistan. Factors Opposing—The minority communities of Hindus of Jammu and the Buddhists of Ladakh would object the outcome. Kashmiri Pandits who

	were forced out of Kashmir by militants are also a major topic to consider.
Kashmir becomes an independent sovereign republic	As an independent state, the region would most likely be economically viable with tourism probably being the largest source of income, however being a landlocked country, it would be heavily dependent on India and Pakistan. Factors Opposing—The outcome is unlikely because it requires both India and Pakistan (and potentially China) to give up territory.
A smaller independent Kashmir	A smaller independent Kashmir formed out of the current strip of Kashmir (administered by Pakistan) and the Kashmir valley (controlled by India). This would leave the Northern areas with Pakistan while India retains Jammu and Ladakh. However this region should maintain good relations with both India and Pakistan as it is landlocked and is covered with snow in winter. This region can also have its defence and foreign relations jointly handled by India and Pakistan. Factors Opposing—The outcome is unlikely because it requires both India and Pakistan to give up territory.

Re-evaluation

The insurgents who initially started their movement as a pro-Kashmiri independence movement, have gone through a lot of change in their ideology. Most of the insurgents portray their struggle as a religious one.

Indian analysts allege that by supporting these insurgents, Pakistan is trying to wage a proxy war against India while Pakistan claims that it regards most of these insurgent groups as "freedom fighters" rather than terrorists.

Internationally known to be the most deadly theatre of conflict, nearly 10 million people, including Muslims,

Hindus, and Buddhists, have been fighting a daily battle for survival. The cross-border firing between India and Pakistan, and the terrorist attacks combined have taken its toll on the Kashmiris, who have suffered poor living standards and an erosion of human rights.

Kargil crisis

Attempts to restart dialogue between the two nations were given a major boost by the February 1999 meeting of both Prime Ministers in Lahore and their signing of three agreements.

These efforts have since been stalled by the intrusion of Pakistani forces into Indian territory near Kargil in Jammu and Kashmir in May 1999. This resulted in intense fighting between Indian and Pakistani forces, known as the Kargil conflict. Backed by the Indian Air Force, the Indian Army successfully regained Kargil. A subsequent military coup in Pakistan that overturned the democratically elected Nawaz Sharif government in October of the same year also proved a setback to relations.

In 2001, a summit was called in Agra; Pakistani President Pervez Musharraf turned up to meet Indian Prime Minister Atal Behari Vajpayee. The talks fell through.

On June 20, 2004, with a new government in place in India, both countries agreed to extend a nuclear testing ban and to set up a hotline between their Foreign Secretaries aimed at preventing misunderstandings that might lead to a nuclear war.[22]

India has granted Pakistan unilateral "most favoured nation" trade status under WTO guidelines, but Pakistan is yet to reciprocate. As of early 2005, both countries are committed to a process of dialogue to solve all outstanding issues. Baglihar Dam issue was a new issue raised by Pakistan in 2005.

Indo-Pak Dialogue to Present

At last, the foreign secretaries of India and Pakistan are meeting on 14 November, 2006 in New Delhi, to resume the composite dialogue process that was put on hold in the wake of the 11 July serial train blasts by terrorists in Mumbai, which killed around 181 innocent people. The Havana summit meeting between Prime Minister Manmohan Singh and President Pervez Musharraf not only broke the deadlock on the resumption of bilateral dialogue, but also paved the way for the creation of an "India-Pakistan institutional mechanism to identify and implement counter-terrorism initiatives and investigations". Both leaders seem to have covered some distance in bridging their differences, agreeing on measures to curb terrorism, and exploring ways towards conflict resolution. But the future prospects of the whole process depend on how far Islamabad tries its best to satisfy India in curbing India-specific terrorism and cross-border infiltration on the one hand, and on whether New Delhi appropriately responds to the flexibility being shown by President Musharraf on the tedious issue of Kashmir, on the other.

Followed by the Havana summit and yet-to-be-created joint anti-terrorism institutional mechanism, India has formally charged 11 Pakistanis for having allegedly carried out the Mumbai blasts, implicating the Inter-Services Intelligence (ISI), two Pakistan-based outlawed militant outfits, and the banned Students Islamic Movement of India (SIMI). Addressing a conference of armed forces' commanders, Prime Minister Manmohan Singh has "put Pakistan on notice that any democratic government of India would find it difficult to continue on the present path (of dialogue) to address all outstanding issues unless the government of Pakistan clearly deals with the issue of terrorism". While India has provided "evidence" to other powers, Islamabad has yet not received any kind of brief on

Indian investigations into the Mumbai blasts. It has to be appreciated, however, that it was President Musharraf who raised the issue of hostility among the intelligence services of the two countries against the backdrop of charges and counter-charges of interference in each other's internal affairs, and who proposed, in his interview with Frontline, that "the intelligence agencies of both sides should reach an agreement to stop interfering in each other's internal affairs".

Expressing their resolve at the Havana summit to sustain the peace process and underlying the importance of its success for the whole South Asian region, Mr. Singh and Mr. Musharraf decided "to continue the joint search for a peaceful settlement of all issues between India and Pakistan, including the issue of Jammu and Kashmir, in a sincere and purposeful manner". In the context of the dispute over Kashmir, they agreed to "build on convergences and narrow down divergences". What are the convergences and divergences, one might ask, over a most divisive issue?

Already, the two sides have drawn their bottom lines: India is not ready to alter borders and any further divide on religious lines; and Pakistan is not ready to accept the Line of Control (LoC) as an international border permanently dividing the Kashmiris. However, both have agreed to make LoC "irrelevant" or, as Manmohan Singh said on 25 May 2006, "just a line on the map". If President Musharraf has spoken about the "joint management" of the two parts of Kashmir, Mr. Singh prefers the expression, "institutional arrangements". On the Kashmiris' right to self-rule, Musharraf is for "self-governance" and India is traditionally for maximum "autonomy", barring sovereignty. Both are against conceding "independence" to the Kashmiris. The divergences are on what areas constitute Kashmir; whether Jammu, Ladakh, and the Northern Areas will be out of it; the quantum of autonomy; exact nature of joint-management/institutional arrangement between the two parts of Kashmir; the autonomy component and residual powers to be retained by the two countries; and the Indo-Pak coordinating "superstructure" and the nature of Kashmiris' representation, demilitarization/end to militancy and security, etc.

If there is enough political will on both sides, as convergences expand, the remaining divergences can be bridged and certain patterns and legal frameworks can be adapted from the resolution of other such disputes, as on Kashmir, to suit our peculiar circumstances. The dispute over Kashmir has lingered on for too long and has cost too much, not only for the Kashmiris, but also for 1.4 billion people in the Subcontinent. It may take time to set an irreversible process in motion to settle the issue, but it must be resolved and removed from the gambit of Indo-Pak relations. Given their past animosity, even the most ancillary issues have turned into perennial issues, such as Siachin and Sir Creek, which could be solved without haggling over details and wasting time. On water issues, both countries remain committed to the Indus Water Treaty.

The real issue, or what we can describe as the core issue, is what kind of relationship the twin-brothers of the Subcontinent might evolve while overcoming past enmities and the mindset of enmity. No doubt, the bloody partition of the Subcontinent left deep scars on both sides, yet the countries could have healed the wounds and started a new chapter of a fraternal relationship. But this did not happen because the Indians refused to accept the new reality and the Pakistanis continued to perceive India as an eternal enemy, while both sides took opposite roads in entering into hostile international alignments. This approach did not come to an end even after the end of the Cold War.

The time has come to evolve a new paradigm of fraternal

and mutually beneficial partnership and cooperative relationship in the region and on the world stage. Both Mahatma Gandhi and Quaid-i-Azam Mohammed Ali Jinnah wanted a fraternal relationship between the two independent states. Instead of competing in an arms race and planning to destroy each other, they need to develop cooperative security, including measures to stabilise the nuclear regime, and universal nuclear disarmament while in the same boat. Indeed, there are particular legitimate national interests to pursue, but why should they be brought into conflict with our shared destiny?

As India and Pakistan continue their efforts to peacefully resolve their contentious issues, all areas of potential cooperation, both bilateral and regional, should be fully exploited to the best advantage of our respective peoples. If Pakistan should grant Most Favoured Nation (MFN) status to India and allow trade and investment between the two countries, India needs to lower its tariffs and remove non/para-tariff barriers to trade. While New Delhi repeatedly claims that India offers a great economic opportunity to its neighbours, it should be taking concrete measures to translate its words into deeds. Both big brothers of South Asia must, in the meanwhile, continue the process of converting SAARC into a vibrant economic union.

The next phase of dialogue should be made productive and useful while narrowing down the areas of differences to be resolved at the political level and fully implementing the agreements already reached and various joint statements signed between the two sides since 6 January, 2004. For this to happen, Pakistan and India must jointly curb the scourge of terrorism that threatens both countries, show greater forebearance and patience for a better tomorrow, and not let terrorists derail the peace process. In the meanwhile, let the two sides remove all hurdles in the way of people-to-people contact by radically liberalising their visa regimes and removing all curbs on the free flow of people and information across our borders to strengthen solidarity and friendship among the people. Together with other South Asian countries, India and Pakistan must strive to make the region yet another powerhouse of economic growth and prosperity, side by side with our neighbour China, and not let others make Asians fight Asians.

References

1. Pakistan acknowledges suspect in Mumbai attacks is a Pakistani.
2. Pakistan on full military alert after hoax call.
3. Instrument of Accession.
4. Pakistan is given evidence on attacks, AP story in NYT, 2009-01-05.
5. In Sharing Mumbai Findings, India Exhorts Pakistan to Act, Washington Post, 2009-01-06.
6. Budania, Rajpal, "India's Pakistan Policy: A Study in the Context of Security," South Asian Studies, Vol. 30:2,1995.
7. Burke, S.M., Mainsprings of Indian and Pakistani Foreign Policies, Minneapolis, University of Minnesota, 1974.
8. Brines Russel, The Indo-Pakistan Conflict, London, Pall Mall Press, 1968.

Chapter 17

INDIA-CHINA-RUSSIA—A TRIANGULAR RELATIONSHIP

Possibility and Perspective

*Col. O. P. Singh**

Introduction

The idea of establishing a strategic triangle between Russia, China and India as a counterweight to the United States was first mooted by former Russian Prime Minister Yevgeny Primakov during a visit to New Delhi in December 1998. Back then, Primakov's grand plans did not find much purchase: Russia was in the throes of a disastrous economic meltdown, while China and a newly nuclear India both rejected the idea of such an axis outright. At that juncture it was difficult to perceive a convergence of strategic interests between India, Russia and China. With the prospects of extended U.S. military presence in the Central Asia, Russia revived its three year old proposal to rope India and China

* Army Officer.

into a trilateral power axis in 2002. The fact that these three countries occupy such a strategic position—both in terms of geography and dynamics of international politics—and that these three countries share common Asian wisdom, fully qualifies it as an entity to reckon with. The commonality of the key national interests and the long-term friendly relations in the field of economy, culture, science and technology create a real possibility for cooperation between these great Eurasian powers.

Any cooperation between India, China and Russia would have to take full cognisance of the relationship of all the three with the U.S. and the West. This does not imply that the relations between any of these countries and the US should be construed as hurdle in political cooperation amongst them.

In Feb 07, representatives from India, China and Russia met in New Delhi for a summit to promote international peace and discuss energy and economic cooperation between their nations, which encompass approximately 40% of the world's 6.5 billion people. The discussions included Iran and North Korea's nuclear programs, rebuilding Afghanistan, and the war in Iraq besides tripartite cooperation in trade and energy. The joint statement at the conclusion of the summit emphasised that the trilateral cooperation was not directed against the interests of any single country and was, on the contrary, intended to promote international harmony and understanding. The three countries fervently insisted that this meeting was not the genesis of a new coalition seeking to remedy an imbalance of power due to U.S. international policy. However, they stressed a "strong commitment" to utilizing "multilateral diplomacy". Analysts seem to agree that this is a thinly veiled threat in response to real or perceived unilateral actions of the United States ir recent years. As India, China and Russia enjoy economic growth and development never seen before in their nations, they appear to be growing a louder voice on the world scene—especially when it comes to America's international policies. Russian President Vladimir Putin has been highly critical of America's policy on international affairs. The recent warnings by Russia against deployment of missile defence by US in Poland are an indicator of things to come.

There is a need to study the intangibles in international relations to arrive at a reasonable prognosis on the emerging triangular relationship between Russia, India, and China. Will this group of nations unite to pressure the United States economically? Will other nations do the same, attempting to balance the scales of global influence with the formation of another superpower? Only time will tell.

BASIS FOR COOPERATION

Triangular cooperation between China, India and Russia has a rich and positive potential based on common or similar positions on a broad range of international issues such as democratisation of international relations, formation of a multi polar world, opposing hegemony, countering international terrorism, extremism, separatism, organised crime and illegal circulation of drugs. Economic cooperation to include energy security and access to each other's markets are other areas of cooperation. Trilateral cooperation has become a reality not only due to the need of speedy development, but also due to the objective prerequisites for its implementation, namely:

Together our countries are self-sufficient from the economic point of view. They possess the richest natural resources enabling them to be powers to reckon with.

More than one-third of mankind lives in these countries. It is well known that the people of Russia, China and India are extremely industrious, highly intellectual, inventive, and skilled and are self sacrificing in attaining goals.

Russia—as successor and heiress of the Soviet Union, which was one of the best technically and scientifically developed states, maintains a major part of its potential and may become a locus in the acceleration of scientific progress in all three countries.

There is an urgent need to counter the US policy of pre-emption and hegemony as it poses a grave danger to the world peace. Invasion of Iraq despite adverse world opinion is a case in point.

AREAS OF COOPERATION

National Missile Defence (NMD)

Indian, Chinese and Russian coordination, informal discussions and their demonstration of a resolve to stand together by their shared ideas on this subject has clearly made its impact felt in the US. Recent history of US led NATO bombing in Kosovo and its bombing of Chinese embassy in Belgrade, its continued support and military supplies to Taiwan, tenor of revised US-Japan Defence Cooperation Guidelines, Cox report of 1999 which alleged China of nuclear spying and their general and regular anti-China human rights campaign keeps China's policy makers vary of US motives. Russia had its own concerns about NATO expansion, invasion of Iraq and emergence of new nuclear weapons states. New Delhi carried anxieties of being defamed before even building their nuclear deterrent. The plan by the United States to develop a NMD system is seen as a US bid to seek unilateral military and security advantage. As a result, responses of these countries had emerged as the most formidable challenge for the US NMD initiative. Reactions of India-China-Russia were widely seen to have the potential of making US NMD programme a dangerously counterproductive pipedream, if not totally nullifying this ambitious US vision.

Polycentric World Order

The three countries would like to see emergence of coalition of interests among equals rather than alliances or partnerships built on hegemony. A polycentric order will involve countries from Asia, Europe, the Americas and Africa, even though the precise shape would depend to a great extent on the several political, economic and social processes under way in the countries of these regions. A polycentric world would be based on a plural order built upon a cooperative approach supported by an overlapping network of institutions among governments and civilian societies, and strengthened by openness, democracy and transparency. A requisite for effective functioning multilateralism is that international political, economic and financial institutions operate under commonly accepted regulations with which all can willingly and enthusiastically abide. The United Nations and more particularly, its primary organ, the Security Council, needs to be reformed to more accurately reflect the realities of a world that has changed so much from the era of World War II. China's and Russia's support to Indian claim of permanent membership of UN Security Council can also be seen from this perspective.

Terrorism

India, China, Russia strategic triangle reflects the essential oriental thinking of seeking security in peace and not peace in security which eludes most western experts. There is unanimous recognition about the need for international cooperation to combat the menace of terrorism, but it is felt that some elements of the US approach to an international coalition against terrorism require caution. USA seems to be motivated by triple goals: to eliminate Islamic extremism; enhance its status as sole super power; increase control over energy sources of Middle East and Central Asia. In fact, China, India and Russia are sitting on the fringes of Islamic or neo Islamic countries and are directly affected by the scourge of terrorism. All three have bilateral dialogue with each other on counter-terrorism. Trilateral exchange of experience, intelligence, skills and ideas would help greatly. The three countries could also evolve a regional plan to deal with terrorism.

Security Cooperation

In a wide area that encompasses West Asia, Central Asia, South, South-East and East Asia, causes of conflict have not been removed. In fact new tensions have emerged, weapons of mass destruction have proliferated, their means of delivery and the threat of addition of new systems either exist or could come into being. It needs no elaboration that China, India and Russia have a deep and vital interest in peace, stability and prosperity of this vast region. All three countries accept the new security concept that advocates mutual security based on trust and disarmament. They are opposed to strengthening and enlarging existing military alliances, including expansion of the NATO, as well as forming new military blocs. In order to enhance mutual understanding and trust, each country can keep others posted about new developments in their bilateral relations. Each of the three can also inform the other two in time on new developments in their relations with other major powers. There are therefore, good reasons for a conceptual shift from old paradigms of competitive security to new ones of cooperative security in the region. The extensive network of treaties and agreements between India, China and Russia including the treaty forming the Shanghai Cooperative Organisation (SCO), are major contributions to a new paradigm of cooperative security.

Cooperation at UN

The United Nations has played a tremendous role in safeguarding peace and security, promoting cooperation and development in the world, thereby enjoying enormous authority in handling major international issues. However, the UN is faced with some new challenges: the position and authority of the U.N. are being challenged, principles of the U.N. Charter violated, and the UN's responsibility to solve development issues neglected. The new changes in the international situation call for strengthened international cooperation, particularly global cooperation. The idea of strengthening cooperation and coordination of China, Russia and India in the UN touches on all these issues. We all are aware of the status of the three countries in the UN. Both China and Russia are permanent members of the UN Security Council. India is striving for the permanent membership of the UN Security Council. China and Russia understand India's aspirations very well and are willing to see India play a bigger role in the UN and have lately supported India's claim for permanent membership in the Security Council. The three nations share wide-ranging interests in many major areas and international issues as all of them are committed to building just and fair new international political and economic order. These issues include anti-unilateralism, advocating peaceful coexistence, and respecting the right of developments to change the unfair international trade regime. As stated earlier the informal consultations on the sidelines of the UN General Assembly in September, 2002 was a good beginning. This arrangement though informal has become a regular feature amongst the three nations.

The meeting of the Foreign Ministers in September 2003 on the sidelines of UN General Assembly Meeting, an initiative that was launched in 2002, was hosted by Indian External Affairs Minister Mr. Yashwant Sinha and was attended by his Chinese and Russian counterparts, Li Zhaoxing and Igor Ivanov. Mr Sinha stated that India would be working with the China and Russia on a new resolution on Iraq that is to be placed before the Security Council. The three ministers also discussed the need to reform the UN. According to Sinha, "We have adopted a common approach and we have asked our ambassadors at the UN to work together on this and, if necessary, take the help of experts to firm up a proposal". The Russian and Indian ministers supported the proposal of China to adopt a UN General Assembly resolution aimed at strengthening international public-health cooperation and, in particular, in the fight against such illnesses as Severe Acute Respiratory Syndrome (SARS). The meeting has shown that on many issues of the international agenda, the positions of India, Russia and China are close or coincide. It was also pointed out that this partnership is not directed against other states and corresponds to the interests of maintaining regional and global stability. Interest was expressed in continuing the trilateral dialogue with a view to coordinating their positions and upholding multilateral approaches on the international scene.

Cooperation at Regional Level

Since the three countries have taken part in different regional organisations, they can inform each other on the development of these organisations and make a study on possible initiatives for coordination and cooperation between these organisations. China and Russia will support India's participation in the APEC. Since all the three countries are members of ASEAN Regional Forum (AFR), they can coordinate their stand as preventive diplomacy. As known, the Shanghai Cooperation Organisation Charter provides for accession of new members, though with a step by step procedure. India is more and more often named as a possible candidate by Russia.

Economic Cooperation

The recurrent financial crisis in different regions of the world led to much criticism of the IMF. The countries that followed the IMF textbook solutions, like Russia and Argentina, had more serious economic crisis than countries that did not do so, like China, India and Malaysia. The second area of concern is the management of the multilateral trading system. China's entry into the World Trade Organisation (WTO), actively supported by India, has strengthened the WTO. As a major trading power, China has an important role to play in shaping the WTO and the global trading system. Hopefully, Russia will also soon become a WTO member. The inability of the World Trade Organisation to address the challenge of developing economies and arrest the trend of protectionism in the developed world is a matter of continued concern. The effective functioning of WTO, and a development oriented agenda for WTO are issues of concern for the three countries. In these circumstances comprehensive China - Russia - India cooperation is the best option. In the global recession after 11 Sep, sustained economic development of China, Russia and India has become the 'engine' of global economy. More objectively, following our economic development and structural changes, there is emergence of more and more demand. The scale of economic contacts between the three countries is becoming bigger and bigger, ties are becoming closer, contradictions and clashes are also decreasing. In the face of economically developed countries and trans national companies, an economy lacking in strength and experience trying to negotiate is an unequal contender. Hence, in our context trilateral dialogue is a must to counter this challenge.

Challenges of Economic Development

There are many similarities in the socio economic conditions of the three countries. Face to face with economic globalisation, the problems the three are encountering also have commonalities. For example, traditional agriculture and industry are hit by the low-priced goods of trans national companies. Developed countries are abusing regulations, non-tariff barriers and are draining science and technology personnel. Definitely a very high price will have to be paid. There is no way of reversing it, but this must be resisted. One must depend on one's own strengths, but we also cannot fight single-handedly. Jointly tackling challenges should be the foundation of trilateral cooperation. This kind of cooperation also transcends purely geopolitical goals because behind the cooperation there is a great motivation of interests: first is to reduce the damage caused by unreasonable regulations; second is to provide an alternative for economic development; and third is to look for a buffer zone in order to avoid economic crisis. All these can become a great impetus for trilateral cooperation. Indeed, the goal of trilateral cooperation is mutual benefit and most likely will conform to the interest of each country.

Energy Cooperation

Cooperation in the field of energy among Russia, China and India can proceed along several lines. All three countries are in different stages of development of their energy sectors. Sharing their experience, for example, in the regulation of the sector and the policies aimed at promoting investment, can help each one in fine tuning the policies pertaining to that sector. However, an important distinction is that while Russia is a net energy exporter and has huge reserves of hydrocarbons, China and India are net energy importers. Thus, Indian and Chinese companies exploring the Russian hydrocarbon basins for their domestic requirements can cooperate effectively.

In fact, efforts are already on in this direction, ONGC Videsh Limited (OVL), an arm of the Indian national company Oil and Natural Gas Cooperation (ONGC) has a stake in the Sakhalin venture in Russia operated by Exxon Mobil. OVL acquired 20 per cent participating interest in Sakhalin-I project, in the Russia Far East for US $ 1.7 billion. The field is estimated to have 2-8 billion barrels of oil reserves. The crude oil expected from the field is good quality low sulphur oil, comparable to Brent (North Sea) and Bonny Light (Nigeria) streams, and thus will command a premium in the international oil market and will directly enhance the supply security of the country. Cooperation is also envisaged in the downstream segment, especially in pipeline transportation. Transportation of petroleum or natural gas via the sea does not look very economical, especially to India, due to geographical constraints and the relative attractiveness of other such options. An oil and/or gas pipeline from Russia to India via China, however, looks feasible enough to warrant a closer look.

The three nations to join together and make the oil and/or gas pipeline from West Siberia in Russia to India, passing through China a reality, the economics would have to make tremendous sense and the political climate would need to be reciprocative. There are challenges galore, as is the case with many other cross-country pipelines, but the benefits can certainly be huge. Russia, which holds the world's largest proven reserves of natural gas and crude oil, will be able to reduce its dependence on Europe for markets and on Iran for trade routes. India will be able to accelerate economic development and growth in a sustainable way and so will China.

Cooperation in Science and Technology

Even though, plenty of research activity is undertaken in the three countries, it is still inadequate. Cooperation in research though a very complex issue needs to be undertaken with full vigour to be able to make a mark in the developing and developed world.Trilateral dialogue on intellectual property rights is another important strategic area of cooperation. While consultative channels on conventional and dominant intellectual property rights (IPR) issues exist, not enough attention appears to have been paid by us on the moves initiated by the US and some other countries on the patenting of research tools and techniques. Such a patent regime will have far reaching implications on research and development activities in Russia, India and China, and therefore require special trilateral attention. One may also take note of technological innovations arising out of traditional or experiential knowledge, the value and importance of which is recognised in India and China.

Technology Missions in India are end-to-end programmes covering the entire chain, from research and development to actual delivery aimed at making a major national impact on the economic and social conditions of large sections of the Indian population. These missions, such as, to provide safe drinking water, immunisation of children and increasing the availability of edible oil, were guided by non-commercial motivations. Indeed many such programmes that impact on several areas of development are not amenable to a straightforward cost-benefit analysis.

The strategy in such technology mission programmes, is to bring all the strengths, administrative, engineering, research and management together, to bear upon its success. This integration is usually possible in programmes that have high societal visibility and impact. The three countries have their strengths and have an excellent track record of end-to-end missions in areas such as space and atomic energy. Can we not take up a trilateral technology mission that has a major societal impact like the Indian Technology Mission? The development of inland waterways is an example of such a technology mission, in which all the three nations have strengths. The three countries together present a unique combination of administrative, managerial, engineering, research expertise and opportunity in this area. The environmental and other development benefits of inland waterways are well known and need not be stated. There is a need to show to the world the joint expertise of India, Russia and China in Science & Technology. The recent success in Indo-Russian BrahMos missile venture is a good example of such cooperation.

Environmental Pollution

Ecologists have been calling to stop the pollution of the planet with industrial wastes and other products of human activities. The growing rate of general radioactivity poses a threat for the global biosphere. In the context of the growing anthropogenic impact on the environment, keeping the latter clean is vitally important for human health. With the magnitude of medical, biological and socio-economic consequences, caused by radiation and chemical malfunctions and catastrophes of the twentieth and early twenty first centuries are alarming. To ensure security and safety of the population, economic facilities and the natural environment must be ranked as a critical task of the twenty first century. The idea is that Russia, China and India could set forth an initiative to draft the special code type document for East, Central and South Asia. The given document must be designed to prevent accidents and catastrophes as well as to eliminate their consequences. This alliance should also seek US as a signatory to Kyoto Protocol on environment.

Another aspect is the effort to make US and Western countries reduce their Greenhouse gases emissions and contribute significantly towards restoring the damage caused to the environment. The recent effort by India in this regard duly supported by Russia and China is laudable.

Appreciated Indian Point of View

On its part India should pursue the idea of trilateral cooperation with vigour for three reasons. Firstly, such cooperation would provide India space for manoeuverability in its negotiations with the West. It would also bring about greater balance in its policy. Secondly, from the perspective of its deep geopolitical and security interests in the Central Asian Region, trilateral cooperation holds enhanced significance. The level of activity in the Central Asian Region has intensified. On the one hand is the military presence of the West and on the other hand Russia is making serious attempts to build new security structures in the region. The Shanghai Cooperation Organisation has been institutionalised and President Putin hopes to create a Collective Security Treaty Organisation. How these two organisations will shape up and how effective an instrument they will emerge is difficult to say at this juncture, but India could be left out from an area that is of vital importance to it. Thirdly, the role of Asia is growing in international politics and as one of the major Asian countries India could derive benefits by cooperating with other major Asian countries. From this perspective India should make serious effort to see that trilateral cooperation moves forward.

Conclusion

In the grim situation facing the world today when the United States has turned into a new imperial power by unleashing a war on Iraq to gain control of its oil wealth, the Eurasian vision of cooperation is the only hope for humanity to overcome the crisis into which it has been plunged. The creation of Russia-China-India Strategic Triangle of Cooperation for executing mega projects of infrastructural development of railroad and gas pipelines, for constructing a land bridge across Eurasia alone has the potential to extricate the world economy from depression. The Eurasian perspective of ensuring security through intensified peaceful cooperation among India, China, Russia and the Central Asian Republics offers a viable paradigm for building a system of Asian security. The forging of the Eurasian trilateral cooperation of the basis of peaceful coexistence and strategic partnership is directed at restoring the missing equilibrium in the present international security environment which has been vitiated of late on account of the aberrant behaviour of the United States which is hell-bent on attaining its objective unilaterally, bypassing the UN and riding roughshod not only over world public opinion but also the opinion of its alliance partners. In such a situation the deepening of tripartite Eurasian Cooperation is both timely and opportune. By 2015 US share of world gross product will amount to 18.6 per cent, the same as that of India and China together. The United States will only be serving its own interests in the first place by having mutually beneficial cooperation with each of the three countries forming the Eurasian triangle.

The India-Russia-China triangle is destined to become a reality sooner than many skeptics think. That the triangle is not a fleeting idea is becoming clearer with the growing strategic relationship and multi-faceted cooperation between three countries as to warrant a specific mention by Prime Minister Vajpayee in his address to the commanders of the three services. Vajpayee's China visit followed by an equally successful visit to Russia has made a significant contribution to the forging of cooperation among three great powers to usher in a multipolar world order. The movement towards forging trilateral cooperation between India, China and Russia has acquired urgency on account of the growing realisation by the three powers that the United States was only exploiting concerns over the menace of terrorism to further its hegemonistic goals.

Strengthening of this India-China-Russia strategic triangle remains the only hope if Asia has to find its voice and make any positive contribution towards the evolution of global framework for security and peace. Looking at the issue realistically, mutual interests, the greatest of all purposes, may become the cement of this alliance. There is, thus, a motivation in all three capitals to cooperate on strategic, security and economic issues.

Chapter 18

ISLAMIC EXTREMISTS IN BANGLADESH

*Dr. O.P. Shukla**

Introduction

A series of coordinated blasts of 459 bombs in 63 out of 64 districts on August 17, 2005 firmly established Bangladesh as another hotbed of terrorism. While the police blamed the Jamaatul-Mujahideen Bangladesh (JMB), Minister of Industries and Jamaat-e-Islami leader Maulana Matiur Rahman Nizami put the blame on India's RAW and Israel's Mosad. Later on, former Islamic Foundation Director, Molana Fariduddin Masud, detained for suspected links to the August 17 blasts reportedly pointed out Nizami's involvement in the country-wide explosions.

The Jagrata Muslim Janata Bangladesh (JMJB) and the JMB, whose leaflets were found at some of the ports, could be telling the Dhaka government that their influence is not

* Editor, Guest Lecturer, Deptt. of Defence Studies, University of Lucknow, Lucknow.

confined to one particular region. The bombs showed that Bangladeshese could no longer deny the direction their country had taken and that unless it was changed, there was going to be only one outcome.

What is disturbing is the threat that the perpetrators of the violence pose to civilized values in Bangladesh. The ominous signals came from the choice of their targets. Institutions that represent civil liberties and democratic values—such as government offices, courts, universities and Press clubs —were the prime targets. The message was that Islamic Law must be founded in Bangladesh on the ruis of all secular and democratic institutions. And terror must be the key to the setting up of the new dispensation.

'Tolerant' Government

The sporadic actions of the government of Bangladesh against the extremist have been more to do with addressing international concerns rather than rooting out the Islamic terrorist groups. JMJB led by Bangla Bhai and JMB were banned hours before the meeting of the donors in Washington on February 23-24, 2005. But Bangla Bhai roamed freely after the ban.

The violence also buttressed the Indian standpoint that Dhaka has been tolerant with Islamic fundamentalist outfits, who rally support by fanning anti-India sentiments. These outfits also have a nexus with militant outfit such as the United Liberation Front of Assam (ULFA) and the National Liberation Front of Tripura (NLFT) operating in India's north-east and provide them shelter.

A major arms haul of April 2004 in Chittagong was quietly buried by Dhaka although the western media had pointed to an Al-Qaida connection. One of the boats that carried the arms was allegedly owned by a senior Bangladeshi politician. Earlier, another big weapons haul too went unnoticed. In June 2003, when the police intercepted a truck carrying assault rifles and RDX among pineapples in Bogra in Bangladesh, the matter was reportedly hushed up, pointing a needle of suspicion to the top echelons in Dhaka.

Terror Network

Apart from the JMB and the JMJB, another outlawed group—the Able Hadith Andolon Bangladesh (AHAB) of Muhammad Asadullah AI Galib—was under scrutiny for the bombings. These three Islamic militant groups are interlinked, and have connections with Islamic groups in Muslim countries in west Asia and Pakistan. One school of opinion in intelligence circles believes AHAB is a mass platform of the JMB and most AHAB workers are involved in JMB activities. Another school says JMB militants through Galib have utilised the facilities of some 700 mosques built across the country by the Revival of Islamic Heritage Society (RIHS). This Kuwait-based NGO, they say, has funded Galib with crores of takas over the last one decade. Worried citizens felt that August 17 was perhaps the last warning before the country spirals into a vortex of violence.

Root Causes

From opposing the Bangladesh liberation war by participating in the genocide and mass murder of the intelligentsia, Jammat-e-Islami has come a long way to become a partner of the government since 2001. The growth of extremism in the last four years can be found in the following facts.

- The international community, including India, failed to address violence against religious and ethnic minorities, which furthered religious extremism and provided a sense of impunity to the zealots. The attacks on minorities, forcible occupation of land and atrocities against Hindus were allowed with impunity.

- The government has been openly siding with extremist elements. On January 8, 2005, the government banned all publications of the Ahmadiya community , including the Koran and any translations or interpretations of it to appease the fundamentalists. The ban on the Ahmadiya publications was in clear contempt of the High Court's orders. On August 17, 2005 nearly 15,000 fundamentalists equipped with sticks, iron rods and other sharp weapons attacked the Ahmadiya community, injuring over 50 people, including women and children at Sundarban Bazar of Shyamnagar upazila, Satkhira.
- State support to madrasas , which are increasingly being held responsible for fomenting extremism across the world, has increased exponentially during the current BNP- Jamaat rule. It is not only Saudi funds, the government of Bangladesh has been using assistance for education from UN agencies, western donors and other multilateral financial institutions to fund the madrasas. According to Bangladesh Economic Review, from 2001 to 2005, the number of madrasas increased by 22.22 per cent in comparison to the 9.74 per cent growth of the general educational institutions. There are about 15,000 Qawmi madrasas under the Bangladesh Qawmi Madrasa Education Board which are totally out of government control and have their own curriculum. Thousands of other Madrasas are not registered under any organisation.
- Extreme fundamentalists have a grip on the present

government. Salahuddin Kader Chowdhury, infamous for his role against the Bangladesh liberation war and suspected arms smuggling to India, serve as the advisor for Parliamentary Affairs to the Prime Minister. Chowdhury's hold on the government is such that he was also nominated for the post of Secretary General of the Organisation of Islamic Conference, much to the consternation of international community. There are many known extreme fundamentalists who hold important positions in the goverment.

- There is power vacuum in Bangladesh. Political authorities do not exercise full control over the Army and other security forces. There is a strong nexus between the extremists and local authorities, Political leaders and Directorate General of Bangladesh Forces' Intelligence. There have been countless incidents in which Islamic extremists were apprehended, sometime with arms and explosives, only to be released by the authorities.

Electoral Alliance with Extremist

The Jammat-e-Islami and other fundamentalist groups remain indispensable in Bangladeshi electoral politics. During the last parliamentary elections in 2001, BNP received 40.97 per cent of the vote against 40.13 per cent received by the Awami League. BNP's landslide victory was ensured because of partner of the government. Islamic fundamentalists have further expanded their support base. Given the power vacuum, polarisation of the Awami League and BNP, state support to fundamentalist groups against the non-Muslims and increased indispensability of the Jamaats in electoral politics, Islamic terrorists in Bangladesh are unlikely to be rooted out.

Taliban Connection in Bangladesh: Threat to India's Security

For a long period now, Bangladesh rulers have been in denial mode—denying the existence of Islamic fundamentalism, which has now led to the virtual Talibanisation of Bangladesh. They have denied that Islamic fundamentalist parties and the madrasas, funded with Arab money, were mushrooming in the country. They have denied the existence of training camps where Pakistani and Bangladesh ex-servicemen have trained cadres for jehadi service in Myanmar and further into South East Asia. Similarly, there is bland denial that Indian insurgent groups have been provided shelter in Bangladesh. Whenever in trouble, deny and be brazen about it, seems to be the motto.

Like the ISI in Pakistan, the ruling dispensation in Bangladesh has encouraged Wahabi-oriented and Saudi Arabia-funded groups like the JMJB that swears allegiance to the Taliban. The Harkat-ul-Jihad al-Ilami (HUJI) is a founding member of Osama bin Laden's International Islamic Front for "Jihad against Jews and Crusaders".

It was the BNP-led coalition that seems to have emboldened al-Qaeda and Taliban sympathisers to raise slogans like "Amrasobai hobo Taliban Bangla hobe Afghanistan" meaning 'We will all become Taliban and Bangla will become Afghanistan.' Some ambition that!

There are now more than 30 religious militant organisations that have set up countrywide networks with the main aim of establishing an Islamic State. Many of the cadres have been given training on how to conduct jehad and they have many veterans from the Afghan, Lebanon and Palestine theatres.

Training is mostly given in the jungle of the Chittagong Hill Tracts and the north of the country. Recruits could be from Bangladesh, Myanmar or South-East Asia. The favourite districts of the extremists are Naogaon, Rajshahi , Kushtia, Bogra and Pabna, bordering West Bengal. The JMJB claims the allegiance of 30,000 activists while the JMB boasts 10,000 full-time, and 100,000 part-time workers. In Chittagong the disticts are Rangamati, Cox's Bazar, Bandarban and Khagrachari bordering Mizoram, Tripura and Myanmar where the main activities are those by HUJI and the Osama-inspired international Islamic Front. It has 25,000 trained activists.

Financing the Extremists

Several NGOs and Qawmi madrasas have received huge sums of money from shady Kuwaiti, UAE, Saudi and Pakistani sources since 1989, ostensibly for opening mosques, schools and hospitals. Instead, they finance militancy. Funds are also diverted into business ventures and it is estimated that these NGOs earn about 1,200 crore taka annually.

India's Concerns

As a neighbour, India is naturally concerned with the rise of violence and the growth of Islamic fundamentalist politics. This trend worries the liberal and secular elements in Bangladesh but their voice is lost in the din of jehadi fervour.

With a porous border between the countries running to some 4,000 kilometers, religious fanatics in Bangladesh can threaten India's security. The influx of illegal migrants from Bangladesh into India has long been a major irritant in bilateral relations between the two neighbours. Dhaka's refusal to accept the fact is justifiably seen in New Delhi as an act of connivance. The other issue of the North-East militants using Bangladeshi territory for arms training and shelters has caused even greater tension.

Bangladesh has become a hatchery for terrorist groups

and insurgents. As fresh evidence of the existence of militant camps across that country surface, India needs to act tough with its errant neighbour. Bangladesh currently hosts over 190 camps belonging to almost two dozen insurgent groups. It is home to 180 top insurgent leaders, including fugitives like ULFA honchos Paresh Barua and Anoop Chettia.

The establishment in Dhaka nurtures an anti-India sentiment and the divide is growing. The Bangladesh Army's war doctrine focuses on a fight against a fictional country Fox land, which is India. The border guarding force, Bangladesh Rifles (BDR), has had repeated skirmishes with India's BSF.

While India should enhance cooperation with Bangladesh in areas like promoting interaction at the people's level and removing protectionist trade barriers, the overall approach should be one of carrot and stick. The growing presence of Islamic terrorist groups in Myanmar necessitates much closer cooperation with Yangon to finalise a coordinated strategy to deal with insurgencies and separatist movements.

Comments

Is India being soft towards Bangladesh? Maybe it is time Delhi took a hard look at that. India needs to take a calibrated view of its Bangladesh policy. What is required is a need to revisit issue, including illegal immigration, water sharing and cattle smuggling, which are costing India dearly. More importantly, a stern message needs to go through a concerted international pressure, which may force Bangladesh into a course correction.

The government in Dhaka is professedly hostile to India, and is acting as an eastern arm of Pakistan or at least its sinister intelligence agency, the ISI. If Pakistan is being forced to dismantle the terror structure in territories it controls, the same are now being rebuilt by the ISI in Bangladesh, where the rebels of Indian northeast are being trained.

The Zia regime must take the blame for the country's dangerous drift. Many countries and civil liberties organizations had warned Dhaka of the danger of Islamic fundamentalism in Bangladesh. Murderous attacks on secular politicians, journalists, writers and women activists of non-government organizations had become routine and were aimed at destroying all challenges to Islamic regimentation.

Chapter 19

NEPALESE CIVIL WAR AND COMMUNIST PARTY OF NEPAL

*Dr. R.B. Singh**

The Nepali Civil War (labelled People's War by the Maoists)[1] was a conflict between government forces and Maoist rebels in Nepal which lasted from 1996 until 2006. The war was started by the Communist Party of Nepal (Maoist) on February 13, 1996, with the aim of overthrowing the Nepalese monarchy and establishing the "People's Republic of Nepal." It ended with a Comprehensive Peace Accord signed on 21 November 2006 which is now monitored by United Nations Mission in Nepal.

Overview

More than 12,800 people were killed (4,500 by Maoists and 8,200 by the government)[2] and an estimated 100,000 to 150,000 people were internally displaced as a result of the

* Editor, Guest Lecturer, Department of Defence Studies, University of Lucknow, Lucknow.

conflict. This conflict disrupted the majority of rural development activities and led to a deep and complex Left Front which, together with the Nepali Congress, was the backbone of the broadbased movement for democratic change. However, communist groups uncomfortable with the alliance between ULF and Congress formed a parallel front, the United National People's Movement. The UNPM called for elections to a Constituent Assembly, and rejected compromises made by ULF and Congress with the royal house. In November 1990 the Communist Party of Nepal (Unity Centre) was formed, including key elements of constituents of UNPM. The new party held its first convention in 1991, they adopted a line of "protracted armed struggle on the route to a new democratic revolution" and that the party would remain an underground party. The CPN(UC) set up Samyukta Jana Morcha, with Baburam Bhattarai as its head, as an open front ten contest elections. In the 1991 elections, SJM became the third force in the Nepali parliament. However, disagreements surged regarding which tactics were to be used by the party. One sector argued for immediate armed revolution whereas others (including senior leaders like Nirmal Lama) claimed that Nepal was not yet ripe for armed struggle.

In 1994 CPN(UC)/SJM was split in two. The militant sector later renamed itself the Communist Party of Nepal (Maoist). The Maoists labeled the government forces "feudal forces," and included in this accusation the monarchy and the mainstream political parties. The armed struggle began soon afterwards with simultaneous attacks on remote police stations and district headquarters. Initially, the Nepali government mobilized the Nepal Police to contain the insurgency. The Royal Nepal Army was not involved in direct fighting because the conflict was regarded as a matter for the police to sustain control. Furthermore, controversy grew regarding the army not assisting the police during insurgent attacks in remote areas. The popularly-elected prime minister resigned his post, due to the refusal of the Royal Army to take part in the conflict. This situation changed dramatically in 2002 when the first session of peace talks failed and the Maoists attacked an army barracks in Dang District in western Nepal. Overnight, the army was unleashed against the insurgents. At the same time, the king of Nepal maintained a puppet democratic government which depended upon him for their status to remain legitimate. Under the aegis of the global War on Terrorism and with the stated goal of averting the development of a "failed state" that could serve as a source of regional and international instability, the United States, European Union, and India, among other nations, have provided extensive military and economic aid to the Nepali government. This material support to the Nepali government dried up after King Gyanendra seized full control in February 2005 to get rid of civil war for once and all.

The government responded to the rebellion by banning provocative statements about the monarchy,[3] imprisoning journalists, and shutting down newspapers accused of siding with the insurgents. Several rounds of negotiations, accompanied by temporary cease-fires, have been held between the insurgents and the government. The government has categorically rejected the insurgents' demand for an election to the constituent assembly; it would result in the abolition of the monarchy by a popular vote. At the same time, the Maoists have refused to recognize the installation of a constitutional monarchy. In November 2004, the government rejected the Maoists' request to negotiate directly with the King Gyanendra rather than via the Prime Minister Sher Bahadur Deuba; their request for discussions to be mediated by a third party, such as the United Nations was dismissed.

Throughout war, the government controlled the main cities and towns, whilst the Maoist dominated the rural areas. Historically, the presence of the Nepali government has been limited to town and zonal centers. The only state apparatus present in most small villages, where most of the inhabitants of Nepal live, were a health post, a government school, a village council, and a police booth. Once the insurgency began, the schools were all that remained, indicating that the Maoists had seized control of the village. The Royal government powerbase is located in the zonal headquarters and the capital Kathmandu. Unrest reached Kathmandu in 2004 when the Maoists announced a blockade of the capital city.

Three Maoist rebels are waiting on top of a hill in the Rolpa district to get orders to relocate to another location.

Intense fighting and civic unrest continued well into 2005, with the death toll rising to 200 in December 2004. On February 1, 2005, in response to the inability of the relatively democratic government to restore order, King Gyanendra assumed total control of the government. He proclaimed, "Democracy and progress contradict one another... In pursuit of liberalism, we should never overlook an important aspect of our conduct, namely discipline."

On November 22, 2005, the joint CPN(M)-United People's Front conference in Delhi issued a 12-point resolution, stating that they "...completely agree that autocratic monarchy is the main hurdle" hindering the realisation of "democracy, peace, prosperity, social advancement and a free and sovereign Nepal." In addition, "It is our clear view that without establishing absolute democracy by ending autocratic monarchy, there is no possibility of peace, progress, and prosperity in the country."[4]

An understanding had been reached to establish absolute democracy by ending monarchy with the respective forces centralizing their assault against autocratic monarchy thereby creating a nationwide storm of democratic protests. This marked a departure from the previous stance of the CPN(M), which had so far vehemently opposed the gradual process of democratization advocated by the UPF.

As a result of the civil war, Nepal's greatest source of foreign exchange, its tourism industry, suffered considerably. iExplore, a travel company, published rankings of the popularity of tourist destinations, based on their sales, which indicated that Nepal had gone from being the tenth most popular destination among adventure travellers, to the twenty-seventh.[5]

The conflict has forced the young and able to seek work abroad in order to avoid the Human Rights Violations committed by the Government forces and the crimes committed by the Maoists. These labourers work predominantly in the Gulf (Qatar, Saudi Arabia, etc.) and Southeast Asia (Malaysia etc). The regular flow of remittances from these labourers has permitted the country to avoid serious economic crisis or economic bankruptcy. The economy of Nepal is heavily dependent on the infusion of foreign income from the labouring class (similar to the Lebanese economy during its civil war).

Use of Child Soldiers

To achieve their goals of removing the king and establishing a secular communist republic, the Maoists resorted to mass underage recruitment, particularly of young students, usually between 12 and 16 years old. At the conclusion of the war, an estimated 12,000 Maoist soldiers were below 18 years of age, and Human Rights Estimates that the majority of the current militia joined as minors. The United Nation Mission in Nepal (UNMIN) has verified nine thousand child soldiers currently in Maoist cantonment training camps.

Maoists used children as soldiers, messengers, cooks, porters and suppliers. Regardless of role, all children received rudimentary military training concerning explosives, so they would be able to recognize and avoid land mines. The Maoists, however, continue to deny that any soldiers were less than 18 years of age. They claim that they have cared for orphans of adult soldiers killed in the war, and that these children were not placed in danger.

Children, including girls, were deployed in combat situations, often to help provide ammunition or assist with evacuating or caring for the wounded. A 16-year-old boy from Dang district in Western Nepal reported that he was forced to carry wounded Maoist combatants to India for treatment. He revealed how he and six others of the same age managed to run away. A 14-year-old girl explained how arms training took place by torchlight during the night.

Throughout the war, the Royal Nepal Army captured Maoist child soldiers. Captured youth were often tortured for information or forced to become spies for the Nepal government working undercover in Maoist militias. There were also numerous accounts of government police and army abducting, raping, and killing Maoist girl soldiers.

Timeline

1996

- February 13: Initiation of "the people's war" by the Communist Party of Nepal (Maoist)
    - Kathmandu: A soft-drink bottling factory owned by a multi-national company is attacked and the building torched.
    - Gorkha District
        - A foreign liquor factory is completely destroyed.

- The office of the Small Farmer's Development Programme of the state-owned Agricultural Development Bank in Chyangli VDC (Village Development Committee) is ransacked.

- Kavre District: A moneylender's house is raided at night, properties and cash reportedly worth 1.3 million rupees seized, and loan documents worth several million rupees reportedly destroyed. 7 members of the moneylender's family are killed , all shot to death.
- Rolpa, Rukum & Sindhuli Districts: One police outpost raided in each district. The outpost at Holeri, Rolpa has its stores seized, including a substantial amount of high explosives. Athbiskot-Rari, Rukum is also raided. The Sindhuligarhi post in Sindhuli is reportedly raided without . 17 Police personnel are killed in total, and only one Maoist guerrilla is killed in retaliation.

2001

- January: The government creates the Armed Police Force to fight the insurgents.
- May 28: Chairman Prachanda gives an interview with the Communist journal A World to Win.[6]
- June 1: Crown Prince Dipendra reportedly kills King Birendra and most of the royal family in the Nepali royal massacre. Dipendra, comatose after a failed suicide attempt or assassination attempt by palace guards, is crowned king, according to tradition. He dies on June 4, Gyanendra is crowned King.[7,8]
- August 3: The first round of peace talks begin.

- November 23: Peace talks collapse when the Maoists withdraw and launch a ferocious attack on Police and Army posts in 42 districts , in which 186 Army and Police personnel are killed, in return for only 21 Maoists killed during resistance by Army and Police personnel.
- November 26: The government of Sher Bahadur Deuba declares a Nationwide State of Emergency and employs the Nepal Army in attacking the Maoists.[9]

2002

- The United States Congress approves US$12 million to train Royal Nepal Army officers and supply 5,000 M16 rifles.[10]
- May: Peace talks collapse.[11]
- May: Large battle fought between Army and Maoist forces at Lisne Lekh along boundary between Pyuthan and Rolpa districts.
- May 11: A photograph is discovered by Nepal government soldiers in western Nepal. The photograph depicts Nepal's Maoist rebel leaders Baburam Bhattarai, Hisila Yami, Ram Bahadur Thapa (alias Badal), and Pushpa Kamal Dahal (alias Prachanda).[12]
- May 22: King Gyanendra, acting on the advice of Prime Minister Sher Bahadur Deubà, dissolves Parliament and orders new elections. The reason given for the dissolution is opposition to the state of emergency.
- July 11: Information leaks out that the Belgian weapon manufacturer FN Herstal is allowed to deliver 5,500 M249 Minimi rifles to the Nepali monarchy, a decision made by all coalition parties.

Minister of External Affairs Louis Michel speaks of "a country in a pluralistic democracy."

- October 4: King Gyanendra deposes Prime Minister Deuba and the entire Council of Ministers, assumes executive power, and cancels the elections for the dissolved House of Representatives, which had been scheduled for November 11.
- October 11: King Gyanendra appoints Lokendra Bahadur Chand as Prime Minister.

2003

- January: The United States hold exercises with the Nepali army.[13] Maoist insurgents kill the Inspector General of Police, Lokendra Dhwaj Chhetri, his wife and his bodyguard, Head Constable Subhash Bahadur Gurung of the Armed Police Force Nepal, while on their morning walk, as they used to do on Sunday mornings, intending to represent general safety to fellow citizens. The Inspector General and his wife, who was a teacher at an international school in the capital, were both unarmed. They were riddled with bullets from Type 56 Rifles and G3 rifles used by the Maoists.
- January 29: A second ceasefire is established and peace talks begin.[14]
- May 13: Code of conduct jointly declared by the government and the Communist Party of Nepal (Maoist) for the mutually agreed period of cease-fire.[15]
- August 17: Killing of 39 Maoist rebels in the Ramechhap District of central Nepal during an offensive launched jointly by the Army , Police and Air Force of Nepal. 7 Soldiers of the Nepali Army and 5 Constables of the Armed Police are also killed in the operation.[16]

- August 24: The Maoists set an ultimatum, threatening to withdraw from the cease-fire if the government does not agree within 48 hours to include the question of the Maoists participating in the Constituent Assembly.[17]
- August 26: The Maoist ultimatum expires.[18]
- August 27:
  - Strike: The Maoist call for a three-day strike to denounce the Army's attacks on their cadres[19]
  - The Maoists unilaterally withdraw from the January 29 cease-fire. Prachanda's statement revives the rebels' demand for an end to monarchic rule in favour of a people's republic, stating, "Since the old regime has put an end to the forward-looking solution to all existing problems through the cease-fire and peace talks, we herein declare that the rationale behind cease-fire...and peace process has ended."[20]
- September 27: "Fifteen people including 8 Rebels and 4 Policemen were killed on Saturday and suspected Maoists bombed five government utilities despite the guerrillas' plans for a nine day truce from October 2, officials said. Eight Maoists were killed in a gun battle with security forces at Chhita Pokhara in the Khotang District, 340 kilometres east of Kathmandu, a police officer said. 4 Policemen were also martyred. Elsewhere in eastern Nepal, the Maoists killed two Policemen, Constable Purna Prasad Sharma and Head Constable Radha Krishna Gurung, and a woman selling beetle nuts, Kali Tamang, in the Jaljale-Gaighat area, an official said. 'A group of seven Maoists descended from a public bus when police were checking the passengers and suddenly

opened fire from automatic pistols, killing the three and wounding two others,' said Sitaram Prasad Pokharel, the chief administrator for the region. In Janakpur, an industrial hub on the Indian border 260 kilometres south-east of Kathmandu, the Maoists under the direct command of Prachanda carried out five early morning bombings that disrupted telephone service and power, police said. No one was killed directly by the blasts but an elderly man died of a heart attack after hearing the explosions, Police Deputy Superintendent Bharat Chhetri said. He said the sites that were bombed included the offices of the roads department and the Nepal Electricity Authority and a telecommunications tower. Police personnel and Maoists traded fire for nearly 40 minutes after the blasts but the rebels escaped and 37 people were injured, Mr Khadka said."[21]

- October 13: At least 42 Police Recruits and 9 Maoists are killed when an estimated 3,000 Maoists attempt to storm a Police Training Center in Bhaluwang. "'The rebels had snapped telephone cables, set up roadblocks by felling trees or blowing up highway bridges to prevent reinforcements from coming,' a witness, Krishna Adhikary, told Reuters."[22]
- October 27: "Colonel Adrian Griffith and six Nepali nationals were freed last week 42 hours after being taken captive in Baglung, 300 km (190 miles) west of Kathmandu, while on a drive to recruit young Gurkha soldiers to serve in the British army." Party chief Prachanda said, "We are sorry for the incident that took place against the policy of the party."[23]
- November 11: The government Defence Ministry accuses the Maoists of abducting twenty-nine 9th- and 10th-grade students from Riva Secondary School

in Mugu District, western Nepal during the previous week.[24]

- November 19: According to a Nepal army official, four people were caught at the Chinese Khasa border point, 114 kilometers northeast of Kathmandu, smuggling weapons from Tibet into Nepal. The official named Hirala Lal Shrestha and Gyaljen Sherpa and said they were taken for interrogation in the Tibetan town of Xigatse.[25]

2004

- February 5: An Army raid is carried out by the Bhairavnath Battalion on a village in Bhimad, Makwanpur District. Reports emerge that 45 suspected Maoist activists and two civilians have been extra-judicially executed. Amnesty International later wrote a letter to Prime Minister Surya Bahadur Thapa and Brigadier-General Nilendra Aryal, Head of the Royal Nepal Army (RNA) human rights cell, demanding an immediate inquiry.[26]
- February 10: Two central committee members of Communist Party of Nepal (Maoist), Matrika Yadav and Suresh Paswan, are reported to have been handed over by India to Nepal. They were reportedly arrested in Lucknow after Nepal provided information.[27]
- February 13: Ganesh Chilwal leads an anti-Maoist protest on this day, the ninth anniversary of the commencement of the revolution.[28]
- February 15: Ganesh Chilwal is shot dead in his Kathmandu office by two suspected Maoists.[29]
- February 15: Fighting erupts at a Maoist jungle base in Kalikot District, 360 km west of Kathmandu. The

base is said to hold 5000 Maoist troops. On February 17, a security official says that a private helicopter flying troops to Kalikot was hit by Maoist fire but that it returned safely to Kathmandu. On February 18, 65 Maoists are reported killed, though this conflicts with other reported death tolls of 35 and 48.[30]

- February 15 and 16: State radio report 13 rebels killed in seven separate small clashes across the kingdom.[31]
- February 18: Lawmaker Khem Narayan Faujdar, a member of the parliament dissolved by King Gyanendra in 2002, is shot dead by two suspected Maoists riding a motorcycle in the Nawalparasi District, 200 km southwest of the capital, according to the police.[32]
- April 2: The largest rallies since 1990 begin in Kathmandu. They are variously labelled "pro-democracy" and "anti-monarchy."[33,34]
- April 3: More than 12 trucks are burnt while waiting at a western Nepal border post to pick up petrol from India. India condemns the attacks and vows to fight terrorism.[35]
- April 4: "Some 150 demonstrators were struck during a police baton charge" during demonstrations in Kathmandu[36]
- April 4 "Hundreds of Maoist rebels" attack a Police outpost in Yadukuwa, Jadukhola killing at least 13 Policemen. 35 Policemen are reported missing, 13 dead, and 7 wounded. 8 to 9 Maoists are reported dead. "Witnesses said more than 500 rebels attacked the Police post and began firing Assault Rifles and RPG-7 rockets. at around 9 p.m. (1515 GMT) on Sunday night. The fighting lasted two to three hours." Other reports state 400 rebels.[37,38,39]

- April 4: In the west of the country three Indian traders are shot and injured and have their vehicles burned.[40]
- April 5: A three day national strike begins, called by CPN(M) and opposed by an "alliance of five political parties" who are protesting in Kathmandu against the monarchy and say the strike will hamper the movement of demonstrators in Kathmandu. Prachanda said, "The time has come to win a united struggle against the feudal forces as the king is trying to take the nation back to the 18th century."[41, 42]
- April 5: In the morning, 3 soldiers are killed and 7 injured by a CPN(M) landmine activated by their vehicle at Dhalkhola, 50 km east of Kathmandu.[43]
- April 5: At least 140 people are injured in clashes in Kathmandu as "about 50,000" demonstrators confront the police. Demonstrators try to break through a police barricade close to the royal palace. The police respond with tear gas and protesters are reportedly injured by police batons. Rocks and bricks are thrown by both sides. Demonstrations also occur in Lalitpur and Bhaktapur. Meanwhile, king Gyanendra has reportedly been away touring villages in western Nepal.[44]
- April 5: The Indian government announces that it will no longer provide police escorts to Indian officials shopping in Nepal, as a means to discourage such trips. Fears are based on the CPN(M) targeting Indians. "We are worried about possible reprisals here if the Maoists continue to target Indians inside Nepal," said a senior police official.[45]
- August 16: The Soaltee Hotel, a popular luxury hotel in Kathmandu, is bombed, after refusing a demand from the Maoists that the hotel close.

- August 18: A bomb explodes in a marketplace in southern Nepal. The blast kills a 12-year-old boy and wounds six others, including three policemen. In addition, Maoist rebels, demanding the release of captured guerrillas, stop all road traffic near Kathmandu by threatening to attack vehicles. Some Nepal businesses are shut down because of threats.
- September 10: A bomb explodes at the United States Information Service office in Kathmandu.
- September 13: U.S. Peace Corps suspends operations and non-essential U.S. Embassy personnel are evacuated from Nepal.
- December 15: Twenty government security personnel are killed in the western district of Arghakhanchi when the Maoists mount a surprise attack.
- December 16: Sixteen Maoist rebels are killed in clashes with Nepali security forces in the western district of Dailekh.
- December 23: Maoist forces launch blockade of Kathmandu.
- December 26: Over 15,000 hold peace rally in Kathmandu.

2005

- January 2: Nepali media falsely reports two children being killed in Dailekh District by a Maoist bomb.
- January 4: Three government security personnel and between two and twenty-four Maoist rebels reported killed in fighting.
- January 8: Maoists detain and later release 300 passengers from six buses that defy their blockade of Kathmandu.
- January 10: Prime Minister Deuba said he would

increase defence spending to fight the Maoists unless they come forward for talks with the government.

- January 11: Protests and blockades over the government fuel price increases between 10% and 25%.
- January 15: Maoists allegedly detain 14 Indian Gurkhas from Chuha village in Kailali.
- February 1: King Gyanendra dissolves the Deuba government and bans all news reports. The army begins arresting senior political leaders, journalists, trade unionists, human rights activists and civil society leaders. All telephone and internet connections are cut.
- February 28: The Indian Army intervenes and is first spotted in Nepal, killing 32 Maoist rebels.
- June 6: Badarmude bus explosion: Some 38 civilians are killed and over 70 injured after a packed passenger bus runs over a rebel landmine in Chitwan District.
- August 9: Maoist rebels kill 40 security men in midwestern Nepal.
- September 3: The Maoists declare a three-month unilateral ceasefire to woo opposition political parties.
- November 19: After negotiations, the Maoist rebels agree to work with opposition politicians in a common front against the rule of King Gyanendra of Nepal.[46, 47]

2006

- January 2: Rebels decide not to extend a four month ceasefire saying that the government had broken the ceasefire with numerous attacks on Maoist villages.[48]
- January 14: Maoists launch coordinated attacks of

five military and paramilitary targets in the Kathmandu Valley. The first demonstration of their ability to organize violence within the Valley, prompting curfews at night for the next several days.

- March 14: Nepali rebels extend road blockade; nationwide strike called for April 3.[49]
- April 5: General strike begins with Maoist forces promising to refrain from violence.
- April 6, 7: Protesters clash with police, hundreds arrested, dozens injured.
- April 8: A curfew is imposed in Kathmandu from 10 p.m. to 9 a.m. The king orders protesters violating the curfew to be "shot on sight."[50]
- April 9: General strike scheduled to end. Government extends curfew, BBC reports. Three dead in two days of unrest, as thousands of demonstrators defy curfews.[51]
- April 27: Maoist insurgents, responding to a demand by the newly appointed Prime Minister Girija Prasad Koirala, announce a unilateral three-month truce after weeks of pro-democracy protests in Kathmandu, and encourage the formation of a new constituent assembly tasked with rewriting the nation's constitution.[52,53]
- May 3: Nepal's new cabinet declares a ceasefire. The cabinet also announces that the Maoist rebels will no longer be considered a terrorist group. Rebels are also encouraged to open peace talks.[54]
- November 21: Peace talks end with the signing of the Comprehensive Peace Accord between Prime Minister Girija Prasad Koirala and Maoist leader Prachanda. The deal allows the Maoists to take part in government, and places their weapons under UN monitoring.[55]

Communist Party of Nepal

The Communist Party of Nepal-Maoist (CPN-M), currently a proscribed outfit, was formed in 1995 following a split in the Communist Party of Nepal-Unity Centre. A radical faction led by Pushpa Kamal Dahal alias Comrade Prachanda and Baburam Bhattarai set up the CPN-Maoist and denounced the Communist Party of Nepal (Unified Marxist-Leninists) or the CPN (UML) and other mainstream communist factions as 'renegades' and 'revisionists' due to their participation in the parliamentary process. It resorted to an armed struggle on February 13, 1996, by attacking police stations in the Rukum and Rolpa districts in northwestern Nepal and thereby declaring a 'People's War' in Nepal.

Earlier, various communist groups had actively participated in the People's Movement of 1989-90 operating under the umbrella organisation of United National People's Movement (UNPM). However, after the conclusion of the People's Movement, these groups were not satisfied with the multi-party democratic system under constitutional monarchy. In order to contest the May 1991 elections, they formed a two-tier organisation, revolutionary front and political front, known as the Communist Party of Nepal-Unity Centre and United People's Front of Nepal (UPFN) respectively. The UPFN emerged as the third largest group in the Parliament and also performed well in the local bodies' elections of 1992. Gradually, however, ideological and personality clashes led to the disintegration of Unity Centre and the UPFN split into two factions, led by Nirmal Lama and Niranjan Govind Vaidiya at one end and Comrade Prachanda and Bhattarai on the other end. Subsequently, the decision by Prachanda not to participate in the 1994 elections led to the creation of CPN-M in 1995 as an underground outfit.

Objectives

The Maoists announced a 'People's War' on February 13, 1996, with the slogan "let us march ahead on the path of struggle towards establishing the people's rule by wreaking the reactionary ruling system of state." They strongly believe in the philosophy of Mao Tsetung that "Political power grows out of the barrel of a gun." They also draw inspiration from the 'Revolutionary Internationalist Movement' and Peru's left wing extremist guerrilla movement, the Sendero Luminoso (Shining Path). The radical communist parties from different parts of the world have provided ideological sustenance for the Nepali Maoists.

The 'People's War' aims to establish a 'New Democracy' in Nepal and constitutes an "historical revolt against feudalism, imperialism and so-called reformists." The immediate reason given by the Maoists for declaring the 'People's War' was the failure of the Nepalese Government to respond to a memorandum presented by its representatives to Prime Minister Sher Bahadur Deuba on February 4, 1996. The memorandum listed 40 demands related to "nationalism, democracy and livelihood". These included among others the abolition of royal privileges and the promulgation of a new constitution, and the abrogation of the Mahakali treaty with India on the distribution of water and electricity and the delineation of the border between the two countries.

Leadership, Cadre and Command Structure

The chief of operations of the CPN-M is its Chairman, Pushpa Kamal Dahal (better known as Comrade Prachanda). He is also Chairman of the 'Central Committee', Member of 'Standing Committee' and 'Supreme Commander' of the People's Liberation Army.

Another front ranking leader Baburam Bhattarai heads the political wing of the Maoists called the United People's Front (UPF). Bhattarai alias Lal Singh @ Jitbir @ Mukti Manab, a 'Politburo and Standing Committee' member, is reportedly responsible for planning and foreign affairs, and was co-ordinator of the dialogue team in 2003. According to the Nepal Police Website, he is in-charge of mid central command (since 3rd cc meeting in September 2004).

Mohan Pokharel Vaidya @ Kiran @ Agam, a founder of the party and a 'Politburo and Standing Committee' member, is widely reported to be the political ideologue and is also in-charge of the Kathmandu valley and eastern central command. Another important Maoist leader is Post Bahadur Bogati @ Diwakar @ Ranadhoj who serves as a 'Politburo and Standing Committee' member and is also in- charge of the western central command.

Ram Bahadur Thapa alias Badal @ Lakhan @ Bhimsen @ Prem, another 'Politburo and Standing Committee' member, is reported to be special central command in-charge. Krishna Bahadur Mahara @ Amar Singh @ Chattan, who acts as the Maoists' spokesperson, is in-charge of the 'Foreign Section (India)'.

The top-level commanders of the insurgents include among others, Yan Prasad Gautarri alias Alok, Chitranarayan Shrestha, Shashi Shrestha, Hisila Yani, Man Bahadur Mahara, Santhosh Bura, Lekhraj Bhatt, C.P. Gajurel. In the political wing, the important Maoist leaders include, Comrade Parvati (a nom de guerre of Baburam Bhattarai's wife Hsila Yemi), Matrika Yadav, Deb Bahadur Gurung, Krishna Dhoj Khadka, Rekha Sharma, Rabindra Shrestha, Bamdev Chhetri and Mumaram Khanal.

The apex military institution of the Maoists is the Central Military Commission of the Communist Party of Nepal (Maoists), which was constituted in 1998.

Government estimates provided in early 2003 on the CPN-M strength indicated that there are approximately 5,500 combatants, 8,000 militia, 4,500 cadres, 33,000 hard core followers, and 200,000 sympathizers.

The main fighting and support forces consist of Magars, Tharus, Janjatis (Gurungs, Rais, Limbus, Tamangs, Dalits, Brahmins and Chhetris, the last two also providing the political and military leadership). Among the Maoist fighters —about 60 per cent—are deployed in the mid-west and west in their strongholds. Another 10 per cent are in the far west with around 10 per cent in Gorkha, the rest is located in Kathmandu valley and east of it.

A considerable number of retired Gurkha soldiers of the British and the Indian Army inhabit many of the Maoist-affected areas and Nepalese security agencies have suspected that these former soldiers along with those retired and deserters from the Royal Nepalese Army (RNA) have/are involved in training the insurgents.

Women have been prominent in the recruiting profile. Available reports indicate that one-fifth to one-third of the cadre and combatants may be women. Reportedly, every village has a revolutionary women's organisation. According to a Jane's Intelligence Review report of October 2001, there are usually two women in each unit of 35-40 men, and they are used to gather intelligence and act as couriers. Baburam Bhattarai was quoted as saying in Spacetime on April 18, 2003, that fifty per cent of cadres at the lower level, thirty per cent of soldiers and ten per cent of members of central committee of the outfit were women. Durgha Pokhrel, Chairman of National Women's Commission, who visited more than 25 Maoist-affected districts, stated on July 3, 2003, during a talk delivered at the Nepal Council of World Affairs that percentage of women cadres could be as high as forty. A women's group, the All Nepal Women's Association

(Revolutionary), is alleged to be a front outfit of the CPN-M.

The All Nepal National Independent Students' Union (Revolutionary), or ANNISU-R is the student wing of the Maoists. Its membership comprises students from school to the university level. The general success in all the strikes called by ANNISU-R, especially in the educational institutions, (at present it is also one of the key student organisations in the anti-King agitation) shows the stronghold of the organisation. According to a report of June 2003, the ANNISU-R comprises approximately 400,000 members.

Reportedly, weaponry in their possession include AK-47 rifles, self-loading rifles, .303 rifles, country guns, hand grenades, explosives, detonators, mortars, and light machine guns. Nearly 85 per cent of these weapons are reportedly looted from the police and RNA.

Structurally, the CPN-M consists of the standing committee at the top, followed by the politburo, central committee, regional bureaus, sub-regional bureaus, district committees, area committees, and cell committees. The Politburo issues directives with the assistance of an approximately 25-member central committee. The main armed component reportedly consists of six guerrilla battalions, which launches military action in response to instructions relayed through their individual chief commissars (one per battalion), who are central committee members. The politburo and standing committee reportedly formulate most of the political and strategic policies. The standing committee, with approximately ten members, is the most powerfull body in the CPN-M. There are five regional bureaus: eastern, central, Kathmandu valley, western and international department.

Organisational structure of the CPN-Maoist

Party	*People's Army*	*United Front*
Standing committee	Central military commission	United people's district committees
Politburo	Regional military commissions	United people's area committee
Central committee	Sub-regional military commissions	United people's village committees
Regional bureaus (five)	District military commissions	United people's ward committees
Sub-regional bureaus (in some places special sub-regional bureau)	Included in this are: Temporary battalion	
District committees	Companies	
Area committees	Platoons	
Cell committees	Squads (separate people's militias also exist under united village people's committees)	

Source: Sudheer Sharma, "The Maoist Movement: An Evolutionary Perspective," in Deepak Thapa, ed., Understanding the Maoist Movement in Nepal, Kathmandu: Martin Chautari, 2003.

Areas of Operation

The guerrillas operate to varying degrees in 68 of the 75 districts that comprise Nepal. Their influence varies between moderate to extreme in these districts. In the districts of Rolpa, Rukum, Jajarkot, Salyan, Pyuthan and Kalikot in mid-western Nepal, Government presence is limited to the district headquarters with the rest of each district under Maoist control. The Nepalese Home Ministry has designated these districts as 'sensitive class A'. Nine districts, namely Dolakha,

Ramechhap, Sindhuli, Kavrepalanchowk, Sindhupalchowk, Gorkha, Dang, Surkhet and Achham, are classified as 'Sensitive Class B', while 17 'Sensitive Class C' districts are Khotang, Okhaldhunga, Udaypur, Makwanpur, Lalitpur, Nuwakot, Dhading, Tanahu, Lamjung, Parbat, Baglung, Gulmi, Arghakhachi, Bardiya, Dailekh, Jumla and Dolpa.

The Maoist insurgency initially commenced in the three districts of Rolpa, Rukum and Jajarkot and eventually spread throughout Nepal. Maoists have very strong bases in Western and mid-Western region and partially in Eastern region.

External Linkages

According to available information, the Maoists of Nepal have well-established linkages with Indian left-wing extremist organizations, primarily with the People's War Group (PWG) and Maoist Communist Centre (MCC). The first signs of contacts were reportedly registered during 1989-1990, when the two groups started collaborating in order to expand their influence. Towards this end, they began the process of laying a corridor, which is now widely referred to as the Revolutionary Corridor (RC) extending from Nepal to across six Indian States, including Bihar, Chhattisgarh, Jharkhand, Andhra Pradesh, Orissa and Madhya Pradesh. This entire area has been identified in Maoist literature as the Compact Revolutionary Zone (CRZ). The CRZ was organized by the Nepal and Indian members of the Naxalite (the popular term for left-wing extremism in India—the movement originated in Naxalbari [hence the term Naxal] in the State of West Bengal in the late 1960s) Movement, in a meeting at Siliguri in the Indian State of West Bengal during August 2001.

Gradually, the interaction between Maoist insurgents and the PWG increased with the sharing of knowledge about guerrilla warfare, bomb manufacturing techniques and arms training. Nepalese Maoists had sent their delegates to the March 2001 Congress of PWG held at Abuz Marh in the Bastar region of Chhattisgarh. The establishment of CRZ gave a wider space and platform for all the proscribed Nepal and Indian left-wing extremist organizations to strengthen their bases in both the countries.

The more radical forces in South Asia, including both the PWG and Nepalese Maoists, are members of the Revolutionary Internationalist Movement (RIM). In July 2001, about 10 extreme Left Wing (Maoist) groups in South Asia formed the Coordination Committee of Maoist Parties and Organization of South Asia (CCOMPOSA), in which the Nepalese Maoists, PWG, MCC, Purbo Banglar Movement (Bangladesh), Communist Party of Ceylon (Sri Lanka) and other Indian left-wing extremist parties became members. The appearance of graffiti in remote villages in Naxalite-strongholds, in Rayakal and Mallapur mandals (administrative unit) of Karimnagar district in Andhra Pradesh, hailing CCOMPOSA points the spread of the idea of a common front of left-wing extremist groups in South Asia. Moreover, the Central Committee of the Maoists, in late-January 2002, passed a resolution stating that it would work together with the PWG and the MCC in fighting the ban imposed on the latter two organisations in India, under the Prevention of Terrorism Act, 2002. A year earlier, in 2001, the Maoists had sent a senior leader named Gaurav as a fraternal delegate to attend the 9th Congress of the PWG. Reports indicate that the Maoists and the PWG have also formed the Indo-Nepal Border Region Committee to coordinate their activities in North Bihar and along the India-Nepal border.

For quite some time, the Maoists have also been working closely with the MCC for unification, consolidation and expansion of Maoist movement in India and across South

Asia. A careful examination of expansion of Naxalite activity in Bihar in the last two years would reveal that the growing linkages between the MCC and the Nepali Maoists are part of their larger strategy to create a 'Compact Revolutionary Zone' stretching across Andhra Pradesh, Chhattisgarh, Jharkhand, and Bihar to Nepal. The porous Bihar-Nepal border, the general breakdown of rule of law, poor governance and incapacity of the police force provides a context for these left extremist groups to operate with ease.

In February 1996, the MCC Central Committee had reportedly published a paper welcoming the Maoist movement in Nepal. Reports of April 2000 indicated that the MCC and Maoists were holding joint training camps in Hazaribagh and Aurangabad. In September 2000, MCC leader Pramod Mishra is alleged to have visited Nepal for extensive discussions with Maoist leaders. In December 2001, the MCC and the PWG, in their joint meetings, held in the Jharkhand forests, resolved to support the Maoist insurgents in Nepal. In the same year, the MCC, PWG and Maoists formed an "Indo Nepal Border Regional Committee" to coordinate their activities in the border areas.

The porous Bihar-Nepal border is easily permeable. Bihar has eight districts and 54 police stations situated on the border. In the recent past, the Bihar police have arrested a number of Nepalese Maoists in the border districts of West and East Champaran, Sitamarhi, Sheohar and Madhubani. Taking advantage of a general breakdown of law and order, the Nepalese Maoists have reportedly set up bases at several places along the border. Reports indicate the existence of training camps in the forests of Bagha in the West Champaran district, which has emerged as a safe haven for the Nepalese insurgents. The Bihar police also suspect that some top leaders of the Nepalese Maoists, including Baburam Bhattarai, were/are hiding in Bihar.

Not much is known about the Maoist links with other militant or left-wing extremist groups operating in India, besides that they are linked to a few Naxalite groups through CCOMPOSA. Besides, a left-wing extremist group, the Communist Party of India—Marxist-Leninist (CPI-ML) Janashakthi, which has a marginal presence at least in six Indian States, but is very active in isolated and limited number of pockets in Andhra Pradesh, expressed support to the Maoists. It is a co-signatory, along with 41 other left-wing extremist groups ranging from South America to South East Asia, to resolution that 'condemned and opposed the malpractice of the fascist state of Nepal' and demanded 'life security' for imprisoned Maoist cadres, leaders and sympathisers.

The Maoists, with the help of Pakistani Inter Services Intelligence (ISI), have been attempting to establish links with Naxalite groups such as the PWG and the MCC by using the Siliguri corridor in West Bengal. Media reports of December 29, 2002, indicated that three members of a Maoist-affiliate, All Nepal National Free Students' Union-Revolutionary, were arrested at the Siliguri bus station, while on their way to Bihar to attend a meeting convened by the PWG.

The growing influence of Nepalese Maoists in other parts of India was unearthed after four of its cadres were arrested in West Bengal on February 26, 2003. The arrested Maoists confessed during interrogation of their plan to use West Bengal as a corridor between their areas of domination in India and Nepal. Darjeeling and Siliguri are the important transit routes. Also they are in a process of consolidating their presence in West Midnapore district, Bankura and Purulia especially in North Bengal with the help of Kamatapur Liberation Organisation (KLO).

The substantial population of nearly eight million Nepali residents in India (primarily in Sikkim, Darjeeling,

Siliguri, Shillong, Dehradun, Himachal Pradesh and Gorakhpur-Lucknow belts) have established a countrywide organization called the Akhil Bharatiya Nepal Ekta Samaj (ABNES). It was banned under the Prevention of Terrorism Act (POTA) in July 2002 by the Government of India. ABNES was registered with the stated objective of securing unity among immigrant Nepalese residing in India and working for their welfare. However, it gradually became involved in subversive activities and began to function as a front for the Maoist insurgents of Nepal. It is also believed that the organization is working for the idea of a greater Nepal.

There is also some reportage about the Nepalese Maoists' links with insurgent groups active in India's North-east like United Liberation Front of Asom (ULFA), Kamtapur Liberation Organisation (KLO), Gurkha National Liberation Front (GNLF) and Gurkha Liberation Organisation (GLO).

Though the exact nature of the relationship is not known, the Maoists are also reported to have some links with the Liberation Tigers of Tamil Eelam (LTTE) in Sri Lanka. However, it is suspected that the Maoists have received arms training from the LTTE operatives in the past and this may be continuing. Links between these two may have been facilitated through the PWG, which has a record of co-operation with the LTTE in arms procurement and training (especially in the use of Improvised Explosive Devices). The arrest of Chandra Prakash Gajurel alias Gaurab, a member of the Maoist politburo, at Chennai airport in Tamil Nadu in August 2003 while trying to travel to Europe to lobby for a political solution to the seven-year-old insurgency in Nepal needs to be seen in this context.

Reference

1. Interview with Prachanda
2. Ed Douglas. "Inside Nepal's Revolution..... (just to check..!!!)". National Geographic Magazine, p. 54, November 2005. Douglas lists the following figures: "Nepalis killed by Maoists from 1996 to 2005: 4,500. Nepalis killed by government in same period: 8,200."
3. "Anti-king remarks intolerable: Lohani". Nepal News: The Kathmandu Post. December 20, 2003. http://www.nepalnews.com.np/contents/englishdaily/ktmpost/2003/dec/dec21/. Retrieved 2006-11-22.
4. "12-Point Understanding between Parties and Maoists". eKantipur.com. http://www.kantipuronline.com/kolnews.php?&nid=57858.
5. "Top Ten World Travel Destinations in 2004". iExplore. January 10, 2005. http://www.iexplore.com/about/pr_2005-01-10.jhtml.
6. "However tortuous the road may be, the victory of the world proletarian revolution is certain". Human Rights Server. May 28, 2001. http://www.humanrights.de/doc_en/archiv/n/nepal/politics/170202_interview_pra.htm.
7. Greenwald, Jeff (June 13, 2001). "Murder and intrigue in Kathmandu". World Tibet Network News. http://www.tibet.ca/en/wtnarchive/2001/6/13-2_3.html. Retrieved 2006-11-22.
8. Onesto, Li (June 17, 2001). "Nepal: Murder in Palace, Maoists in Mountains". Revolutionary Worker Online. http://rwor.org/a/v23/1100-99/1107/nepal_royals.htm. Retrieved 2006-11-22.
9. a b c d e f g h i Pokharel, Tilak P (August 27, 2003). "Nepali Rebels Walk Away from Peace Talks". World Press. http://www.worldpress.org/Asia/1478.cfm. Retrieved 2006-11-22.
10. A.B. Miglani, Sanjeev (August 18, 2003). "Nepal's Maoist cauldron draws foreign powers closer". ReliefWeb. http://www.reliefweb.int/w/rwb.nsf/0/511eca17e4fc4a6d49256d860018432c?OpenDocument.

11. Adhikari, Bipin (March 19, 2003). "Code of conduct as a point of departure". The Kathmandu Post. http://www.nepalnews.com.np/contents/englishdaily/ktmpost/2003/mar/mar19/features1.htm.
12. "More die in Nepal Maoist insurgency despite truce call". ABC News Online. September 28, 2003. http://www.abc.net.au/news/newsitems/s955264.htm.
13. "37 killed as Maoist army attacks camp". The Telegraph. October 14, 2003. http://www.telegraphindia.com/1031014/asp/foreign/story_2458810.asp.
14. Sharma, Sushil (October 27, 2003). "Maoists 'sorry' UK officer held". BBC News. http://news.bbc.co.uk/2/hi/south_asia/3216993.stm.
15. "How anti-monarchy movement took shape". The Independent. http://independent-bangladesh.com/news/apr/27/27042006re.htm#A2.
16. "China arrests four Nepali Maoists for arms smuggling". Daily News. November 20, 2003. http://www.jang.com.pk/thenews/nov2003-daily/19-11-2003/world/w2.htm.
17. "Nepal: Extra-judicial killings inquiry urgent". Scoop. February 18, 2004. http://www.scoop.co.nz/stories/WO0402/S00154.htm. Retrieved 2006-11-22.
18. "India hands over two Maoist leaders to Nepal". The Times of India. February 10, 2004. http://timesofindia.indiatimes.com/articleshow/488699.cms.
19. a b "Nepal anti-rebel leader shot dead". BBC News. February 15, 2004. http://news.bbc.co.uk/2/hi/south_asia/3490725.stm.
20. a b "48 Maoist rebels killed in Nepal army attacks". KuraKani. February 17, 2004. http://www.kurakani.tk/Article163.phtml.
21. "Chronology of decade-long conflict". ReliefWeb. November 22, 2006. http://www.reliefweb.int/rw/rwb.nsf/db900SID/VBOL-6VSKJU?OpenDocument&RSS20=02-P.
22. Sharma, Gopal (April 9 2004). "Nepal parties plan anti-monarchy rally". Independent Online. http://www.int.iol.co.za/

index.php?set_id=1&click_id=3&art_id=qw1081491841355B251.

23. a b "140 Injured As Clashes Rock Nepal's Capital". INDOlink. http://www.indolink.com/displayArticleS.php?id=040404100829.
24. a b c d "Maoist rebels storm police post in Nepal, kill 9". Utusan Online. April 5, 2004. http://www.utusan.com.my/utusan/content.asp?y=2004&dt=0406&pub=Utusan_Express&sec=World&pg=wo_05.htm.
25. "9 policemen dead as Maoists storm post in Nepal". INQ7. April 5, 2004. http://www.inq7.net/wnw/2004/apr/06/wnw_4-1.htm.
26. "Rebels storm police post, kill nine officers". Gulfnews. April 6, 2004. http://archive.gulfnews.com/articles/04/04/06/117143.html.
27. "Maoists kill 9 policemen". The Telegraph. April 5, 2004. http://www.telegraphindia.com/1040406/asp/foreign/story_3092324.asp.
28. Singh, Kedar Man (April 3, 2004). "Anti-monarchy protesters pack streets of Kathmandu". INQ7. http://www.inq7.net/wnw/2004/apr/04/wnw_3-2.htm.
29. "Major parties take to the streets in Nepal". The Hindu. March 14, 2004. http://www.hindu.com/2005/03/15/stories/2005031503781400.htm.
30. "Police want 'shopping trip' slowdown in Nepal". The Statesman. April 5, 2004. http://www.thestatesman.net/page.arcview.php?clid=2&id=68320&usrsess=1.
31. "Nepal rebels ready to surrender under UN supervision". The Times of India. November 20, 2005. http://timesofindia.indiatimes.com/articleshow/1301467.cms. Retrieved 2006-11-22.
32. Sharma, Nagendar (November 18, 2005). "Nepal opposition in Maoist talks". BBC News. http://news.bbc.co.uk/2/hi/south_asia/4450438.stm. Retrieved 2006-11-22.
33. Pasricha, Anjana (January 2, 2006). "Nepal Rebels Call Off Four-Month Truce". Voice of America. http://www.voanews.com/english/archive/2006-01/2006-01-02-

voa14.cfm?CFID=3777224&CFTOKEN=93126810. Retrieved 2006-11-22.

34. "Nepal rebels call for indefinite strike against king". The Boston Globe. February 18, 2006. http://www.boston.com/news/world/asia/articles/2006/02/18/nepal_rebels_call_for_indefinite_strike_against_king/.
35. Gurubacharya, Binaj (April 8, 2006). "Anti-monarchy rallies spread in Nepal". The Boston Globe. http://www.boston.com/news/world/asia/articles/2006/04/08/anti_monarchy_rallies_spread_in_nepal/.
36. "Violent clashes amid Nepal curfew". BBC News. April 10, 2006. http://news.bbc.co.uk/2/hi/south_asia/4894474.stm. Retrieved 2006-11-22.
37. "Nepal Maoist rebels declare truce". BBC News. April 27, 2006. http://news.bbc.co.uk/2/hi/south_asia/4949066.stm. Retrieved 2006-11-22.
38. "Nepal's Maoists Declare Ceasefire". Voice of America. April 27, 2006. http://voanews.com/english/archive/2006-04/nepal-ceasfire.cfm?CFID=3777874&CFTOKEN=10318971. Retrieved 2006-11-22.
39. "Nepal calls ceasefire with rebels". BBC News. May 3, 2006. http://news.bbc.co.uk/1/hi/world/south_asia/4969422.stm. Retrieved 2006-11-22.
40. "Peace deal ends Nepal's civil war". BBC News. November 21, 2006. http://news.bbc.co.uk/1/hi/world/south_asia/6169746.stm. Retrieved 2006-11-22.

Chapter 20

NATIONAL SECURITY MECHANISM

*Dr. R.B. Singh**

Does India have the national security mechanism it needs? What are the inherent strengths and weaknesses of the mechanism it has presently? What modifications are required to remove the weaknesses while at the same time preserving and further adding to the strengths? What are the lessons which we can learn from the mechanisms of other countries? These are some of the questions that need attention in any debate on national security.

National security, which, in Israel, is treated as synonymous with national survival, has the following five major components—diplomatic, military, internal security, economic and intelligence. These components are closely inter-linked and even if one of them is weak, national security as a whole will be correspondingly weakened. National security management is the art and technique of integrating these components and making them function in a co-

* Editor, Guest Lecturer, Department of Defence Studies, University of Lucknow, Lucknow.

ordinated, effective and harmonious manner in times of normalcy as well as in times of crises.

The post-Second World War evolution of the concept of national security management has identified certain other sub-components, which need equal attention for preserving national security and well-being. These are risk management, disruption control management, disaster mitigation and management, whether the disaster is natural (the recent Tsunami which struck Indonesia, Thailand, Sri Lanka, India, Myanmar and the Maldives in the Asian region) or man-made (the Bhopal gas tragedy of 1984), and consequence and national resilience management.

As unconventional threats to nation-States from non-State actors such as insurgents and terrorists, trans-national criminals, narcotics smugglers, counterfeiters etc have increased, there has been a realisation that techniques and tradecraft, which served us fairly adequately against predictable State adversaries, may not be adequate against often unpredictable non-State actors, and that new analytical tools are required to meet the new threats. The old concept of threat analysis has been supplemented by risk analysis and vulnerability analysis. Lucid analysis—whether of threats, risks or vulnerabilities—is the starting point of effective national security policy-making, implementation and co-ordination.

Al Qaeda's terrorist strikes of September 11, 2001, in the US homeland had important lessons not only for the US, but also for the rest of the world. Among these lessons, one could mention:

- Without effective internal security, even the most powerful political, economic and military power in the world would be at the mercy of inimical forces.
- The globalisation of terrorism and the consequent externalisation of internal threats to security have

underlined the importance of an integrated approach to national security. Such an integrated approach has always had an importance in national security management but it has acquired added importance post-9/11.

The US was the first to realise the importance of such an integrated, well-structured approach. This realisation was reflected in the creation of the National Security Council (NSC) with a dedicated national security staff in 1947. The New Delhi-based Indian strategic analysts' community often projects that the NSC is the most innovative part of the US system as it came into being in 1947. This is not so. It is nothing but a small group of members of the Presidential Cabinet designated by law as the NSC to examine in depth national security issues, strategic or tactical, and come up with policy responses for approval by the President and subsequent implementation by different departments concerned with national security. The belief that an examination in depth of national security issues would be possible only in a small group of members of the Presidential Cabinet instead of in the large Cabinet as a whole and that secrecy of decision-making, which is important in national security matters, could be better ensured in a small body than in a large one was behind this decision. Many countries have had such small bodies, by whatever name they were called, long before the US decided to set up the NSC.

The most innovative part was the setting-up of a dedicated NSC staff to service the work of the NSC by coming up with policy options in response to national security situations for consideration by the NSC. Initially, the staff was set up by taking officers on deputation from the State and Defence Departments. Subsequently, the recruitment process was expanded to include inductions from the non-governmental world of universities, think-tanks, media and others. The NSC staff were expected to think in terms of the Government and the nation as a whole instead of in terms of the limited vision of any individual department of the Government concerned with national security. It was meant to weed out parochial tendencies in national security policy making and implementation, without weakening the policy initiatives of independent departments.

Between 1947 and 1953, the NSC staff headed by an individual designated as the Executive Secretary of the NSC, essentially concerned itself with the effective co-ordination of the policy-making and implementation process on behalf of the President. The Executive Secretary was expected to be a co-ordinator par excellence and not a policy innovator and adviser. The additional role of policy adviser to the President came into prominence in 1953 when the then President Dwight Eisenhower revamped the NSC and the NSC staff mechanism and re-designated the Executive Secretary as the Assistant to the President for National Security Affairs. This post has come to be popularly referred to as the National Security Adviser (NSA).

The NSA, who is a member of the executive office, is not subject to Congressional control in the same way as other senior bureaucrats are. The nomination of the NSA by the President is not subject to confirmation by the Senate and he or she has no obligation to testify before Congressional committees if called upon to do so. It is for the President to decide whether national interests demanded that he or she should testify if called upon to do so and his decision cannot be called into question by the Congress. What advice the NSA gives to the President is a matter between him/her and the President and the Congress has no right to know it.

There have been 19 NSAs in the USA since the post was created in 1953—six under President Ronald Reagan, three under Eisenhower, two under Presidents Lyndon Johnson,

Ford and Clinton and only one under Presidents Kennedy, Nixon, Carter and George Bush Sr, the father of the present President. Brent Scrowcroft had the unique distinction of serving as the NSA under two Presidents—under Ford from November 3, 1975 to January 20, 1977, and under Bush Sr throughout his term. Many analysts consider Scrowcroft as the best model of how an NSA should function—a low-profile and effective policy co-ordinator, facilitator and problem solver.

At the beginning of his term, every President issues an order specifying the duties of his NSA, though Reagan never issued such an order. He downgraded the role of the NSA during his first term and made the NSA report to him though his Chief of Staff (Ed Meese), thereby even depriving him of the right of direct access to the President. He came to office with a feeling that under Carter, Zbigniew Brzezinski had been allowed to wield enormous power as the NSA at the cost of the powers and initiative of individual departments. He wanted to correct it. Under Kennedy and Johnson, the role of the NSC as a whole in national security policy-making was considerably circumscribed by their individual style—particularly in the case of Johnson—of taking important decisions during informal discussions with close confidantes. They avoided formalised procedures. It was under Nixon (Kissinger) and Carter that the NSA acquired an enormous clout in the field of foreign and defence policies and an aura, which tended to stifle departmental initiative and innovation in policy-making. The NSA's post has since then been denuded of such aura, but foreign Governments, including that of India, while emulating the US system, tend to emulate the Kissinger and Brzezinski style aura than the substance of the system.

A perusal of the orders issued by various Presidents since 1953 would indicate that all of them saw the principal task of the NSC system, with the NSA acting as its manager and facilitator, as essentially to integrate the foreign and defence policies in such a manner as to protect national security and advance US national interests abroad. The following quotations from the official history of the NSC system would be relevant in this connection:

- "Since the end of World War II, each Administration has sought to develop and perfect a reliable set of executive institutions to manage national security policy. Each President has tried to avoid the problems and deficiencies of his predecessor's efforts and install a policy-making and co-ordination system that reflected his personal management style. The NSC has been at the centre of this foreign policy co-ordination system, but it has changed many times to conform with the needs and inclinations of each succeeding Chief Executive."
- "The view that the Council's role was to foster collegiality among departments also gave way to the need by successive Presidents to use the Council as a means of controlling and managing competing Departments."
- "The structure and functioning of the NSC depended in no small degree upon the interpersonal chemistry between the President and his principal advisers and Department heads. But despite the relationships between individuals, a satisfactory organisational structure had to be developed, for without it the necessary flow of information and implementation of decisions could not occur. Although a permanent staff gradually began to take shape, the main substantive work occurred in the Departments."
- "For 50 years, 10 Presidents have sought to use the NSC system to integrate foreign and defence policies

in order to preserve the nation's security and advance its interests abroad. Recurrent structural modifications over the years have reflected the presidential management style, changing requirements and personal relationships."

In this system, the NSA performs two roles. Firstly, he or she is the adviser to the President on all matters concerning national security. Secondly, he or she co-ordinates the functioning of the national security mechanism on behalf of the President. For the performance of these tasks, he or she depends on the dedicated NSC staff, who function through various committees consisting of the heads or representatives of the heads of different departments concerned with national security.

The orders relating to the NSA also lay down that the Director of the Central Intelligence Agency (CIA), in his capacity as the Director, Central Intelligence, will act as the intelligence adviser not only to the President, but also to the NSC. Similarly, the Chairman, Joint Chiefs of Staff, acts as the military adviser to the NSC. With the recent revamping of the US intelligence system, the incumbent of the newly-created post of National Intelligence Director is expected to act as the intelligence adviser to the President as well as the NSC.

The important roles assigned to the Director, Central Intelligence, and the Chairman, Joint Chiefs of Staff, as advisers to the NSC and not to the NSA tended to circumscribe the role of the NSA and keep it confined to the field of foreign policy and, in some instances, defence policy as well. Till 9/11, the role of the NSAs in the fields of internal security, intelligence management and economic security and well-being was limited to co-ordinating the decision making and implementation process. The NSAs had no advisory role in matters relating to intelligence, internal security and economic policy. Any role in economic matters, however limited, was taken away by President Clinton through a newly-created National Economic Council (NEC) to be serviced by an Assistant to the President for Economic Policy.

A study of the background of the NSAs since 1953 would show that the majority of them barring exceptions such as Gen. Colin Powell, Admiral Pointdexter, Brent Scrowcroft, Anthony Lake etc, came from a non-governmental background, who were chosen because of their area expertise and their expertise in foreign policy matters. They felt comfortable dealing with foreign policy and State actors.

The US has never had as an NSA someone who was an expert in intelligence, internal security or economic matters. The NSAs, with no experience or expertise in these important components of national security, felt uncomfortable dealing with subjects such as terrorism, law enforcement, the various aspects of internal security, economic security and well-being etc and with non-State actors. They tended to over-focus on foreign policy matters, leaving other aspects of national security, particularly internal security, to their subordinates. The inevitable result: 9/11. One only has to read the book "Against All Enemies", written by Richard Clarke, who was the counter-terrorism co-ordinator in the NSC staff before and during 9/11, to see how out of depths Ms.Condoleeza Rice, the then NSA, was in matters relating to counter-terrorism and how helpless she looked.

She was essentially a Russian-speaking expert on Russia from the academic world , who had served with some distinction under Scrowcroft when he was the NSA under Bush Sr, but her exposure to internal security policies and non-State actors-related issues was very limited. After 9/11, the Homeland Security related issues have received much greater attention in the US, but this is yet to be reflected adequately in the composition of the NSC staff and their areas of focus.

In the Indian strategic analysts' community, there is an uncritical admiration for the US national security system as epitomised by the NSC and its staff. They romanticise the American system and attribute to it virtues, which even American analysts do not ascribe to it. These analysts tell us that the NSC and its staff spend more time focussing on strategic, long-term studies than on tactical fire-fighting tasks which are left to the departments concerned, whereas, in reality, most of their time is spent on day-to-day fire-fighting than in long-term studies.

Apart from the pre-1988 success against the erstwhile USSR in Afghanistan and the collapse of international communism, how many other strategic successes can you attribute to the NSC and its staff? Vietnam, Iran, 9/11, post-9/11 developments in Afghanistan, Pakistan and Iraq are not testimonials to the good functioning of the US national security system.

The British Model

The Cabinet Secretary was the linchpin of the British model as it existed before 9/11 and co-ordinated the functioning of the national security apparatus, including the intelligence agencies, civilian as well as military. He was assisted in this task by the Permanent Secretaries Committee on the Intelligence Services, the Chairman of the Joint Intelligence Committee (JIC), who wore a second hat as Director, Security and Intelligence Matters, and the heads of the set-ups for disaster and consequence management. The JIC Chairman was responsible for the assessment of the intelligence provided by the agencies, for monitoring their performance and for co-ordinating physical security.

The Cabinet Secretary had a very limited role in the

formulation and implementation of foreign and defence policies, which were largely managed by the respective political and professional heads of the Foreign Office and the Defence Department. The Cabinet Secretary's role was more as a facilitator and co-ordinator of national security policy-making than as an adviser to the Prime Minister on foreign and security policies.

Post-9/11, the need for a dedicated co-ordinator of security and intelligence, who would not be involved in the day-to-day running of the intelligence and security agencies and who would not be burdened with other responsibilities as the Cabinet Secretary was, was felt. Accordingly, Prime Minister Tony Blair created in 2002 a post of Security and Intelligence Co-ordinator and Permanent Secretary in the Cabinet Office to take over from the Cabinet Secretary the responsibilities till then performed by the latter in matters relating to security and intelligence. It was, however, laid down that he would report to the Cabinet Secretary and through him to the Prime Minister. The order creating the post said: "This new Permanent Secretary Post is being created to enhance the capacity at the centre of Government to co-ordinate security, intelligence and consequence management matters and to deal with risks and major emergencies should they arise."

His functions were laid down as follows:

- The Principal Accounting Officer for a Single Intelligence Account (that is, preparation of a consolidated budget for all the intelligence agencies).
- Chairing the Permanent Secretaries' Committee on the Intelligence Services (PSIS), which advises on intelligence collection requirements, on the agencies' programmes and expenditure, and on co-ordination issues such as the promotion of joint working between the agencies and other Departments.

- Chairing the Central Official Committee to ensure the implementation of CONTEST, the Government's five-year counter-terrorism strategy.
- Deputy Chair of the Civil Contingencies Committee.
- Co-chairing the US-UK Joint Contact Group on Homeland Security.
- Chairing the Official Committee on Security to ensure the implementation of the Government's Protective Security Strategy (that is, physical security).
- Oversight of the Civil Contingencies Secretariat and support for the Home Secretary in his role as the Chair of the Civil Contingencies Committee.

It was also laid down that the JIC Chairman will report to the Cabinet Secretary and the Prime Minister in matters relating to intelligence assessment and to the Security and Intelligence Co-ordinator in all other matters.

The order creating the post of Security and Intelligence Co-ordinator also stipulated as follows: "The appointment of the Security and Intelligence Co-ordinator does not affect the statutory relationships between the heads of the intelligence agencies and their Secretaries of State nor the statutory sole responsibility of the agency heads for the direction of the operations of their agencies and their right of access to the Prime Minister."

Both the incumbents of this post since its creation came from the Home Office. Sir David Omand, the first holder of this post, had previously served as the Director of the Government Communications Headquarters (GCHQ), the technical intelligence agency, Deputy Under Secretary of State For Policy at the Ministry of Defence, Chairman of the Government's Centre for Management and Policy Studies and Permanent Secretary at the Home Office.

Bill Jeffrey, who succeeded Sir David and is the present

incumbent of the post, had served as the Deputy Head of the Economic and Domestic Secretariat in the Cabinet Office, Political Director in the Northern Ireland Office and then as Director-General of Immigration and Nationality.

The Security and Intelligence Co-ordinator has no role in foreign and defence policy matters. The Prime Minister has in his office an Adviser on Foreign Policy. He assists the Prime Minister during his meetings with foreign dignitaries, advises him on foreign policy matters and undertakes any special diplomatic tasks assigned to him by the Prime Minister. He has no role as the co-ordinator of foreign policy formulation and implementation. This task continues to be performed by the political and professional heads of the Foreign Office. Recently, Prime Minister Tony Blair has reverted to the practice which prevailed before the Falklands War of nominating a serving officer (William Ehrman) of the foreign service to function as the Chairman of the JIC.

Thus, post-9/11, the British Prime Minister has three senior officials assisting him in matters relating to national security—the Adviser on Foreign Policy, the Security and Intelligence Co-ordinator in respect of intelligence, internal security, crisis management and disaster management, and the JIC Chairman in respect of assessment of intelligence. While the Adviser on Foreign Policy reports directly to the Prime Minister, the other two report through the Cabinet Secretary, who continues to be the linchpin of the national security mechanism. The Adviser to the PM on Foreign Policy and the Security and Intelligence Co-ordinator are both members of the JIC.

While the JIC Chairman has a dedicated staff called the Joint Intelligence Organisation to help him in the assessment of intelligence and in performing other tasks relating to the intelligence agencies, the Adviser on Foreign Policy and the

Security and Intelligence Co-ordinator do not appear to have any dedicated staff. The Adviser on Foreign Policy makes use of the available staff in the Prime Minister's office and the Co-ordinator is serviced by the staff of the Cabinet Office.

The British model is thus characterised by an avoidance of excessive institutionalisation of the national security apparatus in order to retain a certain flexibility, a preference for serving officers to perform the roles of co-ordination and as foreign policy advisers instead of retired officers and non-governmental experts, an attempt to preserve the position of the Cabinet Secretary as the linchpin of the national security mechanism and to refrain from weakening the leadership role of the Departments concerned with national security in their respective policy domains and of the heads of the intelligence agencies and avoidance of any changes, which could come in the way of the privileged one-to-one relationship between the Prime Minister and the heads of the intelligence agencies, even while keeping them under the administrative control of the departments of which they are part—the Home Office in respect of the Security Service (MI-5) and the Foreign Office in respect of the Secret Intelligence Service (SIS—MI-6) and the GCHQ.

The Israeli Model

The Israeli model, of which not many details are available, seems to be patterned more after the US model, while avoiding the excessive structurisation of the US in order to retain flexibility in policy making and implementation. There is a post of NSA to the Prime Minister created in 1999. He is assisted by four Deputy NSAs, of whom one looks after foreign policy, one after security policy, one after operational matters and one is responsible for administration and accounts. One does not know what kind of staff they have to service them and how they function.

The Indian Model

Till 1999, in India too, as in the UK, the Cabinet Secretary was the linchpin of the national security mechanism and exercised his leadership role in national security matters through the Committee of Secretaries and the JIC. However, in contrast to the UK, the role of the Indian Cabinet Secretary was circumscribed by the following factors:

- The heads of the Intelligence Bureau, the internal intelligence agency, and the Research & Analysis Wing (R&AW), the external intelligence agency, enjoyed greater autonomy of functioning than their counterparts in the UK and had the same privileged direct access to the Prime Minister as their UK counterparts. The control of the Home Secretary over the IB was limited to administrative and financial matters, with practically no control over operational and policy matters. Similarly, the control of the Cabinet Secretary over the R&AW was limited to administrative and financial matters, with very little say in operational and policy matters.
- As in the USA during the years of the Kennedy and Johnson Administrations, many important decisions in foreign policy and national security matters were taken by the Prime Minister of the day during informal consultations with a small group of confidantes, with the Cabinet Secretary playing very little role in such consultations. Among those who played an important role in this informal consultations preceding important decision-making, one could mention V.K.Krishna Menon, the then Defence Minister, and B.N.Mullick, the then Director of the IB, during the prime ministership of Jawaharlal Nehru, D.P. Dhar, P.N. Haksar, T.N. Kaul, the then

Foreign Secretary, R.N. Kao, the then head of the R&AW, and G. Parthasarathi, a former journalist turned diplomat, during the prime ministership of Indira Gandhi and Shri Gopi Arora, an Indian Administrative Service officer serving in the Prime Minister's Office, Shri Ranen Sen, an officer of the Foreign Service then serving as the Joint Secretary in the PMO, Shri G.C. Saxena, the then chief of the R&AW, and Shri A.K. Verma, who also became the chief of the R&AW subsequently, and Shri M.K. Narayanan, the then Director of the IB, during the prime ministership of Rajiv Gandhi.

- The post-1982 institutionalisation of the role of Senior Adviser to the Prime Minister in national security matters. R.N. Kao under Indira Gandhi and Shri G.C. Saxena under Rajiv Gandhi performed this role after they had retired from service. Their role was restricted to national security matters and did not extend to foreign policy though Indira Gandhi did depend upon Kao for performing certain diplomatic tasks of a confidential and sensitive nature through his contacts at the senior levels of the intelligence communities of other countries. As Senior Advisers, Kao and Shri Saxena functioned from the office of the Cabinet Secretary, but they did not have to report to him. This practice of appointing a Senior Adviser on Security was discontinued in 1990.

It was under Rajiv Gandhi and Shri V.P. Singh as Prime Ministers that a tentative beginning was made to revamp the Indian national security mechanism by borrowing and adapting to Indian requirements certain features of the NSC mechanism of the USA. The exercise remained a non-starter.

On coming to office as Prime Minister in 1998, Shri A.B. Vajpayee set up a special Task Force headed by Shri K.C.

Pant and consisting of Shri Jaswant Singh and Air Commodore (retd) Jasjit Singh, the then Director of the prestigious Institute of Defence Studies and Analyses (IDSA), to study the national security mechanisms prevalent in other countries and to submit recommendations on a revamping of the Indian system. Such a revamping was considered necessary in view of the emergence of India as a nuclear power and its expected emergence as a major power of the region, if not the world.

The details of the recommendations of the Task Force are not available and one does not know to what extent they were accepted. After examining the recommendations, the Government set up a revamped national security mechanism in 1998-99, the main features of which were:

- A National Security Council chaired by the Prime Minister and consisting of a small number of members of the Cabinet to discuss in depth national security issues and take decisions.
- A Strategic Policy Group (SPG) headed by the Cabinet Secretary and consisting of the professional heads of the Ministries concerned with national security and the chiefs of the intelligence agencies and the Armed Forces to work out policy/decision options and submit them to the NSC for consideration.
- A National Security Advisory Board (NSAB), consisting of non-governmental experts, to provide policy inputs to the National Security Council Secretariat (NSCS).
- The NSCS to service the work of the NSAB, the SPG and the NSC and to take over the role of assessment of intelligence and co-ordination of the functioning of intelligence agencies, previously performed by the JIC, which ceased to have a separate and

independent existence.

- The creation of the post of NSA to oversee the functioning of the new mechanism and to advise the PM and the NSC in national security matters.

This was a mix of features from the American and British models. The ideas of the NSC, the NSA, the NSCS and the NSAB were borrowed from the US model. The NSAB was patterned after the National Intelligence Council of the CIA, a body of non-governmental experts to prepare long-term studies, without getting involved in day-to-day national security issues. The NSCS was patterned after the NSC staff in the US. The SPG was meant to retain the role of the Cabinet Secretary in national security policy making and co-ordination, as in the UK.

The working of this new system during the last six years has come in for the following criticism:

- SELECTIVE IMPLEMENTATION: The NSC did not meet even once and the previous as well as the present Governments preferred taking major decisions on national security at meetings of the Cabinet Committee on Security and not in the NSC.
- NEGLECT OF STRATEGIC ISSUES: One of the purposes of setting up the NSC system was to provide an institution for bringing about a strategic, long-term approach to policy and decision making. The idea was that the new system should focus on such strategic issues, leaving the day-to-day tactical handling to the Ministries concerned. In actual practice, the new system over-focussed on tactical issues to the neglect of strategic policy-making.
- WEAKNESSES IN THE ASSESSMENT MACHINERY: A bane of the Indian national security mechanism has generally been the weak analytical

capability. The merging of the JIC with the NSCS has proved counter-productive by removing even the limited analytical capability which we had before 1998. The independence and objectivity of the assessment process has been affected by entrusting the same body with the responsibility for assessment and follow-up action thereon.

- FAILURE OF NSCS TO COME UP TO EXPECTATIONS: The NSCS has failed to develop the kind of expertise required on a broad range of national security issues in order to be able to make a meaningful contribution to the decision and policy-making process. It tends to work more as a post office for collecting the views of other departments/agencies, collating and analysing them and passing them on to the SPG. There is very little innovation and new thinking in the policy-making process, the ground work for which has to be done in the NSCS.
- WEAK FOLLOW-UP AND COORDINATION: The follow-up action on the decisions of the Cabinet Committee on Security on the recommendations of the SPG has been weak. While the NSCS does the ground work for the examination of issues by the SPG, once a decision has been taken by the Cabinet Committee on Security, it has limited responsibility for the follow-up action and for coordinating and monitoring the implementation of the decisions. This job is done by the office of the Cabinet Secretary. In the USA, once a decision is taken by the NSC on a policy paper put up by the NSC staff, it is the responsibility of the staff to have necessary Presidential directives issued and to ensure implementation.
- WEAK CONTROL OVER THE NSCS: The NSCS

does the ground work for the examination of national security issues by the SPG, but the Cabinet Secretary, who presides over the SPG meetings and takes the necessary follow-up action, has very little control over the functioning of the NSCS and is hence not in a position to improve the quality of its performance. The NSCS is headed by the Deputy National Security Adviser (DNSA), an officer of the rank of Secretary to the Government. He is accountable to the NSA and not to the Cabinet Secretary. Initially, the NSCS was part of the Cabinet Secretariat, but in 2002, it was transferred to the PMO.

- WEAK CONTROL AND COORDINATION OF THE INTELLIGENCE AGENCIES: On the recommendation of the Special Task Force on the Revamping of the Intelligence Apparatus set up by the Government in 2000 under the chairmanship of Shri G.C. Saxena, the responsibility for monitoring and co-ordinating the performance of the intelligence agencies has been entrusted to the NSA. He is assisted in this task by the NSCS. Neither the NSCS nor the DNSA have expertise in intelligence matters. As a result, the performance of this task continues to be weak and without focus.
- UNSATISFACTORY PERFORMANCE OF THE NSABs: The NSABs were meant to ensure a continuous flow of non-governmental advice and inputs of a strategic nature for decision making. This purpose was defeated by the predominance of retired Government servants in it and by the inadequate representation given in it to those who have never had any association with the Government, either as serving or retired officers. The NSABs were New Delhi-centric with excessive

representation for New Delhi-based experts and with very little representation for experts from other parts of India, who could have brought in the perspectives of different States. They lacked focus and were left to fend for themselves with no carefully laid-down terms of reference.

- EXCESSIVE CONCENTRATION OF RESPONSIBILITIES IN ONE INDIVIDUAL: The decision of Shri A.B. Vajpayee to combine the duties of the Principal Secretary to the PM and the NSA in the same officer (Shri Brajesh Mishra) proved counter-productive. As the Principal Secretary to the PM, he was responsible for the smooth functioning of the Prime Minister's Office and for monitoring all developments in the country—whether security related or not—on behalf of and for the benefit of the Prime Minister. This was by itself a more than a full-time job. The entrustment to him of the additional responsibilities relating to the smooth functioning of the national security mechanism resulted in the dilution of the attention paid to national security tasks. Under Shri Vajpayee, the NSA was responsible for facilitating and co-ordinating policy and decision making in respect of national security, for monitoring and co-ordinating the functioning of the intelligence agencies, for the smooth functioning of the nuclear command and control mechanism and for discharging special diplomatic responsibilities relating to India's relations with China, Pakistan, the USA, Russia and other major powers. Shri Brajesh Mishra's (he is a retired officer of the Indian Foreign Service) familiarity and comfort level with foreign policy related issues and his relative unfamiliarity with internal security related issues led to unsatisfactory

> results in matters concerning internal security, which has in recent years become the most important component of our national security. The consequence: Positive results in the field of foreign policy due to the effective leadership role played by him, but not so satisfactory results in the field of internal security. Moreover, the effective discharge of internal security responsibilities in a federal state like India demands familiarity and acquaintanceship with those in charge of security and law enforcement in the States of the Federation. Neither the NSA nor his Deputy, who was also from the Foreign Service, enjoyed this kind of familiarity and acquaintance-ship. They largely remained strangers to those responsible for security and law enforcement in the States.

The new Government headed by Dr. Manmohan Singh came to office with a promise to correct the inadequacies in the national security mechanism. It appointed J.N. Dixit, former Foreign Secretary, as the NSA and created an additional and independent post of Special Adviser to the Prime Minister on Internal Security to which post, it appointed Shri M.K. Narayanan, former Director of the IB. Dixit was not given additional responsibilities as the Principal Secretary to the PM. A separate officer was appointed to that post.

There are no indications that any serious effort has been made so far to address the deficiencies noticed in the functioning of the new national security mechanism set up in 1998-99 and to have them corrected. The creation of the new post of Adviser on Internal Security has definitely laid the ground work for more focussed attention to internal security, but in the absence of a dedicated staff of his own, the NSA as well as the Adviser on Internal Security have both to depend on the NSCS for the effective discharge of their responsibilities. But, the NSCS is accountable to the NSA and it should not be a surprise if it gives priority to the requirements of the NSA in external matters than to those of the Adviser on Internal Security in internal matters. If an Adviser on Internal Security has to be effective, he has to have a say in the monitoring and co-ordination of the performance of the intelligence agencies, but this task continues to be performed by the NSA.

Dixit, being a Foreign Service officer, was perceived by some analysts and sections of the general public as following on the footsteps of his predecessor by over-involvement in foreign policy related issues resulting in inadequate attention to other issues. As a result, the public perception is that there has been no qualitative improvement in the functioning of the national security mechanism since the new Government came to power in May last.

After the tragic death of Dixit in harness on January 3, 2005, the Government has asked Shri Narayanan to hold additional charge as the NSA before it makes up its mind on the successor to Dixit. This interregnum should be utilised to examine whether any changes in the existing system are required. While making such an examination, the following points have to be kept in mind:

- With no apparent change in Pakistan's policy of continuing to wage a proxy war against India in order to get Jammu and Kashmir, with the continuing spread of Maoist terrorism to more and more areas in the country and with the unrest in the North-East showing little signs of abating, the internal security, intelligence and military components of national security would continue to need maximum attention. Consequently, any NSA would not be as effective as he or she ought to be, unless he has the required familiarity with these components.

- The expertise in matters relating to these components of national security in the NSCS has to be strengthened and the independence, objectivity and vigour of the assessment process has to be restored either by separating the JIC mechanism from the NSCS or through other means.
- The Prime Minister does require an expert in the diplomatic component of national security to handle the on-going back channel negotiations with Pakistan and China and for interacting continuously with his counterpart in the USA. A back-channel negotiator drawing his authority directly from the Prime Minister and enjoying his confidence and not subject to the kind of leakages which are not unusual in the Foreign Office would find greater acceptance from our foreign interlocutors than a run of the mill diplomat from the Foreign Office.
- Is it advisable to make a water-tight division between internal and external security at a time when there is an increasing realisation of the need for an integrated approach to national security? In 1983, Indira Gandhi bifurcated the JIC and created two JICs—one for internal security and the other for external security. Her hopes that this would result in better attention to internal security were belied. Rajiv Gandhi reversed her decision and merged the two.

How to achieve our objectives? By continuing to follow the US model despite the inadequacies noticed so far, hoping that the new incumbent as the NSA would be able to sort out the inadequacies in course of time? By separating the diplomatic and the other components of national security and entrusting the responsibilities to two different experts as the British have done? By abolishing the post of the NSA as suggested by some and reverting to the pre-1999 model of the Cabinet Secretary co-ordinating the national security mechanism by acting through the respective heads of the Ministries concerned?

After 9/11, it has been accepted practically in all the countries of the world that the Governments do need a single nodal point for dealing with national security issues and that the expert in charge of this should not have any responsibility for the day-to-day running of the various ministries and departments performing national security related tasks. Reversion to the pre-1999 model would, therefore, be retrograde.

Chapter 21

INDIA'S FOREIGN POLICY CHALLENGES

*Dr. R.B. Singh**

Introduction

India's foreign policies, fortunately, have enjoyed bipartisan political support domestically, markedly from the 1990s onwards. The year 2004 witnessed a change of political complexion of the Government in India raising uncertainties in international quarters that under a Congress-led Government foreign policies may revert back to the Nehruvian mould. Initial pronouncements by the new Government and especially its new Foreign Minister created some confusion. However, international realities and global security environment soon forced the new Government to prudently stick to the earlier general direction.

India's foreign policies first significant change in

* Editor, Guest Lecturer, Department of Defence Studies, University of Lucknow, Lucknow.

direction, attendant with change in India's economic policies took place under the stewardship of a Congress Prime Minister from South India and not belonging to the Nehru-Gandhi dynasty, namely Prime Minister Narasimha Rao, who recently passed away. He was the initiator of India's 'New Look' foreign policies.

Foreign policies of any nation do not function in a vacuum. They are a product of the prevailing international environment and the country's indices in terms of its geo-strategic location, economic health, military strength and domestic stability. Hence PM Narasimha Rao's 'New Look' foreign policies arose from the prevailing international environment at the end of the Cold War, the disintegration of the former Soviet Union and its global countervailing power and the need for India to detach its foreign policies from domestic minority vote bank considerations and also to focus on neglected regions. Hence the thrust for a strategic partnership with Israel in West Asia and the "Look East" foreign policy. So also was the quest for a substantive relationship with the United States. This was not to the liking of many of the Congress Party hierarchy.

The latter half of the 1990s till 2004 witnessed a BJP Government in power. Its tenure coincided with the post-Cold War era, the major rise of United States unilateralism and the new American policies of pre-emption and military intervention in global affairs without restraint. The Vajpayee Government of the BJP continued with the overall general direction of foreign policies of the Narasimha Rao Government. However greater intensity was accorded to the build-up of US-India strategic cooperation, normalising and enlarging cooperation with China, besides Vajapayee's personal commitment to bring a military adventurist and terrorism proxy-war nation like Pakistan to the dialogue table.

India's Foreign Policies-Imperatives for a Change of Direction/Nuances

Constancy of operational factors / considerations are not the hallmark of the international situation. It is a rapidly changing world, where increasingly the global security environment undergoes changes rapidly and new equations are struck and new doctrines postulated by United States unilateralism, at times in immoral contradiction of its established and declaratory policies e.g. Compromising on counter-terrorism against Islamic Jehad and condoning Pakistan's WMD proliferation.

While the turn of the millennium augured well for the general direction of Indian foreign policies under two separate political dispensations with an over-emphasis on a US-India strategic partnership, the last few years of the 21st Century indicated otherwise.

The last few years of the 21st Century in terms of international / political developments impacting on India's foreign policies presents the following broad picture:

- United States with its tactical obsession with Pakistan has placed the emerging USA-India strategic partnership on the back-burner. India is no longer a priority for USA.
- Russia at long last has realized that it is no longer a "natural ally of the West". The post-Cold War knee-jerk reaction of forging a strategic alliance with China has not brought the desired fruits. Russia may look for resurgence on its own strengths.
- China despite a phenomenal rise in trade with India and a flurry of visits by senior Chinese leaders to India has yet to give up its strategic nexus with Pakistan. China continues with the military build-up of Pakistan and establishing the infrastructure of

a Chinese military presence in Pakistan.

- The Indian sub-continent or so called South Asia, presents a dismal security environment. Pakistan strategically buoyed by American political, economic and military aid continues with its illusions of strategic parity with India and has not displayed any indicators of political maturity or conflict resolution. Turmoil and conflict continues in Nepal and Sri Lanka. Bangladesh under the present political dispensation is anti-Indian and emerging as an alternative base for Pakistan's proxy war against India.

The indicators above present significant challenges for India's foreign policies in 2005 as they generate imperatives calling for a change in direction/nuances of India's existing foreign policy thrusts. The thrust of this paper is to present a perspective analysis of India's foreign policy challenges for 2005.

United States-India Relations Under Challenge of Continued Engagement

The turn of the millennium effervescence in United States-India relations has evaporated and so also the prospects of a meaningful strategic partnership emerging in the future. This is the stark reality in 2005 notwithstanding the rhetoric emerging in Washington and New Delhi.

This situation is not of India's making. This situation has been generated by United States and an avoidable one at that strategically. The United States had a choice to make and that was whether the emerging United States-India strategic partnership could be jettisoned in favour of enlisting the dubious services of Pakistan to further American strategic expediency with relation to Al Qaeda and Osama bin Laden. The United States chose the latter. To add insult to injury, the United States has moved further ahead with weapon-systems and military equipment aid in an effort to placate Pakistan's military rulers call for conventional parity with India. Pakistan was also surreptitiously designated as a Major Non-NATO ally without taking India into confidence.

In Indian perceptions the above has seriously eroded United State's credibility in terms of its declared policies, intentions and deviations from the two foregoing. It is galling for Indians to see the American President extolling the Pakistani military dictator as a valiant fighter against terrorism and a steadfast ally. Indians have not forgotten General Musharraf's role as the architect of the Kargil War (1999), the proxy war by the Pakistani Army in Jammu and Kashmir and the American condonation of Musharraf's WMD proliferation.

American policy makers are likely to dismiss the above as Indian whining. They forget that all of the above has:

- Endangered and ruled out a United States-India strategic partnership.
- Will force India to look for alternatives to preserve its national security interests.
- Likely to make India resist US pressures against development of her ICBM and SLBM arsenal.

India's major foreign policy challenge in 2005 would be how to walk the tight-rope in keeping alive India's engagement with the United States and not let them go on the glide-path towards estrangement. The responsibility on India is heavy as the United States is not likely to make India's task any easier with their narcissistic obsession with Pakistan. On the contrary, the United States may exert avoidable pressure on India on the Kashmir issue to placate the Pakistani military dictator. India would need strong political will to ward off such pressures.

For more on this, readers may refer to this author's paper: "United States-India Relations on Glide Path Towards Estrangement?" (SAAG Paper No. 1183 dated 10-12-2004).

Russia-India Relations Present Hope of Re-kindling of Strategic Partnership

Russia no longer presents the strategically dismal picture as it did in 1991 or in 1996. It may be economically down, but not down and out. The Russian Federation has reasonably weathered its national crises one after the other. Its strategic assets are intact and it cannot be ignored in any global strategic calculus. Within Russia, the Atlanticists with their slogan of "Russia as the natural ally of the West" have lost the debate and Russian foreign policy is veering towards its traditional focus.

In terms of India's foreign policy formulations, Russia presents the following perspectives:

- Russia has had a history of strategic relationship with India.
- India's armed forces have a 60-75% dependence on Russian military inventories.
- Russia seems to intend to re-kindle a strategic partnership with India as evident from President Putin's recent visit to India.
- Russia could emerge as a major source of energy security for India.

If the above factors were not enough the recent American policies of being insensitive to India's national security interests (Pakistan-specific) is likely to prompt India too in re-kindling its strategic partnership with Russia.

This issue stands elaborated in this author's paper entitled: "Russia Re-kindles Strategic Partnership With India" (SAAG Paper No.1180 dated 07-12-2004).

The challenge of re-kindling Russia-India strategic partnership should be pursued forcefully by Indian foreign policy planners in 2005.

India's Challenge in Relations With China—Enlargement With Vigilance

China's policies towards India changed significantly after India's nuclear weapons tests in 1998. China after its initial hysterical reactions on India's nuclear weaponisation settled down to accept the new strategic reality on its Southern frontiers.

China's new approaches towards India manifested itself in the following ways:

- China ensuring peace and tranquility on the Sino-Indian frontiers.
- China-India economic cooperation and two way trade registering a phenomenal growth which is likely to touch US $10 billion.
- Increased China-India military-to-military contacts.

All of the above augurs well for Sino-Indian relations, but at the same time India cannot ignore the following Chinese moves:

- China's slow movement on the boundary dispute dialogue.
- China's continued military build-up of Pakistan.
- China's strategic military cooperation in South Asia with Pakistan and Bangladesh, both adversarial with India.
- China's development of naval infrastructure on India's flanks—Gwadur (Pakistan) and Chittagong (Bangladesh).

China therefore prevents a significant foreign policy

challenge to India in 2005. India's foreign policy planners need to aim at:

- Enlargement of Sino-Indian relations.
- Attempt dilution of Sino-Pakistan strategic nexus by imaginative diplomatic manoeuvers.
- Emphasising the strategic realities on China of the choices of cooperating with a rising major power like India as opposed to building up a regional spoiler state in the form of a pygmy state like Pakistan.

Concurrent with India's attempts to enlarge and enhance its relationship with China, India needs its utmost to exercise vigilance and detailed scrutiny of China's strategic moves in South Asia, till such time China shows definite signals of change of priorities in its South Asian policies.

India and the European Community and the Potential for Multi-polarity

The European Community with specific reference to France and Germany offers the potential for working towards a more multi-polar world. The European Community with the rising value of the "Euro" and its attraction as an alternative to the US dollar in terms of global nesting of financial reserves and trading leads to the prospects of the emergence of an alternative "Euro Trading Area" to the Dollar.

The rising economic strength of the Euro coupled with the political independence of countries like France and Germany offers an attractive foreign policy challenge to India. India also enjoys the luxury of being a lucrative market for European defence equipment sales. A selective use of this option by India could help Indian foreign policy planners to elicit favourable political responses for India's national security and economic interests.

India and West Asia-Strategic Interests Should Outweigh Political Platitudes

India's new Congress government under the influence of its constituent partners of the coalition like the Communists and the Muslim League besides the Nehruvians in the Cabinet have tried to veer India's foreign policy in West Asia towards platitudinous approaches on the Palestine issue and opposed to Israel. This has caused concern within the Israeli government.

India's national security interests are best served by its intensifying the strategic cooperation with Israel followed by the Narasimha Rao Government and the Vajpayee Government.

The challenge in 2005 for India's foreign policy on West Asia are going to be:

- Re-assure Israel that India values its existing strategic cooperation with it and would like it to be made more substantive.
- India would politically support the territorial integrity and sovereignty of Israel.
- Emphasise to Israel that it must invest in a continued Israel-India strategic partnership.
- Emphasise to Israel that the above should not become a hostage to the tenor of US-India relations.

For greater elaboration of this subject, see this author's paper: "Israel-India Strategic Cooperation And Prime Minister Sharon's Visit: The Added Dimensions (SAAG Paper No. 777 dt 02-09-03)".

India's foreign policy planners for West Asia have a bigger challenge in keeping alive its good relations with Iran in the face of stiff opposition from the United States. The United States till such time it militarily intervenes in Iran (prevented by its military overstretch) has embarked on international isolation of Iran. India should not be a part of any such effort.

Both India and Iran must continue to pursue vigorously the thrust enshrined in the Teheran Declaration and the Delhi Declaration.

For different reasons, Israel and Iran assist India's natural security interests and these two should be the focus of India's foreign policy in 2005.

South East Asia—The Need for Two-Tier Diplomatic Engagement: India's "Look East" policy devised by late Narashimha Rao has borne fruit in the last decade and a half. India today enjoys good relations with all the countries in the region. India has good interface with ASEAN in various capacities as well as setting up regional economic and development groupings like BIMSTECH and Mekong-Ganga Project.

While these over arching efforts need to be reinforced and pursued vigorously, relationships with all the countries cannot be pursued with the same intensity.

India's foreign policy challenge in 2005 would be to fashion a two-tier diplomatic engagement with the region. Tier 1 countries should be those with which India has more substantive political, economic and military links. These include Vietnam, Thailand and Singapore. Tier II countries should incorporate the remainder of the region. Vietnam has strategic convergences with India and has extended strategic cooperation all along. India needs to build further and enlarge on this base its ties with Vietnam.

EAST ASIA AND SOUTH PACIFIC CHALLENGES

The challenge here is that the major countries located in this region i.e. Japan, South Korea and Australia are strong United States allies linked to USA with substantive defence ties.

Hence their attitudes towards India will be determined by existing US attitudes towards India.

However of late it seems that Japan while attaching value to the Japan-US security linkages is embarking on a more independent political course. Under the Vajpayee Govt. high-level exchanges have taken place from both sides. India and Japan have also agreed to work together for demanding a UN Security Council Permanent Membership with full veto powers.

Japan has revived interest in significant investments in India's infrastructure and enough convergences exist in the strategic area also.

India's foreign policy challenge in 2005 should be to vigorously pursue Japan towards a strategic partnership with India.

South Asia Foreign Policies Should Ignore Pakistan and Dwell on the Rest of the SAARC Countries

In the last five years, India's foreign policies in South Asia, under American prodding or pressure has led to the following:

- Legitimising Pakistan's military dictatorship by inviting Musharraf for the Agra summit.
- Equating Pakistan with India by engaging in unconditional talks with a terrorist and proxy war state and an implacable foe of India.
- Seeking peace with a country whose very existence which has been framed by the Pakistan Army and its Generals as a "Warrior State" not amenable to peace in South Asia.
- Misreading Pakistani masses yearning for peace with India as the political aspiration of the Pakistani military dictatorship.

India should long ago have dispensed with its Pakistan-centric South Asian foreign policies. It is high time that India's foreign policy planners ignore Pakistan totally from their strategic calculus for South Asia. India should concentrate in a focused manner to improve and enhance its relationships with Nepal, Bhutan, Bangladesh, Sri Lanka and the Maldives. The political stability of these countries is more critical for a South Asian stable security environment than pandering to an inflated egoist state like the militarized Pakistan.

India if it has to exercise political magnanimity in South Asia, it should be towards these countries and not Pakistan as American interlocutors suggest.

Pakistan even under a combination of a rabid Mullah-cum-Pakistan Army dictatorship cannot pose more military threats to India than it has done so far.

Pakistan should be left in the American lap, a situation relished by both. Let USA take care of Pakistan's stability and India should concentrate on the rest of South Asia.

Concluding Observations

The old adage in foreign affairs stipulates that a nation does not have permanent friends or foes; only its national interests are permanent. India's foreign policy challenges for 2005 arise squarely from this precept.

In terms of the above, the prevailing global security environment, the existing global power structure and the United States redefinition of its South Asian priorities suggest:

- India's proximate relations with the United States, and particularly the strategic partnership which it so assiduously pursued in the last decade, no longer serve India's national security interests.
- Russia and India which veered off their quarter of a

century old strategic partnership (USA as a causative factor due to political and economic inducements to both separately) have enough convergence of interests to re-kindle their strategic partnership.

- China, for whatever reasons, has invested heavily in an enlarged economic relationship with India. It needs to further invest in an enhanced political relationship with India by divesting its South Asian policies of its Pakistan strategic nexus policy priorities. Pakistan is squarely in America's lap as a major non-NATO ally. One of the underlying aims of NATO is the containment of China. China needs to take notice of Pakistan's new anti-China status.

India's foreign policy challenges in 2005 therefore lie in going in for course-corrections of the overall foreign policy directions followed by the Narasimha Rao Govt and the Vajpayee Government.

India's quest for strategic partnerships lie elsewhere than the United States and it is this challenge which India's foreign policy planners must face in 2005 and craft policies which while keeping USA engaged politically, look elsewhere for countervailing power, counter-pressure points and multi-polarity.

Chapter 22

REVOLUTION IN MILITARY AFFAIRS AND NATURE OF FUTURE WAR

Brig. S.K. Singh

> 'In the Information Age, Technological Ideas are becoming the new Index of Power, instead of brute Military Force.'
>
> — *Alvin and Heidi Toffler*

Introduction

(17) RMA capabilities imply forces fighting through a total transparency of the battle field, exploiting information superiority through a fused network of satellites, UAVs, air and ground based radars and other 24 hour surveillance systems. Seamless connectivity through computer based communications, generating a command and control which is networked rather than hierarchical, would form the second aspect. Both battle field transparency and command and control will be integrated with all the three Services, rather than separate stand-alone systems for each Service, accept for those in the tactical battle space with limited ranges.

Integrated fire support will the third arm of an RMA based force. Air, artillery, missiles and armoured guns will be fized through digital target integration for precision strikes and higher lethality munition to cause destructive rather than neutralizing effect. The aim would be not only to destroy military targets but also disrupt the strategic command and control by emgaging leadership targets through use of special forces, if required. Intimate support platforms need to be provided to the army for total range of army aviation capabilities from surveillance, utility, command and control and even deep attacks by UAVs. All this will be supported by effective logistics of modular repairs and replacements in the field. Intelligence, speed, manoeuvre, lethality and precision will be the key parameters on which an RMA force will have to operate. Soldier's survivability in an urban environment would be the other key to an RMA based force. Soldier empowerment down stream to digitized ghataks(infantry) will imply permisasion of the RMA to the grassroots level, enhancing the potency of our forces. A link between urban operations in the conventional sphere with the counter-insurgency forces will have to be effectively established to attain the synergy in capacity building of diverse forces.

Definition

(5) RMA is a major change in the nature of warfare brought about by the innovative application of new technologies, which combined with dramatic change in military doctrine, and organisational adaptation fundamentally alters the character and conduct of military operations.

Classification of RMA

(6) RMAs can be classified as Minor or Major RMA

depending upon their extent of affect. These are as follows:-

(a) Minor RMA. Minor RMAs are initiated by small, individual technology and they occur in short periods. These can be shaped and controlled by those who can understand them. All Minor RMAs need not be pursued. Those applicable in one's context should be identified and adopted.

(b) Major RMA. Major RMAs are result of combined multiple technological, economic, social and cultural changes. These usually occur over a relatively large period. Incorporation of rifled weapons in the 19th century is an example of Major RMA. Major RMAs cannot be controlled and therefore they cannot be ignored.

Current RMA

Genesis of the current RMA can be attributed to the CHIP. A series of minor RMAs are underway, driven by military application of Chip technology. We are at the threshold of a major RMA resulting from multiple minor RMAs. Information Technology is in its third phase of technological development giving rise to new tools and processes for waging war like C4I2SR systems and IW etc.

Elements of Current RMA

Defence analysts in various countries have carried numerous reviews of the current RMA. Major elements of current RMA can be classified as follows:

(a) Improved C4I2SR. (Command, Control, Communications, Computers, Intelligence, Inter-operability, Surveillance and Reconnaissance). This is the most important aspect of controlling warfare and avoiding the fog of war to take timely and correct decisions.

Current RMA makes it possible to put in place a robust information grid providing situational awareness at all levels i.e. from tactical to national. Another important aspect is reduction in sensor to shooter time. This is possible with effective RSTA systems (i.e. Reconnaissance, Surveillance and Target Acquisition systems).

(b) Information Warfare. IW can be defined as any action taken to deny, exploit, corrupt or destroy enemy's information, while protecting ourselves against enemy action against own information. In this type of warfare Information is all three i.e. Resource, Target and the Weapon. IW can be broadly classified into four types. These are as follows:-

(i) Against enemy C4I2SR.
(ii) Against Communication links of society (e.g. TV, Radio, Tel and power grid).
(iii) Cyber ops.
(iv) Psyops.

(c) Joint War Fighting. Jointmanship is the key to ensure effective and optimum utilisation of RMA. Interoperability is the key word for the present and future warfare. Needless to say that a joint doctrine is unavoidable.

(d) Standoff, Precision and Stealth Capability. These capabilities are important for strike and reconnaissance activities by aircraft, UAV, ships and cruise missiles.

(e) Space warfare. Space is likely to be the battlefield of the future. The aim would be to provide air space superiority to provide freedom to attack and freedom from an attack. This includes all the activities facilitated by space vehicles (i.e. Reconnaissance, Int Gathering, Missile Defence, Navigation, Data

Transmission and Communication etc).

(f) Focused Integrated Logistics. RMA demands more than basic logistics skills. Rapid responsive forces of the future would require an equally agile logistic-support network. Total logistic visibility, flexible and rapid distribution and transportation would be essential components of such a logistics system.

Cutting Edge Technologies

Nano-technology, Bio-technology and Robotics with Artificial Intelligence are the cutting edge technologies of the future. Genetic studies are being undertaken to learn the information-storing secrets of DNA, which can compress enormous amounts of data into microscopic spaces. These techniques are being applied to computer microchips to create information systems much smaller, faster, and more capable than existing ones. The micro and nano-technologies are being used to develop miniature flying and/or crawling systems capable of performing a wide variety of battlefield sensor missions.

Nano-technology. The field of nano-technology is a rapidly expanding arena. It deals with structures and machines on the atomic and molecular scale. These nano-structures include electrical, mechanical, mechanical-electrical, and quantum devices with the promise to revolutionise the way we develop and manufacture technology and interact with the environment. Potential capabilities include the proliferation of sensors and actuators leading to "clothes that respond to the weather, interface with information systems, monitor vital signs, deliver medicines, and automatically protect wounds; airfoils that respond to airflow; buildings that adjust to the weather; bridges and roads that sense and repair cracks" and so on.

Miniaturisation. The trend toward miniaturisation is

already well under way in numerous research projects. At the extreme, some crystal gazers envision "fire ant warfare," with the battlefield dominated by millions of small semi-autonomous machines, a few inches to feet in size, networked together and capable of rendering an area impassable to troops or conventional mechanised formations. Researchers are in the process of building small robotic devices to extend reach on the battlefield: tiny unmanned aircraft, insect-like crawlers to carry sensors, and long-loiter high-altitude drones. It is expected that these devices will be tied into our battlefield information networks, and that they will be inexpensive enough to be used on routine missions. As useful as these miniature devices are likely to be, they provide only a glimmer of what may be possible in the longer term. Rather than robots several inches in size, some ambitious researchers are talking about machines built atom by atom, measuring only a few nanometers (billionths of a meter) across. Such nanotechnology is in its infancy and it may be decades before this research leads to useful nano-devices. However the research is producing remarkable advanced manufacturing techniques and molecular structural materials, and is likely to result in machines that are highly miniaturised if not actually microscopic.

Biotechnology. Biotechnology is a topic of extensive interest, particularly in the wake of successful efforts to clone adult mammals. Currently the emphasis is on therapeutic applications of genetic technology and on the ethics of procedures such as in-utero genetic testing, genetic intervention to "cure" conditions such as short stature, and human cloning. What underlies all this is rapid advances in our understanding of how biological organisms function at the cellular and molecular level. It is likely that such progress will accelerate over coming decades and a clearer and detailed picture would emerge regarding functioning of complex organisms. In future, the merger of biotechnology, miniaturisation, and information processing will produce machines that perform today's military tasks farther, faster, better, and maybe even cheaper.

Military Critical Technology List

Few technologies that have been identified as to be military critical are listed below :

(a) Nuclear Systems Technology.
(b) Chemical and Biological Systems Technology.
(c) Guidance, Navigation and Vehicle Control Technology.
(d) Armaments and Energetic Materials Technology.
(e) Materials Technology.
(f) Directed and Kinetic Energy Systems Technology.
(g) Electronics Technology.
(h) Manufacturing and Fabrication Technology.
(j) Information Systems Technology.
(k) Sensor and Laser Technology.
(l) Power Systems Technology.
(m) Ground Systems Technology.
(n) Marine Technology.
(p) Aeronautics Systems Technology.
(q) Information Warfare Technology.
(r) Signature Control Technology.
(s) Space Systems Technology.
(t) Weapon's Effects and counter-measures Technology.

(21)The RMA and the Indian Armed Forces

The reason why the velocity of the battles is so high or the OODA Loop so fast is that, firstly, technology enables the commander to see the battlefield more fully, and secondly, broadband communications makes it possible to link all commanders to a comprehensive tactical picture. The latter enables the staff process to be shortened to such an extent that the velocity of battles can be increased. How the commander 'see' more, or become omniscient? As before, he dominates the high ground; but today it is in the form of satellite surveillance, fixed wing reconnaissance, Unarmed Aerial Vehicles (UAVs), infra red devices—all this information being instantly available on the Command Information Decision Support System (CIDSS).

During the era of technology, India fought a minor war at Kargil which undoubtediy was won by the valour of the junior of the army. The victory at Kargil assured the higher command that everything was alright. There was, therefore, no need for serious introspection, and the few changes in the corps and divisional set up at Kargil was all that was required to correct whatever had gone wrong. The Subramaniam Committee dealt with events 'leading up' to Kargil, and the Reddy is an internal enquiry. However, the acquisitions during Kargil and Post-Kargil, indicated that apart from items like cold weather clothing, the army was seriously deficient in Thermal Imagers (TI) night vision devices, laser designators, 155mm terminal homing rounds, counter battery radar, electronic warfare equipment, UAVs, troop carrying helicopters, night flying equipment, Global Positioning System(GPS), digital maps and reliable communication sets.

Joint Operations

If the RMA is to be imposed on a reluctant service, the best method is to impose the RMA through the integrated staff. As warfare changes, single service operations become weaker and more irrelevant without joint service facilities. Satellite surveillance, satellite communications, Joint Electronic Warfare (EW) and joint photo interpretation have already begun to shift to the integrated staff along with the Defence Intelligence Agency (DIA).

NEW DIMENSIONS OF WAR

Information Warfare

Information warfare constitutes another revolutionary aspect of the new era warfare—quickly disrupting or destroying an adversary's command and control system, intelligence, information propaganda abilities, and general situational awareness. Info War is not the same as intelligence operations, although it is clearly related to intelligence. Information warfare is an attack on an adversary's entire information, command and control, and, indeed, decision-making system. Information warfare is "any action to deny, exploit, corrupt, or destroy the enemy's information and its functions; protecting ourselves against the actions; and exploiting our own information operations." Information warfare is directed at shrinking or interfering with the enemy's Observe, Orient, Decide, Act (OODA) loop while expanding and improving our own. Strategists now speak of information as a "strategic asset," and planners describe the objective of information war as "information dominance."

Cyber Ops

Cyber war is the operational extension of information war however; it is becoming a major constituent of warfare. In fact it is the sixth dimension of war in addition to the existing dimensions of Land, Water, Air, Underwater and Space Warfare. It involves tactical disruption, then domination, and perhaps even the reordering, of an enemy's decision-cycle. All this has obvious implications for command and control warfare against an adversary. The cyber ops in future would be fought by Cyber Warriors controlling the cyber space with encapsulated software entities. These entities would have their own identity, state, behavior, thread of control, and ability to interact and communicate with other entities, including people, other agents, and legacy systems. Essentially "cyber vehicles," also referred to as "info craft", would operate in the cyber domain similar to the way air and space vehicles operate in the atmosphere.

Space Warfare

Space warfare involves dominating the "high ground" of space to deny its advantages to the adversary and to use it to implement one's own command, control, communications, navigation, reconnaissance, air defence, missile defence, warning, and weather forecasting. Space assets can become a key to the future digitalisation of the battlefield where some of the fog and friction of war is removed for the side dominating space. Space warfare includes aspects of the other three emerging warfare areas, but has the potential to become a qualitatively distinct warfare area of its own. Military's increasing reliance on support from space-based systems for its everyday operations and especially during times of conflict has highlighted the importance of space operations. However, space assets could provide more than support for the terrestrial war fighter in the future. The space environment offers the possibility of conducting worldwide military operations in a greatly reduced time frame. Effective utilisation of space would have following advantages:-

(a) An effective anti-satellite (ASAT) capability could lead to the ability to achieve aerospace control or superiority in order to deny an opponent the ability to operate in or from space.

(b) Properly placed and employed, space assets could perform missions in much less time than state-of-the-art aircraft. One possible mission is to use space forces to project power to directly achieve national objectives (operational or strategic) in a particular theater.

(c) Space strike systems based on satellites or on trans-atmospheric vehicles could enable precision strikes whose quantitative advantage in speed would result in a qualitative difference in capability.

(d) Future capabilities in space transport may also make possible the movement of critical forces and equipment from one theater to another in time frames and order of magnitude faster than with current sea and air transport.

(e) Further, the altitude advantages provided by space greatly improve surveillance and reconnaissance coverage of the earth and, as a result, could offer the means to command and control operations in theaters where distance and terrain complicate or confound terrestrially based systems.

INFORMATION OPERATIONS

(20)Recent advances in the fields of Information and Communication Technology (ICT) and Information and Communication Systems (ICS) have ushered in an era of 'Information Age' which is fast progressing towards the 'Knowledge Age'. Information has become the new currency of power and Information Operations, the preferred mode of conducting warfare. Information Operations are conducted on 24X7 basis by all nations, industries and other organization, including terrorists. It is therefore important to understand its nuances and applications.

The Changing Role of Information in Warfare

The battle for the information realm will be the first and most important battle, victory in which will virtually ensure victory in the other realms. Information systems for command, control and communication become so essential to combat operations that warfare becomes, conceptually, contests between these systems rather than between strike systems, with information systems themselves as the most critical targets.

Information dominance and denial will be the area of focus in future conflicts. At the national level, information warfare could be viewed as a new form of strategic warfare, where the key issue would be the question of how to attack the enmy systems while protecting one's own. This is aided by the C4I2SR systems. The aim of IW is to attack the enemy's "Observe, Orient, Decide and Action" (OODA) cycle, make it bigger in time and space causing physical and psychological damage simultaneously protecting and shrinking one's own OODA cycle. One of the most potent components of IW is Cyber War, which refers to conducting military operations according to information related principles.

- High-power microwave weapons will be able to "destroy the opponents' electronic equipment."
- Information superiority is "more important than air and sea superiority."
- "We must gain air and sea superiority, but win information superiority first of all."
- Deterrence will be a new operational concept

Like nuclear deterrence, "information deterrence" will be vital, especially if "the power with a weaker information capability can deliver a crippling attack on the information system of the power with a stronger information system." In a very important point, Chang stresses, "Even if two adversaries are generally equal in weapons, unless the side having a weaker information capability is able effectively to weaken the information capability of the adversary, it has very little possibility of winning the war.

(4) This new military strategy had its genesis during the 1970s when it was developed as part of what has been called the 'offset strategy'. The strategy was envisaged as a counter to the perceived threat of an armoured assault by the Warsaw Pact forces in Central Europe where the NATO forces were disadvantaged both in terms of personnel and armoured equipment by a three to one ratio. The NATO forces therefore leveraged the use of technology as a force multiplier by building better weapon systems using current technology, and supporting these systems on the battlefield with newly developed equipment that multiplied their combat effectiveness. Thus a lethal combination of cutting edge technology and state of the art equipment gave the coalition forces a significant competitive advantage over their opposing counterparts.

The three basic components of information, viz. collection, processing and dissemination are complementary and each of them is essential to understand and assimilate a given situation. Thus, mere possession of infinite intelligence data does not transform into an advantage unless the mechanism to sift and collate this data into crucial information exists. Just as important is the need to communicate this information to its intended destination. This two-pronged approach will allow a commander to mas combat power effectively, use economy of force to sustain offensive action, surprise the enemy and correctly manoeuvre his forces to defeat the enemy.

The advantage with Information Operations is that it has both offensive and defensive capabilities. It can be administered during peace time, in crisis and at all levels of warfare to inflict severe damage on the enemy with exceptionally low levels of violence. Information Operations weapons be they non-lethal technology weapons to disrupt a nation's decision making process, soft bombs to cause systemic failure to electrical distribution and telecommunication facilities or electronic intrusion/ hacking of these systems to gain control of these infrastructure, have critically upset the traditional offence-defence that has been heavily in favour of defence for the last two decades owing to power projection and deterrence capabilities of nuclear weapons. Information dominance is therefore poised to supplement nuclear dominance as the key measure of international power in 21st century.

The remarkable success story of the coalition forces in the Gulf War was chiefly built on five critical components, viz. command, control, communications, intelligence (C3I) and precision guidance. During Desert Storm, military commanders had excellent situational awareness owing to the massive deployment of C3I components. Intelligence sensors, navigation systems and communication systems gave coalition battlefield commanders the exact location of friendly forces, opposing forces and own troops. The United States effectively used its various space satellite systems to generate data for maps, locate military units, identify military systems and pin point the location of command and control installation of Iraqi forces. Communication were additionally put in place to transmit military data and weather satellites were used to plan assault. Further, air borne reconnaissance systems—both manned and unmanned—were utilised to supplement the satellites that were constrained by the laws of orbital mechanics and hence could not provide continuous coverage of the specific area.

An important aspect of Information Operations

illustrated during Desert Storm was the immense capability displayed by a new generation of tactical reconnaissance systems, viz. E-3 Sentry AWACS (Airborne Warning and Control System) and E-8A JSTARS (Joint Surveillance and Target Attack Radar System).

AWACS were successfully deployed to enhance the development of an 'air-picture' for coalition military leadership and forces thus giving them a significant advantage over Iraqi fighters in the air-to-air combat during the first week of war. The AWACS could detect low flying aircraft more than 200 miles away. It could also locate, identify and track hundreds of targets at once and direct friendly war planes to intercept incoming aircraft.

JSTARS performed a function similar to that carried out by AWACS i.e. detection and location of stationary and mobile ground vehicles. JSTARS could track and detect troop, tank and helicopter movements opto 120 miles. The plane's radar and 17 operating consoles were connected by an electronic data link with a ground station that the Army used, and movements spotted by the operators were relayed to the commanders on the ground. The vehicle used by the Iraqi forces to meet their logistics requirements were sensed by JSTARS and the target data was transmitted to strike aircraft. This helped immensely in cutting supply bases from the Iraqi forces.

JSTARS were deployed successfully to detect enemy ground movements during the five day ground war with almost negligible loss of coalition tanks. These were also used successfully in detecting and targeting Scud launchers.

Satellite communication systems and digital radios were also used extensibly during Desert Storm to supplement the standard military radios as well to collect and process intelligence data. The need to transmit voluminous data including high-resolution pictures throughout the duration of war was achieved by the combined efforts of Defence Satellite Communication System, commercial satellites and couriers.

Objectives and Components of Information Operations

The objective of Information Operations is to augment national capability by promoting and protecting own information, information systems and information infrastructure while exploiting or degrading the adversary's information, information systems and information infrastructure to gain and maintain a state of information superiority. Its key components are Information Dominance (Offensive), Information Assurance (Defensive) and Perception Management.

Information Dominance

Information Dominance is achieved by coordinating, supporting and conducting information network attack operations with the aim of investigating, breaching, denying or otherwise compromising the adversary's information systems. In this process it also provides the battlefield commander with the status and characteristics of the adversary's information systems. In other words, Information Domination means domination of the adversary's 'Information Space'. Information Space has no boundaries or borders and is omnipresent. It is the nation's responsibility both to protect this space as also to have definite capability to launch sustained offensive in this space. This is the very essence of Information Operations.

Information Assurance

This is the defensive component ensures Network Availability, Information denial and Information

Availability. A formal definition of Information Assurance is: "Information Operations protect and defend information and information systems by ensuring their availability, integrity, Authenticity, confidentiality and non-repudiation. This includes providing for restoration of information systems by incorporating protection, detection and reaction capabilities. It also includes defensive measures as well as pro-active offensive activities.

Perception Management

The aim of Perception Management is to induce or reinforce foreign attitudes and behaviours favourable to own objectives by conducting planned operations to convey selected information to the target audiences to influence their emotions, motives, objective reasoning and ultimately, the behaviour of foreign governments, organizations, groups and individuals. The capabilities in the fields of public affairs, public information and diplomacy fall in this sphere.

(17)Flow of Information : Bottom-up or Top-down

Military maxim holds that the best intelligence comes from soldiers in contact and that reports from these engagements flow up the chain of command, being filtered and consolidated at each echelons along the way. Weapons and tactics have expanded the battlefield well beyond the range of human eyes, ears and of the electronic sensors owned by battalions, brigades and regiments. Manoeuvre warfare absolutely depends on accurate and timely intelligence about entities and events that are no longer easily or quickly sensed from the front lines: events at the full depth of the theatre of operations and often beyond the reach of sensors under the direct control of combat commanders.

Infantry no longer trudges a dozen miles a day. They ride swiftly into battle at speeds upto 40 miles per hour. At night and poor weather,, when optical sensors are blind. Further, well-disciplined forces may ride silently into few formations, limiting the usefulness of sensors sweeping the spectrum for signs of activity. These new deep thrusts can be detected only by air and space-borne systems. These are controlled at theatre or even at national levels, serve multiple users and other purposes and their use must be prioritized. Spy satellites are a good example of sensors that have other, often competing, tasks to perform.

(10) Information—The Weapon of Future Wars

Strategic information attacks, using virus, logic bombs and hackers will be the mode of attack in future wars. An information attack on military communication networks, air control systems, financial networks and Internet system can cripple a nation's military, economic, communication and defensive systems and cause a paralysis amongst its decision makers. Such an attack using a host of viruses, logic bombs and Trojan Horses on an enemy's information system may well be the opening salvoes of a war in the 21st century; just as artillery and air attacks on similar targets often heralded the opening shots of wars fought in the previous one. Alvin Toffler summed it up succinctly when he stated, "The tools of warfare will be no longer tanks and artillery, but computer viruses and micro-robots."(New Military Perspectives for the next century, Military Science Publishing House, 1997)

The individual soldier would be equipped with his personal information management systems along with personal weaponry. Soldiers will carry conventional, light weight rifles, grenades and small missiles and also have multi-media electronic equipment. This system would have radio, fax and video communication, global positioning system, identification friend and foe (IFF) system and a battle field management system, which would provide instantaneous locations of own and enemy forces on a digital display. Information would be available virtually at the finger tips.

Stealth Technology

Stealth technology to prevent the adversary from obtaining information will thus be widely used. Stealth aircraft and ships are already in production. This technology would soon extend to tanks. Light vehicles, UAVs, guns and even combat uniforms. This century may also see the arrival of robot troops possessing artificial intelligence, which may replace soldiers in many hazardous duties. Information denial could see the rise of weapons such as electromagnetic weapons using millimeter waves or electromagnetic pulses that destroy enemy equipment and corrupt their network by 'soft' kills. 'Soft' kills would acquire greater significance than the physical destruction of the targets.

This will bring about major changes in operational concepts. The size of divisions, formations, units and sub-units will reduce drastically as the combat potential will increase exponentially due to technology. Large scale attacks using tanks, aircraft and heavy artillery would reduce, as 'smart' precision munitions will attain the same result at a fraction of the expenditure. The existing command and control system would become more flexible and decision making would be de-centralised even at the lowest level but with a high degree of coordination in the upper echelons of command. Small team operations will be the norm.

Responsive Communication

Responsive communications are critical to intelligence's fundamental mission of supporting commanders. Regardless of the amount of data collected, the targets identified or the accuracies achieved, information has no value unless the commanders and appropriate fire support elements receive it in time to react, either through fire, manoeuvre or both. The joint surveillance target attack radar system with its ground station module and the Guardrail common sensor with its commander's tactical terminal are examples of the types of systems to meet these needs.

The ground station module will be deployed to each corps in sufficient numbers to provide key command and control and fire support nodes down to division, armoured regiments and even manoeuvre brigades. The module is designed to downlink raw radar data from the joint surveillance target attack radar system aircraft and tailor the data to the echelon and function of the node it is supporting. Army intelligence intends to build into the ground station module the ability to downlink live video (television or forward looking radar) from its family of unattended aerial vehicles. The module will also users to view the unattended aerial vehicle video through windows on the same screen depicting the joint surveillance target attack radar system moving target indicator and/or synthetic aperture radar data. Over time, Army intelligence will downlink additional sensors to the ground station module, as it evolves the station to the common ground station.

(3) Network Centric Warfare

(24) Network Centric Warfare (NCW) is a concept of operations that generates increased combat power by networking sensors, decision makers and shooters to achieve shared awareness and synchronized activity. NCW uses information for the benefit of the war fighters in peace and in war. The military calls it "situational awareness" which implies awareness regarding terrain (including objectives and targets), enemy and own forces. This information is passed from the sensors deployed on the ground, at sea, in

the air and in space (satellites, unmanned aerial vehicles, aircraft, radars etc) through broadband digital communication networks to front line units and the decision makers in the rear in real or near real time frame thus making the battlefield transparent and reducing response time.

Network Centric Operations have also been described as high tempo, precise, agile style of manoeuvre warfare focused on effects-based operations (EBO) that derive their power from robust networking of geographically separated entities. EBO are themselves coordinated sets of actions directed at shaping the behaviour of friends, foes and neutrals in peace, crises and war. This implies timely, appropriate and skillful use of all or selected element(s) of national power which include political and diplomatic, economic, technological, social, psychological, information/media and military among others. In essence, therefore, NCW advocates and enables integration and "jointmanship" in which the three Services, in the Indian context, are lagging behind despite all their diplomatic eloquence from time to time. The final is to achieve strategic (political) objectives of war with the least amount of tactical effort which incidentally is also the essence of "Operational Art". Hence, "jointness" and "integration" together with innovative Operational Art are vital parameters of this type of warfare. At the national and military strategic levels we are continuing to underplay and ignore these issues. Our so-called "Jointness" is neither functional nor formalized.

NCW would aim at providing real-time, accurate information available to all friendly forces so that they can make fast, effective and better informed decisions. It visualizes a huge network of computers with three components, namely the quick deployable ground sensors that generate and integrate real time images, military commanders making decisions aided by decision support systems and lastly the shooters—the response systems to destroy the enemy assets.

At the more elementary level the soldier of the future will have the necessary equipment to make him a networked enabled "smart warrior". Using the helmet-mounted-drop-down eye piece, he will see a virtual. GPS linked display showing his current location and that of friendly and hostile units in the area. He will be able to switch the display to watch live video feeds from Unmanned Aerial Vehicles (UAVs) coming via a secure data link. His rifle-mounted Thermal Weapon Sights will not only help him identify enemy positions in the dark, but also pass on the same information to allied units on the network. The soldier utilizes data fed in by sensors like UAVs, fifth generation air crafts, satellites and other sensors, to identify important targets and detect potential traps or hostile units. He wont fire unless absolutely necessary, rather relying on combat robots or Unmanned Combat Aerial Vehicles (UCAVs) to do the job. Once the target has been identified, the soldier will deploy robots or UCAVs to destroy it. The individual soldier thus becomes a powerful component of a huge grid, much more powerful than the soldier of today, with his safety ensured.

Challenges Related to Network Centric Environment

The threat to India from traditional adversaries requires preparation and readiness for high intensity conventional conflicts which are likely to be rare. In the near and mid-term, the armed forces are more likely to fight non-traditional conflicts involving, counter terrorism on land, at sea or in the air; Proxy Wars supported and encouraged by adversarial neighbours; and home grown insurgencies as part of India's turbulent internal security situation. Additionally, the armed forces may be called upon to stabilize the volatile strategic environment around India through benign presence and if required through force projection. Force may also have to be projected to secure our off-shore assets, island territories, assets and Indian diaspora abroad, and to assist friendly nations when invited. Hence, the nature of wars, in the future, is going to compel us to think big but with smaller, more maneuverable, more precise, more agile forces and above all integrated forces. This will come about because technology will allow large forces to be replaced by 'precision' and 'information' highlighting the time factor as the critical issue.

A more challenge lies in the realm of our currently well defined command and control structure which would need a review because in a Network Centric Environment (NCE) the military guideline of 'one up and two down' may not remain relevant. Moreover, the dividing line between strategic, operational and tactical levels, will meet the same fate because the nature of net-centric operations will allow prosecution of operations in a simultaneous and non-linear manner, throughout the battle space, thus hastening the process of achieving the strategic aims and objectives of war.

Another challenge is that while the three Services are modernizing their respective networks and suitable gateways are being factored for limited integration at appropriate levels, the communication networks existing currently do not allow the type of inter-operability required. The completion of the Defence Communication Network (DCN) will help in this regard if effective tri-service architecture is well conceived, developed and put into place by a suitably designated team of operational and technical experts of the three services.

Key Concepts of NCW

NCW is a product of convergence of computers and communications and its exploitation to bring to bear maximum combat power at the right time and right place.

Two key concepts, relevant to NCW, need to be emphasized.

- The first key concept is the use of a geographically dispersed force. As the ranges of sensors and weapons increase and as ability to move information rapidly improves, military forces are no longer geographically constrained. With NCW, one can have the same thing at more than one place at the same time. This is because a sensor or shooter can now be in a position to engage many different targets without having to move.
- The second key concept is the fact that the force is knowledgeable. A knowledgeable force depends upon a steady diet of timely, accurate information, and the processing power, tools and expertise necessary to put battle space information into context and turn it into battle space knowledge.

The biggest changes that network enabled capability will deliver are within the information domain and the way decisions are made. In linking sensors, decision makers and weapon systems, the salient change will be how commanders and staff use this linked information. This has the potential to challenge current command doctrine and procedures. With the rapid emergence of NCW concepts, the focus has progressively shifted from 'massing the forces' to 'massing of effects'. This paradigm shift will also reflect in the way command will need to be exercised in war.

(13)NCW : Superiority Enabled Concepts

Information and Communication Technologies (ICT) have shrunk the globe into a village through powerful and versatile networks. This has resulted in a very different security paradigm; an entirely way to conduct business and a unique way of executing warfare commonly known as

Network Centric Warfare (NCW). In short, ICT and the consequent spread of networks have ushered in the information age, wherein information has become the currency of power, the battle field transformed into a digital domain and information superiority has emerged as the single most important battle winning factor. This information superiority is gained from the information operations that protect our networks and hence our ability to collect, process and disseminate information without any interruption whatsoever while at the same time exploiting/ denying an adversary's ability to do the same. NCW is, thus, an information superiority-enabled concept at the heart of which lie communication networks and the ability to process information most expeditiously.

NCW, in essence, therefore is the exploitation of communication networks by conveying the right information, faster to the forces - who in turn take the right action, faster and against the right objective. It shortens, what is often called the "kill chain"—detect, decide, attack and assess—and reduce the amount of resources required to move through each link. Information superiority in today's battlefield is achieved by integrating sensors, shooter and decision-makers through the seamless working of three major networks: Sensor Grid, Shooter Grid and the Information Grid. In the present context, warfare will be national from the very first moment and will be waged in different dimensions, land, air, water, underwater, space and cyber-space concurrently, under the gaze of media with extremely increased velocity, lethality and reach.

Conducting Network Centric Operation

The four fundamental requirements (capabilities) for conducting network centric operations are Network Communications, Information Sharing, Advanced

Information Technology such as Agents and Decision Support Algorithms and Network Enabled Platforms (Vehicles, tanks, ships, aircrafts and other systems). The Indian armed forces are neither integrated nor do they possess these capabilities, regardless of some "stand alone" capabilities existing within each service. Our desire to acquire the capabilities is loudable but if we wish to move along this of an Indian RMA than our promises must be backed by agencies and agents of implementation. The military instrument of NCW will have to be forged on suitably integrated organizations, new technologies, joint concepts and doctrines, and joint training and joint communication architecture. Hence, the important issues that the services need to examine in far greater are:-

- Jointly evolved communication architecture.
- Joint/ integrated organizations.
- Joint concepts and a joint doctrine to fight future conflicts.
- Induction of new technologies.
- Network-enabled platforms (tanks, ships, air crafts, etc).
- Attitudinal change to accommodate the concept of NCW.

Integrate New Technologies as War Fighting Systems

Technology which is one of the principle factors that drives the change in the method of war fighting is one of the most important component of NCW. India is facing an entirely new technology era, generated through advancements in the field of miniaturization, digitization, material science, bio-technology, sensor technology, stealth, communication and information technology. India needs to integrate new technologies as war fighting systems for which the requirement is to first evolve a new joint war fighting doctrine and concepts of joint war fighting and then decide upon the weapons and other systems to suit the former. Employment of fully integrated task forces in the future would require, in the first instance, introduction of three key technologies. The first one involves Long Range Precision (LRP) Firepower on the pattern used by the Americans in the Gulf War, the war in Kosovo and in Afghanistan. The strikes which were carried out from naval platforms, pass through the medium of air, were guided by space based assets, the struck land targets. In the Indian context also there will be a variety of platforms.

The second dominant technology trend is in the field of Integrated Technologies. The advances in the field of communication, computers, command and control, information and interoperability (C4I2) have provided the military a capability to view the battle space as one composite whole and thus targets can be tackled jointly or singly by any weapon of any service, which is within range. Interoperability will be the essence for the different C4I2 systems of the three services. The third most important field relates to Intelligence, Surveillance and Reconnaissance (ISR) that will keep track of enemy and own forces movements through advanced sensors and platforms like aircrafts, UAVs, and Satellites assisted by Global Positioning Systems (GPS). These advances are making the battlefield more transparent and the wars more precise.

(25)Communication Infrastructure: The Essence of NCW Capability

With rapid changes in technology, the armed forces have also altered their warfare strategies and are today poised for conducting network centric warfare. In fact, the technological revolution has driven the current RMA and brought about a paradigm shift in national security planning the world over.

New technologies are constantly impacting the nature of military capabilities and how they are used in support in national interest. Modernisation of defence communication means, providing in battle the capability to see, decide and quickly communicate with all land, sea and air units. In this way the whole military force performs more effectively than the simple sum of its individual parts.

Communication Infrastructure Required

Modern and future wars will be fought in a digital battlefield wherein the side that dominates both the electromagnetic space and the cyber space will be the winner. This will call for changes in strategy encompassing the full range of warfare from NBC to asymmetric in the likely battlefield environment of tomorrow. The stress will be on training and availability of necessary skills, change in attitude and quick decision making, management of information to ensure there is no information overload, transformation in organization and so on. Central to NCW is the availability of communication infrastructure that is responsive, robust and survivable, and will ensure quick transfer of information from the soldier upwards. This infrastructure will be in the form of strategic, backbone, tactical and access networks, integrated seamlessly to make available a "Network of Networks" to the commanders in the field and at the strategic level. The battle field entities and the critical national assets will plug and play on to this network in accordance with the operational plan.

Tactical Networks

At the strategic and the backbone level, linkages will have to be given to the national infostructure, that is, network managing the nation's economic, power, transformation and other such assets. This is particularly so in the present global environment wherein the concept of borders has become non-existence. The most critical amongst these networks are the tactical networks, which have to provide all telematic services with almost instant response time, long ranges, environment configuration and re-configuration, even as they remain exposed to complete onslaught of anti-technology by the advisory. The key requirements of these networks therefore are physical survivability, information assurance and risk management, management of battlefield electromagnetic space, power management and so on.

National Information Infrastructure

India lives in three ages concurrently—agrarian, industrial and information—with a distinct shift towards the information age with its young population and a very high rate of IT literacy coupled with a very fast developing communication infrastructure. India, today, has one of the largest optical fiber network in the world, is the biggest holder of submarine cables; the fastest growing cellular telephony network in the world with over eight million connections per month, one of the largest satellite and microwave/ Ultra High Frequency (UHF) network, and the largest TV viewer ship in the world. The country boasts of the largest and state-of-the-art private networks with island of excellence in the frontiers of information and communication technology. India has made good use of being a late starter by leapfrogging in the field of technology, thus reducing the digital gap.

National Information Infrastructure, which consists of different networks at the national, strategic, operational and tactical levels, will be at the heart of waging such a warfare and will, in fact, determine the nation's capability as also the vulnerability to execute such a war across the spectrum of warfare with NBC Warfare at one extreme and the

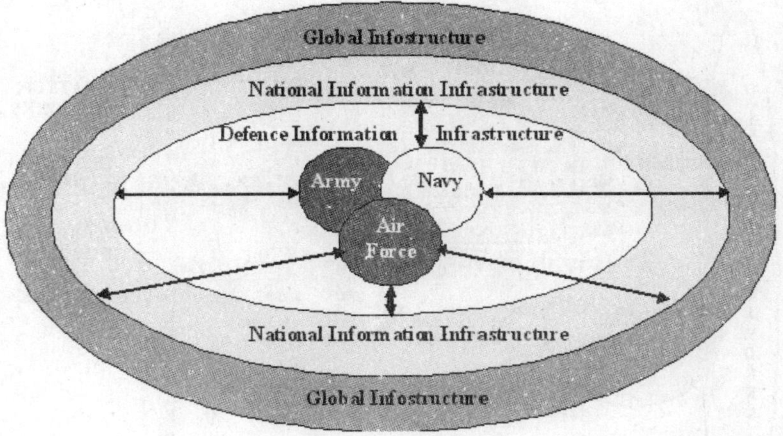

FIG: NETWORK OF NETWORKS–THE NATIONAL INFORMATION GRID

Asymmetric warfare at the other.

Concurrently, plans have to be ready for Disaster Management and synergizing the defence forces efforts with those paramilitary forces, state police organisations, and home guards and so on to bring to bear complete national capability on the adversary. Networks are the very means for bringing about such synergy.

Futuristic Defence Networks

Modernisation of defence communications will call for equipment to have a high degree of serviceability, reliability and availability along with miniaturization, encryption and interoperability. At the tactical level, the emphasis will be on fully integrated C3I systems and tactical data networks with the aim of transforming the soldier on the ground to a digital warrior.

Futuristic defence networks will be bandwidth hungry and any credible network centric infostructure will be aimed

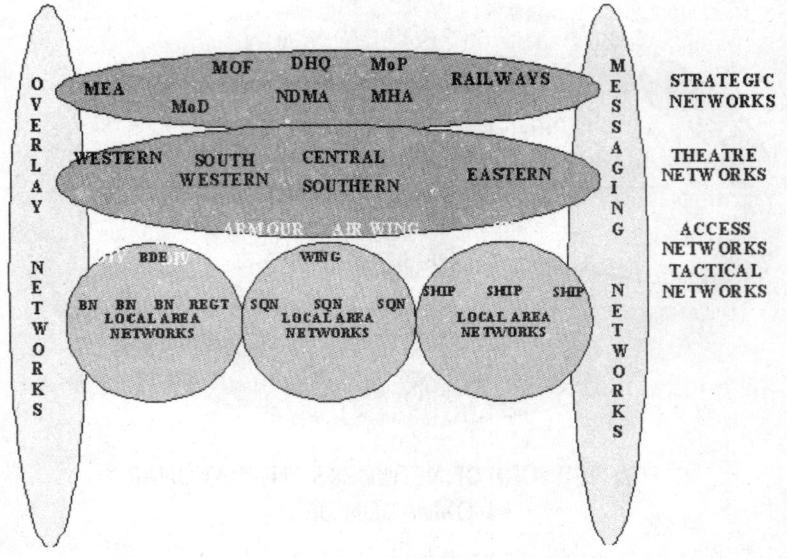

FIG: NATIONAL SECURITY INFORMATION GRID–
A SYSTEM OF SYSTEMS

at delivering requisite bandwidth down to the end user. Voice centric networks are passé- and integrated networks catering to voice, data and steaming video applications are the order of the day. The widening gap between spectrum availability and spectrum requirement will call for highly spectrum efficient communication systems. While optical fiber cable will replace copper in the backbone and access networks, copper will continue to be used for structured cabling. Ten gegabytes per second over copper is a reality, but even this may not be adequate in the years to come. To increase mobility and enhance speed of deployment and re-deployment of field forces, wireless communications will be an inalienable requirement.

Network Centricity

Modernisation of defence communications will be

meaningless if networks are developed in isolation. Network-centricity basically relies on 'network of network'. Hence, to be truly network centric, every network should be capable of integrating into one whole network. The infostructure should integrate with the infostructure, which in turn must integrate the national infostructure. This will only be possible with 'open source systems' which follow well established and internationally acceptable standards. The migration path from current platform-centric systems to network centricity will call for a high degree of transition management. Modern systems will have to co-exist with legacy systems. In fact, there will be three generations of technologies that will co-exist—current, futuristic and legacy.

ARTIFICIAL INTELLIGENCE

Historical Perspective

Early work in AI focused on using cognitive and biological models to simulate and explain human information processing skills, on "logical" systems that perform common-sense and expert reasoning, and on robots that perceive and interact with their environment. This early work was spurred by visionary funding from the Defence Advanced Research Projects Agency (DARPA) and Office of Naval Research (ONR), which began on a large scale in the early 1960's and continues to this day. Basic AI research support from DARPA and ONR—as well as support from NSF, NIH, AFOSR, NASA, and the U.S. Army beginning in the 1970's—led to theoretical advances and to practical technologies for solving military, scientific, medical, and industrial information processing problems.

By the early 1980's an "expert systems" industry had emerged, and Japan and Europe dramatically increased their funding of AI research. In some cases, early expert systems success led to inflated claims and unrealistic expectations: while the technology produced many highly effective systems, it proved very difficult to identify and encode the necessary expertise. The field did not grow as rapidly as investors had been led to expect, and this translated into some temporary disillusionment. AI researchers responded by developing new technologies, including streamlined methods for eliciting expert knowledge, automatic methods for learning and refining knowledge, and common sense knowledge to cover the gaps in expert information. These technologies have given rise to a new generation of expert systems that are easier to develop, maintain, and adapt to changing needs.

Today developers can build systems that meet the advanced information processing needs of government and industry by choosing from a broad palette of mature technologies. Sophisticated methods for reasoning about uncertainty and for coping with incomplete knowledge have led to more robust diagnostic and planning systems. Hybrid technologies that combine symbolic representations of knowledge with more quantitative representations inspired by biological information processing systems have resulted in more flexible, human-like behavior. AI ideas also have been adopted by other computer scientists—for example, "data mining," which combines ideas from databases, AI learning, and statistics to yield systems that find interesting patterns in large databases, given only very broad guidelines.

Case Studies

The following four case studies highlight application areas where AI technology is having a strong impact on industry and everyday life.

- *Authorizing Financial Transactions:* Credit card providers, telephone companies, mortgage lenders, banks, and the U.S. Government employ AI systems to detect fraud and expedite financial transactions, with daily transaction volumes in the billions. These systems first use learning algorithms to construct profiles of customer usage patterns, and then use the resulting profiles to detect unusual patterns and take the appropriate action (e.g., disable the credit card). Such automated oversight of financial transactions is an important component in achieving a viable basis for electronic commerce.
- *Configuring Hardware and Software:* AI systems configure custom computer, communications, and manufacturing systems, guaranteeing the purchaser maximum efficiency and minimum setup time, while providing the seller with superhuman expertise in tracking the rapid technological evolution of system components and specifications. These systems detect order incompleteness and inconsistencies, employing large bodies of knowledge that describe the complex interactions of system components. Systems currently deployed process billions of dollars of orders annually; the estimated value of the market leader in this area is over a billion dollars.
- *Diagnosing and Treating Problems:* Systems that diagnose and treat problems—whether illnesses in people or problems in hardware and software—are now in widespread use. Diagnostic systems based on AI technology are being built into photocopiers, computer operating systems, and office automation tools to reduce service calls. Stand-alone units are being used to monitor and control operations in factories and office buildings. AI-based systems

assist physicians in many kinds of medical diagnosis, in prescribing treatments, and in monitoring patient responses. Microsoft's Office Assistant, an integral part of every Office 97 application, provides users with customized help by means of decision-theoretic reasoning.

- *Scheduling for Manufacturing.* The use of automatic scheduling for manufacturing operations is exploding as manufacturers realize that remaining competitive demands an ever more efficient use of resources. This AI technology—supporting rapid rescheduling up and down the "supply chain" to respond to changing orders, changing markets, and unexpected events—has shown itself superior to less adaptable systems based on older technology. This same technology has proven highly effective in other commercial tasks, including job shop scheduling, and assigning airport gates and railway crews. It also has proven highly effective in military settings—DARPA reported that an AI-based logistics planning tool, DART, pressed into service for operations Desert Shield and Desert Storm, completely repaid its three decades of investment in AI research.

Military Applications of AI

The military and the science of computers has always been incredibly closely tied - in fact, the early development of computing was virtually exclusively limited to military purposes. The very first operational use of a computer was the gun director used in the second world war to aid ground gunners to predict the path of a plane given its radar data. Famous names in AI, such as Alan Turing, were scientists that were heavily involved in the military. Turing, recognized as one of founders of both contempory computer science and artificial intelligence, was the scientist who broke the German's Enigma code through the use of computers.

As computing power increased and pragmatic programming languages were developed, more complicated algorithms and simulations could be realized. For instance, computers were soon utilized to simulate nuclear escalations and wars or how arms races would be affected by various parameters. The simulations grew powerful enough that the results of many of these 'war games' became classified material, and the 'holes' that were exposed were integrated into national policies.

Artificial Intelligence applications in the West started to become extensively researched when the Japanese announced in 1981 that they were going to build a 5th Generation computer, capable of logic deduction and other such capabilities.

Inevitably, the 5th Generation project failed, due to the inherent problems that AI is faced with. Nevertheless, research still continued around the globe to integrate more 'intelligent' computer systems into the battlefield. Emphatic generals foresaw battle by hordes of entirely autonomous buggies and aerial vehicles, robots that would have multiple goals and whose mission may last for months, driving deep into enemy territory. The problems in developing such systems are obvious—the lack of functional machine vision systems has lead to problems with object avoidance, friend/foe recognition, target acquisition and much more. Problems also occur trying to get the robot to adapt to its surroundings, the terrain, and other environmental aspects.

Nowadays, developers seem to be concentrating on smaller goals, such as voice recognition systems, expert systems and advisory systems. The main military value of such projects is to reduce the workload on a pilot. Modern pilots work in incredibly complex electronic environments -

receiving information not only from their own radar, but from many others (principle behind J-STARS). Not only is the information load high, the multi-role aircraft of the 21st century have highly complex avionics, navigation, communications and weapon systems. All this must be organized in a highly accessible way. Through voice—recognition, systems could be checked, modified and altered without the pilot looking down into the cockpit. Expert/advisory systems could predict what the pilot would want in a given scenario and decrease the complexity of a given task automatically.

Besides from research in this area, various paradigms in AI have been successfully applied in the military field. For example, using an EA (evolutionary algorithm) to evolve algorithms, to detect targets given as radar/FLIR data, or neural networks differentiating between mines and rocks, given as sonar data in a submarine.

Genetic Programming

Genetic programming is an excellent way of evolving algorithms that will map data to a given result when no set formula is known. Mathmaticians/programmers could normally find algorithms to deal with a problem with 5 or so variables, but when the problem increases to 10, 20, 50 variables the problem becomes close to impossible to solve. Briefly, how an GP-powered program works is that a series of randomly generated expression trees are generated that represent various formulas. These trees are then tested against the data, poor ones discarded, good ones kept and breed. Mutation, crossover, and all of the elements in genetic algorithms are used to breed the 'highest-fitness' tree for the given problem. At best, this will perfectly match the variables to the answer, other times it will generate an answer very close to the wanted answer.

Neural-networks

Neural networks (NN) are another excellent technique of mapping numbers to results. Unlike the EA, though, they will only output certain results. A NN is normally pre-trained with a set of input vectors and a 'teacher' to tell them what the output should be for the given input. A NN can then adapt to a series of patterns. Thus, when feed with information after being trained, the NN will output the result whose trained input most closely resembles the input being tested.

This was the method that some scientists took to identify sonar sounds. Their goal was to train a network to differentiate between rocks and mines—a notoriously difficult task for human sonar operators to accomplish.

Morality: A Quick Thought

All these systems are quite impressive, and perfected models could prove incredible assets on the battlefield. Artificial Intelligence may only get developed to a certain level due to the threat humans feel as computers get more and more intelligent. The concept behind movies such as Terminator where our robotic military technology backfires on us and destroys us are rampant. Are there moral issues that we must confront as artificial military intelligence develops? As Gary Chapman puts it:

"Autonomous weapons are a revolution in warfare in that they will be the first machines given the responsibility for killing human beings without human direction or supervision. To make this more accurate, these weapons will be the first killing machines that are actually predatory, that are designed to hunt human beings and destroy them".

The applications of AI in the military are wide and varied, yet due to the robustness, reliability, and durability required for most military programs and hardware, AI is not yet an intregral part of the battlefield. As techniques are refined and improved, more and more AI applications will filter into the war scene—after all, silicon is cheaper than a human life.

The Future

AI began as an attempt to answer some of the most fundamental questions about human existence by understanding the nature of intelligence, but it has grown into a scientific and technological field affecting many aspects of commerce and society. Even as AI technology becomes integrated into the fabric of everyday life, AI researchers remain focused on the grand challenges of automating intelligence. Work is progressing on developing systems that converse in natural language, that perceive and respond to their surroundings, and that encode and provide useful access to all of human knowledge and expertise. The pursuit of the ultimate goals of AI —the design of intelligent artifacts; understanding of human intelligence; abstract understanding of intelligence (possibly superhuman)—continues to have practical consequences in the form of new industries, enhanced functionality for existing systems, increased productivity in general, and improvements in the quality of life. But the ultimate promises of AI are still decades away, and the necessary advances in knowledge and technology will require a sustained fundamental research effort.

(12) PSYWARFARE

"Kill one frighten ten thousand"

Psychological Operations has sssumed great importance throughout the history of wearfare. This operation does not involve exchange of lethal fire power causing physical destruction, but aims at far more damaging results by affecting, capturing ans conditioning the minds of the people. It makes people think the way one wants them to think. The intelligentsia of a nation can be subverted and ambiguity can be created in their minds for deception at strategic levels by means of such operations. This has been theorized Sun Tzu- "Attack the mind of enemy leader".

Op desert Storm

Allied Actions. The success of Psychological War during Desert Storm can be judged from the fact that 87,000 Iraqi soldiers surrendered, most of them clutching the leaflets dropped by Americans. Perhaps an Iraqi General gave the best testimony to propaganda operations when he stated, "Psychological operations was a great threat to troop morale, second only to the coalition bombing campaign." The Psychological operations also included use of overt and covert propaganda, exploitation of the opponenent's vulnerabilities, insightment of religious and racial sentiments through management of perceptions and manipulation of evidence, political and economic black mail, mischievious feed back and security slips.

Highlights. The Gulf War highlighted the following Psychological dimensions of future warfare:

- The use of mass media and technical information machinery as an effective tool of war in gaining full control over electronic and print media.
- Effective and suitably deployed propaganda tools can easily destroy the image of political and military commanders.
- Persistence need for a well orchestrated propaganda campaign based on realistic themes.

- Need for immediate and effective counter propaganda campaign.
- Effective jammimg/ destruction of enemy's communication system, which resulted in total collapse of communication between field commanders and leaders leading to panic and disinformation.
- Well trained and equipped Psychological operation teams functioning alongside field formation working under an effective coordinating headquarters.
- Operational plans supported by realistic psychological operation plans pay handsome dividends in winning a war.

The Future Warfare

The examples enumerated above highlight the success achieved by various commanders throughout the history of warfare and as such psychological operations are established military norms, as a tool, in conflicts of varying intensities. Historically, the application of Psychological operations, in one form or another has proven to be almost as essential to the successful waging of war as the use of manpower and weaponry.

An analysis of recent conflicts has demonstrated the value of psychological war on and off the battle field. As a result, most military authorities accept the fact that psychological operation is very special combat weapon, one that every military commander must consider employing and defending against, if he is to accomplish his mission with minimum losses.

Psychological War as a Weapon of War

The chief weapon of psychological war is propaganda. The essential ingredients of propaganda are source, time, audience, subject and mission. Only the effective integration of these ingredients will result in successful propaganda and fulfilment of the objective. Thus, the credibility of the source, the timing, the characteristics of the audience and the credibility of the message are of paramount importance.

An effective psychological operational campaign must be based on through research and intelligence; it must be consistent with government, military and political policy; it must stem from a deep understanding of the target audience and must get the right message of the right audience at the right time. Propaganda is the crucial factor of any psychological operation and should be based on information which to the enemy, is credible. It should be presented in a form which will both attract and excite, while exploiting the physiological and Psychological needs of the target, which it should then seek to satisfy.

Themes

The crux of a psychological war is the "theme" or the message. A deliberate disinformation campaign would essentially encompass analysis of the target audience, vulnerabilities, an assessment of its susceptibility to being influenced, selection of this dissemination tools and subsequent themes. Disinformation themes could attempt to mislead capabilities, intentions, time frame, scope of operations besides a broad spectrum of strategic factors including information on politico-sociological facets, economy, technological potential, transportation and communication means in addition to the armed forces.

Weapon of Future War

To influence the behaviour of a state, it is necessary to develop a strategy aimed at affecting the decision-makers. The distinctive nature of psychological operation derives from the fact that they do not attempt to manipulate material objects, but try to influence the way in which the material objects are perceived and interpreted.

Internet

Such is the logic behind psychological war, a combat weapon that targets the mind. And within this era of information, a lot of disinformation and misinformation is generated which can be very corruptive to our personal and collective lives. The imagined becomes the real for many people, particularly if it is perpetuated in the cross-flow of special interest groups via internet or other data basis.

Internet is the most influential means of reaching the minds of the public across the world with speed.

The Future Strategy

The critical facet of any psychological war strategy focus will remain towards the human being and to the human mind in specific.

(16) POWER LAWS

Scientists have found a "law of war"—one that can be used to predict the likelihood of attacks in modern conflicts. An international team has developed a physics-based theory that might be helpful in pre-empting crisis situations, from conventional battles to global terrorism. The theory is based on how the advantage can be taken of rise in the amount of information available of conflicts, by filtering hundreds of online news sources and government reports, and an emerging field, called complexity science. Advanced computer simulations and mathematical models are used to create a plausible microscopic mechanism to explain the collective behaviour observed in a wide range of human conflict situations—from ongoing insurgent wars and terrorism, through to street-gangs and even online games.

The "Power Laws" describe mathematical relationships between the frequency of large and small events. This finding is remarkable given the different conditions, locations and durations of these separate wars. The last thing one would expect to find within the chaos of war zone are mathematical patterns. Wars are supposed to be chaotic places with random attacks, disorder and violence, yet patterns do exist and these are the same for different wars all round the world from Sierra Leone to Iraq, Colombia and Afghanistan. The way in which modern wars and terrorism are being waged has less to do with geography or ideology, and more to do with the day-to-day mechanics of human insurgency—it is simply the way in which insurgent groups of human beings fight when faced with a much stronger, but more rigid opponent.

(15) ROLE OF MEDIA

The Kargil War is a glowing example of war in the Information Age. The country watched the battle of the Tiger Hill virtually sitting in their drawing rooms. The various news channels have made the society more aware and involved in the process of war. They demand transparency and public accountability of the higher military leadership. Today, media and public opinion largely influence not only national but military strategies. USA exploited media to build up public opinion against Weapons of Mass Destruction (WMD), supposedly stockpiled in Iraq and used it as an excuse to invade her. By the time the world realized that there were no WMDs in Iraq, it was too late.

'Media Strategy' is, therefore, crucially important to shape the environment. One who wins the Information campaign prevails. Information is the key to modern warfare—strategically, operationally, tactically and technologically. If that be so, then shouldn't we be focusing on training our future higher commanders in the 'Art of Interaction with Media' more than the 'Operational Art'?

Degrading the capability of the enemy to use Information does not require physical destruction. Partial blockage of the information flow, corruption of data, or the ability to alter decision maker's behaviour will, in the end, degrade a nation's ability to wage war across the operational continuum. Theoretically, the crushing of front line forces, destruction of the will of the enemy and occupation of territory may no longer be necessary to win a war. The purpose of war will remain that of imposing one's will on the opponent, but the nature of war will considerably change. The emphasis will not be on the 'Function of Command', but on maintaining the 'Supply' and 'Value' of Information.

(26)Implication of IT - RMA and Some Conceptual Flaws

RMA has some flaws which must be taken notice of. Some strategic and technical constraints are as follows:-

- Conventional ground forces do matter. After all the one-sided pounding in Afghanistan, ground troops were needed and their efforts are still continuing.
- Despite total battlefield-IT supremacy in Afghanistan, the US forces have attacked allied troops, wrong targets and even civilian marriage parties.
- Even if heavy bombers operate out of the main base to provide the main air-to-ground punch, other aircrafts will be needed for counter air operations. RPV have a short range and, hence, air superiority will remain a must till 2020 and beyond.

- Future ground forces may not have to be as heavy as in the past.
- IT-RMA is prohibitively expensive.
- Robotics can be a huge help in investigating in the rear of the enemy. Acoustic sensors can pick up snipers and HF microwave radar can "see through" a wall.
- All sensors have limitations. Visible light and IR detectors cannot see through heavy clouds. Most have short ranges specially X-ray and particle beam sensors. Practically, none of the sensors can deeply penetrate metal, concrete or most soils and even heavy foliage (tree trunks). It cannot discriminate between camouflaged heavy equipment from trucks and other civilian vehicles.
- Efforts to promote IT-RMA will create new significant vulnerabilities that do not currently exist.
- IT-RMA is unlikely to provide useful responses to the threats that India faces. The utility and limitations of IT-RMA have been exposed in the 9/11 attack on the US and the war on Taliban that followed.
- IT-RMA violates the principle of 'need to know'. Too much information is as dangerous as too little information. Harsh ground realities once known down the chain may well lower the morale of troops, reduce faith in senior leadership and ignite a breakdown in discipline where a unit is facing heavy odds, whether in defence or in attack.
- IT-RMA will encourage the enemy to 'eavesdrop' or contaminate or disrupt the information flow. The dilemma between easy access and robust security will be a bugbear for formations.
- Enemy will try asymmetric strategies and computer virtuoso with access to critical nodes that can bring an entire system down.

- A radically structured force for IT, if denied high quality information, will not be able to deliver the goods and will be less resilient than a conventional force.
- RMA is not only about weapons, doctrines but also about organization which is not hierarchical. Till now, information is tied to a function and a function to a rank and appointment. A flattened structure will cause problems of micro- as well as macro-management. Sri Lanka Operations were botched to a great degree by the unwanted and unwarranted deleterious effects of interference in decision making by the bureaucrats and politicians.
- A barrage of e-mails, faxes and cell phones from and to soldiers will all hamper operations.
- Complications created due to increasing contracts with civilian technicians to install, maintain, update and repair complex technical systems can be visualized. The civilian technical staff cannot be expected to have the same sense of discipline as a man in uniform, increasing the risk of theft, sabotage and espionage.

BATTLEFIELD OF THE 21ST CENTURY

How will the Warfare be Waged?

In the environment that is likey to be prevalent in this century there may not be large-scale wars or the concept of 'Total War'. Wars will be restricted in place, time and scope and prosecuted against non-state and conventional adversaries. Yet war will not be confined only to the military forces. It will be waged using the arm of diplomacy, finance, cyber war, terrorism, psychological and media wars and even resource and cultural warfare to safeguard the interests of the nation. These actions can be termed as "Non-military War Operations" and will be conducted as a prelude to military actions.

Consequences of Automated Warfare

On the automated battlefield, weapons would be used at an extremely fast rate. This would put heavy premium on establishing large scale production of un-manned vehicles, smart bombs, missiles and other systems. With the acquisition of automated weapons, wars can be more violent and damaging which means more casualties. Another issue is that wars may be continuous—both by day and night and thus exerting psychological stress with no respite to troops.

A doubt could arise as to whether complex technologies would work? Experience shows that TV sets, modern cars, household appliances, computers, aircraft rarely break down and therefore, new technologies need not break down. The main problem with automated weapon systems, it is stated could be organizational and not technical. Pulling together a large of sub systems to make them function is like a jig saw puzzle.

Effect of Stealth Technology on Combat Tactics

Combat tactics would be tailored around smaller, more flexible sub-units who have the ability to call on resources anywhere in the theatre and even beyond the theatre of operations. The battlefield would not conform to any fixed geographical boundaries, and concept of 'Point, Line or Area' battles will be replaced by battles fought across the entire spectrum of the enemy nation. The very concept of waging war will change from the existing norms of slow lumbering buildup, intensive air attacks followed by large scale ground operations. Instead we would have small rapidly deployed forces being utilized in the wake of an electronic 'blackout' that would seize key targets. The aim would be to strike the enemy's psyche rather than physical destruction. Means other than war would be utilized and aspects of economic war, cyber war, terrorism, ideological warfare and even ecological warfare will be used in conjunction with military operations.

The battlefield in 2020 would witness high technology in almost every department of war. The impact of technology on conduct of warfare would appear in a number of dominant trends; namely, extension in the reach and range of weapons, volume and accuracy of fire, systems integration, and increasing transparency on the battlefield. Unlike past wars, when the accuracy of the weapon systems was compensated by heavy volume of fire, the future development of guided weapons will add a new dimension altogether. Induction of various kinds of missiles, laser-aided weapons, target designators, and smart munitions will add to the achievement of precision fire. Two to three rounds of PGMs would be able to achieve the same destruction power that 300 conventional artillery rounds were able to achieve earlier. Thus, with an increase in the induction of PGMs, there will be a major reduction of logistics required to support an army during combat. In addition, high technology will be an influencing factor on organizations, tactics, equipment, and planning differentials between the combat arms and the logistic units. Advances in communication technology, computers, information systems, and surveillance and target acquisition systems will provide field commanders much better means of command and control over large formations during battle. However, no matter how advanced information technology may become, it would not totally eliminate the human angle and uncertainties in the fog of war. By compressing greater fire power, a smaller force will be able to achieve decisive results, as a consequence of greater lethality, accuracy, mobility, and extended range of weapon systems. Manoeuvre capabilities will also increase manifold, with an ability to converge speedily at a decisive point. In the 2020 battlefield scenario it will also be possible to process intelligence using advanced communication and computer systems, thus, expanding the commander's vision and detection ranges, besides improving the quality of information and instant dissemination to sub-ordinate commanders via real-time digital transfer. Micro processing technology will enable an army to conduct and dominate sophisticated information operations; in other words, to observe, to orient, to decide, and to act (OODA).

(18) New Concepts of Land Warfare

Military analysts have deliberated on a fourth generation of warfare in which the target, it is said, will be the whole of the enemy's society (ideology, culture, political, infrastructure and civil society). This generation of warfare will be characterized by dispersion, increased importance of actions by small groups of combatants, decreasing dependence on centralized logistics, a high manoeuvre. Concentrations of men, material and fire power may become a disadvantage as they would be easy to target. Small, highly manoeuvrable, agile forces will tend to dominate the battlefield. The aim will be to cause the enemy to collapse internally rather than destroy him physically. There will be a little distinction between war and peace. Wars will be non-linear, possibly to the point of having no definite battlefields or fronts. Major military and civil facilities will become targets and success will depend heavily on joint operations. By combining these general characteristics with new technology, a possible outline of a new generation of warfare becomes apparent.

A New Battlefield Environment

A new battlefield environment is emerging due to the advent of stand-off, multi-spectral sensors with real time communications that give situational awareness so that targets can be acquired, prioritized and destroyed, by day or by night, in all weathers, throughout the battlefield, with stand-off weapon systems firing precision attack munitions. This threat extends throughout the area of operations. Hence, stand-off engagements from aircraft, UCAVs and long range artillery can relieve ground elements including armour from the role of destroying enemy's combat elements at close quarters. Moreover, due to the high threat posed by the above systems, ground elements may find it difficult to close in with their intended objectives without neutralising the opponent's deep attack systems. The last factor, among other factors, will also mandate tri-service integration which is currently lacking. Furthermore, the Indian Armed Forces do not possess such technologies at present even though they are progressively moving towards this direction.

Platform-centric to Network-centric

Warfare is changing from Platform-centric warfare to Network-centric warfare. Translated in simple terms it means that greater task can be achieved with lesser resources by working smarter and centralize force multipliers.

Alteration of Time - Space Paradigm

Technology is causing a reduction / compression of (Observe, Orientate, Decide and Act) OODA / IDA (Information, Decision and Action) cycle. This is in turn is expanding the space of influence and reducing the time period. The whole concept is pictorially depicted in the figure 3 below.

TIME-SPACE PARADIGM

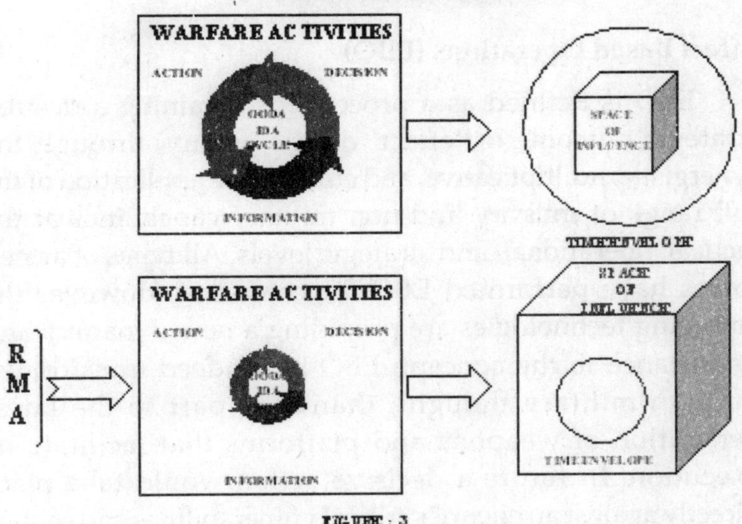

FIGURE : 3

Blurring of Three Levels of War i.e. Tactical, Strategic and Operational Art

The levels of war viz Tactical, Operational and Strategic are getting blurred. This is complicating the nature of military planning and decision-making. The operational level of war links tactical and strategic levels. At the operational level, the essence of technology application so far has been the quest for speed and knowledge through application of digital information technology. Emerging technologies have exponentially expanded the battle space and the areas of interest and influence at various levels . As a result there is diffusion and merging of the three levels of war.

Future may bring more radical change to the operational art. It may make the operational level of war fighting, at least in its old manifestation, less relevant. The rapid tempo of future wars may change the importance of the operational level of war fighting as currently defined. Fundamental alterations in the nature of the operational art may occur even more rapidly than expected.

Effect Based Operations (EBO)

EBO is defined as a process for obtaining a desired strategic outcome or 'effect' on the enemy, through the synergistic, multiplicative, and cumulative application of the full range of military and non military capabilities at the tactical, operational, and strategic levels. All types of armed forces have performed EBO for centuries. However the emerging technologies are providing a new dynamics and importance to the concept. EBO has indeed transformed modern military thought, thanks in part to the latest generation of weapons and platforms that facilitate its execution. In future a decisive action would take place directly against an enemy's critical vulnerabilities and centers of gravity in order to achieve "effects" formerly attainable only after long periods of tactical and operational attrition.

Parallel Warfare

Strategic centralized, including states, have a small number of vital targets at the strategic level. If a significant percentage of them are struck in parallel, the damage becomes insuperable. Contrast parallel attack with serial attack where only one or two targets come under attack in a given day (or longer). The enemy can alleviate the effects of serial attack by dispersal over time, increasing the defenses of targets that are likely to be attacked, concentrating his resources to repair damage to single targets, and conducting counteroffensives. Parallel attack deprives him of the ability to respond effectively, and the greater the percentage of targets hit in a single blow, the more nearly impossible is response. Application of new technologies to systems and weapons entrali for targeting enemy centers of gravity is making parallel warfare a reality.

Simultaneous, Accelerated and Non-linear Operations

Technology is becoming a predominant battle-winning factor through achieving asymmetry between contending forces. It is providing the force multipliers required to make the forces more and more potent. It is bring following changes in the conduct of battle:-

(a) *Simultaneous Operations:* Simultaneity means operations across entire geographical jurisdiction of force i.e. entire frontage and in depth. It also encompasses all the dimensions of war. The battles of the future would be fought on a wholly integrated battlefield in all its dimensions. The battlefield at any instant would be active in all zones from the contact to the strategic levels, in the ground, air, cyber zone and electronics spectrum. This would demand totally integrated operations and a matching integrated surveillance system.

(b) *Accelerated Operations:* The pace of operations has increased manifold and this trend is likely to continue. Accelerated pace and rhythm of war and its increased intensity with swift, sharp and intense engagements are likely to be the order of the day. This is due not only to faster aircraft, better tanks and vehicles and highly centralized ships and submarines, but enhanced communications and intelligence facilities have also contributed substantially. This has shrunk and is continuing to shrink the decision loop, thus increasing the tempo of operations.

(c) *Non-Linear:* The battlefield of the future is likely to be nonlinear involving simultaneous conduct of operations in the contact, tactical, operational and strategic zones. The various areas of the battlefield will not necessarily maintain their geographical relationship with each other, but will tend to merge or change places. All parts of the battlefield would remain activated simultaneously. The battlefield would be one of high fluidity, erasing our traditional notions of front, flank and rear. This would demand and also enable application of combat power throughout the battlefield.

Effect of Technology on the Tactical Aspects of Warfare

Fluidity: With the kind of mobility possible in the future nonlinear battlefield, the battle is going to be extremely fluid. This implies that targets would be, mostly, on the move and would offer very little time for reaction by our combat and fire support elements.

Manoeuvre: Improved manoeuvre capability contributes to the capability to move over increasingly dispersed area and converge quickly at the decisive point, thus concentrating the effects of both fire and manoeuvre. Manoeuvre refers to the employment of forces on the battlefield through movement in combination with fires, to achieve a position of advantage with respect to the enemy in order to accomplish the mission.

Dominating Manoeuvre: One of the more recently identified potential new warfare areas is dominating manoeuvre. Manoeuvre has always been an essential element in warfare, but the RMA potentially offers the ability to conduct manoeuvre on a global scale, on a much-compressed time scale, and with greatly reduced forces. Dominating manoeuvre can be defined as the positioning of forces—integrated with precision strike, space warfare, and information war operations—to attack decisive points, defeat the enemy center of gravity, and accomplish campaign or war objectives. Dominating manoeuvre would be distinct from manoeuvre in several ways.

Firepower and Lethality: In earlier days the lack of accuracy of weapon systems was compensated by heavy rate of fire. Increased lethality, accuracy, mobility and extended range of weapon system provide a lethal punch to the armed forces. Guided weapons have added a new dimension to the battlefield. Precision weapons allow the economical destruction of virtually all targets—especially strategic and operational targets that are difficult to move or conceal. They change the nature of war from one of probability to one of certainty. PGMs allow entralize of the destructive power and reduction in collateral damage. Further increased inventory of PGMs reduces the logistics infrastructure.

Reach: Improved mobility and greater range and effectiveness of weapons have increased the areas of influence and scope of manoeuvre in the battlefield. The battlefield is expanding in depth as well as frontage. The area covered by a unit has increased more than ten fold and seems to be still increasing.

Redefinition of Mass and Surprise by Stealth and Precision. For the first time in the history of warfare, a single entity can produce its own mass and surprise. It is this single entity of PGM delivery from a stealthy platform that makes parallel warfare possible. Surprise has always been one of the most important factors in war—perhaps even the single most important, because it could make up for large deficiencies in numbers. Surprise was always difficult to achieve because it conflicted with the concepts of mass and concentration. In order to have enough forces available to hurl enough projectiles to win the probability contest, a commander had to assemble and move large numbers. Of course, assembling and moving large forces in secret was quite difficult, even in the days before aerial reconnaissance, so the odds on surprising the enemy were small indeed.

Stealth and precision have solved both sides of the problem; by definition, stealth achieves surprise, and precision means that a single weapon accomplishes what thousands were unlikely to accomplish in the past.

Battlefield Transparency: Advances in surveillance and target acquisition technologies, satellites, unmanned aerial vehicles and various kinds of radars and sensors have made the battlefield transparent to a very large extent.

Future Battlefield and Likely Operational Environment

Future battlefield and likely operational environment could be summed up as follows:

(a) Numbers alone would not indicate strength and capabilities. Intangibles like computing power, communications etc will count. Technology will be an increasing battle winning factor through achieving asymmetry between the contending forces.
(b) Battle front comprising dug in positions would be replaced by a totally fluid front extending in all dimensions of distance, altitude and time.
(c) War would progress with accelerated pace and rhythm even at night resulting in rapid depletion of assets.
(d) Battlefield transparency would increase with quantum improvement in real-time surveillance and effective C4I2. Information technology advances would fundamentally alter techniques and methods of command and control allowing centralized planning and co-ordination of multi functions.
(e) Command and control over space technology will provide the cutting edge in future battle fields.
(f) There will be a quantum jump in precision and lethality of weapon systems, thereby increasing the rate of attrition.

(g) Accent will be on manoeuvre and mobility, rather than on attrition warfare.

(h) Extended geographical area of operations, simultaneity of operations at all levels and non-linearity of the battlefield and the modus operandi to fight in this environment will assume greater importance.

(j) Integrated operations would lay more emphasis on jointness. Much higher degree of coordination and integration between the air force and surface forces would be required.

Synergy in Operations

(3) The challenges and threats are likely to be thrown up owing to an increase in Information Operations undertaken by the three Armed Forces of our country is likely to enhance the concept of interoperability or joint operations. Synergy in operation enables different services, branches and weapons to fight effectively together by marshalling their unique capabilities. It also helps to avoid inefficiencies and wastes that arise when a multiplicity of agencies in the defence and intelligence communities generate their own ideas and philosophies.

SECURITY OUTSIDE BATTLE ZONE

(19)Rear Area Security

The reality of modern conventional warfare is that formations and units are much more dependent on logistic and technical support than ever before. While it may be possible to provide some immediate maintenance support by air, the bulk would have to move overland and workshops and other rear area facilities would still have to be set up on the ground. Rear area protection is not exciting, high profile or attractive, but without rear area security a modern mechanized force is likely to find itself as effective as a beached shark. The solution to this problem needs to include three elements:

- Static security—for protection of elements deployed in rear areas and for key infrastructure facilities.
- Convoy and route security—to ensure the unhindered flow of supplies.
- Rapid response units—to engage enemy special forces or other elements employed to disrupt the logistic support of the main force, and to hunt down and destroy the raiding forces.

Static Security

The matter of providing local security for static elements in the rear areas is a simple one for most field commanders, at least in theory. The support elements must be deployed in such a way as to minimize the need for protection forces. In addition, where possible these elements should provide their own sentries, local patrols, protection and local reaction forces. Infantry elements are to be provided where the area is too large for logistic and technical units to protect themselves.

Convoy and Route Security

The planning for convoy and route security must include:

- Careful route and waypoint selection with an eye to the ordinary driver finding his way even in the absence of military police waypoint teams, keeping in mind the security risks and the practicalities of quick reinforcements for a convoy that strikes trouble.

- Careful route reconnaissance, route surveillance and ongoing route patrols.
- Properly co-ordinated and brief escort teams.

The responsibility for communications protection should be of a unit that is integral to the formation and is specifically tasked, organized, trained and equipped for that role. An integral unit will be vastly more effective than a unit merely attached for the purpose since the former would have a better understanding of the style of functioning of the formation.

Rapid Response Units

These teams would have the specific of pre-empting, ambushing or pursuing enemy special forces and airborne elements that may attempt raids. The troops employed for this task would need a combination of specialized knowledge, training, experience and weapons and equipment to outmatch their adversary. In effect they would need to be trained to a standard similar to that of special forces, albeit with a different focus on training, organization and equipment.

UAV Support

Surveillance can vastly enhance the effectiveness and efficiency of rear area security forces. Obtaining air support for rear areas tasks is even more difficult. One possible option is the use of UAVs.

(22)Indian Imperatives in the Future Combat Milieu

The future battlefield has the following challenges:

- *Preparedness:* It mandates the reduction of the force generation time, which is currently tardy.

Mobilisation has to include a strategic air lift or a methodology that ensures the correct positioning of forces before the onset of open hostilities.

- *Battlefield Tempo:* This axiomatically can alone be achieved if force generation in the tactical realm is swift, concentrated and in the correct combat mix, free of logistic encumbrance, and a wieldy axis of maintenance.
- *Battlefield Domination:* It can be achieved through a flexible man-machine mix, the mix being dependant on the situation at that moment and the elements of the mix retaining the flexibility to detach and be applied swiftly elsewhere. Or, having the wherewithal to degrade, defeat or neutralize the enemy activity to a time frame where own forces can be applied to overwhelm the enemy with minimum combat application, relying more on dislocating, demoralizing and shocking the enemy into submission.
- *Dispersal and Convergence Capable:* The nuclear scenario dictates the capability to be widespread and yet rapidly convergence-capable.
- *Discarding Archaic Modes:* Obviously, the graduated application for 'battle progression syndrome' in such a scenario is of a 'dinosauric vintage'.
- *Simultaneity:* Simultaneity in addressing the 'centre of gravity' has to be the credo with greater focus on the selection of the enemy's 'centre of gravity'. The aim must be to win the campaign rather than the battles. That would mean losing a few battles en route, for the greater of winning the campaign. Hence, there has to be the mental resilience in the event some of the battles are lost with the aim furthered as a result of it.

- *Stand Off Capability:* Robotic substitution in military and combat application is a must for accomplishing missions that are dangerous and time consuming through the conventional mode.
- *Real Time Intelligence, Surveillance and Reconnaissance (ISR) Capability:* The field force, for effective and timely force generation and battlefield domination, has to be armed with a real time IRS capability.

(23) Future Challenges and Role of the Indian Army

The current role of the Indian Army is to preserve national interests and safeguard territorial integrity and unity of the country, against any external or internal threats. In the future, greater may be put on the preservation of the sovereign rights, protection of innocents, preservation of environment and right to free trade and protection of our economic interests. These challenges and role demand a full spectrum capability for waging and winning future conflicts and wars. Full spectrum capability includes the types of conflicts that the army is currently involved in and the type of operational missions that it may be ordered to undertake in future. These include the following types of operations, both offensive and defensive (conventional and unconventional/asymmetric):-

- Under threat of use of nuclear weapons.
- Full scale of conventional conflict.
- Limited and sectoral conflicts.
- Border skirmishes.
- Defence of island territory and/or dislodging an adversary from our island territory.
- Low Intensity Conflict Operations (LICO) including counter insurgency operations, counter proxy war operations, counter terrorist operations against

global/regional terrorist groups who may in due course even possess chemical weapons and other weapons of mass destruction and internal conflicts caused by internal dissent fanned by unscrupulous political factions.

- Out of Area Contingency missions to assist friendly nations and to stabilize adverse situations in the region.
- Military reaction to unforeseen contingencies demanding a pro-active (including pre-emptive) or reactive response, inside or outside the country.
- Other forms of warfare such as information war (including media war), psychological war, cyber and space war.
- UN peacekeeping or enforcement operations.

Nature of Wars

The nature of future war may be summarized as under:-

- Future wars will be highly uncertain.
- Technology will play a pre-dominant role in designing the conduct of war.
- The costs involved and the complexities of war waging may force nations to join allies/coalitions thus requiring expertise in combined warfare methods.
- The high costs of waging wars and of individual weapon systems will demand total synergy between various components of national power and the various elements of the armed forces themselves.
- Weaker states will use "asymmetric warfare" to fight more powerful opponents while the more powerful states will positive asymmetry the C4ISR capabilities to deliver significant lethal and non-lethal effects

with precision, speed and crushing power.

- Globalisation and interconnectedness will makes war transparent thus challenging the political utility of using armed forces.
- Military power is likely to be used selectively, in an integrated and synergetic manner and with increasing indiscrimination in choosing means as well as ends.
- There will invariably an international pressure on warring parties due to the fear of escalation, especially if the nuclear armed states are involved, and hence wars are likely to be short but of high intensity.
- Two or three generations of warfare will coexist, that, is, high technology as well as low technology components.
- American-led world order and democratic states will continue to be challenged by Islamic terror networks, sheltered mostly by weak authoritarian states and funded by the richer nations of Islamic world.
- The strategy of global leadership and engagement by the US, based on assumption that such a role is natural, will continue for the foreseeable future.
- A balance between the measures of active security building and restraint will have to be maintained with a better awareness of their respective strengths and weaknesses.
- Care will have to be taken to work within the limits of international law, including its percepts on the minimum use of force and proportionality of response.

(11) TECHNOLOGY ADVANCEMENT, 2020

(11) Battlefield Milieu, 2020

Getting down to the specifics of a likely battlefield milieu in a war with either Pakistan or China, the following merit considerations:-

- With advances in satellite imagery as well as aerial and ground based sensors, there will be an increase in the 'warning period' available before the outbreak of hostilities.
- Effective night vision devices will add a new dimension to night fighting capability; particularly so in the plains and semi-desert areas of Punjab and Rajasthan, in the context of an India-Pakistan war; and slightly degraded in mountainous terrain in the case of the Sino-India War.
- Whereas mechanized forces will have a major role in a war with Pakistan, they will have limited utility in a war against China. Instead, air mobile forces will play a predominant role in the latter case.
- Wars will be short, swift and limited against a nuclear back drop. However, the tempo will be enhanced on both sides, using hi-tech night vision and surveillance devices, and a broad spectrum of sensors.
- The integration of command, control, communication and intelligence (C3I) systems would lead to faster decision making and responses.
- Besides forces earmarked for conventional battle, we should expect to see 'rapid action' forces, lightly armed and equipped and backed up by a sound infrastructure of tactical airlift aircraft, intelligence agencies, and counter terrorist organizations which would infiltrate, close in, and destroy those who

engage in unconventional warfare, such as Pakistan.

- A land battle launched by China, though unlikely in any great measure due to terrain and logistics restraints, would see the employment of airborne forces targeted to seize deep objectives, duly supported by PGM sans sea borne weapon systems.
- Whereas an India-Pak war is more likely to be fought inside Pakistani territory, the reverse would be likely in the case of a Sino-India War, which would be fought on Indian soil and over the skies above.
- The stronger power would attempt to lengthen the duration of war to its advantage, this would imply a longer duration war with China than one with Pakistan.

TABLE : MILITARY REVOLUTION

Ser	*Name*	*Innovation*	*Date*
1.	Infantry	Longbows - enhanced range and ability	14th century
2.	Artillery	Cannons, gun barrels, gun powder	15th century
3.	Sail and Shot	Sail ships replaced cars and warships Carried artillery	14th to 17th century
4.	Fortress	Defensive fortifications to withstand artillery bombardment	16th century
5.	Gun Powder	Archers replaced by infantry units with muskets and artillery	16th to 17th century
6.	Napoleanic	Standardisation of equipment and Mass Armies	18th century
7.	Land Warfare	Rail - enhanced strategic mobility Telegraph - Rapid transmission of information Rifles - increased aim Accuracy of artillery	19th century
8.	Naval/ Steamship	Metal hulled ships with turbine engines Long range artillery	19th to 20th century

9.	Interwar	IC Engines Aircraft designs Mechanisation Carrier aviation Amphibious warfare Radio and radar exploitation Blitzkrieg Nuclear bombs	20th century
10.	Nuclear	Coupling of nuclear warheads to ballistic missiles	20th century
11.	Technology	Information Warfare Network Centric Warfare	20th and 21st century

REFERENCES

1. Brig RM Khaire, "Doctrinal Changes Necessitated by the Changing Contours of Conventional Warfighting", TRISHUL DSSC Wellington, Spring 2007, p. 13.
2. Frank Barnaby, "The Battle Field of the Future" Chapter five of "Future War—Armed Conflict in the Next Decade", Edition 1984, p. 72.
3. Lt Cdr A. Anand, Information Technology —The Future Warfare Weapon, Ocean Books Private Limited, p. 97
4. Lt Cdr A Anand, Ibid., p. 16.
5. Gp Capt AK Sharma, Impact of RMA in future wars in the Indian Context including limited and Anti-Insurgency Operations, College of Air Warfare Journal, Summer 2003, p. 26.
6. Steven Metz and James Kievet, Strategy and the Revolution in Military Affairs: from theory to policy, US Army War College, 1995, p. 19.
7. Bharat Karnad, "India's Future Plans and Defense Requirements" published in "Emerging India—Security

and Foreign Policy Perspective" by N.S. Sisodia and C. Uday Bhaskar, Promila Publications, 2005, p. 63.

8. Bruce W Watson, *Military Lessons of the Gulf War*, Lancer International, 1991.
9. Maj Gen V.K. Madhok, Battlefield of the Early Twenty First Century, M/S SUJAY, Mathura Road, New Delhi, 1987, p. 17.
10. Col Ajay Singh, Warfare in the 21st Century, War College Journal, Army War College, autumn 2007, p. 22.
11. Lt Gen Vijay Oberoi, PVSM, AVSM, VSM , "Army 2020, Shape, Size, Structure and General Doctrine for Emerging Challenges", Knowledge World & Centre For Land Warfare Studies, p. 33.
12. Brig T.K. Kaul, "Psychological Warfare as a Weapon of War in 21st Century", NDC Papers 1/2001, National Defence College, New Delhi, p. 58.
13. Lt Gen(Retd) Davinder Kumar, "Key to National Security", SP's Land Forces, 2/2008, a SP Guide Publication, p. 1.
14. Brig Vinod Anand, "Decision Making in Era of RMA", PINNACLE The ARTRAC Journal, Vol. 3, No. 2, October 2004, Army Training Command, India, p. 72.
15. Col A. Bajpaye, "Military Leadership and Management in the Information Age", PINNACLE The ARTRAC Journal, Vol. 3, No. 2, October 2004, Army Training Command, India, p. 101.
16. Editorial Team, "Experts find Law that can Predict Wars" Article published in Times of India Newspaper dated 29 June, 2008, p. 15.
17. Alan D. Campen, "The First Information War", Bookmart Publishers, New Delhi, 2000, p. 52.
18. Lt. Gen. (Retd) V.K. Kapoor, "New Concept of Land Wrafare", SP's Land Forces Vol. 2, No. 5, A SP Guide Publication, 2005, p. 6.

19. Helmoed-Romer Hietman, "Rear Area Security Conundrum", SP's Land Forces, Vol. 2, No. 5, A SP Guide Publication, 2005, p. 10.
20. Lt. Gen. (Retd) Davinder Kumar, "Information Operations: Key to National Defence", SP's Land Forces, 6/2005, a SP Guide Publication, p. 10.
21. Rear Admiral (Retd) K.R. Menon, "The Revolution in Military Affairs and the Indian Armed Forces", PINNACLE The ARTRAC Journal, Vol. 1, No. 2, September 2002, Army Training Command India, p. 7.
22. Brig (Retd) S.K. Raychaudhari, VSM, "India's Quest for Revolution in Military Affairs (RMA)", PINNACLE The ARTRAC Journal, Vol. 1, No. 2, September 2002, Army Training Command, India, p. 27.
23. Lt Gen (Retd) V.K. Kapoor, "Do we have full Spectrum Capability", SP's Land Forces, 5/2007, a SP Guide Publication, p. 10.
24. Lt Gen (Retd) V.K. Kapoor, "Network Centric Warfare: Situational Awareness is the Key", SP's Land Forces, 5/2007, a SP Guide Publication, p. 12.
25. Lt. Gen. (Retd) Davinder Kumar, "Communication Infrastructure: The Essence of Network Centric Capability", SP's Land Forces, 2/2006, a SP Guide Publication, p. 3.
26. Maj Gen Ashok Joshi, VSM (Retd.), "RMA and its Relevance Today for Indian Armed Forces", PINNACLE The ARTRAC Journal, Vol. 1, No. 2, September 2002, Army Training Command, India, p. 84

1. Times of India, 11 March 2000. (www.timesofindia.com/today/11home2-htm).
2. Dixit, J.N., Security in South Asia—Trends and Directions. APH Publishing Corporation, 2004. Ed. Vandana A & Ashok Shukla.

3. Chapman Graham P. The Geopolitics of South Asia. Ashgate Publishing Ltd. UK. 2003, p. 262.
4. Hymans,Jacques E.C. Why Do States Acquire Nuclear Weapons. Nuclear India in the Twenty First Century. Eds D.R. Sardesai and Raju Thomas. PalgraveMcMillan . USA. 2002, p. 144.
5. Perkovich, George. What Makes the Indian Bomb Tick. Nuclear India in the Twenty First Century. Ed D.R. Sardesai and Raju G.C. Thomas . Palgrave – McMillan, England. 2002, p. 26.
6. Ibid., p. 27.
7. Ibid.
8. Lavoy, Peter ; The Cost of Nuclear Weapons in South Asia. Nuclear India in the Twenty First Century. Ed D.R. Sardesai and Raju G.C. Thomas. Palgrave – McMillan, England. 2002, p. 261.
9. Subramanyam K, *India and the International Nuclear Order*. Nuclear India in the Twenty First Century. Ed D.R. Sardesai and Raju Thomas, Palgrave- McMillan, New York, 2002, pp. 74-75.
10. Perkovich., *op.cit.*, p. 39.
11. Perkovich, *op.cit.*, p. 46.
12. Jaswant Singh, Foreign Minister of India after India carried out the nuclear tests at Pokharan, Rajasthan in May 1998.
13. Rama Lakshmi & Glenn Kessler, "International Group Backs Nuclear Accord for U.S., India," *The Washington Post*, September 7, 2008, www.washingtonpost.com.
14. Siddharth Varadarajan, "India and the Additional Protocol," The Hindu, March 7, 2009, www.hindu.com/ 2009/ 03/ 07/ stories/ 2009030755691000.htm.
15. "India Working on Ratification Procedures," *The Hindu*. April 13, 2009, www.hindu.com/ 2009/ 04/ 13/ stories/ 2009041360211100.htm.

16. www. The bulletin.org. Bulletin of Atomic Scientists Jan/ Feb., 2002, p. 71.
17. Spector. Leonard S Spector, Nuclear Ambitions; Carnegie Endowment, Western Press; 1990, p. 34.
18. www. thebulletin.org. Bulletin of Atomic Scientists Jan/ Feb 2002, p. 71.
19. www. The bulletin.org. Bulletin of Atomic Scientists Nov/ Dec 2003, p. 77.
20. Perkovich, George. India's Nuclear Bomb. Oxford University Press. New Delhi. 2000, p. 298.
21. Dr. Raja Mohan C., "A Nuclear Strategy for India". USI National Security Series 1999. Ed Basrur, Rajesh M.
22. Majumdar Anindyo J. Nuclear India into the New Millennium. Lancer's Books, New Delhi, 2000, p. 178.
23. Joshi, Arun. Hindustan Times, 28 October 2004, New Delhi, p. 4.
24. Pervez Hoodbhoy and Zia Mian www.The India-Pakistan conflict—Towards the failure of nuclear deterrence.
25. www.dae.gov.in
26. Abani. Dr. M.C. Nuclear Emergency: Preparedness and Response, N.B.C. Defence Journal. June 2002. CME Pune, p. 3.
27. Nair, Brig Vijai K. Nuclear India. Lancer International, New Delhi, 1992, p. 67.
28. www.indiadaily.com. 16 Oct 04.
29. Hindustan Times. New Delhi, 02 August 2004, p. 4.
30. www.un.org
31. United Nations Documents S/628, January 2, 1948
32. United Nation Document S/646, January 15, 1948
33. United Nations Documents S/**2017 March 30, 1951**

Secondary sources

1. Stephen P. Cohen, Sergei Kamenev, Vladimir

Moskalenko and Leo Rose, Afghanistan and Kashmir (New York: The Asia Society, and Moscow: The Russian Oriental Institute, 1993).

2. Devin Hagerty, "The Powers of Suggestion: Opaque Proliferation, Existential Deterrence, and the South Asian Nuclear Arms Competition," Security Studies, 2:3/4, Spring/Summer, 1993, 256-283.
3. Raju Thomas, ed., Perspectives on Kashmir: The Roots of Conflict in South Asia (Boulder: Westview Press, 1992).
4. Sumit Ganguly and Kanti Bajpai, "India and the Crisis in Kashmir," Asian Survey, Vol. 34, No. 5, May 1994.
5. Vijay Khare 'Dr. B.R. Ambedkar and India's National Security', Kilasoo Books, New Delhi-2005.
6. Michael Krepon, Mishi Farugues, eds., Conflict Prevention and Confidence Building Measures in South Asia: The 1990 Crisis. The Henry L. Stimson Center, Occasional Paper No. 17, April 1994.

INDEX